The State of
Working America

The State of Working America

1998-99

LAWRENCE MISHEL

JARED BERNSTEIN

JOHN SCHMITT

ECONOMIC POLICY INSTITUTE

ILR Press
an imprint of
Cornell University Press
Ithaca and London

First published 1999 by Cornell University Press
First printing, Cornell Paperbacks, 1999

Printed in the United States of America

Library of Congress Cataloging-in-Publication Data

Mishel, Lawrence R.
The state of working America, 1998-99/Lawrence Mishel, Jared Bernstein, John Schmitt.
p. cm.
Includes bibliographical references and index.
ISBN 0-8014-3613-3 (cloth: alk. paper).—ISBN 0-8014-8582-7 (paper: alk. paper)
1. United States—Economic policy—1993- 2. United States—Economic conditions—1981- —Regional disparities. 3. Fiscal policy—United States. 4. Income distribution—United States. 5. Cost and standard of living—United States. 6. Young adults—United States—Economic conditions. 7. Unemployment—United States. 8. Labor market—United States. I. Bernstein, Jared. II. Schmitt, John. III. Title.
HC106.82.m575 1998
338.973--dc21   98-43250

Recommended citation for this book is as follows: Mishel, Lawrence, Jared Bernstein, and John Schmitt, THE STATE OF WORKING AMERICA, 1998-99. An Economic Policy Institute Book. Ithaca, N.Y.: ILR Press, an imprint of Cornell University Press, 1998.

Cornell University Press strives to use environmentally responsible suppliers and materials to the fullest extent possible in the publishing of its books. Such materials include vegetable-based, low-VOC inks and acid-free papers that are recycled, totally chlorine-free, or partly composed of nonwood fibers. Books that bear the logo of the FSC (Forest Stewardship Council) use paper taken from forests that have been inspected and certified as meeting the highest standards for environmental and social responsibility. For further information, visit our website at www.cornellpress.cornell.edu.

Cloth printing   10 9 8 7 6 5 4 3 2 1
Paper printing   10 9 8 7 6 5 4 3 2

To my children, Eli and Julia, who inspire me by their accomplishments.
—LARRY MISHEL

To Kay.
—JARED BERNSTEIN

For Walter.
—JOHN SCHMITT

VISIT EPINET.ORG

The Economic Policy Institute's web site contains current analysis of issues addressed in this book. The DataZone section presents up-to-date historical data series on incomes, wages, employment, poverty, and other topics. The data can be viewed online or downloaded as spreadsheets.

Table of Contents

Acknowledgments

The preparation of this publication required the intensive work effort of many people on EPI's research staff. Monica Hernandez played a key role in organizing the document and preparing much of the tables and text. Yonatan Alemu prepared all of the graphs and provided extensive research assistance. David Webster and Danielle Gao did an enormous amount of excellent computer programming and database management. The library staff, Terrel Hale and Violetta Loyevsky, were a great help as well. Our colleagues provided much needed advice. In particular, Dean Baker helped with particular sections, and Ruy Teixeira, Jeff Faux, Eileen Appelbaum, and Nan Gibson provided useful comments on drafts.

It has been a pleasure to continue the partnership with Kim Arbogast and Patrick Watson in the development and production of this book. Pat reviewed every word we wrote and effectively edited, checked, made consistent, and substantially improved the text and presentation. Kim produced and designed the book. Joe Procopio proofread, and Nan Gibson, Brian Lustig, Marcus Tonti, and Linda Ellis worked to provide a large audience.

Many experts were helpful in providing data or their research papers for our use. We are particularly grateful to those who provided special tabulations: Ed Wolff and Peter Gottschalk. Others who provided data, advice, or their analysis include Dale Belman, Steve Camarota, Timothy Smeeding, Mark Keese, Daniel Aaronson, Ann Ferris, Ken Hudson, Frank Sammartino, Julie Day, Chuck Nelson, Ed Welniak, Howard Hayghe, Al Davis, Bruce Fallick, Jack McNeil, Gordon Merman, Tom Nardone, Marion Nichols, Anne Polivka, Larry Rosenblum, Wayne Shelley, and John Stinson.

We are grateful to the Ford Foundation, the John D. & Catherine T. MacArthur Foundation, Carnegie Corporation of New York, the Charles Stewart Mott Foundation, and the Rockefeller Foundation for providing support for the research and publication of this volume. We also wish to thank the Russell Sage Foundation as well as the Rockefeller Foundation for their support of our work on the relationship between wage inequality and technology.

The State of
Working America

Executive summary

USING A WIDE VARIETY OF DATA ON FAMILY INCOMES, TAXES, WAGES, UNEMPLOYMENT, wealth, and poverty, *The State of Working America 1998-99* examines the impact of the economy on the living standards of the American people. The story we tell is one of great disparities.

As this book goes to press, the economy is in an expansion, but many of the economic problems first evident in the 1980s continue to be felt. For example, despite growth between 1989, the year of the last business cycle peak, and 1997 in gross domestic product, employment, and hours worked by the typical family, median family income in 1997 was still only $285 higher than it was in 1989. The significant improvements in 1997 and 1998 in wages for most workers have still left wage trends in the 1990s no better than they were for most workers in the 1980s. Wage declines have also pulled down new groups of workers in the 1990s, including many white-collar workers and recent college graduates. Women workers in the middle and upper-middle part of the wage distribution, who saw real wages rise significantly in the 1980s, have experienced a sharp deceleration in the 1990s.

At the same time, jobs have become less secure and less likely to offer health and pension benefits. Middle-class wealth (the value of tangible assets such as houses and cars, plus financial assets, minus debts) has also fallen. These same factors have kept economically less-advantaged families in poverty despite an extended economic recovery.

American workers might be able to take some solace if their sacrifices now would eventually guarantee an improved standard of living for themselves or their children. Unfortunately, the country has little to show for the belt-tightening of the last two decades: productivity growth has been lackluster; only corporate profits, the stock market, and top-executive pay are doing better than in the past.

To be sure, some bright spots have appeared. The unemployment rate in mid-1998 stood at about 4.5%. Inflation had fallen to below 2% per year. Changes to the tax code in 1993 reversed some of the inequities built into the federal tax structure in the 1980s. After a decade of neglect, four increases in the minimum wage in the 1990s have boosted the earnings of millions of low-wage workers. The simultaneous expansion of the earned income tax credit has further improved the earnings of low-wage workers in the poorest families.

Nevertheless, the typical American family is probably worse off near the end of the 1990s than it was at the end of the 1980s or the end of the 1970s, despite an increase in the productive capacity of the overall economy. To the extent that the typical American family has been able to hold its ground, the most important factor has been the large increase in the hours worked by family members.

The following is a summary of the economic realities that characterize the state of working America.

Family incomes: slow and unequal growth

Since 1979, the most important development regarding American incomes has been slow growth and increasing inequality. In the most recent period for which we have data, 1989-97, median family income rose by only $285, or 0.6%. Income stagnation of this magnitude is unprecedented in the postwar era. In every other postwar expansion, the income of the typical family had, at this point, already far surpassed the level reached in the preceding peak.

In any event, the restoration by 1997 of a family income level obtained in 1989 is disappointing on two further counts: first, the typical married-couple family with children worked 247 more hours (about six more full-time weeks) per year in 1996 than in 1989 and, second, the productive capacity of the economy improved about 8% over the same period. American families are working harder to stay in the same place and are seeing little of the gains in the overall economy.

Why have income trends continued to be so poor in the 1990s? Along with overall slow growth, the primary reason is the continuing wage deterioration among middle- and low-wage earners, now joined by white-collar and even some groups of college-educated workers. Despite a reversal over the last two years in these long-term trends, a longer-run view underscores continuing problems in the 1990s. Over the full 1989-97 period, for example, wages fell faster for the median worker (-0.4% per year) than they did in the 1979-89 period (-0.2%) per year.

Another key factor in understanding recent trends is the deceleration in the growth in the hours of paid work performed by members of working families. In the 1980s, many families compensated for falling hourly compensation, which was particularly steep for male workers, by working more hours. Some families increased the number of family members in the paid workforce. In other families, the number of hours worked by members already in the labor force increased. The annual hours worked by all family members in the typical married-couple family with children grew 368 hours per year (more than nine weeks of full-time work), from 3,236 hours per year in 1979 to 3,604 hours per year in 1989. After a large increase in the annual hours of paid work in 1979-89, many working families had less scope for increasing the number of hours of additional work that they could provide. The annual hours of paid work performed by the typical family grew an additional 247 hours, to 3,851 per year in 1996, a substantial extra time commitment for working families, but not enough to keep pace with the hours growth of the 1980s or enough to counteract the simultaneous squeeze on wages.

Younger families have been especially hard hit by overall slow family income growth and widening inequality. A cohort, or intergenerational, analysis of income growth shows that recent groups of young families have started out at lower incomes and obtained slower income gains as they approached middle age. One result of this trend has been to constrain income mobility, which had worked in the past to offset increasing income inequality.

Another major factor fueling growing inequality in the 1990s has been the acceleration of capital income growth, which resulted from a surge in profitability in the 1990s. This growth has generated a stock market boom that has overwhelmingly benefited the richest families. The increase in the rate of profit (the return to capital or interest and profits per dollar of plant and equipment assets) has also squeezed wage growth since 1979, but especially since 1989. Had profitability grown only at historically normal levels, then hourly compensation could have been 7% higher in 1997 than it actually was.

Some analysts have suggested that changes in the demographic composition of American families have been a major cause of the income problems documented above, implying a lesser role for economic causes such as wage decline. While the increased share of economically vulnerable families (e.g., female-headed families with children) has without a doubt put downward pressure on income growth, this process is a dynamic one that has not been constant over time. Moreover, some demographic factors, such as the increase in educational attainment, have led to increased family income. Contrary to the conventional wisdom, which has typically assigned the primary role to changes in family type, we find clear evidence that, while the shift to less well-off family types has put downward pressure on incomes, educational upgrading has more than compensated for this effect. Most importantly, on net, during the 1979-96 period, when income inequality was increasing most quickly, the demographic factors we consider (i.e., age, education, and race of the household head, along with family type) led to rising, not falling, household incomes. Thus, we should discount explanations that depend on demographic change to explain income decline.

Taxes: a further cause of worsening inequality

The effective federal tax rate for a middle-class family of four has changed little since 1980. In that year, this family paid about 23.7% of its income in federal income tax and Social Security and Medicare contributions. By 1985, the contribution had increased slightly to 24.4%, a level maintained through 1995.

While average federal tax rates for most Americans have changed little since 1979, effective tax rates have changed substantially for those with the highest incomes. Between 1977 and 1985, for example, changes in tax laws reduced the tax bill for the wealthiest 1% of families by an average of $97,250 per family relative to what these families would have paid in the absence of those changes. Meanwhile, these same changes increased the tax payments of the bottom 80% of families by an average of $221 per family relative to what they would have paid without the new tax code. Progressive tax changes in 1986 and again in 1993 partially reversed some of these inequities. On net, however, the wealthiest 1% of families have seen their tax bills fall by $36,710 since 1977, thanks to changes in the law.

The sharp reduction in the effective federal tax rates facing the richest 1% of taxpayers has contributed to the rise in income inequality since 1979. Nevertheless, since the typical family faces the same effective tax rates in the mid-1990s as in the late 1970s, changes in tax policy cannot account for the decline in living standards of the broad middle class. Most of the rise in inequality and the fall in living standards, then, reflects what employers are putting into paychecks, not what the government is taking out.

Wages: working longer for less

Since wages and salaries make up roughly three-fourths of total family income (more for the broad middle class), wage and salary trends are the primary determinant of the recent slow growth in income and the accompanying rise in income inequality. While the last two years have seen significant growth in real wages at all levels, especially at the bottom, these increases have generally not yet been sufficient to counteract the two-decade-long pattern of stagnant and declining wages. After adjusting for inflation, hourly wages stagnated or fell between 1989 and 1997 for the bottom 60% of all workers (wages over the 1990s did increase 1.4% for workers at the 10th percentile). In real terms, earnings of the median worker in 1997 were about 3.1% lower than they were in 1989.

As in the 1980s, men generally experienced more difficulties than women. Wages for the bottom 80% of men were lower in 1997 than in 1989. Median male workers' real wage fell about 6.7% over the 1989-97 period, a rate of decline was almost as rapid as that of the 1980s. Women's wages, however, rose between 1989 and 1997 at all levels of the wage distribution (with the exception of a slight decline at the 20th percentile). The growth in real wages for low-paid women (up 2.7% between 1989 and 1997) stood in strong contrast to the steep declines over the 1980s (down 18.2% between 1979 and 1989). Wages for women at the middle and the top grew in the 1990s, but at rates that were far slower than those achieved in the 1980s. The share of jobs paying less than a "poverty-level wage" (i.e., less than the hourly wage that is required to keep a full-time, full-year worker's annual income at the poverty line for a family of four) did not change between 1989 and 1997. This stagnation in the distribution of wages suggests either that job creation between 1989 and 1997 largely followed that of the 1989 wage distribution, or, if new jobs were somehow "better" than average, as some have claimed, that the wages paid on "existing" jobs deteriorated.

Including nonwage fringe benefits, such as employer health care and pension costs, does not change the overall picture. The hourly cost of benefits grew slightly faster than wages in the 1980s, but slightly slower than wages in the 1990s (primarily due to health care cost containment). Moreover, analyses of the average costs of health care benefits can conceal both the decline in the share of workers receiving employer-provided health care (down 7.6 percentage points between 1979 and 1997) and the disproportionate loss of benefits among low-wage workers (10.7 percentage points of high-school-educated workers lost health care coverage between 1979 and 1997, compared to only a 4.6 percentage-point drop among of college-educated workers).

The worst declines in wages have been for entry-level jobs. Between 1989

5

and 1997, for example, the average hourly wage for men with a high school degree and one to five years of work experience fell 7.4%; among comparable women, real wages fell 6.1%. Even young college graduates have suffered. Male college graduates with one to five years' experience earned 6.5% less in 1997 than in 1989. Their female counterparts were earning 7.4% less in 1997 than in 1989 (after an 11.2% increase in the 1980s).

Meanwhile, corporate chief executive officers (CEOs) have seen their pay skyrocket. In 1965, the typical CEO made about 20 times more than the average production worker; in 1989, the ratio had almost tripled to 56; by 1997, relative CEO pay had more than doubled again to 116 times the pay of the average worker. A separate estimate of CEO pay shows that the salary, bonus, and returns from stock plans of the average CEO grew 100% between 1989 and 1997. Extraordinarily high CEO pay appears to be a uniquely American phenomenon, with U.S. CEOs earning, on average, more than twice as much as CEOs in other advanced economies.

While economists continue to grapple with explanations for falling wages and widening wage inequality, a number of factors appear to account for most of the shifts in the wage structure. These include severe drops in the 1980s and 1990s in the number (and bargaining power) of unionized workers; an erosion through the 1980s in the inflation-adjusted value of the minimum wage, which has only been partially corrected in the 1990s; the decline in higher-wage manufacturing jobs and the corresponding expansion of low-wage, service sector employment; the increasing globalization of the economy through immigration and trade; and the growth in contingent (temporary and part-time) and other nontraditional work arrangements.

Many policy makers have cited a technology-driven increase in demand for "educated" or "skilled" workers as the most important force behind wage inequality. The evidence suggests that the overall impact of technology on the wage and employment structure was no greater in the 1980s and 1990s than in the 1970s. Productivity growth, for example, was lackluster in the 1980s and 1990s, not what we would expect if technology were inducing a widespread restructuring of the economy. It is also difficult to reconcile the idea that technology is bidding up the wages of "more-skilled" and "more-educated" workers, given the stagnation since 1989 in the wages of many college graduates and white-collar workers. Technology has been and continues to be an important force in shaping the economy, but no evidence exists that a "technology shock" during the 1980s and 1990s created a demand for "skill" that could not be satisfied by the ongoing expansion of the educational attainment of the workforce.

Jobs: slow growth and greater insecurity

The good news is that the average unemployment rate since the beginning of the business cycle in 1989 has been lower than during any business cycle since 1967-73, and, by mid-1998, the unemployment rate stood at about 4.5%. While falling unemployment has undoubtedly helped boost wages in the last two years, even current low levels of unemployment have not fully restored workers' sense of job security or reduced the share of workers in contingent or nonstandard jobs.

Data through the mid-1990s show that job stability (based on objective measures of job duration) and job security (based on more subjective measures) have been deteriorating over the last two decades. This conclusion generally reflects a decline in job stability for men and simultaneous gains (from low levels) for women. The median time that a 35-44-year-old male worker has been with his current employer, for example, fell from 7.6 years in 1963 to 6.1 years in 1996, with most of the decline (nine-tenths of a year) taking place between 1987 and 1996. The corresponding female worker saw her time with the same employer rise from 3.6 years to 4.8 years between 1963 and 1996, with most of the increase (eight-tenths of a year) taking place before 1987.

The share of workers in "long-term jobs" (those lasting at least 10 years) fell sharply between 1979 and 1996. Long-term jobs accounted for 41.0% of all jobs in 1979, but just 35.4% in 1996. Again, the worst deterioration has taken place since the end of the 1980s. The decline in long-term jobs affected men most. Just under half (49.8%) of men held long-term jobs in 1979, but this proportion had fallen 9.8 percentage points to 40.0% by 1996. Gains for women over the same period were much smaller, rising 1.2 percentage points, from 29.1% in 1979 to 30.3% in 1996.

Another measure of job stability, involuntary job loss (not for cause), was higher in the economic recovery years of 1993-95 than it was in the period 1991-93, which included the trough of the current business cycle. In 1996, 11.4% of the working-age population reported losing a job at some point in 1993-95, when the unemployment rate averaged 6.2%. In 1993, the share that reported losing a job sometime in 1991-93, when the average unemployment rate was 7.3%, was lower (10.9%).

With more than one-third of current workers with their current employers for at least 10 years, long-term jobs continue to be an important part of the economic landscape. And with only about 10% of workers losing their jobs in any given three-year period, most workers appear isolated from the threat of losing their job. Nevertheless, the sharp decline in the share of long-term jobs and the persistent high rate of job displacement despite a fall in the national unemployment rate have understandably affected workers' perceptions of job security.

Survey data show rising feelings of job insecurity through 1996, despite economic growth and falling unemployment. In 1989, only 8.0% of workers thought that it was very or fairly likely that they would lose their jobs in the next 12 months; by 1996, the figure had risen to 11.2%, despite the almost identical unemployment rate in the two years (5.3% in 1989, 5.4% in 1996). Over the same period, the share of workers who reported that it would be "very easy" to find other jobs with the same income and benefits as their current jobs fell 7.1 percentage points, from 34.2% to 27.1%.

Data on the economic consequences of job loss justify workers' anxieties. Displaced workers face difficulties finding new employment (more than one-third were out of work when interviewed one to three years after their displacement). When they do find work, their new jobs pay, on average, about 13.0% less than the jobs they lost, and more than one-fourth of those who had health insurance on their old jobs don't have it at their new ones.

Given that the unemployment rate is relatively low, we should probably look elsewhere for the source of workers' insecurity. One of the prime suspects is the increasingly contingent nature of much of the work available in the 1990s. Almost 30% of workers in 1997 were employed in situations that were *not* regular full-time jobs. These "nonstandard" work arrangements ranged from independent contractors and other self-employed workers to workers employed by temporary agencies or as day laborers. While many of these workers appreciate the flexibility of their current arrangements, nonstandard workers generally earn less than workers with comparable skills and backgrounds who work in regular full-time jobs. Nonstandard workers are also far less likely than regular full-time workers to have health or pension benefits.

Wealth: the rich get richer, the rest get poorer

Stagnant and falling wages and incomes tell only part of the story of rising inequality. A family's ability to plan for the future and to cope with financial emergencies is strongly affected by its wealth (tangible assets such as a house and car plus financial assets such as stocks and bonds).

The distribution of wealth is even more concentrated at the top than is the distribution of income, and wealth inequality has grown worse in the 1990s. Between 1989 and 1997 (projected), the share of wealth held by the top 1% of households grew from 37.4% of the national total to 39.1%. Over the same period, the share of all wealth held by families in the middle fifth of the population fell from 4.8% to 4.4%. What is even more disturbing is that, after adjusting for inflation, the value of this middle group's wealth holdings actually fell between 1989 and 1997, due primarily to a rise in indebtedness. Between 1989 and 1995 (the latest year for which data are available), the share of households with zero or negative wealth (families with negative wealth owe more than they own) increased from 15.5% to 18.5% of all households. By 1995, almost one-third (31.3%) of black households had zero or negative wealth.

The stock market boom of the 1980s and 1990s has had little or no impact on the vast majority of Americans for the simple reason that most working families do not own much stock. While the share of households owning stock has risen in the 1990s, by 1995 almost 60% of households still owned no stock in any form, including mutual funds or defined-contribution pension plans. Moreover, many of those new to the stock market have only small investments there. In 1995, for example, fewer than one-third of all households had stock holdings greater than $5,000. In the same year, almost 90% of the value of all stock was in the hands of the best-off 10% of households. Not surprisingly, then, projections through 1997 suggest that 85.8% of the benefits of the increase in the stock market between 1989 and 1997 went to the richest 10% of households.

Poverty: rates remain high despite economic expansion

Since the mid-1980s, poverty rates in the United States have failed to respond to economic growth. The most recent poverty rate — 13.3% in 1997 — is 0.5 percentage points above the 1989 rate of 12.8%. Even with an economy that grew between 1979 and 1997, poverty rates in those 18 years were high by historical standards, averaging 13.6% for the period 1979-89 and 14.0% for the period 1989-97.

Poverty rates for minorities and children are well above the national average. More than one-quarter of blacks (26.5%) lived in poverty in 1997 (below the 30.7% rate in 1989 and the 31.0% rate in 1979). About one in five (19.9%) children were poor in 1997, up slightly from 19.6% in 1989 and 16.4% in 1979. For minority children, poverty rates are especially high: 37.2% of black children and 36.8% of Hispanic children under 18 were poor in 1997. The poor also appear to be poorer now than at any time in the last 20 years: in 1997, the share of people in poverty whose incomes were below 50% of the poverty line was 41.0%.

Some argue that these rates are artificially high due to erroneous measurement. But a study by a nonpartisan panel of poverty experts shows that an updated measure of poverty would actually increase the number of poor by about 9 million persons (with most of the increase among the working poor). Regard-

9

less of the poverty definition used, poverty rates have been growing faster than economic conditions would predict.

The conventional wisdom typically defines the problem in terms of the supposedly counterproductive behavior of poor people themselves, implying that, with more effort, the poor could lift themselves up by their bootstraps. Recent trends in family structure and low-wage labor markets, however, contradict this analysis. The role of family structure (the shift to family types more vulnerable to poverty) has become increasingly *less* important since the 1970s. The role of family structure (the shift to family types more vulnerable to poverty) is typically cited as the key reason that poverty rates have been unresponsive to economic growth. While it is true that the increase in female-headed families has consistently put upward pressure on poverty rates, its impact has fallen considerably over time. And a countervailing demographic change — the rising educational attainment of heads-of-households in poor families — should have led to consistently larger declines in poverty. A full accounting of the demographic and economic forces responsible for recent poverty problems assigns a relatively minor role to family structure.

In fact, the problems analyzed throughout this book — slow growth, heightened inequality of the income distribution, and, in particular, falling wages — all conspired to keep poverty rates historically high throughout the 1980s and into the 1990s.

Variations across regions

Trends in the nation's 50 states and various regions, in broad terms, mirror those at the national level. Nevertheless, important regional differences exist in the trends for family income, employment, wages, and poverty. These different experiences underscore another dimension of inequality in the United States, one that flows from regional disparities in wage levels and job opportunities.

Over the 1980s, the Northeast outperformed the rest of the country with respect to most important economic indicators, including median hourly wages, median family incomes, poverty, and unemployment. However, despite low unemployment, low-wage workers in some Northeastern states (New York and Pennsylvania, for example) still lost ground. States in the West, particularly California, experienced almost no growth in employment or median incomes, and wages declined for workers at the median and below.

Family income inequality increased persistently at the state level in both the 1980s and 1990s. Over the 1980s, the top-fifth/bottom-fifth ratio grew 2.4 points in New York and 2.1 points in California. Other states where income inequality grew faster than the national average in the 1980s included Indiana, Michigan, Missouri, West Virginia, Mississippi, Louisiana, and Hawaii. Inequality continued to grow in most states in the 1990s, with faster growth in both New York and California. By the end of the period, the average income of the richest fifth of New York families was 13.7 times that of the poorest families in that state. The Southwestern states of New Mexico and Arizona also saw relatively fast growth in inequality over the 1990s; these states ended the period with levels similar to New York (13.0 in New Mexico, 13.8 in Arizona).

California and New York suffered most acutely in the 1990s recession, as these states' incomes and employment contracted and poverty grew. The most recent data show incomes of working families in these large states to be lower than at the previous business cycle peak in 1989. Many other states, however, have clearly benefited from the recent tightening of labor markets. In 1997, unemployment was below 4% in many states (especially in the Midwest), and, thanks in part to increases in the minimum wage, the real wages of low-wage workers in these states have grown over the recovery.

International comparisons: falling behind in wages, productivity

A comparison of the recent economic performance of the United States and other advanced, industrialized countries sheds important light on the U.S. economy over the last two decades. Over the postwar period, the United States has consistently found itself in the middle or the bottom of advanced countries with respect to growth in national income per person. Even in the 1990s, when the United States has been heralded as a model "new economy," national income per person in the United States has grown at only about the same rate as it has in France, Italy, and the United Kingdom and more slowly than it has in Japan, Germany, and the average rate for advanced economies.

A similar story holds for the most important long-run determinant of living standards: growth in labor productivity, or the production of goods and services in an average hour of work. Since at least the early 1960s, productivity growth rates in the United States have averaged only half the rate of other advanced economies. For many years, economists dismissed the more rapid growth in productivity in other countries as evidence only that it is easier for countries with lower levels of output per hour to play "catch-up" with the United States. A new development in the 1990s, however, is that at least four European economies (Belgium, France, the Netherlands, and western Germany) appear to have finally caught-up to average U.S. productivity levels. Thus, it seems that the alleged inefficiencies of more regulated economies have apparently not prevented them from narrowing — and in several cases closing — the productivity gap with the United States.

As productivity differences narrow between the United States and the rest of the advanced economies, the U.S. position at or near the top of the world income chart relies increasingly on working longer, not more efficiently. Between 1990 and 1995, a rise in the average hours worked per year in the United States and an even larger decline in the average hours worked per year in Japan have given the United States the dubious distinction of being the advanced economy with the longest work year. An important contributor to the much longer work schedule in the United States is the lack of legally mandated, employer-paid vacation time, which is typically three to five weeks per year for all workers in most European economies.

Along with slower growth, the U.S. economy has consistently produced the highest levels of economic inequality among the advanced economies. The United States had the highest overall poverty rate among 16 advanced economies in the late 1980s and 1990s. High-income families (those in the 90th percentile of family income) in the United States earn almost six times more than their low-income counterparts (those in the 10th percentile). The average ratio for other advanced economies is under four, with only the United Kingdom (with a ratio of about five) anywhere near the U.S. level. In fact, U.S. inequality is so severe that low-income families in the United States are worse off than low-income families in the 12 other advanced economies for which comparable data exist, despite the higher average income level in the United States. (The United Kingdom is the only country where low-income families are worse off than in the United States). Inequality in the United States (along with the United Kingdom) has also shown a strong tendency to rise over the last two decades, even as inequality was relatively stable or declining in most of the rest of the advanced economies.

Finally, economic mobility for those at the bottom — a factor that, in principle, could counteract the effects of inequality — is actually lower in the United States than in other wealthy economies. The United States, for example, had a lower transition rate out of poverty than France, Germany, Ireland, the Netherlands, and Sweden in the mid-1980s. (Only Canada, which had a lower overall poverty rate, had a worse transition rate than the United States.) Low-wage workers in the United States also appear to be less likely than workers in other economies to move on to higher-wage employment. Among low-wage workers in eight advanced economies in 1986, for example, U.S. low-wage workers had the lowest probability of having moved to high-wage jobs and the highest probability of being unemployed five years later.

The living standards debate

BY MANY IMPORTANT INDICATORS, THE AMERICAN ECONOMY IS SOARING. UNEMPLOY-
ment in early 1998 fell to its lowest point in 30 years. In a reversal of the trend of
the previous two decades, real wages for most workers were finally on the rise,
and productivity — a broad measure of the efficiency of the labor force — was
picking up speed. What's more, these positive developments have been accompanied by a higher level of confidence about the economy across a broad cross-
section of the American public. In sum, it looks as if the economy of 1996-98
has delivered broad-based growth to most workers and their families.

But how significant are these recent changes? Do they represent a reversal
of decades of stagnant family income growth and real wage losses for most
workers? Or are the fundamental problems that have beset working families
over the long term simply on pause, due to current low unemployment and the
increased demand for work?

The evidence presented in this 1998-99 edition of *The State of Working
America* suggests that a marked transformation in the U.S. economy has yet to
occur. When we put recent gains in their historical context, it is clear that the
living standards of many working families have neither fully "recovered" from
the early 1990s recession nor benefited from the overall growth in productivity.
Moreover, whether recent gains continue depends upon whether the factors responsible for the long-term erosion of wages continue to be offset by tight labor
markets, unexpectedly low inflation, and further minimum wage increases.

This introductory essay spells out our assessment of the living standards of
America's working families, both past and present, and attempts to address the
current issues in the public discussion. It begins with a short-term view that
enumerates the impressive gains of the past few years. The second part, which

compares the current 1990s business cycle with that of the 1980s, finds that, by many measures, workers and their families in the 1990s have yet to recover the ground they gained in the 1980s but lost in the 1990s recession. Finally, viewing the long term, we ask whether the gains of the late 1990s are evidence of a new economic order, the "reward" for two decades of economic pain in the form of falling wages and unequal growth. We find no evidence that real wage losses, the increase in economic inequality, and the heightened insecurity of working families are part of some sacrifice that has led to higher productivity, compensation, or per capita income.

The good news about recent wage trends

One of the most important and troubling economic phenomena of the last two decades has been declining wages and stagnant family incomes amidst positive overall economic growth. Even when unemployment was beginning to fall in the middle part of this decade, the economic gains continued to elude most working families. Wages continued to decline through 1995, and family incomes were still far below the level they had reached before the 1990-91 recession.

The 1996-98 period, however, is different. Over the last year and a half, as shown in **Table A**, low unemployment has persisted, and wages have not only grown faster than inflation, they have grown faster at the bottom of the wage scale than at the top.

For example, male wages at the 20th and 50th percentiles fell by about 1% per year in the 1989-96 period (the 20th percentile worker earns less than 80% of the workforce; the 50th percentile, or median, worker earns less than half of the workforce). But from 1996 through the first half of 1998, real wages grew 4.1% per year for low-wage male workers and 2.0% per year for the median male worker, indicating a narrowing of the wage gap between middle- and low-wage men. Wages fell for low- and middle-wage female workers at an annual rate of 0.2% from 1989 to 1996, but reversed course and grew at annual rates of 2.7% and 2.6% respectively from 1996 to mid-1998. Wages for high-wage male and female workers also grew relatively quickly in the 1996-98 period, but, in both cases, wage growth at the 90th percentile was slower than at the 20th. This pattern of growth indicates a narrowing of the wage gap between the top and the bottom of the wage scale, an uncharacteristic pattern given inequality's persistent increase over the past two decades.

The other panels in the table show the primary factors responsible for the recent growth spurt of real wages: falling unemployment, the increase in the real value of the minimum wage, and the decline in the growth of inflation.

TABLE A Wage growth in the 1990s

	1989	1996	1998*	1989-96	Change 1996-98*	1989-98*
Hourly wages ($1998)						
All				*Annualized percent change*		
90th percentile	$23.72	$23.81	$24.63	0.0%	2.3%	0.4%
50th percentile	11.30	10.71	11.13	-0.8	2.6	-0.2
20th percentile	6.79	6.63	6.99	-0.3	3.6	0.3
Male						
90th percentile	$26.41	$26.14	$27.20	-0.1%	2.7%	0.3%
50th percentile	13.22	12.26	12.63	-1.1	2.0	-0.5
20th percentile	7.82	7.32	7.77	-0.9	4.1	-0.1
Female						
90th percentile	$19.55	$20.59	$21.14	0.7%	1.8%	0.9%
50th percentile	9.66	9.51	9.88	-0.2	2.6	0.3
20th percentile	6.25	6.15	6.40	-0.2	2.7	0.3
Unemployment rates				*Total percentage-point change*		
All	5.3%	5.4%	4.5%	0.1	-0.9	-0.8
White	4.5	4.7	3.9	0.2	-0.8	-0.6
Black	11.4	10.5	9.0	-0.9	-1.5	-2.4
Hispanic	8.0	8.9	6.9	0.9	-2.0	-1.1
Young (18-35),						
Minority, high school educated						
Black	15.9%	16.3%	12.8%	0.4	-3.5	-3.1
Hispanic	8.3	9.9	7.9	1.6	-2.0	-0.4
Real minimum wage				*Annualized percent change*		
(1998 dollars)	$4.39	$4.53	$5.15	0.5%	9.0%	1.9%
Consumer price index	124.0	156.9	162.4	3.4	2.3	3.2

* These columns reflect seasonally adjusted data for the first six months of 1998.

Source: Authors' analysis of BLS and CPS data.

The role of low unemployment. The overall unemployment rate was 4.5% in the first half of 1998, down almost a full percentage point since 1996. Moreover, this 0.9-point decline overall was accompanied by larger declines among groups of workers who are traditionally further down the hiring queue. For example, the unemployment rate for African Americans and Hispanics fell by 1.5 and 2.0 points over this period. Looking at a particularly disadvantaged group — young (18-35), minority high school graduates — reveals an even larger decline of 3.5 percentage points for young blacks. Of course, even with these large declines, unemployment rates for young minority workers are still many times higher than the overall rate (e.g., the unemployment rate for young African Americans with a high school degree was more than three times that of whites in each of the years shown). Nevertheless, these improvements provide clear evidence that persistently tight labor markets have greatly increased the employment opportunities of the least well-off.

The role of a higher minimum wage. The Congress mandated two $0.90 increases in the federal minimum wage in the 1990s, the first of which was implemented in 1990/91, the second in 1996/97. By 1996 inflation had eroded much of the value of the first increase, but the second increase, which raised the real value of the minimum wage 9% per year over the 1996-98 period, clearly helped to lift wages at the lower end of the wage scale.

The role of lower inflation. Inflation, as measured by the annualized growth rate of the consumer price index, grew by 3.4% per year in the 1989-96 period but slowed to 2.3% in 1996-98. This unexpected deceleration in inflation means that wage increases given by employers simply to offset anticipated higher inflation translated into real wage increases. Thus, some of the wage growth over the 1996-98 period is a result of inflation temporarily growing more slowly than expected. As inflationary expectations begin to conform more closely to the actual path of price growth, the contribution of lower prices to real wage growth is likely to diminish.

These recent wage and employment trends are a welcome reversal of the long-term trend toward rising inequality. The problem of inequality's persistent growth has led numerous analysts to view low unemployment levels as well as increases in the minimum wage as desirable policies that could be implemented without adversely affecting the economy or hurting the workers they are meant to help. As the data in the table show, low unemployment has not led to runaway inflation, nor has the increase in the minimum wage hurt the job prospects of low-wage workers.

A broader look at the 1990s

The above examination of the past few years provides important insights into the short-term condition of the economy and underscores the importance of persistent low unemployment. But to accurately assess the economy, it is best to examine an entire business cycle (in this case, 1989-98) and compare it to trends over other cycles. We now have enough years of data to evaluate most of the economic landscape of the 1990s.

Unfortunately for working Americans, the 1990s have been, in many ways, an extension of the 1980s. Income and wage inequality have increased (though at a slower rate), families are working longer for less, wealth has become even more concentrated, and poverty has not fallen much in response to overall economic growth. And the 1990s have introduced some new problems with regard to living standards: an increase in job insecurity; a decline in wages for white-collar and entry-level, college-educated workers; wage stagnation for middle-wage females; and, at least through 1996, worse income growth for the typical family.

Family income

By 1997, the most recent year for which data are available as this book goes to press, the income of the median American family was only slightly ($285) higher than it was at the peak of the last business cycle peak in 1989. The initial decline was attributable to the recession that began in 1990, but the median continued to fall as the recovery got under way in 1991 and 1992. In 1994, median family income finally responded to overall growth, and it has increased each year since. The fact that it took eight years for median family income to reach its prerecession level is unprecedented in the postwar era. In every prior recovery, the income of the typical family had, by this point in time, far surpassed its level of the prior peak.

Examining the continued growth of income inequality in the 1990s has been made more difficult because of changes in the survey instrument used by the Census Bureau to track family income. However, we use a specially constructed data set (explained in Appendix A) that allows for a consistent comparison of 1989 to 1996. These data clearly reveal that slow income growth is not the only problem: family income has also become increasingly unequal during this recovery. The inflation-adjusted average income of the top 1% of families, for example, grew by 10% from 1989 to 1996, while the income of the middle fifth fell by 2.1% and that of the lowest fifth fell by 4.0%. Though this is a slower increase in income inequality than occurred over the 1980s, it nevertheless represents considerable growth of income inequality.

Working longer

The primary factor driving these income problems is the continuing wage deterioration among non-college-educated workers, joined in the 1990s by white-collar and even some groups of college-educated workers. This has meant that families have had to constantly boost their hours of work outside the home in order to keep their incomes from stagnating.

Were it not for the extra hours of work provided by working wives, the average income of middle-income, married families would have fallen in the 1990s (**Table B**). Between 1989 and 1996, middle-class husbands and wives increased their annual hours of work outside the home from 3,550 to 3,685, or

TABLE B Family income and hours worked in the 1990s,
middle-income, married-couple families*

	1989	1996	Change	% Change
Income ($1996)	$53,908	$54,515	$607	1.1
Annual hours (husbands and wives)	3,550	3,685	135	3.8
Husbands	2,207	2,227	20	0.9
Wives	1,342	1,458	116	8.6

Percent change in income without wives' added hours: -1.1%

* Data include prime-age (25-54) couples only, to avoid the impact of retirement on average hours worked.

Source: Tables 1.16, 1.17, and Figure 1I.

more than three weeks of extra work per year. And, because of falling wages, this 3.8% increase in hours translated into just 1.1% more family income over seven years. Most of the added hours came from wives, and, without their added work effort, these middle-class families would have lost 1.1% of their income. These middle-income families were not alone: the bottom 80% of families increased their annual hours of work but still managed only to stay even.

Wage erosion

The deterioration in hourly wages is a long-term trend that continued in the 1990s. Between 1989 and 1997 (our last full year of wage data), the median male wage fell 0.9% per year, and the hourly wages of the bottom 80% of male workers were lower in 1997 than in 1989. Wages for females, which grew 0.6% per year at the median in the 1980s, were flat in the 1990s, rising just 0.1% per year from 1989 to 1997.

Adding fringe benefits to these wage data does not brighten the picture (**Figure A**). Since the average value of the benefit package fell relative to wages over the 1990s, the typical worker actually lost more in terms of compensation (wages and benefits) than in wages. From 1989 to 1997, compensation fell 4.2% for all workers, 7.8% for males. By contrast, wages alone fell 3.2% for all workers and 6.7% for males.

The disappointing path of compensation growth is especially clear when compared to productivity, which grew 9% from 1989 to 1997. If economic growth were distributed as equally as in the past, then the growth in productivity would have lifted the income of the typical, middle-class family, whose 4,000 hours of work in 1996 surely made a nontrivial contribution to the rise in this important

FIGURE A Hourly productivity and real compensation growth* in the 1990s

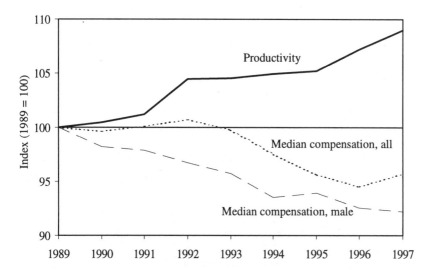

* Because data on the median benefit package are unavailable, we assign the average compensation-to-wage ratio (average compensation divided by average wages and salaries) to the median wage. This method overstates the growth in the median worker's benefits.

Source: Authors' analysis.

indicator. The fact that most families are simply striving to get back to the living standards they enjoyed in 1989 is a telling measure of our diminished expectations.

Much of the conventional economic analysis of the 1990s argues a college degree is a prerequisite to participating in the new technology-driven economy. If this is so, then we would expect the wages of new college graduates to be on the rise, or at least immune from the trend of long-term wage deterioration. But this is not the case. The 1990s have been a bad decade for young, college-educated workers. The hourly wages of entry-level college graduates fell about 7% for both males and females from 1989 to 1997, a sharp reversal particularly for young women graduates, whose hourly wages grew 11.2% in the 1980s. Even young college graduates in scientific and engineering occupations earned lower wages in 1997 than their counterparts earned in 1989; those in computer occupations ended the period with only modestly higher wages.

Thus, while the tight labor market of the last few years has delivered real gains to those who have fallen behind over the last two decades, these gains have been too small to reverse long-term wage and income losses. The real wage of the median worker was 4% lower in the first half of 1998 than in 1979; for the median male worker it was down 15%. On the other hand, the post-1979 period has been a good one for those at the top of the wage and income scales.

There is no "smoking gun" to account for these long-term income and wage losses. Instead, a variety of related factors have, since the late 1970s, interacted to increase inequality and reduce the wages of most workers. All of these factors share a common characteristic: they reflect the general deregulatory, laissez-faire shifts in the economy and forces that have weakened the bargaining power of workers, both union and non-union and both white and blue collar. For instance, the long-term decline in labor market institutions – the falling real value of the minimum wage along with continuing deunionization – can explain one-third of the growing wage inequality among prime-age workers. The expansion of low-wage service-sector employment has contributed perhaps another 20-30%. This shift to lower-paying industries is causally linked to another important contributor to the economic problems of working families: the increasing globalization of the economy through immigration and trade. By itself, globalization may account for 10-20% of the increase in wage inequality (with immigration playing an even larger role in the wage erosion of low-wage workers); the combined effects of globalization and the shift to lower-paying industries can conservatively account for 30% to 40% of the growth of wage inequality. Thus, the weakening of labor market institutions, the impact of globalization, and the shift to low-wage service industries can together account for two-thirds to three-fourths of the growth in wage inequality.

Job security

Another new and disturbing feature of the 1990s recovery has been the decline in job security, defined here as the sense among workers that, as long as their job performance is adequate, their employment situation will remain unchanged.

Workers appear less and less likely to be able to count on the long-term employment attachments that in the past provided opportunities for steady wage growth, fringe benefits, and long-term job security. Between the 1980s and the 1990s, for example, the share of workers who have been at their current jobs for at least 10 years has fallen. Involuntary job loss (layoffs, "downsizing," and other job displacements not for cause) actually *increased* between the recession of 1992 and the recovery through 1995. These objective measures of job stability may have contributed to workers' subjective perceptions that jobs were less secure through most of the 1990s recovery than they were in past recoveries, including those with weaker labor markets. Survey data through 1996 indeed show workers feeling less optimistic than in the past that their jobs would last and more pessimistic about their employment prospects if they lost their jobs. It is not unreasonable to conclude that job insecurity can help explain why wage growth was slow to respond to falling unemployment throughout most of the 1990s recovery.

Given that the unemployment rate is relatively low, we should probably look elsewhere for the source of workers' insecurity. One of the prime suspects is the increasingly "contingent" nature of much of the work available in the 1990s. Almost 30% of workers in 1997 were employed in situations that were not regular full-time jobs. These "nonstandard" work arrangements ranged from independent contracting and other forms of self-employment to work in temporary agencies or as day labor. The most readily documented indicator of this trend is the near doubling of the share of workers employed by temporary help agencies, from 1.3% in 1989 to 2.4% in 1997. While many of workers in nonstandard jobs appreciate the flexibility of their current arrangements, they generally earn less than workers with comparable skills and backgrounds who work in regular full-time jobs. Nonstandard workers are also far less likely than regular full-time workers to have health or pension benefits.

Poverty
The theme of a growing, even booming, economy leaving families behind is perhaps nowhere more evident than in a discussion of American poverty. The fact that poverty did not fall between 1995 and 1996 (the most recent year for which data are available) is one of the many contradictions of the 1990s recovery.

In 1997, 13.3% of the population, or 35.6 million Americans, were poor, a higher poverty rate than in 1989 (12.8%) or 1979 (11.7%). Conventional explanations that blame demographic trends for the uncoupling of the historical relationship between economic growth and falling poverty rates fall short in the 1990s, since these trends, which include not only the shift to mother-only families but also the educational attainment of family heads, worked to lower poverty over this period. Also, including the value of benefits provided to the poor (yet not typically counted in their incomes) fails to explain the disconnection. Rather, the increase in both economic inequality and the share of jobs that pay poverty-level wages have kept the poverty rate from falling as the economy has expanded.

This lack of access to jobs in the 1990s that could lift the poor out of poverty challenges recent shifts in U.S. anti-poverty policy. The welfare-to-work component of welfare reform partially reflects American values regarding the integrity of work as well as voters' distaste for dependence on government support of low-income families. However, the wage and employment opportunities facing poor persons will have to expand considerably before anyone can reasonably expect the poor to work their way out of poverty.

International comparisons

The 1990s have been promoted as a stellar period for the American economy relative to that of other industrialized economies. While this is generally true for unemployment rates, other broad economic indicators, including growth in per capita income and labor productivity, fail to show that the U.S. is economically dominant among the advanced countries (defined as those in the Organization for Economic Cooperation and Development, or OECD). With regard to wage growth and inequality, measures that are more directly relevant to living standards of working families, the U.S. is clearly behind.

Per capita income has historically been higher in the U.S. than in other OECD countries. But in the 1990s, average annual growth in this broad measure of prosperity was just 1.0% in the U.S, compared to 1.3% among the other OECD countries. A similar comparison for productivity shows the U.S. growing more slowly than the OECD average in both the 1980s and 1990s, so that by 1995 the U.S. no longer led the world in productivity levels; by that year, West Germany, France, the Netherlands, and Belgium all had productivity levels slightly above or comparable to those of the U.S.

Enriching the rich: surging profitability and CEO pay

During the 1990s, in the midst of slow income growth, widespread wage erosion, heightened job insecurity, and stubbornly high poverty, corporate profitability and compensation of top executives has surged. And while this surge increased the wealth of the richest households, that of middle-income households was no greater in 1997 than in 1989.

By 1997, the net worth (assets minus debts) of the top 1% was about $10 million, up 11.3% from 1989 (**Table C**). Over the same period, the net worth of middle-class families (those in the middle fifth of the wealth distribution) fell by 2.9%. This pattern of wealth accumulation, facilitated in large part by the stock market boom, enabled the top 1% of households to control 39.1% of total net wealth by 1997, an increase of 1.8 percentage points over 1989 and 5.3 points over 1983.

Note that the stock market boom of the 1990s has not enriched the middle-class household. While the share of households owning stock has risen in the 1990s, by 1995 (the most recent year for which these data are available) almost 60% of households still owned no stock in any form, including mutual funds and pensions, and fewer than one-third of all households had stock holdings greater than $5,000. In the same year, almost 90% of the value of all stock was

TABLE C Wealth, profitability, and CEO pay trends, 1979-97

Wealth	1983	1989	1992	1997*	Percent change 1983-89	Percent change 1992-97	Percent change 1989-97
Net worth, middle-income households (000)	$54.7	$57.9	n.a.	$56.2	6.0%	n.a.	-2.9%
Net worth, upper 1% (000)	$7,065.1	$8,962.1	n.a.	$9,977.9	26.9	n.a.	11.3
					Change in share		
Percent of households with net worth of $10,000 or less (including negative)	29.7	31.8	n.a.	31.9	2.1	n.a.	0.1

	1979	1989	1992	1997	Percent change** 1979-89	Percent change** 1992-97	Percent change** 1989-97
Profitability/stock market growth							
Return on capital	6.4%	7.1%	7.3%	10.4%	0.7%	3.1%	3.3%
Capital share of income	17.4	18.4	16.7	21.6	1.0	4.9	3.2
New York Stock Exchange Index (real $)	126.5	233.0	262.0	456.5	6.3	11.7	8.8
CEO compensation							
Cash wages & bonuses (1989=100)	54.6	100.0	105.9	144.6	5.7%	6.4%	4.7%
Average compensation (000) ($1997)	$999	$1,783	$2,085	$3,565	5.4	11.3	9.0

* Net worth levels are projections; net worth percentages are from 1995.

** Rows 1 and 2 are percentage-point changes; row 3 is annualized percent growth.

Source: Profitability: Table 1.15; CEO compensation: Table 3.51; Wealth: Tables 5.3 and 5.6.

in the hands of the best-off 10% of households. Not surprisingly, then, estimates through 1997 suggest that 85.8% of the benefits of the increase in the stock market between 1989 and 1997 went to the richest 10% of households.

This increase in wealth concentration stems in part from an economic phenomenon that was a much larger factor in the 1990s than in the 1970s or 1980s: the increase in the "return on capital," or corporate profitability. As shown in Table C, the pre-tax profit rate (the profits and interest income earned from plant and equipment assets) grew 3.3 percentage points from 1989 to 1997, to stand at a 30-year high. As a result, the share of income derived from profits and interest (capital income) has also reached historic highs, climbing 3.2 percentage points in the 1990s. Had the growth in profitability been more modest (achieving, for example, the long-term average of the 1960-80s), average labor compensation in 1997 could have been 7.7% higher. Reflecting this increased profitability and the stock market boom, Table C also shows that compensation of chief executive officers (CEOs) doubled from 1989 to 1997 and grew 71% over the 1992-97 recovery.

Whether there has been a payoff to the economy, or to a typical working family, from downsizing, restructuring, deunionization, and globalization is uncertain. What is clear, however, is that CEO compensation, business profitability, and the income and wealth of the top 1% owe much to the economy of the 1990s.

Summing up the 1990s

From the perspective of working families, the economy of the 1990s is woefully similar to that of the 1980s:

- Income growth remains slow, and it has been slower in the 1990s than in previous business cycles; it has taken the median family longer to regain its pre-recession income level in this recovery than in any other since World War II;

- Income inequality has continued to grow in the 1990s, although it has done so more slowly (at about two-thirds the rate) than in the 1980s;

- Despite the 1996-98 spurt in wages, wage growth in the 1990s has been no better than in the 1980s; due to the slowdown in the growth of benefits over the 1990s, median hourly compensation, which was flat over the 1980s, declined in the 1990s.

- Many workers who were able to avoid wage losses in the 1980s succumbed to the long-term trend in the 1990s. Among them were new college graduates, including those in technologically advanced fields (such as engineering) and male white-collar workers.

- The wage premium enjoyed by college-educated workers grew strongly in the 1980s but grew little in the 1990s for men and fell for women. This development challenges the notion that the 1990s was a period in which technological advances led to accelerated demand for highly educated workers.

- Jobs grew more insecure in the 1990s, as downsizing diminished the job stability of white-collar workers.

Is there a 'new economy'?

The economy over the 1979-89 and 1989-97 business cycles brought only modestly higher incomes for middle-income families and lower incomes for those at the bottom of the income scale. Whatever income growth has been generated among middle-income families, particularly married-couple families, has in large part been driven by more family members working and working more hours each year. Thus, American families still face the consequences of a long-term erosion in wages, deteriorating job quality, and greater economic insecurity. To some analysts, however, these are the unfortunate but unavoidable costs associated with a transition to a "new economy," whose promise is expanding living standards for all. In some analyses, the wage and productivity growth of 1996 and 1997 are cited as evidence of a successful transition to a new economy.

The economy is always changing, renewing, and reformulating itself. New products and new ways of producing goods and services are always being developed. Thus, in many routine ways we have a "new economy" every year. The more profound question is whether we are making or have made a transition to a permanently *better* economy, i.e., a more efficient economy leading to increased living standards for working families.

In the post-1979 period, economic policy has moved decisively toward creating a more laissez-faire, deregulated economy. Industries such as transportation (trucking, intercity buses, railroads, airlines) and communications have been deregulated. Management has actively pursued the weakening of union protections, the right to organize, and the right to collectively bargain. Social protections, such as safety, health, and environmental regulations, the minimum wage, government cash assistance (e.g., welfare), and the unemployment insurance system, have been weakened. Increased globalization, including greater international capital mobility and international trade, has given greater scope to managerial discretion. Taxes on capital and the average and marginal tax rates for high-income families and business have been reduced. We have pursued the anti-inflationary policies preferred by investors, Wall Street, and the bond market. In sum, there has been a conscious, decided shift of national policy designed to unleash market forces and empower management decision makers.

The promise of all of these policies was to raise living standards and to generate more overall income growth. As with all policies and economic transformations, there were expected to be, and there have been, losers, as the large redistribution of income, wealth, and wages since 1979 attests. The question is, was there an overall improvement in the economy that would justify all of the social costs? In economists' terms, did the benefits outweigh the costs? Or simply, was the gain worth the pain? Is there reason to believe we are making a transition to a *better* economy?

The issue of whether we have a "new" and "better" economy requires that we specify when the "new economy" originated. Some analysts have identified 1992 as the starting point, while others focus on 1994 or 1996. But regardless of the starting point, it is inherently difficult, given the cyclicality of the economy, to distinguish whether positive trends in any recovery year are due to the cyclical recovery or to the onset of a "new economy." Therefore, we analyze this issue in three ways. First, we examine whether the economy's performance in this recovery and business cycle was better than in earlier ones. The merit of such an approach is that it employs an "apples to apples" comparison that looks beyond the data for a few, selected years. The second part of the analysis addresses whether the solid wage and productivity performance in 1996 and 1997 are indicative of our having ascended to a new information technology era. The third part examines how "knowledge workers," presumably the cutting edge and clear beneficiaries of the new economy, have fared in recent years.

Business cycle comparisons

In comparing one business cycle to another, three indicators are key: the growth of productivity (output per worker), growth in real hourly compensation, and growth in real income per capita. The first, productivity growth (the growth in private nonfarm output per hour worked), allows us to judge the rate at which the private sector is becoming more efficient. Central to the "new economy" idea is that growing inequalities and insecurity have been necessary (or the price paid) for generating a significant acceleration in productivity growth. But productivity growth in the current business cycle (1990-98) has been no better than that of the business cycles of the 1970s and 1980s — between 1.0% and 1.2% annually (**Table D**) – and it pales in comparison to the growth over the five business cycles from 1948 to 1973, when productivity grew from 1.9% to 3.3% annually.

TABLE D Growth in nonfarm business productivity, hourly compensation, and income per capita over business cycles, 1948-98

| Year:qtr | | Annual percent growth | | |
Start	End	Productivity	Real hourly compensation	Income per capita
Business cycles:				
1948:4	1953:3	3.3%	3.3%	3.0%
1953:3	1957:3	1.9	3.0	0.8
1957:3	1960:2	2.1	2.2	1.0
1960:2	1969:4	2.7	2.6	2.9
1969:4	1973:4	2.7	2.0	2.5
1973:4	1980:1	1.2	1.1	1.6
1980:1	1990:3	1.0	0.5	1.6
Current cycle				
1990:3	1998:1	1.2%	0.6%	1.4%
Recoveries:				
1949:4	1953:3	3.2%	3.3%	4.6%
1954:2	1957:3	2.1	3.2	1.9
1958:2	1960:2	2.6	2.6	3.4
1961:1	1969:4	3.2	3.0	3.8
1970:4	1973:4	2.7	2.1	3.7
1975:1	1980:1	1.5	1.1	3.0
1982:4	1990:3	1.3	0.4	2.7
Current recovery				
1991:1	1998:1	1.3%	0.7%	1.8%
1992:2	1998:1	0.9	0.4	1.9

Source: Authors' analysis of BEA and BLS data.

Recent productivity growth is similarly unspectacular in the shorter period that includes only the recovery. Regardless of the time period used to date the current recovery (starting in early 1991, as per the National Bureau of Economic Research, or in mid-1992, when unemployment started falling), its productivity performance has been no better than the recoveries of the 1970s and 1980s and significantly below those of the earlier postwar period. So, in terms of the key indicator of efficiency — productivity — there is nothing new in the new economy.

Some have argued that productivity is mismeasured or understated (particularly in services) and that the payoff will come as we learn to exploit microelectronic/computer technologies. Productivity may or may not be mismeasured, but the only relevant issue here is whether there has been a greater understatement of productivity growth in the 1990s than in the 1980s, 1970s, or earlier periods (otherwise, our comparison of time periods would remain correct). No analysis has shown a growth in mismeasurement. For instance, any errors in measuring productivity in particular service sector industries or in the service sector as a whole have been present for decades, and the expansion of the most difficult-to-measure services, such as finances and health care, has not been sufficient to substantially affect overall trends. The payoff may come eventually, but when? There have been claims ever since the 1950s that computerization will soon transform productivity, and we are still waiting.

The second indicator in Table D is the growth of average real hourly compensation (which includes payroll taxes, pensions, health insurance, wages, and salaries for all nonfarm business sector employment). This measure captures the compensation growth of all workers, from executives to day laborers, and therefore does not reflect trends experienced by "typical workers." Average hourly compensation growth does, however, provide a measure for how fast the compensation pie is growing. Far from posting a better performance, the current business cycle has seen slower compensation growth (0.6%) than during the stagflationary 1970s (1.1%) and the earlier postwar periods (when it ranged from 2.0% to 3.3%). Compensation growth in the current recovery also does not suggest a better performance for the 1990s.

The final measure, income per capita (gross domestic product per person) reflects growth in all types of income and growth in the percent of the population employed. As with compensation growth, per capita income is an average across the population and therefore does not take into account changes in distribution — in other words, it does not reflect trends for a typical family. By this measure, income growth in the current cycle has been no better than that of the 1970s and 1980s and far slower than that of the 1948-73 period. The 1.8% or 1.9% per capita income growth in the current recovery, however, is decidedly inferior to the recoveries of the 1970s or 1980s and just half that of the earlier postwar recoveries with the exception of the mid-1950s.

Thus, if we are in a "new economy" it is not necessarily a better economy in terms of productivity, wage, or income growth.

The last two years

Although productivity and other measures of economic performance have not shown strong or even better-than-average growth over this business cycle, productivity and compensation growth in the last two years has been strong. For instance, productivity grew 1.9% and 1.7%, respectively, in 1996 and 1997. Can or should these trends be interpreted as evidence of the economy ascending to a new, higher rate of productivity growth?

Caution is called for in interpreting short-run gains as evidence of a new economic regime. Simply put, two good years no more proves the existence of a new economy than does the dismal performance of the three prior years (productivity growth of 0.1%, 0.4%, and 0.2%) prove a permanent, lower productivity growth regime. The convention of examining complete recoveries and business cycles remains the most enlightening type of analysis. But the question of why productivity picked up so much in 1996 and 1997 is still an important one. It seems unlikely that the long-awaited gains from the computer revolution, the tax cuts of the 1980s, deregulation, or globalization suddenly took hold in 1996. Rather, a more plausible explanation may be that persistent low unemployment and a spurt in demand pushed productivity up. Business did not expect nor plan for an economy with unemployment below 5.5%, so as demand grew faster than expected there was greater-than-expected capacity utilization (primarily in services) and resulting productivity gains. That is, businesses were faced with the opportunity to sell more goods and services than expected and managed to produce more even though they could not add workers as quickly. This conventional macroeconomics story fits the facts more reasonably, in our view, than does a sudden ascent to a new economy.

'Knowledge' workers

One prominent formulation of the new economy story holds that we are enjoying an information-technology-fueled ascent to a new era. However, this story does not correspond to trends in the labor market. For instance, a transition to a technology economy would presumably be associated with an increased need for highly skilled and educated workers. Yet, our analysis of wage and employment trends for the 1990s up through 1997 shows that this decade has not been a good one for white-collar and college-educated workers compared to the 1980s. For instance, the decades-long shift into white-collar occupations actually ground to a halt in the early 1990s, and it has been slower over the 1989-97 period than in prior decades. Moreover, projections to 2005 show a further slowdown in the shift to white-collar employment. Corresponding to this slow growth are historically high rates of white-collar job displacements from downsizing and greater job instability and insecurity among college-educated men.

Perhaps most disconcerting to a new economy interpretation is that wage trends for white-collar and college-educated workers have not been especially favorable in the 1990s. This is especially true for men over the 1989-97 period: wages for nearly every white-collar occupation group were stagnant or fell; health insurance coverage did not expand; wages among the college educated rose just

1.2%; and the college/high-school wage premium has been flat over the 1992-97 recovery. Remarkably, the entry-level wages earned by new college graduates, male or female, were 7% less in 1997 than in 1989.

Even so-called information technology workers have not done all that well. For example, newly hired engineers and scientists are earning 11% and 8% less in 1997 than their counterparts did in 1989, despite good wage growth over the 1996-97 period. Young college graduates in computer science and mathematics occupations were earning only 5% more in 1997 than in 1989, with all of the gains occurring in 1997 following seven years of wage stagnation.

These trends do not easily fit with a story in which information technology is transforming the workplace, allowing those equipped to participate to enjoy prosperity while those lacking skills lag behind. Rather, it seems that white-collar workers' experiences in the 1990s – wage losses, displacement, and job instability – mirrors the unpleasant experiences of blue-collar workers in the 1980s. This phenomenon might be described as the "blue-collarization" of white-collar worklife in the 1990s. How can a new information-age economy be expected to lift all of our wages when it cannot even do so for white-collar workers and young college graduates working in technical occupations, presumably the best-educated, most computer literate, and most flexible segment of the workforce?

In sum, looking at the current recovery compared to the past, the dramatic changes of the last two years, and the labor market status of key "knowledge" workers, there seems to be little if any evidence that changes in the economy have led to greater long-term capacity to raise incomes or produce goods and services. Thus, the factors causing the pain of greater dislocation, economic vulnerability, and the long-term erosion of wages have not made the economy into a "better" economy, nor has the large-scale redistribution of income and wealth documented throughout this book been associated with improved economic efficiency, compensation, or income growth. For the vast majority, the slogan for the last two decades might be "all pain, no gain."

Conclusion

As the 1990s recovery proceeds, unemployment has fallen sharply and real wage growth has become strong and broad based. These are very favorable developments, coming on the heels of long-term wage losses and stagnating living standards for most working families.

And yet, despite consistent expansion of the economy since 1991, the wage of the median worker remains below its prerecession level, and the income of the median family took longer to recover in this business cycle than in any prior postwar recovery. Income and wealth have become more concentrated, and jobs have become more insecure. Even groups whose wages grew in the 1980s, such as middle-wage women, white-collar workers, and young college graduates, have faced real wage losses in the 1990s.

This critical viewpoint of the 1990s economy has little in common with the conventional wisdom of much contemporary economic analysis, most of which proclaims that we are enjoying the "best economy in 30 years" (or "in 50 years," or "ever"). But it is unclear in such proclamations what the yardstick is for judging the economy, and for whom the economy is considered "best." With real median family income and median compensation still below their pre-recession levels, it cannot be said that this is best economy for working families. And while declining unemployment, accelerating productivity, and rising real wages are evidence of an economy getting better, it is difficult, in light of the longer-term negative trends examined in this book, to call it the "best."

Economic discourse as well as economic policy needs to be explicit about who benefits from economic growth, and which yardstick is used to judge improvements. America's conversation about the economy, and, more pointedly, about the living standards of working families, cannot be limited to short-term analysis with a sole focus on the recent gains in unemployment, productivity, and wages. Nor can the conversation convincingly reference a "new economic order" when the evidence is so starkly lacking. Instead, the economic discourse must recognize and address the scope of wage and income problems that over the last two decades have diminished the quality of life of American families.

Documentation and methodology

Documentation

The comprehensive portrait presented in this book of changes in incomes, taxes, wages, employment, wealth, poverty, and other indicators of economic performance and well-being relies almost exclusively on data in the tables and figures. Consequently, the documentation of our analysis is essentially the documentation of the tables and figures. For each, an abbreviated source notation appears at the bottom, and complete documentation is contained in the Table Notes and Figure Notes found at the back of the book. (In rare circumstances, however, we incorporate data in the discussion that are not in a table or figure.) This system of documentation allows us to omit distracting footnotes and long citations within the text and tables.

The abbreviated source notation at the bottom of each figure and table is intended to inform the reader of the general source of our data and to give due credit to the authors and agencies whose data we are presenting. We have three categories of designations for these abbreviated sources. In instances where we directly reproduce other people's work, we provide an "author-year" reference to the bibliography. Where we present our own computations based on other people's work, the source line reads "Authors' analysis of *author (year)*." In these instances we have made computations that do not appear in the original work and want to hold the original authors (or agencies) blameless for any errors. Our third category is simply "Authors' analysis," which indicates that the data presented are from our original analysis of microdata (such as much of the wage analysis) or our computations from published (usually government) data. We use this source notation when presenting descriptive trends from government income, employment, or other data, since we have made judgments about the appropriate time periods or other matters for the analysis that the source agencies have not made.

Time periods

Economic indicators fluctuate considerably with short-term swings in the business cycle. For example, incomes tend to fall in recessions and rise during expansions. Therefore, economists usually compare business cycle peaks with other peaks and compare troughs with other troughs so as not to mix apples and oranges. In this book, we examine changes between business cycle peaks. The initial year for many tables is 1947, with intermediate years of 1967, 1973, 1979, and 1989, all of which were business cycle peaks (at least in terms of having low unemployment). We also present data for the latest full year for which data are available (usually 1996 or 1997) to show the changes over the current business cycle. Some information was available only for nonpeak years, and we included these data when we considered it important.

Growth rates and rounding

Since business cycles differ in length, we usually present the annual growth rates in each period rather than the total growth. We also present compound annual growth rates rather than simple annual rates. Compound annual growth rates are just like compound interest on a bank loan: the rate is compounded continuously rather than yearly. In some circumstances, as noted in the tables, we have used log annual growth rates. This is done to permit decompositions.

While annual growth rates may seem small, over time they can amount to large changes. For example, the median incomes of families headed by persons age 24 and below fell 2.4% per year between 1979 and 1989; over the full period, however, incomes declined a considerable 21.7%.

In presenting the data we round the numbers, usually to one decimal place, but we use unrounded data to compute growth rates, percentage shares, and so on. Therefore, it is not always possible to exactly replicate our calculations by using the data in the table. In some circumstances, this leads to an appearance of errors in the tables. For instance, we frequently present shares of the population (or families) at different points in time and compute changes in these shares. Because our computations are based on the "unrounded" data, the change in shares presented in a table may not match the difference in the actual shares. Such rounding errors are always small, however, and never change the conclusions of the analysis.

Adjusting for inflation

In most popular discussions, the Consumer Price Index for All Urban Consumers (CPI-U), often called simply the consumer price index, is used to adjust dollar values for inflation. However, some analysts hold that the CPI-U overstated inflation in the late 1970s and early 1980s by measuring housing costs inappropriately. The methodology for the CPI-U from 1983 onward was revised to address these objections. Not all agree that it should have been revised. We chose not to use the CPI-U so as to avoid any impression that this report overstates the decline in wages and understates the growth in family incomes over the last few decades.

Instead of the CPI-U, we adjusted dollar values for inflation using the CPI-U-X1 index, which uses the new methodology for housing inflation over the entire 1967-93 period. The CPI-U-X1, however, is based on small-sample, experimental indices for the 1970s, and there is some slight variation in methods over the entire period. Nevertheless, use of the CPI-U-X1 has become standard (e.g., it is generally used by the Census Bureau in its presentations of real income data). Because it is not available for years before 1967, we extrapolate the CPI-U-X1 back to earlier years based on inflation as measured by the CPI-U.

Some economists have argued that the CPI (both the CPI-U and the CPI-U-X1) overstates the growth of inflation. We are skeptical that this is the case, and we continue to use the CPI-U-X1. See Appendix C, "The Measurement of Inflation," by Dean Baker for a discussion of this issue.

In our analysis of poverty in Chapter 6, however, we generally use the CPI-U rather than the CPI-U-X1, since Chapter 6 draws heavily from Census Bureau publications that use the CPI-U. Moreover, the net effect of all of the criticisms of the measurement of poverty is that current methods *understate* poverty. Switching to the CPI-U-X1 without incorporating other revisions (i.e., revising the actual poverty standard) would lead to an even greater understatement and would be a very selective intervention to improve the poverty measurement. (A fuller discussion of these issues appears in Chapter 6.)

Household heads

We often categorize families by the age or the race/ethnic group of the "household head," that is, the person in whose name the home is owned or rented. If the home is owned jointly by a married couple, either spouse may be designated the household head. Every family has a single household head.

Hispanics

Unless specified otherwise, data from published sources employ the Census Bureau's designation of Hispanic persons. That is, Hispanics are included in racial counts (e.g., with blacks and whites) as well as in a separate category. For instance, in government analyses a white person of Hispanic origin is included both in counts of whites *and* in counts of Hispanics. In our original analyses, such as the racial/ethnic wage analysis in Chapter 3, we remove Hispanic persons from other racial (white or black) categories; using this technique, the person described above would appear only in counts of Hispanics.

CHAPTER 1

Family income: slower growth, greater inequality

THE SLOW AND UNEVEN GROWTH OF FAMILY INCOME SINCE THE EARLY 1970S IS THE most important economic problem confronting American families. In this regard, understanding the dynamics of family income growth is central to the theme of this book. This chapter examines how the economy, through the production of jobs, wages, and returns on investment, has generated slow growth and increasing inequality in family incomes.

The 1990s recovery, despite racking up some impressive numbers on aggregate economic indicators such as unemployment and recent productivity growth, provides an excellent example of the income problem. For the first time in the postwar period, family income fell four years in a row, declining each year from 1989 to 1993. The initial decline was attributable to the recession that began in 1990, but the median continued to fall as the recovery got under way in 1991 and 1992. In 1994, median family income finally responded to overall growth, and it has increased each year since (the most recent available data on family income are from 1997). Nevertheless, the median family — the family in the middle of the income scale — was only slightly better off (by $285 in 1997 dollars) in 1997 than it was at the peak of the last business cycle, in 1989. This is also historically unprecedented: in every prior recovery, the income of the typical family had, by this point, far surpassed its level of the prior peak. But in the 1990s, thanks to the continued surge of income inequality, the relationship between the growing economy and improving living standards has eluded all but the wealthiest families.

Even with the growth that has occurred since 1994, by 1997 the income of the median family was essentially back where it started in 1989, despite a 9% increase in productivity over the period.

The underlying factor driving the income problem is the growth of inequality — the ever-expanding gap between those at the top and the middle and the middle and the bottom of the income distribution. While this pattern of income growth has prevailed since the late 1970s, it departs from the earlier postwar period, which saw a much more equalizing growth pattern. In fact, inflation-adjusted incomes about doubled for each family income "fifth" from 1947 to 1979, but after that incomes stagnated for middle-income families, fell at the bottom, and rose at the top. Even in 1996, when the labor market was finally beginning to reflect the benefits of the continued recovery, the average real income of the bottom fifth of families fell by 1.8%. The strongest growth occurred among the top 5%, whose average income grew 3.1% from 1995 to 1996.

Why have income trends continued to be so negative in the 1990s? Along with overall slow growth, the primary reason, at least through 1996, is the continuing wage deterioration among middle- and low-wage earners, now joined by white-collar and even some groups of college-educated workers. Another key factor in understanding recent income trends is the contribution of working wives.

In the 1980s, many families compensated for the fall in hourly compensation, which was particularly steep for male workers, by working more hours (either through more family members working or through longer hours by those employed). This strategy — working longer for less — is most notable among married-couple families, in part because these families tend to have more potential workers than do families headed by one person. In fact, in the absence of increased hours and earnings by working wives in married-couple families in the 1980s, the incomes of the bottom 60% of families would have fallen.

In the 1990s, however, there was a slowdown in the growth (for some, even a decline) of hours and earnings among working wives in married-couple families, particularly among low- and middle-income women. Unlike the prior decade, wives' contributions were no longer sufficient to offset the lower earnings of husbands, whose wages continued to fall (only husbands in the top fifth experienced wage increases). By 1996, the bottom 80% of married-couple families would have experienced flat or declining incomes in the absence of wives' work; even with wives' contributions, families in the bottom 40% lost economic ground in the 1990s.

The slowdown in wives' hours and earnings also affected inequality growth. In the 1980s, the fastest growth in wives' work effort was among the bottom 60%, and their contributions to their families' incomes counteracted, to an extent, the sharp growth of income among the richest married-couple families. The net effect was equalizing. But since hours and earnings losses were most concentrated among this same middle- and low-income group of wives in the 1990s, their earnings had little impact on the growth of inequality over this period. Over the full period, 1979-96, however, wives' contributions were equalizing.

One difficulty in assessing the progress of inequality in the 1990s stems from an important change in the methodology used by the Census Bureau, the primary source for income data in this chapter. Starting in 1993, Census counters allowed families to report higher levels of income from earnings than in previous years, creating an inconsistency that led to an upward bias in the inequality trend. Below, we have adjusted the data to allow a comparison to 1989, but we still find solid evidence that family income inequality continued to grow in the 1990s — at about half the rate of the 1980s and twice the rate of the 1970s.

Not only have incomes grown slowly, they have declined for younger families. A cohort, or intergenerational, analysis of income growth shows that recent groups of young families have started out at lower incomes and obtained slower income gains as they approached middle age. Consequently, families headed by someone entering their prime earning years after 1976 may not achieve the same incomes in middle age as did the preceding generation. One result of this trend has been to diminish the role of income mobility in offsetting increasing income inequality.

The growth of inequality has also been fueled by large increases in the capital incomes of the wealthy. These gains stem in large part from the increase in the rate of profit, or the return to capital holdings. Profit rates continue to soar in the 1990s, but (as discussed in the Introduction) these gains have not led to increased investment in capital stock, nor have they been accompanied by increases in efficiency, as measured by productivity growth. Their main effect has been to increase the incomes of the richest families at the expense of the broad working class.

In the first few sections of this chapter we examine the changes in income in recent years relative to other periods since 1947. This analysis focuses on changes in median family income for families overall as well as for families differentiated by the age or race/ethnicity of the household head and by family type (families with children, married-couple families, single-parent families, and so on). In the final sections we turn to the growth of inequality and its causes.

Median income grows slowly in 1980s, declines in 1990s

Income growth over the last two business cycles — 1979-89 and 1989-97 — was slow and the gains were unequally distributed. **Tables 1.1** and **1.2** show changes in family income, adjusted for changes in consumer prices, in various cyclical peak (or low-unemployment) years since World War II. (These Census data exclude the impact of the sharp increase in capital gains over the 1980s and 1990s; we adjust for this omission in Chapter 2). As explained in the section on documentation and methodology, examining income changes from business cycle

TABLE 1.1 Median family income,*
1947-97 (1997 dollars)

Year	Median family income*
1947	$20,102
1967	35,076
1973	40,978
1979	42,483
1989	44,283
1997	44,568
Total increases	
1947-67	$14,974
1967-73	5,902
1973-79	1,505
1979-89	1,800
1989-97	285

* Income includes all wage and salary, self-employment, pension, interest, rent, government cash assistance, and other money income.

Source: Authors' analysis of U.S. Bureau of the
Census data. For detailed information on table
sources, see Table Notes.

TABLE 1.2 Annual growth of median family income,
1947-97 (1997 dollars)

Period	Median family income growth		Adjusted for family size*
	Percent	Dollars	Percent
1947-67	2.8%	$749	n.a.
1967-73	2.6	984	2.8%
1973-79	0.6	251	0.5
1979-89	0.4	180	0.5
1989-97	0.1	36	0.1

* Annualized growth rate of family income of the middle fifth, divided by
the poverty line for each family size.

Source: Authors' analysis of U.S. Bureau of the Census data.

FIGURE 1A Median family income, 1947-97

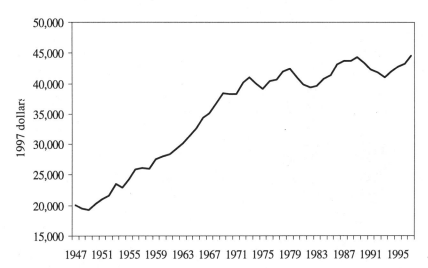

Source: U.S. Bureau of the Census.

peak to business cycle peak eliminates the distortion caused by the fact that incomes fall significantly in a recession and then recover in the subsequent upswing (see **Figure 1A**).

Family income increased substantially in the two decades immediately following World War II (1947-67). During that time, median family income increased by $14,974, for an annual rate of growth of 2.8% (Table 1.2). Family incomes continued to grow into the early 1970s, but since 1973 they have risen slowly. In 1989, the median family's income was $1,800 greater than it was in 1979, translating into growth of just 0.4% per year from 1979 to 1989, or only two-thirds of the sluggish 0.6% annual growth of the 1973-79 period and only one-seventh the rate of the postwar years prior to 1973 (**Figure 1B**). In fact, the $1,800 income growth over the 10 years after 1979 equals the amount that incomes rose every 22 months in the 1967-73 period.

The recession that began in 1990 and ended in 1991 (or in 1992 in terms of unemployment) significantly reduced incomes through 1993. Despite income growth from 1993 to 1997, the median family income in 1996 was only 0.6%, or $285, above its 1989 level. This small 1989-97 income growth appears to reflect more than the unemployment accompanying a normal business cycle downturn. First, considering the mildness of the 1991 recession (unemployment rose by

FIGURE 1B Annual growth of median family income, 1947-97

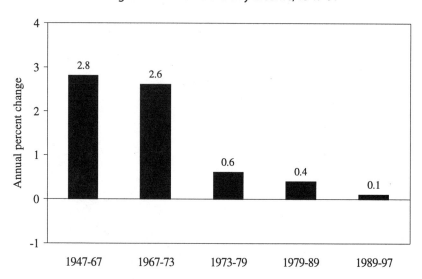

Source: U.S. Bureau of the Census.

2.1 percentage points, which is less than in the usual downturn), we would have expected median family income to recover much sooner, as it did following much deeper recessions. Second, the income decline reflects several ongoing and new structural shifts in income growth, such as the falloff in wages among white-collar and college-educated workers that preceded the recession.

The fact that the median income took eight years to return to its pre-recessionary peak is historically unique. Typically, job growth, falling unemployment, and increasing productivity — all of which occurred in the recovery that began in 1991 — would have helped return median family income to its previous level. But as we show below, increasing income inequality and continued earnings declines through 1996 have eroded the incomes of all but the top 5% of families.

It is common practice also to examine measures of family income growth that adjust for changes in family size, since the same total family income shared by fewer family members can be interpreted as improved economic well-being for each family member. However, trends in incomes adjusted for family size can be misleading, since the recent decline in the average family's size is partially due to lower incomes; that is, some families feel they cannot afford as many children as they could have if incomes had continued to rise at early postwar rates. Yet a family deciding to have fewer children or a person putting off

FIGURE 1C Average number of persons per family, 1947-97

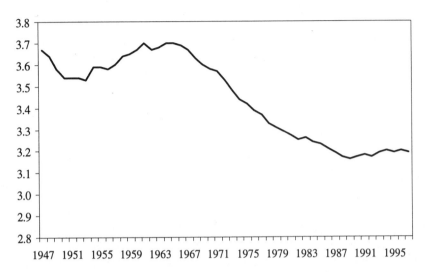

Source: U.S. Bureau of the Census.

starting a family because incomes are down appears "better off" in size-adjusted family income measures. It also seems selective to adjust family incomes for changes in family size and not adjust for other demographic trends such as more hours of work and the resulting loss of leisure.

Nevertheless, even when income growth is adjusted for the shift toward smaller families (Table 1.2, column 3), the income growth from 1979 to 1989 is only slightly higher than the "unadjusted" measure (0.5% versus 0.4%). In fact, the trends in size-adjusted income never diverge more than 0.2% from the unadjusted measure in any period, suggesting that the shrinking size of families has only marginally offset the slow growth of median family income since 1973.

Note that the decline of size-adjusted family income was the same as that of unadjusted income in the 1990s. This stems largely from the fact that family size, after falling continuously over the 1980s, stabilized in the 1990s. **Figure 1C** shows the average number of persons per family in the 1947-97 period. At the beginning of the figure, in 1947, families had on average about 3.7 members. By 1989 the number had fallen to 3.2. Since then the trend has been flat, and so we would not expect size adjustments to play a role in income trends in the 1990s.

We return below to a more detailed investigation of the impact of other aspects of demographic change on family income growth and inequality.

An economic 'generation gap'

Table 1.3 shows that income declines have been greatest among the youngest families. The average income of families headed by someone under age 25 declined at an annual rate of 2.4% from 1979 to 1989 and 0.7% from 1989 to 1997. These young families in 1997 had about $5,000 less income to spend in real dollars than their 1967 counterparts had when they were starting out. This pattern of income loss has meant that the income gap between the median income of these youngest families and those of older persons has expanded since 1979.

Families headed by someone between the ages of 25 and 34 have also fared poorly relative to earlier years. The incomes of these families eroded 0.5% per year from 1979 to 1989 and was flat from 1989 to 1997, in stark contrast to their 3.1% and 2.5% annual growth rates in 1947-67 and 1967-73. Many families in this age group are likely to be bringing up young children and trying to buy a home of their own; their income problems thus represent income problems for the nation's children. Families with household heads age 25 to 34 in 1997 had incomes about $1,900 less than their counterparts had in 1979.

The incomes of the 35-44 and 45-54 age groups grew modestly — 0.5% and 0.8% per year — between 1979 and 1989, compared to growth of about 3% per year between 1947 and 1973. Incomes of families headed by someone over 65 increased at a 2.0% pace from 1979 to 1989, only half as fast as in the 1967-73 period. From 1989 to 1997, families headed by individuals less than 55 experienced income stagnation or losses; only those families headed by older persons saw their incomes grow. Thus, Table 1.3 underscores a post-1979 economic "generation gap," with younger families starting out lower down the income scale and falling further behind, while older families hold their ground.

Income growth among racial/ethnic groups

While sluggish income growth has affected all racial groups, **Table 1.4** illustrates some important differences in income growth by race, particularly in the 1989-97 period, when black families were the only racial group with significant positive median income growth. Hispanic families, however, lost ground at a highly accelerated rate in the 1990s.

White families, who fared the best from 1967 to 1979, experienced modest 0.5% annual growth in their real median income from 1979 to 1989. Black families, whose 1996 median income was 40% lower than that of whites, experienced slower income growth than whites in 1973-79 (0.3% versus 0.6%) and in

TABLE 1.3 Median family income by age of householder, 1947-97 (1997 dollars)

Year	Under 25	25-34	35-44	45-54	55-64	Over 65
1947	$15,553	$19,439	$21,840	$22,815	$21,236	$12,124
1967	25,840	35,792	40,850	42,783	35,558	17,368
1973	27,251	41,506	48,650	51,765	43,461	21,851
1979	28,220	41,877	49,699	54,874	47,532	24,557
1989	22,086	39,960	52,036	59,671	48,724	29,877
1997	20,820	39,979	50,424	59,959	50,241	30,660
Annual growth rate						
1947-67	2.6%	3.1%	3.2%	3.2%	2.6%	1.8%
1967-73	0.9	2.5	3.0	3.2	3.4	3.9
1973-79	0.6	0.1	0.4	1.0	1.5	2.0
1979-89	-2.4	-0.5	0.5	0.8	0.2	2.0
1989-97	-0.7	0.0	-0.4	0.1	0.4	0.3

Source: Authors' analysis of U.S. Bureau of the Census (1996) and unpublished Census data.

TABLE 1.4 Median family income by race/ethnic group, 1947-97 (1997 dollars)

Year	White	Black*	Hispanic**	Ratio to white family income of: Black	Hispanic
1947	$20,938	$10,704	n.a.	51.1%	n.a.
1967	36,407	21,554	n.a.	59.2	n.a.
1973	42,829	24,717	$29,635	57.7	69.2%
1979	44,330	25,103	30,731	56.6	69.3
1989	46,564	26,158	30,348	56.2	65.2
1997	46,754	28,602	28,142	61.2	60.2
Annual growth rate					
1947-67	2.8%	3.6%	n.a.		
1967-73	2.7	2.3	n.a.		
1973-79	0.6	0.3	0.6%		
1979-89	0.5	0.4	-0.1		
1989-97	0.1	1.1	-0.9		

* Prior to 1967, data for blacks include all nonwhites.
** Persons of Hispanic origin may be of any race.

Source: Authors' analysis of U.S. Bureau of the Census (1996) and unpublished Census data.

THE STATE OF WORKING AMERICA

1979-89 (0.4% versus 0.5%). The median income of families of Hispanic origin declined slightly (0.1% per year) between 1979 and 1989.

The ratio of black to white median family income fell from 1967 to 1979 and then remained fairly constant, declining slightly by the end of the 1980s. Interestingly, in the 1989-97 period, the income of the median black family rose at a much faster annual rate (1.1%) than in the prior two periods, while that of the median white family fell. These countervailing trends led to an increase in the black/white ratio. (Chapter 6 reveals similar relative gains by blacks in poverty rates.) Prior to the 1990s, Hispanic family incomes were higher than those of African Americans, but they fell sharply in the 1990s, at an annual rate of 0.9%. Thus, by the end of the period, Hispanic median family income was lower than that of black families and had fallen to a historical low of 60.2% that of white families. In 1997 dollars, the median Hispanic family was $2,206 worse off than in 1989.

Only dual-income, married couples gain

The only type of family that experienced income growth over the 1980s and the 1990s was married couples with a wife in the paid labor force (**Table 1.5**). Incomes among married couples where the wife was not employed declined 0.3% over the 1980s and 0.4% in the 1990s (1989-97). Similarly, the slight fall in income experienced by single-parent families in the 1980s accelerated somewhat in the 1990s. This was a dramatic turnaround for female-headed families, since their incomes grew 1.4% per year in the 1973-79 period. (The effect of this income decline on poverty rates is explored in Chapter 6.)

This pattern of income growth suggests that it was only among families with two adult earners that incomes grew in the post-1979 period. The data in Table 1.5 also show sizable growth in the importance of working wives. In 1979, the share of married couples without a wife in the labor force was about equal to that of those with a wife in the labor force (41.9% versus 40.6% of all families). By 1997, married couples with two earners (assuming the husband worked) made up 47.3% of all families, while one-earner married couples were proportionately fewer in number, 29.3% of the total.

While this shift toward two-earner families has been a major factor in recent income growth, this shift appears to be attenuating, since the rate at which wives (and women in general) have been joining the labor force has slowed in recent years (see Chapter 4). For example, among married-couple families, wives joined the paid labor force at an annual rate of 1.3% in the 1970s, 0.8% in the 1980s, and 0.5% in the 1989-97 period (not shown in table). Furthermore, as we show below, the hours of working wives grew more slowly in the 1990s relative to the 1980s.

TABLE 1.5 Median family income by family type, 1947-97 (1997 dollars)

Year	Total	Married couples		Single		
		Wife in paid labor force	Wife not in paid labor force	Male-headed	Female-headed	All families
1947	$20,619	n.a.	n.a.	$19,472	$14,405	$20,102
1967	37,322	$44,020	$33,652	30,128	18,986	35,076
1973	44,301	51,812	38,826	36,527	19,712	40,978
1979	46,477	53,921	38,403	36,455	21,429	42,483
1989	49,893	58,590	37,209	36,043	21,281	44,283
1997	51,591	60,669	36,027	32,960	21,023	44,568
Annual growth rate						
1947-67	3.0%	n.a.	n.a.	2.2%	1.4%	2.8%
1967-73	2.9	2.8%	2.4%	3.3	0.6	2.6
1973-79	0.8	0.7	-0.2	0.0	1.4	0.6
1979-89	0.7	0.8	-0.3	-0.1	-0.1	0.4
1989-97	0.4	0.4	-0.4	-1.1	-0.2	0.1
Share of families						
1951*	86.7%	19.8%	66.9%	3.0%	9.9%	100.0%
1967	86.4	31.6	54.8	2.4	10.6	100.0
1973	85.0	35.4	49.7	2.6	12.4	100.0
1979	82.5	40.6	41.9	2.9	14.6	100.0
1989	79.2	45.7	33.5	4.4	16.5	100.0
1997	76.6	47.3	29.3	5.5	17.8	100.0

* Earliest year available.

Source: Authors' analysis of U.S. Bureau of the Census (1996) and unpublished Census data.

Married-couple families, although still predominant — they represented 76.6% of all families in 1997 — make up a smaller share of families than they did in the 1950s and 1960s. There has been a continuing rise in the importance of female-headed families; in 1997 they represented 17.8% of the total. Although this phenomenon has been the focus of increased attention in recent years, the share of female-headed families grew more quickly in the 1967-79 period than in the period since 1979. Note also that the median incomes of these female-headed families actually grew over the 1967-79 period, when their share of the population of families was increasing. This pattern suggests that income trends *within* demographic groups were a more important source of income loss than the often-cited shift to female-headed families. (Chapter 6 looks closely at this issue in the context of poverty.)

Examined as a whole, family income growth was stagnant over the 1989-97 period (Table 1.5, last column), with losses experienced by single-headed families and families with wives not in the paid labor force. Families with working wives were the only family type to achieve income growth over this period; their incomes rose a modest 0.4% per year. As we show below, this growth was driven primarily by the increase in annual hours of work by wives.

Growing inequality of family income

The vast majority of American families have experienced either modest income growth or an actual erosion in their living standards in recent years, while the small minority of upper-income families have experienced substantial income growth. The result has been an increase in inequality such that the gap between the incomes of the well-off and those of everyone else is larger now than at any point in the postwar period. The rich have gotten richer, low-income and even poor families are more numerous and are poorer than they have been in decades, and the middle has been "squeezed." This section examines the income trends of families at different income levels and the dramatic growth of income inequality in the 1980s and 1990s.

Table 1.6 shows the share of all family income received by families in different segments of the income distribution. Families have been divided into fifths, or "quintiles," of the population, and the highest income group has been further divided into the top 5% and the next 15%. The 20% of families with the lowest incomes are considered the "lowest fifth," the next best-off 20% of families are the "second fifth," and so forth. The table also shows the trend in the "Gini ratio," a standard measure of inequality, bounded by zero and one, wherein higher numbers reveal greater inequality. Because the Census Bureau raised the "top codes" (i.e., the highest income levels it would record) in 1993, income shares beyond that year are less comparable to those of prior years (a factor we correct for in the next section).

The upper 20% of families received 47.2% of all income in 1997. The top 5% received more of total income, 20.7%, than the families in the bottom 40%, who received just 14.1%. In fact, the 1997 share of total income in each of the three lowest-income fifths—the 29.8% of total income going to the bottom 60% of families—was smaller than the 34.5% share this group received in 1979. As we will see in a later chapter providing international comparisons (Chapter 8), income in the United States is distributed far more unequally than in other industrialized countries.

The 1980s was a period of sharply increasing income inequality, reversing

TABLE 1.6 Shares of family income by income fifth and top 5%, 1947-97

Year	Lowest fifth	Second fifth	Middle fifth	Fourth fifth	Top fifth	Breakdown of top fifth		Gini ratios
						Bottom 15%	Top 5%	
1947	5.0%	11.9%	17.0%	23.1%	43.0%	25.5%	17.5%	0.376
1967	5.4	12.2	17.5	23.5	41.4	25.0	16.4	0.358
1973	5.5	11.9	17.5	24.0	41.1	25.6	15.5	0.356
1979	5.4	11.6	17.5	24.1	41.4	26.1	15.3	0.365
1989	4.6	10.6	16.5	23.7	44.6	26.7	17.9	0.401
1997*	4.2	9.9	15.7	23.0	47.2	26.5	20.7	0.429
Percentage- point change								
1947-67	0.4	0.3	0.5	0.4	-1.6	-0.5	-1.1	-0.018
1967-73	0.1	-0.3	0.0	0.5	-0.3	0.6	-0.9	-0.002
1973-79	-0.1	-0.3	0.0	0.1	0.3	0.5	-0.2	0.009
1979-89	-0.8	-1.0	-1.0	-0.4	3.2	0.6	2.6	0.036
1989-97	-0.4	-0.7	-0.8	-0.7	2.6	-0.2	2.8	0.028

* These shares reflect a change in survey methodology leading to greater inequality.

Source: Authors' analysis of unpublished Census data.

the trend toward less inequality over the postwar period into the 1970s. Between 1979 and 1989, the bottom 80% lost income share and only the top 20% gained. Moreover, the 1989 income share of the upper fifth, 44.6%, was far greater than the share it received during the entire postwar period and even higher than the 43% received in 1947. Even among the rich, the growth in income was skewed to the top: between 1979 and 1989, the highest 5% saw their income share rise 2.6 percentage points (from 15.3% to 17.9%), accounting for the bulk of the 3.2 percentage-point total rise in the income share of the upper fifth. The Gini ratio grew four times faster in the 1980s than in the 1970s, reflecting the acceleration of inequality over the decade.

The increase in inequality continued unabated over the 1989-96 period. For example, the share received by the top 5% grew from 17.9% in 1989 to 20.7% in 1997 (recall that part of this increase — as shown below, perhaps a third — is due to lifting the top code). Comparing the bottom two rows of the table reveals that the rate of share loss among the bottom 80% was slower than that of the 1980s. However, note that these two rows compare a 10-year to a seven-year period; correcting for this difference reveals that inequality grew at a similar

FIGURE 1D Ratio of family income of top 5% to lowest 20%, 1947-97

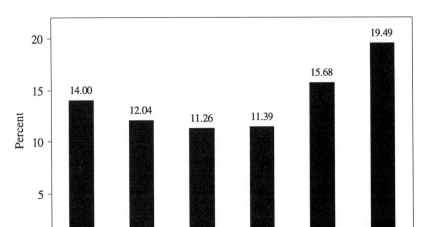

* This ratio reflects a change in survey methodology leading to increased inequality.

Source: Authors' analysis of U.S. Bureau of the Census data.

annualized rate in both periods. The Gini ratio also continued to increase at a similar rate in the 1990s as in the 1980s (accounting for the shorter time period from 1989 to 1996). The top fifth, and in particular the top 5%, continued to gain at the expense of everyone else, including the group in the 80-95th percentile range, whose income share fell 0.2 points in the 1990s.

The increase in the income gap between upper- and lower-income groups is illustrated in **Figure 1D**, which shows the ratio of the average incomes of families in the top 5% to the average income of those in the bottom 20% from 1947 to 1997. The gap between the top and the bottom incomes fell from 1947 to 1979 but grew to a historic high of 19.5 by 1997, reversing three decades of lessening inequality.

Another way of viewing this recent surge in income inequality is to compare the "income cutoff" (the income of the best-off family in each group) of families by income group, as in **Table 1.7**. By focusing on this measure, we are able to discuss income gains and losses for complete groupings of families (e.g., the bottom 40%).

Over the early postwar period, from 1947 to 1973, there was strong and even income growth across the income spectrum. From 1947 to 1967, for in-

TABLE 1.7 Real family income growth by income group, 1947-97, upper limit of each group (1997 dollars)

Year	Lowest fifth	Second fifth	Middle fifth	Fourth fifth	95th percentile	Average
1947	$10,506	$16,952	$22,988	$32,618	$53,536	$23,517
1967	18,167	29,823	39,992	54,827	88,094	38,914
1973	20,678	34,120	47,606	65,468	102,063	46,321
1979	21,388	35,169	49,825	68,607	110,064	48,402
1989	20,714	36,242	52,810	77,079	128,093	53,723
1997	20,586	36,000	53,616	80,000	137,080	56,902
Annual growth rate						
1947-67	2.8%	2.9%	2.8%	2.6%	2.5%	2.5%
1967-73	2.2	2.3	2.9	3.0	2.5	2.9
1973-79	0.6	0.5	0.8	0.8	1.3	0.7
1979-89	-0.3	0.3	0.6	1.2	1.5	1.0
1989-97	-0.1	-0.1	0.2	0.5	0.9	0.7

Source: Authors' analysis of U.S. Bureau of the Census data.

stance, the growth in the top value in each fifth ranged from the 2.5% annual pace obtained by the top 5% to the 2.9% annual pace obtained by those in the second fifth. Because incomes grew slightly faster for lower- and middle-income families than upper-income families (the top 5%) from 1947 through 1967, there was a general decline in income inequality, as shown by the falling Gini ratio in the previous table.

The pattern of income growth since 1973 has been far more uneven and far slower than in the earlier period. From 1973 to 1979 the fastest income growth was the 1.3% annual growth among the top 5% of families, which, though modest, was twice the 0.6% and 0.5% annual income growth among the first and second fifths. Incomes across the spectrum continued to grow slowly in the 1979-89 period, but the pattern of growth was even more unequal. The families with the lowest incomes actually lost ground from 1979 to 1989 (incomes fell 0.3% annually), while the top 5% accelerated to a 1.5% annual rate. In the most recent period, 1989-97, average annual growth slowed considerably, but inequality continued to increase, as the growth went mostly to families at the top of the income scale. The bottom 40% of families lost 0.1% per year, while the top 5% gained 0.9%.

Figure 1E presents a revealing picture of incomes growing together in the first 30 years of the postwar period and growing apart thereafter. The bars in

FIGURE 1E Family income, average annual change

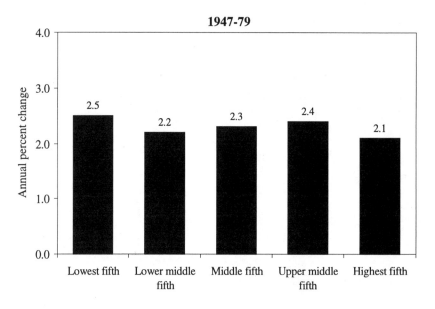

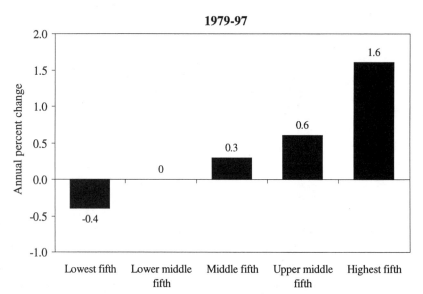

Source: Authors' analysis of U.S. Bureau of the Census (various years).

each panel represent the annual growth rate of average income by income fifth over the periods 1947-79 and 1979-96. The top panel, covering the years 1947-79, shows strong and even growth. In fact, over this period, growth was slightly faster at the bottom of the income scale relative to the top, i.e., growth was equalizing. The bottom panel shows a very different pattern. Since 1979, the annual growth of family income has been negative for the bottom fifth, falling 6.4% per year. Income growth has been flat for the next fifth and positive for the top three fifths. Note that between 1947 and 1979 income grew 0.4% per year more slowly in the top relative to the bottom fifth (found by subtracting one rate of growth from the other); since 1979, income has grown 2.0% more *quickly* in the top relative to the bottom fifth. Thus, the 1947-79 equalizing pattern of growth has sharply reversed in the post-1979 period.

Counter-arguments to the evidence on income trends

A number of questions have been raised regarding the above evidence. First, Census data have undergone some important changes in the 1990s, and these changes have most likely imparted an upward bias to the levels and growth of income inequality in the measures published by the Census Bureau over the 1989-96 period. Thus, while we know that inequality has increased since the late 1980s, the changes in the primary data source (March CPS data) have previously left us uncertain as to the magnitude of the increase. Using data specially prepared by the Census to account for this difference, we address this issue in this section.

Second, some economists argue that consumption, a proxy measure for "permanent" income, is a better measure of family well-being than annual income. This raises the question of whether the inequality of consumption has increased along with that of income.

Finally, some economists argue that it is demographic, not economic, factors that are responsible for the growth and inequality problems documented above. This is an important distinction, because an incorrect diagnosis of the problem will lead to inappropriate policy responses. We explore the validity of this claim below.

How much has inequality really grown in the 1990s?

Most government surveys of income data are "top coded," meaning that, for reasons of confidentiality, the values that respondents report are "capped" (i.e., values above the top code are simply assigned the same top-coded value). Beginning in 1993, these caps were significantly raised. Also, in 1995, the Census

Bureau began to report more fully the earnings of the highest-paid workers (see Appendix B for a more detailed explanation). The impact of these changes is to raise the reported income levels of high earners from the 1996 survey relative to those from earlier years, before these changes went into effect. Thus, researchers have been unable to determine the precise magnitude of the increase in inequality from 1989 to, for example, 1996.

To remedy this measurement issue, **Table 1.8** presents data from a version of the Census Bureau's Current Population Survey dataset specifically prepared to be comparable over the two years 1989 and 1996. It reports average income by income fifth (the same measure underlying the growth rates shown in Figure 1E) and income shares (along with the Gini ratio). The top panel presents changes in average income by income fifth, with the top fifth separated into the 80-95th percentile, the 96-99th percentile, and the top 1%. The bottom panel shows income shares and the Gini ratio, as in Table 1.6.

The table corroborates the above findings that inequality continued to increase in the 1990s. While the increase is smaller once we correct for the change in survey procedure, the inequality-inducing pattern of growth is unmistakable. The average income of families in the first two fifths fell by 4.0%, while that of the middle fifth fell by 2.1%. The only growth that occurred was among the top 20% of families, and even that growth was concentrated in the top 5%. The fastest growth was among the very richest — the top 1% of families — whose incomes increased by 10.0% over this seven-year period.

The changes in income shares also reflect increasing income imbalances. Tracking the gains in the top panel, the only increase in shares — 1.8 percentage points — went to the top 20%, and the top 1% claimed fully one-third of this growth.

Figure 1E above showed that the ratio of the average family income of the top 5% to that of the bottom fifth grew by 3.4 points (19.1 compared to 15.7) from 1989 to 1996. These adjusted data (last column of panel 1) show a growth in this ratio of 2.0 points, about two-thirds that of the unadjusted data. Similarly, while the change in income shares at the bottom of the income scale is about the same from both data sources, the 1989-96 change among the top fifth is 0.4 points lower than that shown in Table 1.6. The Gini ratio grows two-thirds as fast in these data as the growth of this indicator taken from the last column of Table 1.6. This suggests, therefore, that about a third of the growth in family income inequality as presented in the Census Bureau's published series is driven by changes in the top-coding procedure. However, recall that neither these data nor the Census Bureau's series reflect the full gains going to the top 1%, because of both top codes that remain even in the adjusted data and the omission of capital gains.

TABLE 1.8 The growth of income inequality, 1989-96, using comparable data

	Lowest fifth	Second fifth	Middle fifth	Fourth fifth	Top fifth	80 to 95%	96-99%	Top 1%	Top 5%/bottom fifth
Average income									
1989	$12,745	$29,337	$45,212	$64,479	$120,203	$96,319	$164,442	$296,941	15.0
1996	12,234	28,164	44,254	64,037	125,039	97,740	177,436	326,777	17.1
Percent changes	-4.0%	-4.0%	-2.1%	-0.7%	4.0%	1.5%	7.9%	10.0%	2.0*
									Gini ratio
Income shares									
1989	5.2%	11.7%	17.1%	23.4%	42.5%	25.5%	11.6%	5.4%	0.394
1996	4.9	11.1	16.6	23.0	44.4	26.1	12.3	6.0	0.411
Point changes	-0.3	-0.7	-0.5	-0.4	1.8	0.6	0.6	0.6	0.017

* Point change.

Source: Authors' analysis of specially constructed CPS March data; see table note for detailed explanation.

Nevertheless, when examined in tandem with pre-1989 data from the previous section, these data suggest that income inequality proceeded to expand strongly in the 1990s, although it has grown somewhat more slowly — about two-thirds as fast — than in the 1980s.

Inequality as measured by consumption

Some economists express doubts about analyses of income because the incomes of families fluctuate from year to year in response to special circumstances— a layoff, a one-time sale of an asset, and so on. As a result, a family's income may partially reflect transient events and not its economic well-being over the long term. In this view, consumption levels of families provide a better measure of inequality, since families typically gear their consumption to their expected incomes over the long term.

Table 1.9, which presents the ratio of consumption levels at different percentiles, permits a view of this final dimension of growing inequality. Over the 1970s, the distance between levels of consumption of families at the top and the middle of the distribution grew slightly, from 1.87 to 1.90. A countervailing trend (decreasing inequality) occurred among families at the 50th percentile relative to those at the 10th, but these changes were small .

The 1980s, however, saw a large increase in consumption inequality, mirroring the trend in income inequality shown above. As the ratios show, the top pulled away from the middle (the 90/50 ratio grew from 1.90 to 2.13), and the middle pulled away from the bottom (the 50/10 ratio grew from 2.01 to 2.31). Unlike the income data, these consumption data suggest a slight contraction of inequality since 1989 (this analysis is available only through 1993, however). Whether this contraction reflects a true shift in the trend is yet to be determined, but even with it, consumption inequality remains at a historically high level.

The impact of demographic changes on income

It is often suggested that changes in the demographic composition of American families have been a major cause of the income problems documented above, implying a lesser role for economic causes such as wage decline. While it is unquestionably the case that the increased share of economically vulnerable families has put downward pressure on income growth, this process is a dynamic one that has not been constant over time. In addition, some demographic factors, such as the increase in educational attainment, have led to increased family income. It is important, then, to look at the net effect of the different type of demographic shifts in various time periods.

Table 1.10 shows the impact of the following demographic factors on household income: age, education, family type, and race (all refer to the head of the

TABLE 1.9 Distribution of real consumption expenditure, 1972-93

Year	Ratio of consumption between different percentiles*		
	90th/10th	90th/50th	50th/10th
1972/73	3.89	1.87	2.08
1980/81	3.82	1.90	2.01
1989	4.92	2.13	2.31
1993	4.61	2.11	2.18

* Ratios reflect adjustment for family size using equivalency scales.

Source: Authors' analysis of U.S. Department of Labor.

household; households, unlike families, include one-person units). The challenge of this analysis is to quantify the impact of changes in these factors on income trends over time. For example, of the list of factors examined, the two with the largest impact are family type and education level. Over time, as seen in the bottom panel of Table 1.5, a demographic shift has occurred toward family types more likely to have low incomes, such as single-parent families or individuals living alone. A countervailing trend, however, has been the higher education levels of heads of households, a demographic trend that should lead to higher income levels over time.

Which of these two factors — educational upgrading or the shift to lower-income family types — has had a larger impact, and how has the impact varied by income level? (Race and age, while important, have played a secondary role in income trends.) Contrary to the conventional wisdom, which has typically assigned the primary role to changes in family type, there is clear evidence that, while the shift to less well-off families has put downward pressure on incomes, educational upgrading has more than compensated for this effect. Most importantly, on net, during the 1979-96 period when income inequality was increasing most quickly, the demographic factors considered here led to increasing, not falling, household incomes. Thus, explanations that depend on demographic change to explain income decline should be discounted.

The numbers in Table 1.10 show the percent changes in real household income from 1969 to 1996, along with the changes due to these specific demographic factors. For example, the first panel shows that, among families in the lowest fifth of the income scale, the shift to lower-income family types led to a

TABLE 1.10 The impact of demographic change on
household income, 1969-96, by income fifth

	Lowest fifth	Second fifth	Middle fifth	Fourth fifth	Top fifth	Average
Income change (%), actual, 1969-79	8.1%	0.8%	4.8%	10.0%	10.4%	8.1%
Change due to:						
Age	-1.0	-1.6	-1.8	-1.8	-1.8	-1.7
Education	5.6	5.9	5.4	4.5	4.6	4.9
Family type	-15.4	-12.0	-8.8	-5.9	-3.6	-6.5
Race	-1.3	-1.1	-0.8	-0.5	-0.4	-0.6
Total demographic effect*	-8.9	-7.5	-5.4	-2.6	0.5	-2.6
Income change (%), demographics constant**	17.0	8.3	10.3	12.6	9.9	10.8
Income change (%), actual, 1979-89	2.2	3.3	4.3	7.8	16.5	10.3
Change due to:						
Age	1.3	0.6	0.6	0.5	-0.1	0.3
Education	4.9	5.3	4.7	4.5	4.6	4.7
Family type	-5.6	-5.4	-4.1	-3.0	-2.1	-3.2
Race	-1.5	-1.3	-0.9	-0.5	-0.4	-0.6
Total demographic effect*	-1.1	-0.2	0.6	1.4	2.6	1.5
Income change (%), demographics constant**	3.4	3.6	3.7	6.4	13.9	8.7
Income change (%), actual, 1989-96***	-2.6	-5.3	-3.6	-0.6	18.0	6.7
Change due to:						
Age	-0.1	0.5	1.0	1.1	1.2	1.0
Education	5.8	6.7	6.2	5.1	4.8	5.3
Family type	-4.8	-4.5	-3.5	-2.5	-2.1	-2.8
Race	-2.2	-1.6	-0.9	-0.5	-0.5	-0.8
Total demographic effect*	0.2	1.7	2.5	2.9	4.2	3.2
Income change (%), demographics constant**	-2.7	-7.0	-6.1	-3.5	13.8	3.5

Addendum: Household income levels by fifth, 1969-96 (1996 dollars)

	Lowest fifth	Second fifth	Middle fifth	Fourth fifth	Top fifth	Average
1969	$8,289	$21,229	$33,493	$46,742	$80,193	$37,989
1979	8,964	21,390	35,109	51,415	88,497	41,075
1989	9,165	22,103	36,626	55,442	103,105	45,288
1996	9,000	21,284	35,689	55,193	115,801	47,393

*   Components do not sum to the aggregate effect due to interactions between the groups (see table note for further explanation).

** This row—the actual change minus the total demographic effect—shows the impact of income changes within each demographic group.

*** Percent changes are given as 10-year rates so as to be comparable with above panels.

Source: Authors' analysis of March CPS data.

15.4% decline in income from 1969 to 1979. Note also that this effect declines as we move up the income scale; the negative effect of family type in the top fifth was only 3.6% over this period. As expected, however, educational upgrading lifted incomes between 4.5% and 5.9%. The next-to-last row of the panel, which gives the impact of each of the above demographic factors taken as a whole, shows that, on net, the impact of demographic change was negative for all but the highest income group (implying that demographic change served to increase inequality over this period).

Note, however, that the average incomes of all but the second fifth grew significantly over this period (top row). Thus, despite the downward pressure of the negative factors (primarily family type), incomes *within* each demographic group grew enough to offset these losses. The last row of each panel, which shows the percent of income growth within each demographic group by income fifth, quantifies this point. These changes are net of demographic effects and thus represent the impact of economic changes such as real wage trends or the growth of income inequality on household incomes.

During the 1970s, household incomes within demographic groups grew strongly and were equalizing in nature. Net of demographic change, the income of the bottom fifth of households grew 17.0%, while that of the top fifth grew 9.9%. Thus, over the period when demographic pressure was exerting its strongest negative effects, favorable economic growth among low-income households was great enough to more than offset the unfavorable demographic trends. (Chapter 6 finds similar dynamics regarding the impact of demographic change on poverty rates over this period.)

Over the 1980s, the impact of family type, though still negative, was less a factor than in the previous period for each income group, particularly for the least well-off. For example, while shifts in family structure lowered the average income of the bottom fifth by 15.4% over the 1970s, continuing shifts lowered that group's average income by 5.6% in the 1980s. For the middle fifth, the comparable changes were 8.8% in the 1970s and 4.1% in the 1980s. Conversely, the positive impact of educational upgrading fell only slightly for each income group; for the bottom fifth they fell from 5.6% in the 1970s to 4.9% in the 1980s. Thus, in the 1980s, the net impact of demographics (second panel, second-to-last row) was notably smaller than in the previous period, with incomes for the bottom lowered by 1.1% and raised at the top by 2.6%.

Unlike the prior period, however, income growth net of demographic change (i.e., within demographic groups) slowed considerably for all but the wealthiest households. For example, the last row of the middle panel shows that, holding demographics constant, incomes grew by 3.4% for the bottom fifth, 3.7% for the middle fifth, and 13.9% for those at the top of the income scale. Thus, despite the decelerated negative impact of changes in family type, economic growth shifted in such a way as to dampen the growth of income for low-income households within each demographic category.

Over the most recent period, 1989-96, the impact of changes in family type has continued to decline while that of education has slightly increased (the values in this panel are given as 10-year rates so as to be comparable with the earlier periods). Thus, in this time period, net changes in demographics were actually *positive* for each group, though less so at the bottom of the income scale. In the bottom quintile, the negative impacts of family type and race were essentially reversed by the positive impact of education.

At the same time, however, nondemographic factors such as wage decline led to real average income losses for the bottom 80% of households. In the prior period (the 1970s), income growth net of demographic change was slow but positive, meaning low- and middle-income families made some economic progress, controlling for demographic changes (though less so than the 1960s). In the 1990s, within-group incomes fell, as much as 7.0% for households in the second fifth. Thus, most households were unable to take advantage of the positive impact that demographic changes had on their incomes in the 1990s, as their within-demographic-group losses outpaced these gains.

In sum, the message from Table 1.10 is that demographic factors do not account for the scope of income problems documented thus far. Nor do they help explain why income trends were slower and more unequal after 1979 relative to earlier periods. Over the 1970s, while the shift to less-well-off family types was putting significant downward pressure on income growth, incomes grew at a strong pace both at the top (10.4%) and the bottom (8.1%) of the income scale. In the 1990s, however, when changes in family type had the smallest negative impact of each of the time periods we examine, income growth was highly unequal, growing 18.0% at the top and falling 2.6% at the bottom. Additionally, while the negative impact of changes in family type was tapering off, the positive effect of educational upgrading persisted at similar levels in each time period.

The 'hollowing out' of the middle class

Another dimension of income growth is the proportion of the population that has low, middle, and high incomes. Two factors determine the distribution of the population at various income levels: the rate of growth of average income and changes in income equality. As average income grows (holding inequality constant), there will be a greater proportion of the population at higher income levels. However, if inequality grows such that the low-income population re-

TABLE 1.11 Distribution of persons, households, and families by income level, 1969-97

	1969	1979	1989	1997	1969-79	1979-89	1989-97
Under $25,000	27.3	25.8	25.4	25.5	-1.5	-0.4	0.1
$25,000 to $75,000	62.6	58.4	53.5	51.5	-4.2	-4.9	-2.0
Over $75,000	10.1	15.8	21.1	22.8	5.7	5.3	1.7
Total	100.0	100.0	100.0	100.0			
Household incomes							
Under $25,000	35.7	35.3	33.6	34.0	-0.4	-1.7	0.4
$25,000 to $75,000	55.6	52.0	49.5	47.7	-3.6	-2.5	-1.8
Over $75,000	8.7	12.7	17.0	18.4	4.0	4.3	1.4
Total	100.0	100.0	100.0	100.0			
Persons (income relative to the median)							
Less than 50	18.0	20.1	22.1	22.3	2.1	2.0	0.2
50-200	71.2	68.0	63.2	61.6	-3.2	-4.8	-1.6
200 or more	10.8	11.9	14.7	16.1	1.1	2.8	1.4
Total	100.0	100.0	100.0	100.0			

Source: Authors' analysis of U.S. Bureau of the Census.

ceives an unusually low proportion of the income growth and the high-income population obtains an unusually large proportion, then a rise in average income is unlikely to translate into a general upward movement of the population to higher income levels. The following table reveals that, as expected, economic growth has led to a larger share of families with higher incomes, both in absolute and relative terms. However, the growth of inequality, particularly over the 1990s, has also led to increases in the share of families with low incomes. The combination of these two patterns means that fewer families reside in the middle class.

The first two panels of **Table 1.11** show the proportion of families and households (which include one-person units) with low, middle, and high incomes in 1969, 1979, 1989, and 1997. The definition of middle income has been arbitrarily set as a range from $25,000 to $75,000. Over the 1969-89 period, the proportion of families and households with low and middle incomes declined as the shares with incomes beyond $75,000 increased. Income losses since 1989 have led to a downward shift in household income, as 0.4% of households have moved into the lower income group, and the share of families in the top income group has increased by 1.4%.

The third panel of Table 1.11 examines the incomes of people — single and in families — according to the per capita incomes of their families (size-adjusted), with a single person given their individual income. In this analysis, the income of persons is measured relative to the median. Thus, unlike the above panels, which fix the income brackets in real dollar terms, the brackets for the income categories in this panel move with the median income. This approach provides more important insights into inequality, because it measures the relative, as opposed to the absolute, changes in family incomes. Thus, in the first panel, the absolute income level of a low-income family may grow such that they cross from the $25,000 category into the middle group. But if their income grows more slowly than that of the median, they will still fall behind relative to more affluent families. The bottom panel shows evidence of precisely this pattern.

From 1979 forward, more than one-fifth of the population lived in households with income below half of the median. Over both the 1970s and 1980s, this share grew by about two percentage points. As we have stressed throughout the chapter, median income fell over the 1990s, as well as the income levels of those below the median. This led to a slightly larger share of persons in low-income families, as measured by absolute dollar cutoffs (top two panels), while the share of *relatively* low-income families changed little. At the other end of the income scale, there is further evidence of the top pulling away from the rest of the pack. In 1979, 11.9% of the population lived in households whose income was at least 200% of the median; by 1996, that share had increased to 16.1%, an increase of 1.4 percentage points.

Greater capital incomes, lower labor incomes

The fortunes of individual families depend heavily on the sources of their incomes: labor income, capital income, or government assistance. For instance, one significant reason for the unequal growth in family incomes in the 1979-89 period was an increase in the share of personal total income that was in the form of capital incomes (such as rent, dividends, interest payments, capital gains) and a smaller share earned as wages and salaries. Since most families receive little or no capital income, this shift had a substantial impact on income distribution.

Table 1.12 presents data that show the sources of income for families in each income group in 1989. The top fifth received a larger share of its income (13.8%) from financial assets (capital) compared to the other 80% of the population. For instance, the top 1% received 41.0% of its income from financial assets. The other income groups in the upper 10% received from 12% to 19% of

TABLE 1.12 Source of family income for each family income group, 1989

Income group	Labor	Capital*	Government transfer	Other	Total
All	75.3%	12.9%	6.7%	5.1%	100.0%
Bottom four-fifths					
First	46.3%	4.6%	39.9%	9.1%	100.0%
Second	69.6	7.7	14.3	8.4	100.0
Middle	79.1	8.0	6.7	6.2	100.0
Fourth	83.4	8.0	3.9	4.7	100.0
Top fifth	80.0%	13.8%	2.0%	4.2%	100.0%
81-90%	83.6	9.6	2.4	4.3	100.0
91-95%	81.8	12.3	1.9	4.0	100.0
96-99%	74.3	19.4	1.6	4.6	100.0
Top 1%	57.6	41.0	0.4	1.1	100.0

* Includes rent, dividend, interest income, and realized capital gains.

Source: Authors' analysis.

their income from capital. In contrast, the bottom 80% of families relied on capital income for less than 8% of their income in 1989.

Those without access to capital income depend either on wages (the broad middle) or on government transfers (the bottom) as their primary source of income. As a result, the cutback in government cash assistance primarily affects the income prospects of the lowest 40% of the population, but particularly the bottom fifth (see Chapter 6). For instance, roughly 40% of the income of families in the bottom fifth is drawn from government cash assistance programs (e.g., Aid to Families With Dependent Children, unemployment insurance, Social Security, Supplemental Security Income). The income prospects of families in the 20th to 99th percentile, on the other hand, depend primarily on the level and distribution of wages and salaries.

The shift in the composition of personal income toward greater capital income is shown in **Table 1.13**. Over the 1979-89 period, capital income's share of market-based income (personal income less government transfers) shifted sharply upward, from 16.1% to 21.0%. This shift toward capital income was slightly reversed over the 1989-97 period as interest rates and, therefore, interest income fell. In 1997, however, capital income's share of 20.4% was still significantly above its 1979 value. Correspondingly, the share of labor income, including wages and all nonwage compensation (benefits), was still significantly

TABLE 1.13 Shares of market-based personal income by type, 1959-97

Income type*	Shares of income				
	1959	1973	1979	1989	1997
Total capital income	14.1%	14.4%	16.1%	21.0%	20.4%
Rent	4.7	2.5	1.4	1.3	2.4
Dividends	3.4	2.7	2.7	3.2	5.3
Interest	6.0	9.2	12.0	16.5	12.6
Total labor income	72.0%	74.1%	74.0%	70.3%	70.7%
Wages & salaries	69.2	69.3	67.3	63.6	63.8
Fringe benefits	2.8	4.8	6.7	6.7	6.9
Proprietor's income*	13.8%	11.4%	9.9%	8.7%	9.0%
Total market-based personal income **	100.0%	100.0%	100.0%	100.0%	100.0%
Realized capital gains	n.a.	n.a.	1.5%	3.5%	5.0%

*   Business and farm owners' income.
** Total of listed income types.

Source: Authors' analysis of NIPA data.

lower in 1997 than in 1979, 70.7% versus 74.0%, despite a slight increase over the 1989-97 period.

This shift away from labor income and toward capital income is unique in the postwar period and is partly responsible for the recent surge in inequality. Since the rich are the primary owners of income-producing property, the fact that the assets they own have commanded an increasing share of total income automatically leads to income growth that is concentrated at the top.

It is difficult to interpret changes in proprietor's income (presented in Table 1.13), because it is a mixture of both labor and capital income. That is, the income that an owner of a business (or farmer) receives results from his or her work effort (labor income) and his or her ownership (capital income) of the business or farm. To the extent that the shrinkage of proprietor's income results from a shift of people out of the proprietary sector (e.g., farming) and into wage and salary employment, there will be a corresponding increase in labor's share of income (e.g., as farm income is replaced by wage income). This shift out of proprietor's income thus helps to explain a rising labor share in some periods. However, labor's share of income fell from 1979 to 1989 despite an erosion of the share of proprietor's income from 9.9% to 8.7%.

This analysis of personal income understates the shift toward capital income in the 1979-97 period because the data in Table 1.13 do not include the growth of realized capital gains, the profit made when capital assets are sold. Capital gains primarily accrue to the highest-income families since they control most of the wealth (see Chapter 5). Income from capital gains grew strongly in the 1980s (from 1.5% of personal income to 3.5%) and 1990s (up to 5.0%), and thus the share of capital income has grown more strongly in the 1979-89 and 1989-97 periods than is shown in the top panel of Table 1.13. In fact, the inclusion of capital gains in the national income accounts would show an increase in the capital income share in the period 1989-97.

From the point of view of national income (incomes generated by the corporate, proprietor, and government sectors), one can also discern a strong shift away from labor income toward capital income (**Table 1.14**). For instance, labor's share of national income fell from 73.5% in 1979, to 71.9% in 1989, and to 70.8% in 1996. A closer look at the underlying data, however, suggests an even more significant shift away from labor income. First, labor's share of national income rose steadily from 1959 to 1979. One reason for the expanding share of labor income was the steady expansion of the government/nonprofit sector. When the government/nonprofit sector grows, there is a tendency for labor's share of income to grow, since this sector generates *only* labor income and no capital income. For example, the growth of the government/nonprofit sector from 18.3% of national income in 1979 to 19.3% in 1989 necessarily added 1.0 percentage points to labor's share of national income (other things remaining equal). Labor's share of national income also grows as the proprietary sector (farm and nonfarm unincorporated businesses) shrinks, as it did from 1959 to 1979, because labor's share of income in that sector is relatively low (about one-third in 1979). When resources shift from a sector with a low labor share of income, such as the proprietor's sector, to sectors with a higher labor share (all of the other sectors), the share of labor income in the economy necessarily rises. Thus, the changing composition of income across organizational sectors (expanding government, shrinking proprietors) provides momentum for an increase in labor's share of national income and has done so for the entire postwar period.

This analysis suggests that the question to be asked is not only why did labor's share of income fall since 1979, but also why did labor's share of national income not continue to rise over the 1979-96 period, as it had earlier? The failure of labor's share to grow stems primarily from the unique decline in labor's share of the corporate and business sector between 1979 and 1997, reversing the tendency toward more labor income from the 1960s to the 1970s. This is most clearly seen in the bottom panel of Table 1.14 and in **Figure 1F**, which shows the division of incomes in the corporate sector. There, labor's share fell from

TABLE 1.14 Shares of income by type and sector, 1959-97

Sector	Shares of domestic national income					
	1959	1973	1979	1989	1996	1997
National income all sectors						
Labor	68.4%	72.6%	73.5%	71.9%	70.8%	n.a.
Capital	18.9	16.9	17.5	19.9	20.8	n.a.
Proprietor's profit	12.6	10.4	9.0	8.2	8.3	n.a.
Total	100.0	100.0	100.0	100.0	100.0	n.a.
Corporate and business sector						
Labor	44.2%	48.2%	50.5%	48.3%	47.0%	n.a.
Capital	18.7	15.9	16.0	17.8	19.7	n.a.
Total	62.9	64.1	66.5	66.1	66.7	n.a.
Proprietor's sector						
Labor	9.0%	5.2%	4.7%	4.2%	4.6%	n.a.
Capital	0.3	1.0	1.4	2.2	1.1	n.a.
Proprietor's profit	12.6	10.4	9.0	8.2	8.3	n.a.
Total	21.9	16.6	15.2	14.6	14.0	n.a.
Government/ monprofit sector						
Labor	15.2%	19.2%	18.3%	19.3%	19.2%	n.a.
Capital	0.0	0.0	0.0	0.0	0.0	n.a.
Total	15.2	19.2	18.3	19.3	19.2	n.a.
ADDENDUM **Shares of corporate- sector income***						
Labor	78.3%	82.0%	82.6%	81.6%	78.9%	78.4%
Capital	21.7	18.0	17.4	18.4	21.1	21.6
Total	100.0	100.0	100.0	100.0	100.0	100.0

* Does not include sole proprietorships, partnerships, and other private noncorporate businesses. The corporate sector, which includes both financial and nonfinancial corporations, accounted for 58% of national income in 1989.

Source: Authors' analysis of NIPA data.

FIGURE 1F Income shares in the corporate sector, 1959-97

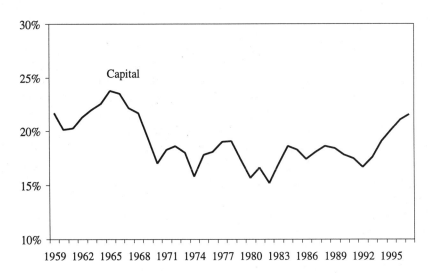

Source: Authors' analysis of NIPA data.

82.6% in 1979, to 81.6% in 1989, and to 78.4% in 1997. These data suggest that there has been a shift away from labor income in the private sector (both corporate and proprietor) that does not show up in national income because of the growth of the labor-intensive government/nonprofit sector.

How important is the shift in the shares of labor and capital income? Between 1979 and 1997, labor's share in the corporate sector fell 4.2 percentage points. A return to the 1979 labor share would require average hourly compensation to be 5.4% greater (82.6 divided by 78.4, less 1), a compensation growth equal to that typically achieved over 10 years, or more than half of the actual growth from 1979-96 (see Chapter 3). Similarly, the shift of income from labor to capital lowered compensation growth by 4.1% over the 1989-97 period. These calculations illustrate that the shift toward greater capital income shares has had substantial implications for wage and compensation growth.

An examination of labor and capital income shares, however, cannot fully determine whether there has been a redistribution of income from labor to capital, or vice versa. This type of analysis assumes that, if labor and capital shares remain constant, then there has been no redistribution. Such an analysis is too simple for several reasons. First, in contrast to most topics in economics, such an analysis makes no comparison of actual outcomes relative to what one might expect given a model of what drives labor and capital income shares. This means we need to look at the current period relative to earlier periods and examine variables that affect income shares. Several trends suggest that, other things being equal, capital's share might have been expected to decline and labor's share to rise. One reason for this expectation is that there has been a rapid growth in education levels and labor quality that would tend to raise labor's share. The primary trend, however, that would tend to lessen capital's share (and increase labor's share) is the rapid decline in the capital-output ratio since the early 1980s (see **Table 1.15**). This fall in the ratio of the capital stock to private-sector output implies that capital's role in production has lessened, suggesting that capital's income share should have fallen in tandem.

Rather than fall, as we have seen the share of capital income has risen: this is due to the rapid growth in the return to capital, before- and after-tax, starting in the late 1980s and continuing steadily through 1997 (Table 1.15 and **Figure 1G**). That is, the amount of before-tax profit received per dollar of assets (i.e., the capital stock) has grown to its highest levels since the mid-1960s, while the after-tax return on capital is as high as in any year since 1959 (the earliest year for which a measure is available). The relationship between the return to capital and capital's share of income is illustrated in the accompanying box.

As discussed in the Introduction, this large increase in profitability does not correspond to a growth in efficiency, as measured by the ongoing growth of

TABLE 1.15 Profit rates and shares at business cycle peaks, 1959-97

	Business cycle peaks				
Corporate sector	1959	1973	1979	1989	1997
Profit-rates*					
Pre-tax	8.7%	7.4%	6.4%	7.1%	10.4%
After-tax	4.6	3.9	3.2	4.0	6.7
Income shares					
Profit share**	21.7%	18.0%	17.4%	18.4%	21.6%
Labor share	78.3	82.0	82.6	81.6	78.4
Total corporate income	100.0	100.0	100.0	100.0	100.0
Capital-output ratio	2.05	1.98	2.23	2.08	1.68

*   "Profit" is all capital income. This measure, therefore, reflects the returns to capital per dollar of assets.

** "Profit share" is the ratio of capital income to all corporate income.

Source: Authors' analysis of NIPA and FRB data.

FIGURE 1G Corporate sector profit rates, 1959-97

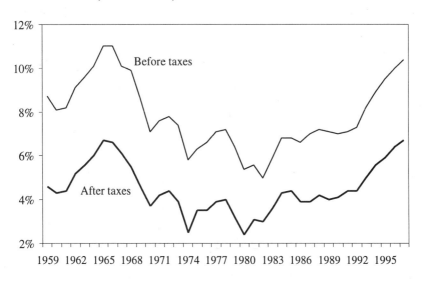

Source: Authors' analysis of NIPA and FRB data.

RISING PROFIT RATES, CONSTANT PROFIT SHARE

There has been some confusion as to the difference between a rise in the *profit rate,* or return to capital (which has risen dramatically in the last 15 years), and a rise in *capital's share of income,* which has grown less. The following exercise is designed to show how these two rates differ and how each can rise or fall at its own pace.

Income is the sum of the returns to capital and labor. It can be expressed in the following equation:

(K * r) + (W * L) = Y

where K is the capital stock, r is the rate of return on capital (the profit rate), W is the average hourly wage, L is the number of labor hours, and Y is income.

Capital's share of income can be calculated by dividing capital income, K * r, by total income, Y. If the capital share remains constant, then the quantity (K * r)/Y doesn't change (nor does the labor share, (W * L)/Y). Capital's share, (K * r)/Y, can also be written as (K/Y) * r, where the quantity K/Y is equal to the ratio of the capital stock to total income. If K/Y falls, as it has over the last 10 years, then r can rise a great deal, even if capital's share remains constant.

For example, if K = $2,000, r = .05, and Y = $1,000, then the capital share of income would be 10%:

(K * r)/Y = ($2,000 * .05)/$1,000 = $100/$1,000 = .10

If the capital stock fell to $1,000 (so that K' = $1,000), the profit rate rose to 10% (so that r' = .10), and income remained unchanged (Y' = $1,000), the capital share would still be 10%:

(K' * r')/Y' = ($1,000 * .10)/$1,000 = $100/$1,000 = .10

In this example, the profit rate doubles, but the capital share of income remains the same because the capital stock has fallen 50%.

Over the last 15 years, the fall in the capital-output ratio has muted the rise in capital's share of income. From 1979 to 1997 the capital-output ratio fell 25% (from 2.23 to 1.68) while the "profit rate," or return to capital, rose from 6.4% to 10.4% (a 62.5% rise). The combined effect of these two trends was to raise capital's income share from 17.4% to 21.6%.

productivity in the economy. That is, this higher profitability has not been a payoff for enhanced private sector efficiency. Rather, higher profitability in the current context implies a larger flow of income to owners of capital out of the same steady stream of income (productivity) that the economy has been generating for several decades.

This growth in profitability has left less room for wage growth, or it might be considered the consequence of businesses successfully being able to restrain (or impose) slow wage growth as sales and profits grew in recent years. If the return to capital in 1997 (10.4%) had been at the average of the cyclical peaks of

1959, 1973, and 1979 (7.5%), then hourly compensation would have been 7.7% higher in the corporate sector in 1997. This is a large loss: its impact on the wages of the typical worker is greater than the impact of the shift to services, globalization, deunionization, or any of the other prominent causes of growing wage inequality (which are discussed in Chapter 3).

Increased work by wives cushions income fall and counteracts inequality

Family earnings growth has not only been slow and unequal, it has also come increasingly from greater work effort — from a rise in the number of earners per family and in the average weeks and weekly hours worked per earner. Thus, "working longer for less" has become a significant source of family stress into the 1980s and 1990s. In this section we examine this phenomenon from the perspective of married-couple families with a prime-age (25-54-year-old) family head. (We exclude families headed by elderly persons to avoid the effect of retirement on hours of work.)

As is well known, the largest increase in work effort in our labor market has come from the long-term increase in female participation in the labor force. In part, this stems from the fact that the impact of historical conventions that once served to reduce female economic independence has lessened, and sex discrimination has probably become less severe. Neither has disappeared, but these changes represent a positive social/economic evolution of women's integration into the labor force.

At the same time, for many families, the increased work effort of their female members (who were either out of the paid labor force or working few hours) has been the only way to keep their incomes from sliding. (Although women have long been the major contributors to nonmarket work, "work" in this section refers exclusively to labor market employment.) As will be detailed in Chapter 3, this increased work effort has occurred simultaneously with a fall in real hourly wages for men and for some groups of women over the decade. The result has been increases in annual earnings primarily through more work rather than through higher hourly wages.

This trend is troublesome for several reasons. As the 1990s results will show, depending on increased work effort as the primary source of income growth is self-limiting, because it can go on only until all adult (or even teen) family members are full-time, full-year workers. The slowdown in the growth in women's labor force participation in recent years may even, in fact, signal the near exhaustion of this type of income growth. Below, we present evidence of this con-

FIGURE 1H Working wives' contribution to family income, 1970-96

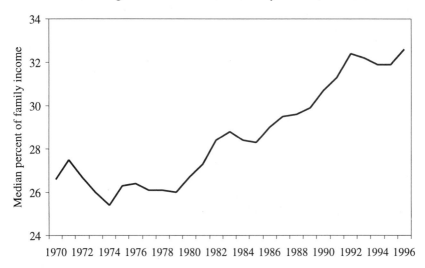

Source: Hayghe (1993) and unpublished updates.

jecture: wives' hours of market work, after growing sharply over the 1980s, grew significantly more slowly over the 1990s, and they even fell for families in the bottom income fifth. Moreover, there are significant costs and problems associated with this growth strategy, one of the most significant being the lack of adequate, affordable child care.

Thus, the problem is not that more women or mothers are working but that many are doing so in part to maintain family incomes in the face of lower real wages. Increased work elicited through falling real wages is a sign of poor performance of the economy. In addition, families are clearly worse off if, to obtain higher incomes, they must work more hours rather than rely on regular pay increases.

Married-couple families (76.3% of all families in 1996, Table 1.5) are most able to increase income through greater work effort because they have two potential adult workers. Single-parent families and individuals, however, can increase work effort only by having the adult work more weekly hours and/or more weeks in a year. It is for this reason that we focus first on the greater work hours of prime-age, married couples.

Figure 1H, which graphs the median percent of total family income contributed by wives' earnings for all families with working wives, shows the growing importance of wives' earnings since 1970. The median percent contribution

TABLE 1.16 Family income, married couple, prime-age families,*
1979-96, by income component

Family income	Lowest fifth	Second fifth	Middle fifth	Fourth fifth	Top fifth	Average
1979	$21,475	$38,676	$50,732	$64,950	$109,129	$56,992
1989	20,453	39,119	53,908	72,000	126,750	62,446
1996	19,911	39,046	54,515	73,057	138,280	64,962
Percent change						
1979-89	-4.8%	1.1%	6.3%	10.9%	16.1%	9.6%
1989-96	-2.7	-0.2	1.1	1.5	9.1	4.0
Dollar change by source:						
1979-89	$-1,022	$443	$3,176	$7,050	$17,621	$5,454
Due to:						
Husbands' earnings	-2046	-2117	-1802	1541	7444	604
Wives' earnings	1117	2574	4725	5466	11146	5006
Other income	-93	-14	253	43	-969	-156
1989-96	$-543	$-73	$607	$1,058	$11,530	$2,516
Due to:						
Husbands' earnings	-656	-1901	-1196	-2329	3547	-507
Wives' earnings	4	1377	1501	3168	5420	2294
Other income	109	451	302	218	2563	729

* Families where the family head is 25-54.

Source: Authors' analysis of March CPS data.

of working wives grew from around 26% of family income in 1979 to just below 33% in 1996. Note that all of the growth in this series occurred after 1980, when family income growth was slowest.

The income growth in total and by type of income among prime-age, married-couple families is shown in **Table 1.16** (the values in the table are averages for each income group). Among the bottom two-fifths, incomes were either stagnant or falling from 1979 to 1989, while the middle fifth achieved modest growth (6.3% over 10 years, or 0.6% annually). In contrast, income growth among married-couple families in the top two fifths grew by 10.9% and 16.1% over this period, again reinforcing the pattern of inequality growth seen throughout the chapter. In the 1990s, average income growth among the bottom 80% of these families slowed, with only the top fifth maintaining its rate of growth (annualized, the average income of this group grew by 1.5% over the 1980s and 1.3% in the 1990s).

The data in Table 1.16 also show the dollar changes in average incomes for each group by three sources: earnings of husbands, earnings of wives, and all other income, including transfers, capital incomes, and the earnings of other family members. Over the 1980s, husbands' earnings fell among the bottom 60%, but the earnings of wives grew in each income fifth. Other income played a small role, but for these families the major determinants of their changing economic fortunes over the 1980s were the poor performance of husbands earnings and the strong growth of the earnings of wives.

Note, for example, that in the lowest fifth, while average family income fell by $1,022 (in 1996 dollars), it would have fallen by another $1,117 from 1979 to1989 were it not for wives' increased earnings. In the second and middle fifth, family income grew by $443 and $3,176, exclusively due to wives' contributions, since average husbands' earnings fell by $2,117 (second fifth) and $1,802 (middle fifth).

In the 1989-96 period, husbands' earnings declined for all but the top fifth of prime-age, married-couple families. In addition, wives' earnings stagnated in the bottom 20% and grew more slowly in the other quintiles. Thus, whereas wives in all income quintiles were able to offset their husbands' losses in the 1980s, this was no longer the case for the bottom 40% in the 1990s. For example, the added $1,377 of average wives' earnings in the second fifth failed to offset the $1,901 decline in husbands' earnings. Only families in the top fifth experienced relatively strong income growth, as the average earnings of both husbands and wives continued to grow, though less so on an annual basis, than in the 1980s.

Table 1.17 presents the growth in annual hours worked by husbands and wives in prime-age families; **Table 1.18** shows average hourly wage rates. Together, these results show that it was more work, rather than higher hourly wages, that fueled income growth over the 1980s and 1990s. (The growth in hours of wives reflects both greater hours of those already working as well as the added hours of wives who joined the workforce over the period.)

Turning first to the hours data in Table 1.17, note that the drop in husbands' annual earnings from 1979 to 1989, shown in the previous table, occurred despite the fact that the average husband was working more, not fewer, hours. Excepting the bottom fifth, where hours were essentially unchanged, husbands in each fifth added at least another week's worth of hours in 1989 relative to 1979. By 1989, the average husband (including some not employed) in the second to top fifths worked more than full time and year-round (2,080 hours, or 40 hours for 52 weeks).

Wives' hours grew a great deal over the 1980s — about 28% — with above-average growth rates among wives in the bottom 60%. The addition of 270 hours

TABLE 1.17 Annual hours of work, husbands and wives in prime-age families,* 1979-96

	Lowest fifth	Second fifth	Middle fifth	Fourth fifth	Top fifth	Average
Husbands' hours						
1979	1,714	2,079	2,155	2,220	2,350	2,104
1989	1,712	2,146	2,207	2,278	2,412	2,151
1996	1,633	2,126	2,227	2,312	2,450	2,150
Change, 1979-89						
Hours	-2	67	52	58	62	47
Percent	-0.1%	3.2%	2.4%	2.6%	2.6%	2.2%
Change, 1989-96						
Hours	-79	-19	20	34	38	-1
Percent	-4.6%	-0.9%	0.9%	1.5%	1.6%	-0.1%
Wives' hours						
1979	555	851	1,003	1,212	1,222	969
1989	756	1,115	1,342	1,451	1,530	1,239
1996	717	1,250	1,458	1,595	1,595	1,323
Change, 1979-89						
Hours	201	264	340	238	308	270
Percent	36.2%	30.9%	33.9%	19.7%	25.2%	27.9%
Change, 1989-96						
Hours	-40	135	116	145	65	84
Percent	-5.2%	12.1%	8.6%	10.0%	4.2%	6.8%

* Families where the family head is 25-54.

Source: Authors' analysis of March CPS data.

to the average family's labor supply added more than six and a half weeks of paid work to the family's income.

For those in the bottom 60% of prime-age, married-couple families, husbands' annual earnings fell in the 1980s because of the erosion of their hourly wages: they fell 7.0% for husbands in the middle fifth and 13.3% for husbands in the lowest fifth (Table 1.18). Only husbands in the best-off fifth of families experienced significant real hourly wage growth (7.1%). Despite these wage gains at the top, the majority of husbands in these families lost ground over the 1980s, even with their increased work effort.

It is useful to note the degree to which an increase in wives' hours is neces-

TABLE 1.18 Hourly wages, husbands and wives in prime-age families,* 1979-96

	Lowest fifth	Second fifth	Middle fifth	Fourth fifth	Top fifth	Average
Husbands' wages						
1979	$8.92	$13.99	$17.46	$20.48	$31.84	$18.54
1989	7.74	12.57	16.23	20.64	34.10	18.26
1996	7.71	11.79	15.55	19.32	35.03	17.88
Wives' wages						
1979	$5.78	$7.71	$9.29	$11.03	$14.44	$9.65
1989	5.72	8.20	10.46	12.99	18.82	11.24
1996	6.05	8.41	10.66	13.80	21.46	12.07
Percent changes:						
Husbands						
1979-89	-13.3%	-10.2%	-7.0%	0.8%	7.1%	-1.5%
1989-96	-0.4	-6.2	-4.2	-6.4	2.7	-2.1
Wives						
1979-89	-1.0%	6.3%	12.6%	17.7%	30.3%	16.4%
1989-96	5.6	2.6	1.9	6.2	14.0	7.4

* Families where the family head is 25-54.

Source: Authors' analysis of March CPS data.

sary to offset the fall in the wages of husbands, given that men earn significantly higher hourly wages. For example, the $1.23 drop in the hourly wage of husbands in the middle fifth from 1979 to 1989 (working 2,207 annual hours) created an annual loss of $2,715. Replacing this income would require a wife in the middle fifth (earning $10.46 an hour) to work 260 additional hours annually, or more than six extra full-time weeks.

Various factors combined to reduced the economic fortunes of the majority of these families in the 1989-96 period. First, both husbands' and wives' hours of work either fell or increased less quickly for most families, with larger declines for those in the bottom 60%. For example, husbands' hours fell by just under 80 hours (two full-time weeks) in the bottom quintile and about 20 hours in the second fifth. Wives' hours also fell in the bottom fifth from 1989 to 1996, and grew much more slowly in each other income class.

In addition, wage decline for husbands (Table 1.18) accelerated on average and was more widespread in the 1990s; only husbands in the top fifth saw an increase. The average hourly earnings of wives grew more slowly over the 1989-

96 period; only for those in the lower fifth did wages, on average, grow more quickly in the 1990s. It appears that the strategy of increasing hours of work to counteract wage decline was less viable for these families in the 1990s relative to the 1980s, and their incomes either continued to decline (bottom fifth), stagnated (second fifth), or grew more slowly as a result.

It is not always obvious how these changes of wages earned and hours worked affected family income. **Figure 1I** and **Table 1.19** bring together the information from the prior tables to identify the role of increased earnings and hours worked by wives on family income growth in the 1980s and 1990s. The first panel of the figure focuses on the 1980s, and the bottom panel examines the 1989-96 period.

As shown in the figure, the average family income of prime-age, married-couple families would have been essentially unchanged in the absence of wives' contributions, growing 0.8% in the 1980s and 0.4% over the 1990s. In the 1979-89 period, the lowest-income families would have experienced twice the income loss that actually occurred (10.0% versus 4.8%) were it not for wives' greater work effort. As Table 1.19 shows, this contribution from low-income wives came exclusively in the form of more hours of work, which raised family income by $1,163 (1996 dollars), or 5.4% (the small decline in the wage rate of wives in this income category lowered family income by $45).

For families in the second and third fifths in the 1979-89 period, average family income would have fallen in the absence of wives' added work effort and higher wage rates. The average income of families in the middle fifth, for example, would have fallen 3.1% had not wives' added contribution led to an increase of 6.3% (Figure 1I). Table 1.19 shows that most of the $4,725 of earnings that middle fifth wives contributed over the 1980s stemmed from more work hours; about a third of this increase came from wives' higher wages. For the top two fifths, incomes would have grown on average even in the absence of wives' earnings. Nevertheless, as Table 1.19 shows, wives' contributions increased family income by 8.4% in the fourth fifth and 10.2% in the top fifth. In both of these cases, wives' wage growth outpaced growth in hours as a primary source of the increase.

In the 1990s, wives' contributions played a smaller role in family income changes. For example, the first two bars of Figure 1I, bottom panel, show that wives' earnings played no role in the 2.7% decline in the income of the bottom fifth of prime-age, married-couple families. Table 1.19 reveals that this lack of effect is attributable to the countervailing roles of the falling hours and increases in the average wage rates of low-income wives. Family income growth in the second fifth was stagnant in the 1990s, but would have fallen 3.7% in the absence of wives' contributions, which came mostly in terms of increased hours, as 2.8% of a 3.5% income gain was due to increased work effort. Only families

FIGURE 1I The effect of wives' earnings on family income,
prime-age families,* 1979-96

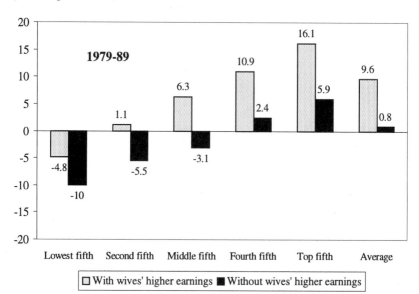

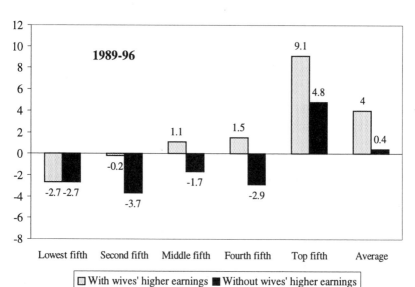

* Families where the family head is 25-54.

Source: Authors' analysis of March CPS data.

TABLE 1.19 Effect on family income of changes in wives' earnings, prime-age families,* 1979-96 (1996 dollars)

Effect on family income of changes in:	Lowest fifth	Second fifth	Middle fifth	Fourth fifth	Top fifth	Average
1979-89						
Wives' earnings and hours	$1,117	$2,574	$4,725	$5,466	$11,146	$5,006
Wives' hours	1,163	2,032	3,153	2,628	4,448	2,606
Wives' wages	-45	542	1,572	2,838	6,697	2,399
Percent:						
Wives' earnings and hours	5.2%	6.7%	9.3%	8.4%	10.2%	8.8%
Wives' hours	5.4	5.3	6.2	4.0	4.1	4.6
Wives' wages	-0.2	1.4	3.1	4.4	6.1	4.2
1989-96						
Wives' earnings and hours	$4	$1,377	$1,501	$3,168	$5,420	$2,294
Wives' hours	-227	1,107	1,209	1,877	1,217	944
Wives' wages	231	269	292	1,292	4,203	1,350
Percent:						
Wives' earnings and hours	0.0%	3.5%	2.8%	4.4%	4.3%	3.7%
Wives' hours	-1.1	2.8	2.2	2.6	1.0	1.5
Wives' wages	1.1	0.7	0.5	1.8	3.3	2.2

* Families where the family head is 25-54.

Source: Authors' analysis of March CPS data.

in the top fifth experienced significant income growth over the 1989-96 period (9.1%), about half of which stemmed from wives increased earnings. As in the prior period, high-income wives gained more from increased wage rates than from added hours. Despite these large gains at the top, the fact remains that wives' contributions, though crucial to their families' economic well-being, were less effective drivers of income growth in the 1990s than they were in the 1980s.

Have the growing earnings of wives contributed to the growth of income inequality? The notion that the growth of "two-earner" families has contributed to growing inequality is intuitively plausible if one thinks that (1) there has been a growth of high-wage employed women marrying high-wage men, and (2) the increase in the hours and earnings of these women has been greater than that of their lower-income counterparts. It is true, in fact, that wives in higher-income families earn more than those in other families and that their hourly wages have grown the quickest (Table 1.18). However, the fastest growth in work hours has been among the wives in the bottom three-fifths (Table 1.17), and, as shown in Table 1.19, the effect of wives' hours on family income growth has been fairly even. The data discussed so far, however, only indirectly relate to whether the pattern of growth of wives' earnings led to greater inequality, and they do not address whether inequality would be higher or lower without any earnings from wives. The following table addresses this omission.

The data in **Table 1.20** allow a direct examination of the effect of wives' earnings on income inequality of prime-age, married-couple families from 1979 to 1996 and on the growth of inequality over that period. The numbers in the table are the shares of total income going to each income group, calculated with and without wives' earnings (note that, in this analysis, the top fifth is broken down into the 80-95th percentile and the top 5%). The difference between shares calculated in this manner reveals the contribution of wives' earnings to inequality. For example, in 1979, wives' earnings led to a more equal distribution of income, since without wives' earnings the lowest fifth would have had a 6.7% share of total income instead of the 7.5% share it had with wives' earnings. Overall in 1979, wives' earnings increased the income shares of the bottom four-fifths and decreased the share of income of the top fifth by 2.3 percentage points. In 1989, wives' earnings had an even larger effect on raising the income shares of the lowest 80% of families and on lessening the income share of the top fifth, which fell by 2.9 points (2.2 points in the top 5%). This pattern continued in 1996, as the size of wives' contributions to the income shares of the bottom 80% continued to grow while that of the top fifth fell further.

The bottom panel reveals that between 1979 and 1989 the income shares of the bottom 60% of prime-age, married-couple families fell, with the largest declines among the bottom fifth. In the absence of wives' earnings, however, income shares would have been 0.2 points lower in the second fifth and 0.3 points lower in the middle fifth. Conversely, they would have been 0.6 points higher in the top fifth, mostly due to the effect seen in the top 5%. This pattern shows that the shifts in wives' hours and wages were equalizing over the 1979-89 period.

In the latter period — 1989-96 — only the top 20% gained income share, with fairly uniform losses among the bottom 80% of families. Note, however, that wives' earnings had no effect in the bottom two fifths and were equalizing in the middle and fourth fifth. Thus, the slowdown in wives' earnings and hours, particularly among lower-income families, had little impact on inequality in the 1990s. Only among the top 5% is there evidence that the pattern of wives earnings dampened the growth of income share, from an increase of 2.4 points without wives' earnings to an actual increase of 1.9 points. The last panel shows the equalizing effects of wives' contributions to family income over the 1979-96 period.

The growth in work hours in the 1979-89 period took place in all families

TABLE 1.20 Effect of wives' earnings on income shares of prime-age,* married-couple families

	Lowest fifth	Second fifth	Middle fifth	Fourth fifth	Top fifth	80-95%	Top 5%
Family income shares							
1979							
Actual	7.5%	13.6%	17.8%	22.8%	38.3%	23.6%	14.7%
Without wives' earnings	6.7	12.9	17.3	22.6	40.6	24.1	16.5
Effect of wives' earnings	0.8	0.7	0.5	0.2	-2.3	-0.5	-1.8
1989							
Actual	6.5%	12.7%	17.3%	23.0%	40.6%	24.7%	15.9%
Without wives' earnings	5.6	11.7	16.4	22.8	43.4	25.3	18.1
Effect of wives' earnings	0.8	1.0	0.8	0.2	-2.9	-0.6	-2.2
1996							
Actual	6.1%	12.0%	16.8%	22.5%	42.6%	24.8%	17.8%
Without wives' earnings	5.2	11.0	15.7	22.1	45.9	25.4	20.5
Effect of wives' earnings	0.9	1.0	1.1	0.4	-3.4	-0.6	-2.8
Change in Income Shares							
1979-89							
Actual	-1.1	-0.9	-0.6	0.3	2.3	1.1	1.2
Without wives' earnings	-1.1	-1.2	-0.9	0.3	2.8	1.2	1.7
Effect of wives' earnings	0.0	0.2	0.3	0.0	-0.6	-0.1	-0.5
1989-96							
Actual	-0.3	-0.6	-0.5	-0.6	2.0	0.1	1.9
Without wives' earnings	-0.4	-0.7	-0.7	-0.7	2.5	0.1	2.4
Effect of wives' earnings	0.0	0.0	0.2	0.2	-0.5	0.0	-0.5
1979-96							
Actual	-1.4	-1.5	-1.0	-0.3	4.3	1.2	3.0
Without wives' earnings	-1.5	-1.8	-1.6	-0.5	5.4	1.3	4.1
Effect of wives' earnings	0.1	0.3	0.6	0.2	-1.1	0.0	-1.0

* Families where the family head is 25-54.

Source: Authors' analysis of March CPS data.

and not just in prime-age, married-couple families (to whom all of the data previously presented applied). In **Table 1.21,** we pool the hours of family work effort across the family and take the average for each fifth. For the three family types in the table, family work effort increased for each income group over the 1980s, with the largest increases among the bottom 80%. Among all families, for example, those in the second fifth worked an average of 182 hours more in 1989 than in 1979, a 8.0% increase. The increase for the top group was 1.7%, though

TABLE 1.21 Changes in family hours worked by family type, 1979-96

	Lowest fifth	Second fifth	Middle fifth	Fourth fifth	Top fifth	Average
All families*						
1979	1,126	2,267	3,020	3,556	4,426	2,969
1989	1,185	2,449	3,206	3,792	4,502	3,093
1996	1,175	2,413	3,287	3,974	4,447	3,117
Percent change						
1979-89	5.3%	8.0%	6.2%	6.6%	1.7%	4.2%
1989-96	-0.9	-1.5	2.5	4.8	-1.2	0.8
1979-96	4.4	6.4	8.8	11.8	0.5	5.0
Married couples with children						
1979	2,190	2,950	3,236	3,711	4,301	3,278
1989	2,400	3,279	3,604	3,914	4,293	3,498
1996	2,333	3,412	3,851	4,131	4,294	3,604
Percent change						
1979-89	9.6%	11.2%	11.4%	5.5%	-0.2%	6.7%
1989-96	-2.8	4.1	6.9	5.6	0.0	3.1
1979-96	6.5	15.7	19.0	11.3	-0.2	10.0
Unrelated individuals						
1979	649	1,387	1,822	2,034	2,170	1,612
1989	759	1,603	1,944	2,091	2,246	1,729
1996	685	1,595	1,940	2,111	2,262	1,719
Percent change						
1979-89	17.0%	15.6%	6.7%	2.8%	3.5%	7.2%
1989-96	-9.8	-0.5	-0.2	0.9	0.7	-0.6
1979-96	5.6	15.0	6.5	3.8	4.2	6.6

* Excludes one-person families.

Source: Authors' analysis of March CPS data.

the potential increase among these families was constrained by their very high levels of work. Note also the large increase in hours worked by middle-class married couples with children (middle panel), as hours among these families in the second and middle fifth increased by 11.2% and 11.4%, respectively. Even unrelated individuals, who by definition cannot increase family work hours by sending more workers into the labor force, saw relatively large increases in their labor supply from 1979 to 1989.

Hours of work were stagnant, on average, for most families in the 1989-96 period; the average for all families rose by 0.8%. Of the family types we examine, only married couples with children were able to increase their average labor supply, and these increases took place only among the middle three-fifths of families. For example, among married-couple families with children in the middle fifth, hours of work grew 6.9%, or 247 hours since 1989. Since 1979, these middle-class families added 615 hours, more than 15 weeks of full-time work to their schedules. While these added hours have surely helped to raise middle-class income, they also leave significantly less time for nonmarket activities.

In sum, the results from this section have both positive and negative implications. On the plus side, there is clear evidence of increased economic progress for female workers. Since 1979, wives have increased their hours of market work; for most wives, wages have also risen. To a large extent, these increases have offset widespread decline in their husbands' earnings. Furthermore, the pattern of these changes in wives' contributions to family income have been equalizing, i.e., the income distribution for prime-age, married-couple families would have been more skewed toward the wealthy in the absence of wives increased contributions.

On the negative side, the evidence also shows that families have been working longer for less. Particularly in the 1980s, family work hours needed to increase quite sharply to compensate for negative male wage trends, explored in detail in Chapter 3. But this is a self-limiting strategy; families cannot indefinitely increase their work hours. In fact, in the 1990s the growth in wives' hours slowed considerably, lowering their ability to offset other factors, such as continued male wage decline, that placed downward pressure on income growth. Finally, the sharp increase in work hours of all families has cut into their time for nonmarket activities.

Falling behind the earlier generations

Until this point we have exclusively focused on cross-section analyses, such as comparing the incomes of high-income, older, or married-couple families in one year to those of another. Although these comparisons accurately portray changes in various dimensions of the income distribution over time, they do not trace the incomes of particular families or individuals. For instance, consider comparisons of income growth by income fifth over a 10-year period. A person or family may be in the middle fifth in the first year but in a higher or lower fifth 10 years later. Thus, a comparison of middle-income families over time actually compares one set of families in the first year to a different set of families in the later year.

It is especially important to note that the incomes of individuals and families generally follow a life-cycle pattern. Typically, a person, after completing schooling, starts earning income in a relatively low-paying entry-level job, sees fast income growth as job changes, accumulated experience, and seniority occur over the next two decades, and obtains slower income growth in his or her later working years. As **Figure 1J** shows, young families (headed by a person in his or her twenties) in 1996 had much lower incomes than families headed by a middle-aged person (in his or her forties or fifties). It also shows that incomes grow relatively rapidly as the household head proceeds through his or her thirties and forties, and that income growth slackens and then declines as the household head approaches retirement years.

Viewed this way, the income growth of families as a whole over a 10-year period depends both on how high incomes are for young families when they start out and on how fast incomes grow as families progress through their life-cycle pattern. In fact, the slow growth of median family incomes in recent years is most accurately portrayed as young families starting off with lower incomes than their predecessors while older families proceed to higher incomes at a historically slow pace.

One way to examine income growth over the life-cycle is to examine the income trajectories of "birth cohorts" (a group of people born in the same years) over time, as in **Table 1.22**. The first column shows the median income, in 1996 dollars, of males age 25-34 in the years 1956 through 1996. The second column tracks the median income of 35- to 44-year-olds over these periods. We focus exclusively on males' median incomes, since trends in female income are confounded by large changes in labor supply over this period.

This type of table allows two related types of analyses. By comparing the income levels down each column, we can compare levels across cohorts, such as the different income levels experienced by 25- to 34-year-olds, at different points in time. Thus, reading down column 1 shows that the median income of young males age 25-34 was about 19% lower in 1996 than in 1976. We can also track a particular cohort's progress through time by reading along the diagonal (more on this approach below).

We saw earlier (Table 1.3) that young persons have been starting out from lower income levels in recent years. Table 1.22 corroborates this, as we see that 25- to 34-year-old males have started out with successively lower incomes in 10-year intervals since 1976 (note that this analysis does not follow the usual peak-to-peak comparisons employed throughout this book). Similarly, the median incomes of males age 35-54 also fell over the past 20 years.

In this context, however, we are most interested in changes that occurred within cohorts (along the diagonal). This table tracks three cohorts over 20 years:

FIGURE 1J Median family income by age of householder, 1997

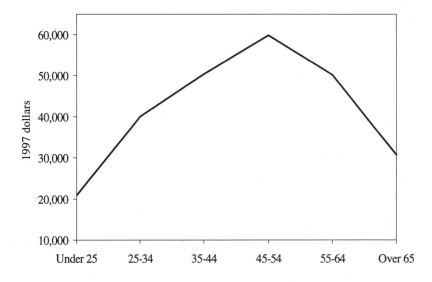

Source: U.S. Bureau of the Census.

TABLE 1.22 Median income by male 10-year birth cohorts, 1956-96

Year	Ages 25-34	Ages 35-44	Ages 45-54
1956	$22,321	$24,251	$22,851
1966	29,004	32,561	30,836
1976	30,949	37,841	37,228
1986	27,432	37,467	39,735
1996	25,179	32,167	36,232
Percent change			
1956-66	29.9%	34.3%	34.9%
1966-76	6.7	16.2	20.7
1976-86	-11.4	-1.0	6.7
1986-96	-8.2	-14.1	-8.8

Source: U.S. Bureau of the Census, Income Website.

the first cohort moves from 1956, when its members were 25-34, with median income of $22,321 (1996 dollars), to 1976, when they were 45-54, with median income of $37,228. Similarly, the second cohort can be tracked from 1966 (median income $29,004) to 1986 (median income $39,735). While each of these cohorts started out higher than the previous one, their incomes grew successively more slowly. For example, the median income of the first cohort grew 67%, that of the second cohort grew 37%, and that of the third cohort grew 17% (from $30,949 to $36,232). In fact, for this third cohort, as it moved from ages 35-44 in 1986 to 45-54 in 1996, its median actually fell, from $37,467 to $36,232, a 3% decline.

In sum, we find that, while each cohort continues to experience some measure of the expected age-income profile revealed in Figure 1J, over the last 20 years each successive cohort has been worse off than the preceding cohort at the same age. This break in upward income mobility across cohorts raises the issue of whether the most recent cohorts (those age 25-34 in 1986 and 1996) will ever achieve incomes in their "prime age" equal to those of the earlier postwar cohorts. Given continued slow income growth and falling real wages, it is possible that the recent (and some future) cohorts will have lifetime incomes inferior to those of their parents' generations.

Income mobility

This section examines a related aspect of the dynamic changes in economic well-being: how much income mobility exists in the economy? If a family is in the lowest fifth in one period, how likely is it to move up to a higher fifth over time? Is this likelihood fixed, or does it tend to fluctuate? These are the questions addressed below.

In order to address these mobility issues we use longitudinal data, or data that follow the same persons over time. Each person is assigned to an income fifth at the beginning and end of the relevant periods of observation based on his or her family's income. Different income cutoffs are used for each period, meaning that the 20th percentile upper limit in, for example, 1979 will be different than that of 1989. This approach to income mobility examines a family's *relative*, as opposed to absolute, position in the income distribution.

In this sense, the analysis tracks how families are doing relative to others they started out with in the same age cohort and income class. If each family's income grew by the same amount (in percentage terms), there would be no change in mobility, i.e., no changes in the relative positions of families in the income distribution. If, however, a family that starts out in the bottom fifth experiences

TABLE 1.23 Income mobility, 1969-94

1969 Income group	1994 Income group					
	First fifth	Second fifth	Middle fifth	Fourth fifth	Top fifth	Total
First fifth	**41.0%**	24.9%	16.2%	12.1%	5.8%	100.0%
Second fifth	22.4	**24.7**	23.9	16.1	13.0	100.0
Middle fifth	16.9	21.0	**23.5**	22.8	15.9	100.0
Fourth fifth	11.3	18.5	19.7	**24.2**	26.3	100.0
Top fifth	9.5	10.6	16.6	24.5	**38.8**	100.0

Source: Unpublished tabulations of the PSID by Peter Gottschalk.

faster income growth than other low-income families, it may move into a higher fifth , i.e., this family will experience upward mobility.

Table 1.23 presents a "transition matrix" for the period 1969-94. Going across each row in the table, the numbers reveal the percent of persons who either stayed in the same fifth or "transitioned" to a higher or lower one. For example, the first entry shows that 41.0% of persons in the bottom fifth in 1969 were also in the bottom fifth in 1994. At the other end of the income scale, 38.8% of those who started in the top fifth stayed there. The percent of "stayers" (those who did not move out of the fifth they started out in) are shown in bold.

Note that large transitions are uncommon. For example, only 5.8% of those who began the period in the first fifth ended up in the top fifth, while only 9.5% fell from the top fifth to the lowest fifth. Those transitions that do occur are most likely to be a move up or down to the neighboring fifth. For example, among the middle three-fifths, slightly less than two-thirds of the transitions were to neighboring fifths.

Though Table 1.23 does not reveal a great deal of income mobility, the data do show that mobility exists and that families can and do move up and down as their relative fortunes change. How does this fact comport with the historically large increases in cross-sectional inequality that we focused on throughout this chapter? In fact, if cross-sectional income inequality is higher in 1996 than in 1979, as we have shown, then, unless mobility has increased, families will grow further apart as time progresses. That is, the increase in cross-sectional inequality means that, at any point in time, a family at the bottom of the income scale is further (in terms of the difference in their incomes) from the family at the top of the scale. But if the chances of moving from the bottom to the top — the rate of income mobility — were to increase, the low-income family would at least have

TABLE 1.24 Income mobility over the 1970s and 1980s*

1969 Income group	1979 Income group					
	First fifth	Second fifth	Middle fifth	Fourth fifth	Top fifth	Total
First Fifth	**61.5%**	24.0%	8.7%	4.4%	1.5%	100.0%
Second Fifth	22.7	**31.3**	27.5	12.9	5.6	100.0
Middle Fifth	9.6	22.5	**29.6**	26.1	12.2	100.0
Fourth Fifth	3.3	17.3	22.4	**31.6**	25.4	100.0
Top Fifth	2.9	5.0	11.9	25.1	**55.2**	100.0

1979 Income group	1989 Income group					
	First fifth	Second fifth	Middle fifth	Fourth fifth	Top fifth	Total
First fifth	**61.0%**	23.8%	9.5%	4.6%	1.1%	100.0%
Second fifth	22.9	**33.2**	27.7	13.5	2.7	100.0
Middle fifth	8.3	25.2	**29.5**	25.7	11.4	100.0
Fourth fifth	4.6	13.0	23.0	**33.2**	26.2	100.0
Top fifth	2.7	4.9	10.8	22.8	**58.8**	100.0

* Unlike the previous table, this table averages family income over three years in order to "smooth out" temporary transitions.

Source: Unpublished tabulations of the PSID by Peter Gottschalk.

a better chance of climbing closer to its distant, more wealthy counterpart (of course, mobility works both ways: increased mobility also means the wealthy family has a greater chance of falling from its privileged heights). If, instead, the rate of mobility is either unchanged or diminished over time, increasing point-in-time inequality will not be offset by changes in mobility. In order to determine whether the rate of mobility has changed, we must compare two transition matrices covering periods of equal length.

Table 1.24 provides such a comparison. It presents two transition matrices, one for the 1970s and the other for the 1980s. (Unlike the previous table, this table uses three years of family income data for each year, e.g., a family's 1969 income is actually the average of its 1968-70 data. This approach is preferred in mobility analysis since it "smooths out" temporary transitions. However, due to data constraints, we were unable to use this approach in Table 1.23.) These tables again show relative stability (the largest shares of persons are "stayers," located along or close to the diagonal). For example, both 10-year periods re-

FIGURE 1K Percent staying in same fifth in each pair of years, 1968-69–1990-91

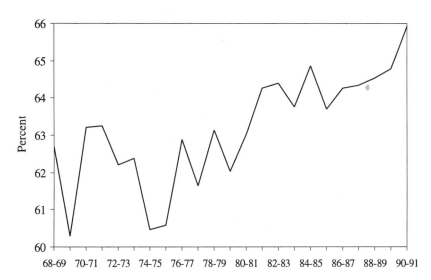

Source: Gottschalk and Danziger (1998).

veal that about 85% of persons in families stayed in the first or second fifths. But more important in this context is the fact that mobility has not increased. The shares of both "stayers" and those who made transitions are very similar in both periods. For example, 61.5% remained in the lowest fifth over the 1970s, and 61.0% remained there in the 1980s. The shares who remained in the middle were also very close (29.6% versus 29.5%), and only a slightly larger share remained in the top fifth in the 1980s. There is no evidence here of an increase in mobility to offset increased inequality.

In fact, as **Figure 1K** shows, the rate of mobility appears to have declined since the late 1960s. This figure uses the same longitudinal data source as above to plot the percent of persons who stayed in the same fifth, one year to the next. Thus, an upward trend suggests declining mobility rates, as persons are less likely over time to make the transition across income classes. For example, in 1969, 62.7% of persons ended up in the same quintile they started in one year earlier, in 1968. At the end of the period, between 1990 and 1991, 65.9% failed to move to either a lower or higher income group. The fact that the graph drifts upward over the period under analysis implies that rate of mobility, as measured by the probability of moving to a different income fifth in an adjacent year, has fallen.

Conclusion

The most important development regarding contemporary income trends is the slow and unequal growth that continues unabated. Over the 1979-89 period, rapid income growth among upper-income families and stagnant or falling incomes for the bottom 60% of families led to sharp increases in inequality. At the same time, the income of the median family grew more slowly (0.4% per year) than over any other postwar business cycle.

Since 1989, median family income growth has been stagnant for most family types, and the 1997 median is just $285 (in 1997 dollars) above its 1989 level. In prior recoveries, the income of the median family had far surpassed its prerecession level by this point in the business cycle. In fact, our analysis of an important source of family income growth in the 1980s — the contributions of working wives — shows that this source was insufficient to counteract the negative hours and earnings trends in the 1990s that beset the bottom 40% of prime-age, married-couple families. Finally, younger families starting out in the 1980s or 1990s have done so from lower income levels than earlier generations, and their likelihood of pulling ahead in later years has fallen.

In the Introduction, we note that the 1997-98 respite from the labor-market problems that characterized the last few decades has the potential to lift family incomes in the latter part of the decade (barring, of course, an economic downturn). Nevertheless, should unemployment begin to rise and the labor market become less "tight," there is, in our view, nothing to prevent a return to the pattern of slow and unequal family income growth that has been the norm since the late 1970s.

The remainder of the book elaborates on the themes established in this chapter. The next chapter focuses on changes in the level and distribution of taxes in order to examine the extent to which the U.S. tax system has exacerbated or ameliorated the slow and unequal income growth of the 1980s and 1990s. The third and fourth chapters examine the labor market trends (wages and employment) that are at the heart of the rise in inequality and sluggish income growth. Chapters 5 and 6 broaden the income analysis by examining trends in wealth and poverty. Chapter 7 examines the impact of wage and income trends from a regional perspective, and Chapter 8 compares trends in the United States to those in other advanced countries.

Taxes: burden on
the wealthy greatly diminished

THE ANALYSIS IN CHAPTER 1 REVEALED THAT THE PRE-TAX INCOMES OF MOST FAMILIES have stagnated while the incomes of wealthy families have grown significantly. This chapter broadens the analysis by examining the role of the tax system in these developments.

Three main conclusions arise from this examination. First, tax changes in the 1980s and 1990s have substantially reduced the taxes paid by the wealthiest 1% of families, while leaving the tax burden on the bottom four-fifths of families almost unchanged. For example, differences in tax laws between 1977 and 1998 lowered the federal tax payments of the top 1% of families by an average of $36,710 (or 14.2% of their average initial tax liability). Over the same period, the bottom four-fifths of families saw their average tax payments fall by just $335 (or 6.9%).

Second, the federal tax changes that contributed to widening income inequality over the full period can be broken into two distinct phases: an early phase, between 1977 and 1985, when the top 1% of families received large tax cuts (an average of $97,250 per family) and the bottom four-fifths saw their average tax burden increase by $221; and a later phase, marked by tax law changes in 1986 and 1993, in which the top 1% lost some but not all of the tax reductions from the earlier period and the bottom four-fifths saw small declines in their tax burden relative to 1977 levels.

The third conclusion is that the widening inequality and the falling standards of living documented in Chapter 1 are, for the most part, independent of any of the changes in the tax structure made during the 1980s and 1990s. The economic problems facing the majority of Americans are, overwhelmingly, a product of their *before*-tax and not their *after*-tax incomes. As mentioned above,

TABLE 2.1 Federal vs. state and local tax burdens,
1959-97 (revenue as a percent of GDP)

	Federal	State and local	Total
1959	17.9%	7.5%	25.4%
1967	18.3	8.9	27.2
1973	19.1	10.5	29.6
1979	20.0	9.8	29.8
1989	19.8	10.3	30.2
1997	21.3	10.7	32.1

Source: Authors' analysis of NIPA data. For detailed information on table sources, see Table Notes.

the tax burden on the bottom four-fifths of the population changed little between 1977 and 1998. Thus, for members of this large group, changes in pre-tax income are the key determinants of their economic well being.

The tax burden: still light overall

Compared to other advanced industrialized countries, the overall U.S. tax burden is light and has increased little in the last 30 years. **Table 2.1** shows the total tax burden in the United States as a percent of gross domestic product (GDP) from 1959 to 1997, broken out by federal and state/local contributions. The overall tax burden increased steadily between 1959 and 1973, then held relatively constant between 1973 and 1989 at around 30% of GDP. Rising levels of state and local taxation, which grew from 7.5% of GDP in 1959 to 10.3% of GDP in 1989 (up 2.8 percentage points) accounted for most of the increase in the overall tax burden. Over the same period, the federal tax burden increased from 17.9% of GDP in 1959 to 19.8% of GDP in 1989 (up 2.0 percentage points). As we show below, the effect of shifting the tax burden to state and local governments is to widen post-tax income inequality.

Between 1989 and 1997 the overall tax burden rose again, from 30.2% of GDP in 1989 to 32.1% in 1997. Over this most recent period, however, the federal tax burden rose faster than the state and local burden, mostly reflecting rising revenues from federal income and corporate taxes. As we will see below, the rise in tax revenues over the 1990s has been progressive, with effective tax rates falling for the bottom 60% of families, rising only slightly for the next 35% of families, and climbing significantly only for the top 1% of families.

TABLE 2.2 Tax revenue* in OECD countries, 1965-93 (as a percent of GDP)

	1965	1979	1989	1995	Percentage-point change 1965-95	Foreign minus U.S. rate, 1995
United States	24.3	26.5	27.0	27.9	3.6	0.0
Japan	18.3	24.4	30.7	28.5	10.2	0.6
Germany**	31.6	37.8	38.2	39.2	7.6	11.3
France	34.5	40.2	43.7	44.5	10.0	16.6
Italy	25.5	26.8	37.9	41.3	15.8	13.4
United Kingdom	30.4	32.6	36.2	35.3	4.9	7.4
Canada	25.9	30.6	35.1	37.2	11.3	9.3
Australia	23.2	27.4	30.6	30.9	7.7	3.0
Austria	34.7	39.8	40.9	42.4	7.7	14.5
Belgium	31.2	45.5	44.1	46.5	15.3	18.6
Denmark	29.9	44.5	50.7	51.3	21.4	23.4
Finland	30.3	36.7	43.4	46.5	16.2	18.6
Ireland	25.9	30.9	35.4	33.8	7.9	5.9
Netherlands	32.8	44.5	44.9	44.0	11.2	16.1
New Zealand	24.7	32.7	39.1	38.2	13.5	10.3
Norway	29.6	41.1	41.3	41.5	11.9	13.6
Portugal	16.2	22.9	30.8	33.8	17.6	5.9
Spain	14.7	23.3	34.6	34.0	19.3	6.1
Sweden	35.0	49.0	55.5	49.7	14.7	21.8
Switzerland	20.7	31.1	31.7	33.9	13.2	6.0

* Including Social Security.
** Western Germany in first three columns; eastern and western Germany in 1995.

Source: Authors' analysis of OECD (1997).

Table 2.2 puts the U.S. tax burden in an international context by showing government revenues as a percent of GDP for the Organization for Economic Cooperation and Development (OECD) countries (the group of advanced industrial countries). The last column shows the difference between foreign and U.S. tax levels in 1995 — a positive number indicates that the foreign tax burden is higher than in the United States. All the numbers in the last column are positive, demonstrating that, in 1995, the United States had the lowest tax burden among the advanced industrial economies. The next-to-the-last column of Table 2.2 gives the percentage-point change between 1965 and 1995 in each country's tax revenue (as a share of GDP). The United States had the smallest increase in the national tax burden over the period.

Despite progressive changes, an increase in regressivity since 1970s

Despite the relative stability of the total U.S. tax burden over time, the tax code has undergone frequent changes that have affected the *distribution* of the tax burden. Since the late 1970s, these changes have combined with changes in pre-tax income to enrich the highest-income families —primarily the top 1% — at the expense of almost everyone else.

In order to incorporate the effect of the most recent round of major tax changes, this section includes an analysis of the Congressional Budget Office's (CBO) projections of the impact of the Omnibus Budget Reconciliation Act of 1993 (OBRA93). These projections generally refer to the distribution of taxes and incomes in 1999 based on projected income levels and tax law in that year. Given the nature of tax law, the tax rate projections are likely to provide an accurate estimate of the distribution of tax burdens. Predicting the distribution of pre-tax incomes, however, is more difficult, so the analysis focuses on changes in tax rates by income class and not on changes in pre-tax income. (Since the years chosen for the federal tax analysis in this section are dictated by the timing of important tax legislation and the availability of data from the Congressional Budget Office, years other than the standard "peak" years, i.e., of low unemployment, appear in some of the tables that follow.)

After-tax family income inequality has increased since 1977, despite recent shifts toward a more progressive tax system (where those with higher incomes pay a larger share of their incomes in taxes). **Table 2.3** looks at the changes in income after all federal taxes between 1977 and 1995, the most recent year for which CBO has conducted analyses using actual, rather than projected, family income data. The average after-tax income of the top fifth of families grew 28.1% from 1977 to 1989, but the most dramatic growth occurred among the wealthiest families: the average income of the top 1% of the income distribution grew 102.2% after taxes during 1977-89. This increase exceeds the growth in pre-tax income (78.0%) by 24.2 percentage points, suggesting that reduced taxation substantially boosted the after-tax incomes of the wealthiest 1% of families in the 1977-89 period. By contrast, the income of the average family in the bottom four-fifths of the income distribution fell by 1.8% before federal taxes and 2.2% after taxes in the 1977-89 period. A closer look reveals that it was the poorest families who bore the brunt of these declines: pre- and post-tax income for the bottom fifth both fell 10.4%. The second fifth saw its pre- and post-tax income slide by nearly the same amount.

The data for 1989-95 reveal widespread declines in both pre- and after-tax incomes. The bottom four-fifths of families saw both their before- and after-tax incomes fall in the most recent period. The declines for this group in 1989-95

TABLE 2.3 Average after-tax* family income growth, 1977-95 (1997 dollars)

Income group	After-tax income				Percent change in income			
					After tax		Before tax	
	1977	1985	1989	1995	1977-89	1989-95	1977-89	1989-95
Bottom four-fifths	$25,824	$24,751	$25,251	$24,427	-2.2%	-3.3%	-1.8%	-5.2%
First	9,718	8,412	8,703	7,751	-10.4	-10.9	-10.4	-11.5
Second	21,604	19,217	19,433	17,781	-10.1	-8.5	-9.8	-8.1
Third	31,789	29,730	30,144	27,775	-5.2	-7.9	-5.3	-6.2
Fourth	41,827	41,603	42,761	39,961	2.2	-6.5	2.4	-4.7
Top fifth	$72,695	$87,231	$93,119	$88,717	28.1%	-4.7%	25.4%	1.0%
81-90%	52,234	55,854	57,152	54,540	9.4	-4.6	9.7	-2.6
91-95%	65,456	71,417	74,645	71,652	14.0	-4.0	14.6	-2.2
96-99%	90,168	105,527	112,176	110,942	24.4	-1.1	22.3	3.9
Top 1%	232,009	407,631	469,200	439,985	102.2	-6.2	78.0	8.5
All	$35,404	$37,024	$38,510	$36,241	8.8%	-5.9%	8.6%	-3.3%

* Federal taxes only.

Source: Authors' analysis of CBO data.

were faster than they were in 1979-89 (-3.3% in just six years compared to -2.2% in the preceding 12 years). The contrast between before- and after-tax incomes for the top fifth of families is striking. The before-tax income of the top fifth continued to grow in the 1990s, but at a much slower rate (1.0% over six years) than in the late 1970s and 1980s (25.4% over 12 years). Increases in the 1990s were concentrated in the top 1% (up 8.5%) and the 96-99% group (up 3.9%). After-tax incomes for the top fifth, however, fell 4.7%, a larger amount than for the bottom four-fifths of families, suggesting a move toward greater progressivity over the period.

Table 2.4 shows that between 1977 and 1989 the after-tax income shares of the bottom 90% of the income distribution fell, while the shares going to the top 10% grew. By 1989, the top 20% of families held almost 50% of total after-tax income, up from 43.9% in 1977 and 44.7% in 1980. Most of the gain to the upper fifth was generated by those in the top 1%, who gained 5.0 percentage points in their share of after-tax income over the 1977-89 period, with most of the shift (60%) occurring in the period between 1980 and 1985.

Over the 1989-95 period, a small, ambiguous shift toward after-tax income equality took place. The wealthiest 5% of families (the top 1% and the 96-99%

TABLE 2.4 Shares of after-tax* income for all families, 1977-95 (1997 dollars)

Income group	1977	1980	1985	1989	1995	Percentage-point change 1977-89	1989-95
Bottom four-fifths	56.1%	55.3%	51.3%	50.6%	50.9%	-5.5	0.3
First	5.7	5.4	4.4	4.3	4.0	-1.4	-0.3
Second	11.5	11.3	10.0	10.0	9.8	-1.5	-0.2
Third	16.3	16.1	15.1	15.0	15.2	-1.3	0.2
Fourth	22.6	22.5	21.8	21.3	21.9	-1.3	0.6
Top fifth	43.9%	44.7%	48.7%	49.4%	49.1%	5.5	-0.3
81-90%	15.5	15.2	15.2	15.0	15.0	-0.5	0.0
91-95%	9.8	9.9	10.0	9.8	9.8	0.0	0.0
96-99%	11.3	11.2	12.1	12.4	12.2	1.1	-0.2
Top 1%	7.3	8.4	11.4	12.3	12.1	5.0	-0.2
All	100.0%	100.0%	100.0%	100.0%	100.0%		

* Federal taxes only.

Source: Authors' analysis of CBO data.

groups) lost a 0.4 percentage-point share (0.2 percentage points each) of total after-tax income, to the benefit of families in the middle and the fourth fifth. At the same time, however, the bottom two-fifths of families saw their income shares decline, albeit by a smaller amount than in the 1977-89 period.

Table 2.5 extends the analysis of after-tax income through 1999, using projections of the 1999 family income distribution made by CBO in 1998. (The data for 1977 and 1989 are identical to those used in the preceding two tables.) The data summarized in the table identify the role of shifts in the tax structure on the growth of after-tax income inequality. Specifically, the table decomposes (i.e., breaks down into their component parts) the changes in after-tax income shares since 1977 into those due to pre-tax income shifts (discussed in Chapter 1) and those attributable to federal tax policy shifts.

Column 1 shows that the bottom 90% of families had a lower after-tax income share in 1989 than in 1977 (as noted in Table 2.4). The bottom 80% of families lost a 5.2% share of total after-tax income during the 1977-89 period, and 4.6 of these points were due to a relative loss of pre-tax income. By contrast, only 0.6 points of the 5.2 percentage-point drop were due to shifts in the distribution of the tax burden. Thus, shifts in the tax burden, though significant,

TABLE 2.5 The effects of tax* and income changes on
after-tax income shares, 1977-99**

| | Change in after-tax Shares | | Change in shares due to: | | | |
| | | | Pre-tax income shifts | | Change in tax progressivity | |
Income group	(1) 1977-89	(2) 1989-99*	(3) 1977-89	(4) 1989-99*	(5) 1977-89	(6) 1989-99*
Bottom four-fifths	-5.2	-0.5	-4.6	-1.9	-0.6	1.3
First	-1.3	-0.4	-1.1	-0.6	-0.2	0.2
Second	-1.8	-0.1	-1.6	-0.5	-0.2	0.4
Third	-0.6	-0.5	-0.5	-0.9	0.0	0.4
Fourth	-1.4	0.5	-1.3	0.1	-0.1	0.4
Top fifth	5.2	0.5	4.6	1.9	0.6	-1.3
81-90%	-0.5	-0.2	-0.4	-0.3	-0.1	0.1
91-95%	0.0	-0.1	0.1	-0.1	-0.1	0.0
96-99%	1.1	0.4	1.1	0.6	0.0	-0.2
Top 1%	4.6	0.4	3.8	1.7	0.7	-1.2
All	0.0	0.0	0.0	0.0	0.0	0.0

* Federal taxes only.
** CBO projections based of 1999 income levels under 1998 tax law.

Source: Authors' analysis of CBO data.

were clearly not the primary mechanism of the overall redistribution of income from 1977 to 1989. Over the same period, the top 1% of families captured a 4.6 point larger share of after-tax income. But, again, most of this improvement (3.8 points) was due to changes in pre-tax income share and much less (0.7 points) to changes in the tax structure.

Column 2 demonstrates that the after-tax income share for the bottom four-fifths of the population is expected to fall 0.5 percentage points over the 1989-99 period. This decline is the result of two countervailing forces. The share of pre-tax income for the bottom four-fifths is projected to fall by 1.9 percentage points, indicating a further growth of pre-tax income inequality. The greater tax progressivity built into 1993 tax changes, however, will partially offset these declines, raising the after-tax income share for the group by 1.3 percentage points.

Table 2.6 summarizes the full extent of the OBRA93 tax changes on expected tax rates and liabilities (using projected 1999 income levels). Unlike the above tables, this table shows the impact of OBRA93 once it is fully phased in

TABLE 2.6 Effect of 1993 tax law* on 1999 tax liabilities and rates (1997 dollars)

Income group	Effective tax rates			Tax liabilities		
	Pre	After	Point change	Pre	After	Percent change
Bottom four-fifths	15.9	15.5	-0.4	$5,510	$5,371	-2.5%
First	7.0	5.0	-2.0	682	487	-28.6
Second	15.0	14.9	-0.1	3,697	3,672	-0.7
Third	19.3	19.5	0.2	7,947	8,030	1.0
Fourth	22.1	22.3	0.2	13,616	13,739	0.9
Top fifth	26.2	27.9	1.7	$40,285	$42,899	6.5%
81-90%	24.6	24.9	0.3	21,503	21,765	1.2
91-95%	25.9	26.3	0.4	30,550	31,022	1.5
96-99%	26.8	27.7	0.9	52,215	53,969	3.4
Top 1%	28.0	33.2	5.2	234,136	277,619	18.6
All	22.8	23.7	0.9	$13,134	$13,653	3.9%

* OBRA93; federal taxes only.

Source: Authors' analysis of CBO projections for 1999.

(in 1998). The decrease of rates and liabilities at the bottom of the income scale and the increase at the top are signs of the progressivity of the 1993 changes. The poorest 20% of families are projected to pay 28.6% less in taxes under a fully phased-in OBRA93 than they would have in the absence of the change in tax law. Conversely, the average liability of the wealthiest taxpayers rises by 18.6%, from $234,136 to $277,619. On average, the bottom 80% of families pays less in taxes (-2.5%) as a result of the change, while the top fifth, on average, pays about 6.5% more.

In summary, the large majority of the growth in income inequality is attributable to shifts in pre-tax income that occurred before taxation. Although the federal tax system exacerbated this trend toward greater inequality between 1977 and 1989, changes in the tax system since 1989, particularly OBRA93, should partly reverse this long-term trend toward more regressive taxation. As we show below, however, given their vast income growth and the failure of even OBRA93 to tax them at past rates, the richest families continue to enjoy a lower federal tax liability than they would have had if the 1977 tax system were in place in 1996.

TABLE 2.7 Effective federal tax rates, 1977-99(p)*

Income group	1977	1980	1985	1989	1992	1999(p)	Percentage-point change 1977-89	1989-99(p)
Bottom four-fifths	16.3%	16.5%	16.7%	16.6%	16.0%	15.0%	0.3	-1.6
First	9.3	8.1	10.3	9.3	8.0	4.6	0.0	-4.7
Second	15.4	15.6	15.7	15.6	14.7	13.7	0.2	-1.9
Third	19.5	19.8	19.1	19.3	19.2	18.9	-0.2	-0.4
Fourth	21.9	22.9	21.7	22.0	21.9	22.2	0.1	0.2
Top fifth	27.3%	27.5%	24.2%	25.6%	26.2%	29.1%	-1.7	3.5
81-90%	23.9	25.2	23.5	24.1	24.5	25.2	0.2	1.1
91-95%	25.3	26.4	24.3	25.6	26.0	27.2	0.3	1.6
96-99%	26.9	28.0	24.3	26.2	26.6	29.0	-0.7	2.8
Top 1%	35.6	31.8	24.9	26.8	27.8	34.4	-8.8	7.6
All	22.8%	23.3%	21.8%	22.7%	22.7%	24.2%	-0.1	1.5

* (p) indicates CBO projections of 1999 income levels under 1998 tax law.

Source: Authors' analysis of CBO data.

The diminished progressivity of federal tax rates

Even though most of the income shifting between 1977 and 1989 occurred before taxes, regressive changes in federal taxes did contribute to the increased inequality of after-tax family incomes over the period. **Table 2.7** and **Figure 2A** present the effective federal tax rates (i.e., the ratio of taxes paid to pre-tax income) by family income group. The average effective tax rate for all families changed little between 1977 and 1989, falling one-tenth of a percentage point, but it is expected to have grown by 1.5 percentage points by the end of the 1989-99 period. A closer look at the table, however, reveals that the small decline in the overall effective federal tax rate in 1977-89 was the result of a steep drop (8.8 percentage points) in the effective rate for the top 1% of families, combined with very small changes, both up and down, in the rates applicable to the other 99% of families. A similar pattern holds in 1989-99. The 1.5 percentage-point increase in overall effective federal tax rates reflects a 7.6 percentage-point rise for the top 1% of families and smaller changes, in both directions, for the rest of families. Changes in the earned-income tax credit (EITC) for low-wage workers, for example, helped drop the effective rate for the bottom fifth of families by 4.7 percentage points in 1989-99.

FIGURE 2A Federal tax burden, 1977-99(p)

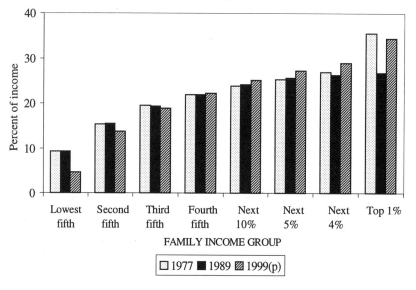

Source: Authors' analysis of CBO data.

A basic conceptual problem, however, leads the numbers in Table 2.7 to systematically understate the deterioration in tax progressivity over the 1977-89 period and to overstate the improvements in tax progressivity in 1989-99. Tables 2.3 through 2.7 use effective tax rates calculated from the income distribution and corresponding tax law for each year. Thus, the effective tax rate for the top 1% of families in 1977 (35.6%; see Table 2.7) is determined by taking the total tax payments for the group in 1977 as a percentage of the total income for the group in the same year. The effective tax rate for the top 1% in 1999 (34.4%) also reflects the projected income and taxes paid in 1999. The change in the effective tax rate, then, is just the difference in the two (-1.2 percentage points). But the *pre*-tax incomes for the top 1% will have grown substantially over the 1977-99 period. These higher real incomes would have been treated differently in earlier years, when tax law included more tax brackets, particularly for high incomes. A better comparison of the tax changes over the period, then, would ask: what would a family with a given income in 1999 have paid in taxes if the 1977 tax law were applied to its (inflation-adjusted) 1999 income?

Table 2.8 presents the conclusions of such an analysis over the period 1977-98. For the bottom 95% of families, the recalculation makes little difference to their effective tax rates (compare with Table 2.7). But for the top 5%, and espe-

TABLE 2.8 Estimated effective federal tax rates on 1998 income under prevailing tax law, 1977-98

Income group	1977	1985	1989	1992	1998	Percentage-point change 1977-89	1989-98
Bottom four-fifths	16.0%	16.7%	16.4%	16.0%	14.9%	0.5	-1.6
First	9.0	10.2	9.2	8.0	4.6	0.2	-4.6
Second	14.2	15.7	15.5	14.7	13.7	1.3	-1.8
Third	18.8	19.1	19.2	19.2	18.9	0.4	-0.3
Fourth	21.8	21.7	21.8	21.9	22.2	0.0	0.4
Top fifth	26.3%	24.0%	25.0%	25.5%	26.4%	-1.3	1.4
81-95%	24.9	23.8	24.6	25.1	25.2	-0.3	0.6
96-99%	28.1	24.3	26.2	26.6	29.0	-1.9	2.8
Top 1%	40.1	25.0	26.7	27.8	34.4	-13.4	7.7
All	18.0%	18.1%	18.1%	17.9%	17.2%	0.1	-1.0

Source: Authors' analysis of Citizens for Tax Justice data.

cially the top 1% of families — those who experienced the largest pre-tax income gains and those affected by the additional, higher tax brackets in 1977 — the impact is substantial. A family in the top 1% of the 1998 income distribution would have paid 40.1% of its income in taxes under the 1977 tax law (versus the 35.6% actually paid by the top 1% of families in 1977). Thus, this alternative calculation shows an even steeper decline between 1977 and 1989 in the effective tax rates for the top 1% (-13.4%) than shown in Table 2.7 (-8.8%).

Most of the preceding tables have grouped families into fifths and examined how changes in tax policy over time have affected these groups. **Table 2.9** and **Figure 2B** use U.S. Treasury Department data that depart from this approach in order to illustrate how federal income and payroll tax changes have affected a family of four with a single earner. In both Table 2.9 and Figure 2B, the "middle-income" family earns the median family income for a family of four with one worker, the "low-income" family earns half the median, and the "high-income" family twice the median. The most striking features of Figure 2B are the steady rise in the effective federal tax rates in 1955-80 and the subsequent flattening out of federal rates thereafter (confirming the pattern observed in the CBO data above). Table 2.9 also makes clear that, as the result of the expansion of the EITC, the effective tax rate for a "low-income" family of four fell 2.8 percentage points in 1989-95.

FIGURE 2B Effective federal tax rate for family of four, 1955-95

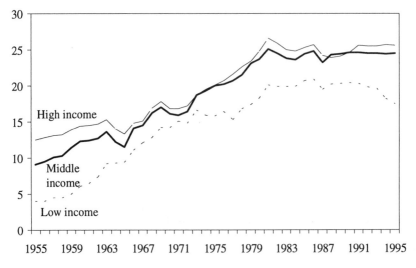

Source: U.S. Department of Treasury (1995).

TABLE 2.9 Effective federal tax rate*
for a family of four with one earner, 1977-95

Income level**	1977	1980	1985	1989	1992	1995***	Percentage-point change 1977-89	1989-97
Low	15.3%	18.3%	20.7%	20.3%	19.9%	17.5%	5.0	-2.8
Middle	20.7	23.7	24.4	24.5	24.5	24.5	3.8	0.1
High	21.6	24.8	25.3	24.1	25.5	25.6	2.5	1.4

*   Average rate for combined federal income, employee plus employer Social Security, and Medicare taxes.
**   Low income is one-half median income for a family of four; middle is median income; high is twice median income.
*** Estimated.

Source: U.S. Department of Treasury (1995).

TABLE 2.10 Effect of federal tax changes on family tax payments, 1977-98(p)*

Income group	Average 1998(p) income before federal taxes	The effect of federal tax changes, 1977-98, on the amount of tax payments, assuming 1998(p) income levels				Difference in taxes, 1977-98(p)	
		1977-85	1985-89	1989-92	1992-98(p)	Dollars	Percent
Bottom four-fifths	$30,481	$221	$-76	$-145	$-335	$-335	-6.9%
First	8,652	104	-87	-104	-294	-381	-48.9
Second	22,002	330	-44	-176	-220	-110	-3.5
Third	36,416	109	36	0	-109	36	0.5
Fourth	54,854	-55	55	55	165	219	1.8
Top fifth	$127,517	$-2,984	$1,358	$650	$1,129	$153	0.5%
81-95%	85,273	-938	682	426	85	256	1.2
96-99%	156,797	-5,958	2,979	627	3,763	1,411	3.2
Top 1%	644,043	-97,250	10,949	7,084	42,507	-36,710	-14.2
All	$49,888	$56	$6	$-139	$-351	$-427	-4.8%

Source: Authors' analysis of Citizens for Tax Justice data.

What federal tax changes mean in dollars

The next step in our analysis is to examine the effect of changes in the tax system on the levels of after-tax income of each income class. The dollar effect of any change in a group's tax rate on the group's actual, after-tax income depends on both the size of the change in the tax rate and on its level of income. **Table 2.10** shows the average projected pre-tax family income in 1998 for each income group (column 1) in constant 1997 dollars. Columns 2 through 5 show the changes in the average amount of taxes paid by each income group due to federal tax changes enacted in different periods between 1977 and 1998 (projected), holding incomes constant at their projected 1998 levels. (The effective tax rates, as in Table 2.8, are calculated using projected 1998 income and applying the tax code in place in each of the earlier periods.) The final two columns show the cumulative effect of changes in the tax code in 1977-98 on 1998 federal tax payments.

The data presented here show that shifts in federal tax policy in 1977-85 were highly regressive, cutting the taxes for the average family in the 96-99% income group by $5,958 and in the top 1% by $97,250. Since 1985, the tax system has been moving to reverse these regressive changes. Tax changes after

1985 caused the tax bill of the top 1% to rise by $10,949 in the late 1980s, and changes after 1989 are expected to increase the tax bill for the top group by an additional $49,591. The effective rate on the top 1%, however, is not expected to return to its 1977 level by 1998: the wealthiest families can still expect to pay $36,710 (14.2%) less in taxes in 1998 than they would have paid under the 1977 system.

The poorest fifth of families benefited from tax changes in the late 1980s and early 1990s (the Tax Reform Act of 1986 and OBRA93). By the end of the period, tax changes led to a $381 cut in their tax bill, or a 48.9% reduction over their liability under 1977 rates. Families in the second fifth ended the 1977-98 period paying, on average, less in taxes ($110, or 3.5%) than they did at the beginning of the period. Over the same period, tax increases for the middle and the fourth fifths ranged between 0.5% and 1.8%.

The causes of changes in the federal tax burden

To show the source of the progressive and regressive changes in the federal tax system, **Table 2.11** decomposes the federal effective rates into their components: the personal income tax, the payroll tax, the corporate income tax, and the excise tax. Personal and corporate income taxes are progressive; the effective rates go up consistently as income rises. Excise and payroll tax rates are regressive, but, as regards the latter, the distribution of Social Security benefits may be a mitigating factor (as discussed below).

Between 1977 and 1989, personal income tax rates fell slightly for the bottom 99% of families and substantially for the top 1% (see **Figure 2C**). After 1989, primarily as a result of OBRA93, personal income tax rates rose for the wealthiest 1% of families (though they did not return to their 1977 levels), fell for the bottom two-fifths of families, and were largely unchanged for the rest. Although the average personal income tax for the richest 1% of families is projected to fall from 25.2% to 22.2% over the full period, the effective rate for the bottom fifth is expected to fall even more steeply, from -0.6% to -6.8%, indicating that the tax system actually transfers money to this group through the EITC.

Between 1977 and 1999, the overall payroll tax rate is projected to rise from 6.5% to 9.2% (Table 2.11 and **Figure 2D**). While the payroll tax is expected to rise for all groups, the bottom 99% will see the largest increases in rates. Payroll taxes have a smaller impact on the wealthiest families, in part because the rich earn much of their income from investments (Chapter 1), which are not subject to payroll taxes, and in part because payroll taxes are capped. In 1998, they applied only to the first $68,400 (1998 dollars) of earnings. The

TABLE 2.11 Effective tax rates for selected federal taxes, 1977-99(p)*

Income group	Personal income tax 1977	Personal income tax 1999(p)	Payroll tax 1977	Payroll tax 1999(p)	Corporate income tax 1977	Corporate income tax 1999(p)	Excise tax 1977	Excise tax 1999(p)
Bottom four-fifths								
First	-0.6%	-6.8%	5.1%	7.9%	1.9%	0.5%	2.9%	2.9%
Second	3.4	0.9	7.5	10.0	2.7	1.0	1.8	1.8
Third	6.9	5.4	8.1	10.8	3.0	1.3	1.5	1.3
Fourth	9.6	8.4	7.8	11.4	3.2	1.3	1.3	1.1
Top fifth								
81-90%	12.0%	11.4%	7.4%	11.1%	3.4%	1.8%	1.1%	0.9%
91-95%	13.9	13.7	6.5	10.3	3.9	2.5	1.0	0.8
96-99%	16.6	16.8	4.4	7.4	5.1	4.3	0.8	0.5
Top 1%	25.2	22.2	1.3	2.7	8.8	9.2	0.3	0.3
All	11.1%	11.1%	6.5%	9.2%	3.9%	3.0%	1.3%	1.0%

* CBO projections.

Source: Authors' analysis of unpublished CBO data and CBO (1998).

FIGURE 2C Personal income tax burden, 1955-99(p)

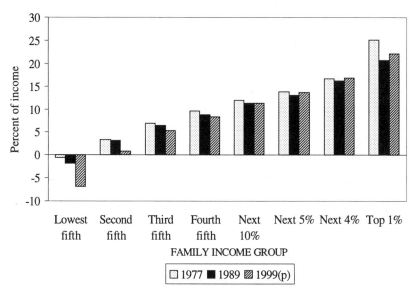

Source: Authors' analysis of CBO data.

FIGURE 2D Payroll tax burden, 1977-99(p)

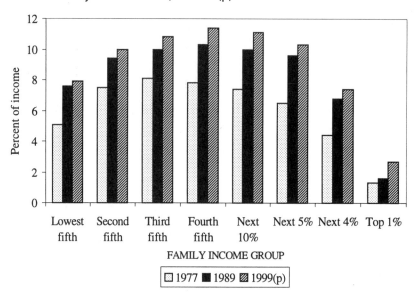

Source: Authors' analysis of CBO data.

payroll tax is by far the largest federal tax paid by the bottom 80% of the income distribution in 1998.

In this analysis, the tax incidence (i.e., those who ultimately bear the burden of the tax) of the payroll tax falls totally on employees; the employer portion is shifted to employees in the form of lower wages. While this is a common and valid assumption of payroll tax incidence, it does not speak to the total redistributive effects of the Social Security system, which incorporate both the taxation and benefit structure. Since retirement benefits are redistributed progressively (less wealthy retirees receive more benefits than they contributed over their lifetimes, while the most wealthy receive fewer benefits than they put in), the benefit structure counteracts the regressive nature of the tax evident in Table 2.11.

However, the age structure of the population is changing so that the number of beneficiaries is rising faster than the number of workers. Some analysts have argued that demographic phenomena will strain the social insurance system's ability to maintain its progressive benefit structure. (For example, the retirement age is already scheduled to rise to 67; researchers have found that the burden of this change is heaviest at the lower end of the income distribution.) Without this redistributive component, the burden of the tax falls on wage earners in the

106

FIGURE 2E Corporate tax burden, 1977-99(p)

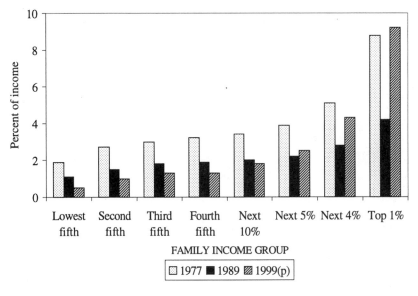

Source: Authors' analysis of CBO data.

present, while its regressive nature is not mitigated for future generations. Therefore, the rise in payroll taxes is considered a regressive change.

Corporate income taxes, which have a progressive structure, declined considerably at all income levels between 1977 and 1989 (see **Figure 2E**). Corporate income taxes are projected to fall, on average, between 1989 and 1999, but the average change masks an increase in the corporate tax burden for the top 10% of families and a decline for the rest. Since corporations are owned by households through shares of stock, households also bear the burden of corporate taxes. In this analysis, it is assumed that half of corporate taxes are borne by stockholders in the form of lower dividends and slower stock appreciation and half are paid by consumers in the form of higher prices.

Excise taxes have fallen slightly since 1977 while maintaining their regressive structure. These taxes — levied on alcohol, gasoline, cigarettes — are the most regressive federal taxes (Table 2.11 and **Figure 2F**). In 1999, the poorest families are projected to pay 2.9% of their income in excise taxes, while the richest fifth, which spend smaller proportions of their incomes on goods subject to excise taxes, pay only 0.3% of their income toward excise taxes.

We have already seen (Tables 2.7 and 2.8) the net effect of the changes in these four categories during the period 1977-99. **Table 2.12** and Figures 2C

FIGURE 2F Corporate tax burden, 1977-99(p)

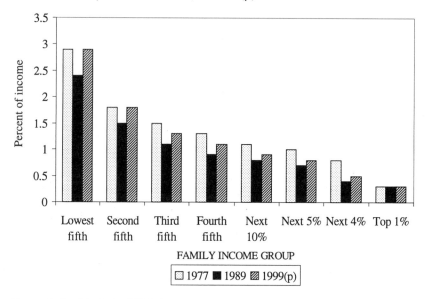

Source: Authors' analysis of CBO data.

through 2F make clear which components of the federal tax structure produced these outcomes. The total effective tax rate on all families is projected to rise by 1.5 percentage points over the period; the only factor contributing to this increase is the 2.7 point rise in payroll tax rates. Declines in the corporate income tax (0.9 points) and in federal excise tax rates (0.3 points) counteracted some, but not all, of the increases in payroll and income taxes. (On average, personal income taxes did not change over the period.) From the standpoint of tax progressivity, most of these developments were regressive. The regressive payroll tax increased substantially, while the progressive corporate income tax decreased.

During 1977-99, the effective federal tax rate for the wealthiest 1% of families is expected to fall by 1.2 percentage points as the result of declines in the personal income tax (-3.0 percentage points) and increases in corporate income tax (0.4 points) and payroll taxes (1.8 points), with no change in the federal excise tax burden. For the bottom four-fifths of families, average effective federal tax rates are projected to fall for all but the fourth fifth, reflecting declining personal and corporate income taxes and rising payroll taxes, with little change in the impact of excise taxes.

TABLE 2.12 Changes in effective federal taxes, 1977-99(p)*

Income group	Personal income tax	Payroll tax	Corporate income tax	Excise tax	Total
Bottom four-fifths					
First	-6.2	2.8	-1.4	0.0	-4.8
Second	-2.5	2.5	-1.7	0.0	-1.7
Third	-1.5	2.7	-1.7	-0.2	-0.7
Fourth	-1.2	3.6	-1.9	-0.2	0.3
Top fifth					
81-90%	-0.6	3.7	-1.6	-0.2	1.3
91-95%	-0.2	3.8	-1.4	-0.2	2.0
96-99%	0.2	3.0	-0.8	-0.3	2.1
Top 1%	-3.0	1.4	0.4	0.0	-1.2
All	0.0	2.7	-0.9	-0.3	1.5

* CBO projections.

Source: Authors' analysis of unpublished CBO data and CBO (1998).

Changes in corporate taxation: the shift to untaxed profits

Although corporate rates have dropped, this decline does not necessarily lead to lower corporate tax liability, since the lower rates could be applied to greater absolute profits (i.e., an expanded tax base). In fact, this was a goal of the 1986 tax reform. However, contrary to the goal of the reform, corporate tax revenue declined through the period because of the growth of *untaxed* corporate income, that is, income from which certain expenses, like interest payments, have been deducted.

Between 1979 and 1997, total corporate profits as a percent of GDP grew from 7.5% to 8.5% of GDP (**Table 2.13**), yet taxed profits fell significantly over this same period, from 7.6% to 6.3%. This phenomenon of rising total profits and falling taxed profits is due to the rise in untaxed corporate profits, which rose from -0.1% of GDP in 1979 to 2.1% in 1997 (Table 2.13 and **Figure 2G**). Over the full period (1967-97), taxed corporate profits dropped, from 8.1% of GDP to 6.3%.

Two factors account for the shift from taxed to untaxed profits: increased indebtedness (along with higher real interest rates) and a more favorable tax

TABLE 2.13 Taxed and untaxed corporate* profits, 1967-97 (as percent of GDP)

	1967	1973	1979	1986	1989	1997
Pre-tax profits	9.8%	7.9%	7.5%	7.3%	7.8%	8.5%
Taxed profits	8.1	7.1	7.6	3.4	4.4	6.3
Untaxed profits	1.7	0.8	-0.1	3.9	3.4	2.1
Net interest	1.1	1.6	1.8	2.2	2.7	1.1
Depreciation allowances	0.8	0.6	-0.3	1.4	1.1	1.0
Other deductions	-0.2	-1.4	-1.6	0.3	-0.3	0.1
After-tax profits	6.5%	5.0%	4.8%	5.6%	6.0%	6.4%
Taxable profits only	4.8	4.2	4.9	1.7	2.5	4.3
Corporate profits taxes**	3.3%	2.9%	2.7%	1.7%	1.8%	2.0%

*   Nonfinancial corporations only.
** Federal, state, and local combined.

Source: Authors' analysis of NIPA data.

FIGURE 2G Taxed and untaxed corporate profits as a percent of GDP, 1959-97

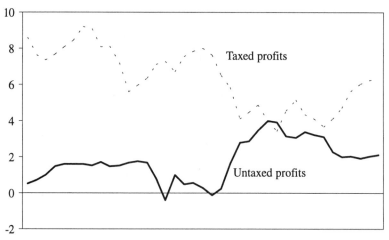

Source: Authors' analysis of BEA data.

treatment of depreciation. Since the late 1970s, corporations have increasingly raised money by selling bonds (i.e., they have borrowed) rather than by selling stocks. As a result, corporations have been paying out more and more of their gross profits as interest payments (on bonds) rather than as dividend payments (on stocks). This trend is reflected in Table 2.13 in the steady increase in net interest payments between 1967 and 1989, from 1.1% of GDP in 1967 to 2.7% in 1989. This trend reversed between 1989 and 1997, probably because of falling interest rates and a shift toward equity financing.

Since interest payments are treated more favorably than dividends by the federal tax system (they are considered an expense for nonfinancial corporations and deducted from taxable profits), and since interest rates were high relative to inflation in the 1980s, the corporate emphasis on debt over equity has lowered the corporate tax burden. Corporate liability is lowered, then, as corporations deduct interest payments from their tax base.

The second reason for lower corporate taxes is the federal tax system's relatively favorable treatment of capital depreciation. With the introduction of the accelerated cost recovery system in 1981, corporations were able to take tax deductions on purchases of new equipment and other investments sooner. Since this accelerated depreciation allowed them to defer some of their taxes for several years, it amounted to an interest-free loan. This tax break grew over the mid-1980s, when untaxed profits due to depreciation allowances grew from -0.3% of GDP in 1979 to 1.4% in 1986 (Table 2.13). Since 1986, Congress has taken back part of this tax cut, reducing untaxed profits in this category to 1.0% of GDP in 1997.

These shifts have led to a growing gap between actual and taxable corporate profits, which has in turn led to a sharp decrease in corporate profits taxes (Table 2.13). As a share of GDP, taxes on corporate profits fell substantially over the period, from 3.3% in 1967 to 2.0% in 1997.

Table 2.14 shows the results of these changes on corporate taxes as a share of profits. Since 1977, corporate taxes have declined from 35.2% of actual profits (defined as the sum of taxable profits, net interest, and the difference between allowable depreciation and true depreciation) to 24.2% in 1997. Moreover, the 1997 effective tax rate, 24.2%, is little more than half of what corporate taxes were in 1959 (Table 2.14 and **Figure 2H**). The beneficiaries of this fall in corporate tax liability relative to true economic profits are largely those who own and lend to corporations: the wealthy.

TABLE 2.14 Corporate profits
tax* rates, 1959-97 (percent)

	Share of:	
	Taxable profits	Actual profits
1959	47.5%	44.7%
1967	41.2	34.0
1973	40.8	36.6
1977	37.8	35.2
1979	35.6	36.2
1986	49.9	23.3
1989	41.7	23.4
1992	35.3	22.8
1997	32.3	24.2

* Federal, state, and local combined.

Source: Authors' analysis of NIPA data.

FIGURE 2H Corporate profits taxes, 1959-97

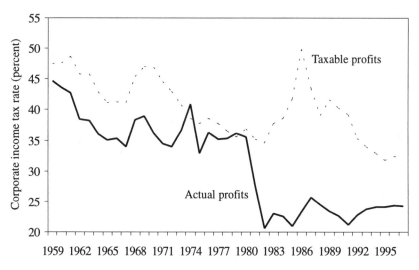

Source: Authors' analysis of BEA data.

FIGURE 2I Total tax receipts as a percent of GDP, 1930-93

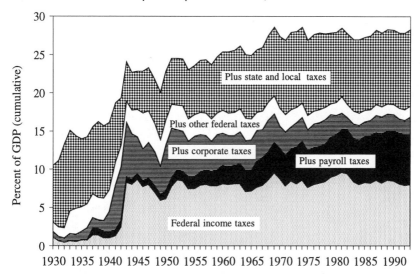

Source: Bajika and Steuerle (1991), updated by original authors (1996).

The shift to state and local taxes

As noted in the beginning of this chapter, the proportion of total tax receipts contributed by state and local taxpayers has grown over time, relative to the federal tax burden (see Table 2.1). **Figure 2I**, which presents total tax receipts as a percentage of GDP, by different components, makes this point graphically. The figure shows that, starting in the postwar period, the growth of tax receipts has been led by state and local taxes (as well as federal payroll taxes, which were discussed above), while the federal income tax shows a relatively flat trend. Since state and local taxes are less progressive than federal taxes, the distribution of the overall tax burden is considerably, and increasingly, less progressive than the distribution of federal taxes alone.

State and local governments rely for their revenues predominantly on regressive taxes, such as sales taxes and property taxes (here regressivity is sensitive to incidence assumptions, discussed below), and on nontax sources of income such as fines and fees (regressive when they apply to consumption). **Table 2.15** gives the effective rates for state and local taxes by family income group for a family of four (the findings are for 1995, the most recent data available). The regressive structure of the state and local burden is shown in the table's final

TABLE 2.15 Effective state and local tax rates in 1995 as
percentage shares of income for nonelderly married couples

Income group	Personal income tax	Corporate income tax	Property tax	Sales & excise tax	Total tax	Total after federal deductions
Bottom four-fifths						
First	1.2%	0.1%	4.5%	6.7%	12.5%	12.4%
Second	2.2	0.1	2.9	5.2	10.4	10.3
Third	2.8	0.0	2.8	4.2	9.8	9.4
Fourth	3.1	0.1	2.8	3.5	9.5	8.6
Top fifth						
81-95%	3.5%	0.1%	2.8%	2.6%	9.0%	7.7%
96-99%	3.9	0.1	2.6	1.8	8.4	6.5
Top 1%	4.6	0.3	1.9	1.1	7.9	5.8

Source: Citizens for Tax Justice (1996).

column: the proportion of income that a family of four paid in state and local taxes fell as its income increased.

However, as with federal income and corporate taxes, state and local income and corporate taxes are progressive. Table 2.15 shows that the average family at the bottom of the income distribution paid 1.2% of its income in state and local personal income taxes, while the wealthiest 1% of families paid 4.6%. The state corporate tax is flat throughout most of the distribution, then slightly progressive at the top.

Conversely, property, sales, and excise taxes are regressive: the percentage of income that is taxed falls as income increases. This burden grew in 1986 when federal deductibility of state sales taxes was removed. In 1995, the poorest families in the average state paid 6.7% of their income in sales and excise taxes. This proportion fell as income increased, until the wealthiest 1% of families paid a combined 1.1%.

The calculation of property tax incidence is particularly sensitive to the assumptions upon which the analysis is based. To the degree that owners of land and structures are able to shift the property tax burden onto tenants, the tax is regressive. Conversely, since ownership of land and capital generally rises with income, the property tax is progressive to the extent that those owners are unable to shift the tax forward onto property users.

TABLE 2.16 Types of federal vs. state and local taxes
as a percent of revenue at each level, 1997

Type of tax	Federal	State & local
Progressive	57.1%	22.8%
Personal income tax	43.6	18.4
Corporate income tax	12.3	4.3
Estate/gift taxes	1.2	0.0
Regressive	42.0%	73.6%
Excise/customs/sales/other*	4.5	39.6
Contributions for social insurance	37.5	10.0
Property	0.0	24.1
Nontaxes**	0.9	3.6
Total	100.0%	100.0%

* Other taxes include vehicle licenses, severance taxes, etc.
** Fines, certain fees, rents, royalties, tuition, hospital fees, etc.

Source: Authors' analysis of NIPA data.

The property tax column in Table 2.15 assumes that homeowners bear the full burden of their property taxes. For residential renters, half of the property tax is allocated to renters and half to owners. These two assumptions lead to the regressive structure reflected in the table, since poorer homeowners and renters devote a larger proportion of income to housing than do the wealthy. The property tax liability on business is assumed to be that part of state property tax revenue not accounted for by residential renters and homeowners.

The shift to state and local governments' revenues, as seen in Figure 2I, is of particular concern from a distributional perspective, since state and local taxes are more regressive than federal taxes. In spite of increases in social insurance taxes, in 1997 57.1% of federal revenues still came from progressive taxes (personal, corporate, and estate), while only 22.8% of state/local revenues were raised progressively (**Table 2.16** and **Figures 2J** and **2K**). (Payroll taxes at the state level are not strictly comparable to those at the federal level, since these state contributions are mostly for pension funds for state and local employees. As such, they are more like personal assets than federal payroll taxes, which are distributed under a pay-as-you-go system. In this regard, they are less regressive than federal payroll taxes.) Almost three-quarters (73.6%) of state/local revenues are raised from regressive taxes, compared with less than half (42.0%) of federal revenues.

FIGURE 2J Federal revenue sources, 1997

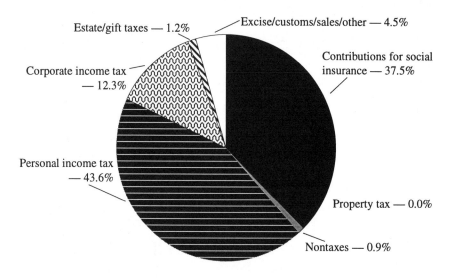

Estate/gift taxes — 1.2%

Excise/customs/sales/other — 4.5%

Corporate income tax — 12.3%

Contributions for social insurance — 37.5%

Personal income tax — 43.6%

Property tax — 0.0%

Nontaxes — 0.9%

Source: Authors' analysis of NIPA data.

FIGURE 2K State and local revenue sources, 1997

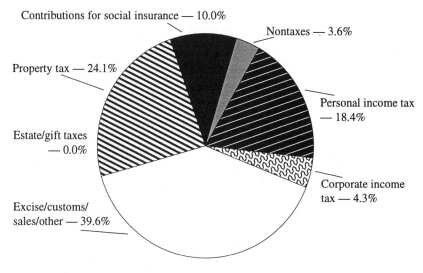

Contributions for social insurance — 10.0%

Nontaxes — 3.6%

Property tax — 24.1%

Personal income tax — 18.4%

Estate/gift taxes — 0.0%

Corporate income tax — 4.3%

Excise/customs/sales/other — 39.6%

Source: Authors' analysis of NIPA data.

TABLE 2.17 Types of taxes as a percent of GDP, 1959-97

Type of tax	1959	1967	1973	1979	1989	1997
Progressive*	13.0%	12.7%	13.2%	13.9%	13.0%	14.6%
Federal	12.3	11.7	11.4	11.9	10.6	12.2
State & local	0.7	1.0	1.8	2.0	2.3	2.4
Regressive**	12.3%	14.2%	16.1%	15.5%	16.7%	16.9%
Federal	5.5	6.5	7.6	7.9	9.0	9.0
State & local	6.8	7.7	8.5	7.6	7.8	7.9
Nontaxes***	0.2%	0.3%	0.3%	0.3%	0.5%	0.6%
Federal	0.1	0.2	0.1	0.2	0.2	0.2
State & local	0.1	0.1	0.1	0.2	0.3	0.4

*   Personal and corporate income taxes; estate and gift taxes.
** Customs, excise, sales, and other taxes (including vehicle licenses, severance taxes, etc.);
    property taxes; contributions for social insurance.
*** Fines, certain fees, rents, royalties, tuition, hospital fees, etc.

Source: Authors' analysis of NIPA data.

Table 2.17 shows the percent of GDP taxed by progressive and regressive taxes, together with nontax revenues, at peaks of business cycles since 1959. While progressive taxes have varied slightly since 1959, regressive taxes have increased their share of GDP substantially — from 12.3% in 1959 to 16.9% in 1997 — as the result of increases at both the federal and state/local levels. Nontax revenues have risen but remain low, at only 0.6% of GDP in 1997.

Conclusion

The federal, state, and local tax systems have done little to ameliorate the growth of income inequality documented in Chapter 1. The federal personal income tax remains a progressive tax structure, but regressive changes in the personal income tax in 1977-89 and the increasing reliance on taxation from other, more regressive sources have limited the ability of the tax system to curb the rise in income inequality since the late 1970s. In fact, between 1977 and 1989, the tax system shifted to the advantage of the wealthiest 1% of families, who received large tax cuts at the expense of the poor and middle class. To some extent, tax changes since 1986 have reversed this trend, particularly regarding income taxes. However, the tax system has still done little to counteract the steep increase in *pre*-tax income inequality, since it generates most revenues from regressive sources. The long-term rise in untaxed corporate profits and a shift to greater dependence on regressive state and local taxes have contributed to the increase in regressivity and after-tax income inequality.

Wages: long-term erosion and growing inequality

WAGE TRENDS HAVE BEEN THE PRIMARY DETERMINANT OF THE SLOW GROWTH IN income and the greater income inequality experienced in recent years. This should not be surprising, since wages and salaries make up roughly three-fourths of total family income; the proportion is even higher among the broad middle class. This chapter examines what has happened to the wage structure and what explains trends in wage inequality.

The widespread deterioration of wages that began in the 1980s continued over the current business cycle from 1989 to 1997, despite some positive wage gains since 1996, as explained in the Introduction. Wage inequality has continued in the most recent period as well, but its character in the 1990s has been different — it has grown between the top and the middle of the wage distribution but has actually diminished between the middle and the bottom. That is, in the 1980s there was increasing divergence between the wages of high-wage and middle-wage workers and between middle-wage and low-wage workers. Since the late 1980s, however, top earners have continued to fare better than middle-wage earners, but low earners have fared better than middle-wage earners.

The deterioration of wages over the 1989-97 period has been broad, encompassing the bottom 80% of men. Wage growth has been stagnant for lower-middle- and middle-wage women in the 1990s, a reversal from the 1980s, when wages for these groups rose modestly. Primarily because of the lifting of the minimum wage, the lowest-wage women saw their wages rise from 1989 to 1997 after falling 18% over the 1979-89 period.

Many high-wage workers, particularly men, failed to see real wage improvements in the 1989-97 period. Male white-collar wages, including those for managers and technical workers, have been stagnant or have declined, and the wages of male college graduates have stagnated and remain below their level of the mid-1980s or early 1970s. The wages of new college graduates have declined by 7% among both men and women over the 1989-97 period despite a recent upturn, indicating that each years' graduates are accepting more poorly paying jobs than their counterparts did at the end of the 1980s.

The deterioration of wages among non-college-educated workers, who make up 75% of the workforce, has continued in the 1990s at the same pace as in the 1980s. Moreover, the wages earned by new high school graduates has continued to decline, although more slowly in 1989-97 as in the 1979-89 period. The result is that the entry-level wages of high school graduates in 1997 were 27.6% less for young men and 18.3% less for young women than in 1979.

These wage declines have not been offset by any growth in nonwage compensation or benefits, since benefits have grown more slowly than wages in the 1990s and have fallen since 1992. Over the 1979-96 period, average compensation (wages and benefits) grew at the same pace as average wages, just 0.5% per year.

One group that has fared exceptionally well in recent years is corporate executives: the wages of chief executive officers grew 44.6% over the 1989-97 period, and their total compensation grew 100.0%. In 1965 CEOs made 20.3 times more than a typical worker; by 1989 this ratio had risen to 56.1, and by 1997 it had reached 115.7. While U.S. workers earn less than workers in other advanced countries, U.S. CEOs make twice as much as their counterparts abroad.

What is driving this long-term widespread erosion of wages among non-college-educated and other workers? Not poor productivity performance: productivity has been growing about 1% per year since 1979, and positive productivity cannot explain falling real wages. Growth in benefits, particularly health benefits, is not responsible, since the trend in compensation (wages and benefits) has paralleled that of wages. However, the modest productivity growth over the 1973-97 period, including that of the 1992-97 recovery, does correspond to growth, albeit slow, in *average* wages and compensation, creating the situation where increases in wage inequality necessarily relegate the losers to falling wages.

There is no "smoking gun," or single factor, that can explain all or even most of the shift in wage inequality. However, a number of factors, in total, seem to account for most of the long-term shifts in wage inequality over the 1979-97 period. Significant institutional shifts, such as a severe drop in the value of the minimum wage and deunionization, can explain one-third of the growing wage inequality among prime-age workers, with the minimum wage primarily affecting low-wage women and weaker unions having the greatest impact on blue-collar, middle-wage men. Similarly, the increasing globalization of the economy — immigration and trade — and the employment shift to lower-paying service industries has created more wage inequality, explaining, in combination, another third of the total growth of wage inequality (industry shifts alone can explain about 20%). Another important factor in the 1990s has been the surge in profitability, which has come partially at the expense of wage growth.

We reject the notion that the growth of wage inequality reflects primarily a technology-driven increase in demand for "educated" or "skilled" workers. There is evidence that the overall impact of technology on the wage and employment structure was no greater in the 1980s or 1990s than in the 1970s. Moreover, skill demand and technology have little relationship to the growth of wage inequality within the same group (i.e., workers with similar levels of experience and education), which was responsible for a significant part of the overall growth of wage inequality in the 1980s. Technology has been and continues to be an important force, but there was no "technology shock" in the 1980s or 1990s, and no ensuing demand for "skill," that could not be satisfied by the continuing expansion of the educational attainment of the workforce.

It is also difficult to see a "bidding up" of the wages of "more-skilled" and "more-educated" workers when the wages of many college graduates and white-collar workers, especially men, have been falling or stagnant since the mid-1980s, except during the most recent year or two of tight labor markets. Moreover, it is misleading to label the group whose wages have been falling as "less educated" or "less skilled," since this group constitutes three-fourths of the workforce and includes many workers with associate-college degrees.

Even so-called information technology workers have not done all that well. Among young college graduates, engineers and scientists are earning 11% and 8% less in 1997 than their counterparts did in 1989, despite good wage growth over the 1996-97 period. Young college graduates in computer science and mathematics occupations were earning only 5% more in 1997 than in 1989, with all of the gain occurring in 1997. These trends do not easily fit with a story in which information technology transforms the workplace so that those equipped to participate enjoy prosperity while those lacking skills lag behind.

More hours and stagnant wages

To understand changes in wage trends, it is important to distinguish between trends in annual, weekly, and hourly wages. Trends in annual wages, for instance, are driven by changes in both hourly wages and the amount of time spent working (weeks worked per year and hours worked per week). Likewise, weekly wage trends reflect changes in hourly pay and weekly hours. In this chapter we focus on the hourly pay levels of the workforce and its subgroups. We do this to be able to distinguish changes in earnings resulting from more (or less) work rather than more (or less) pay. Also, the hourly wage can be said to represent the "true" price of labor (exclusive of benefits, which we analyze separately). Chapter 4 addresses employment, unemployment, underemployment, and other issues related to changes in work time and opportunities.

Table 3.1 illustrates the importance of distinguishing between annual, weekly, and hourly wage trends. The annual wage and salary of the average worker in inflation-adjusted terms grew 0.2% annually between 1989 and 1996 (the most recent year for which data are available). However, all of this growth was due to longer working hours. For instance, the average worker worked 1,868 hours in 1996, 45 more—nearly an additional hour more each week—than the 1,823 hours worked in 1989. Correspondingly, the 0.2% yearly growth in annual wages was driven by a 0.3% yearly growth in annual hours with no growth (actually, a 0.2% decline) in real hourly wages. Any wage analysis that focuses only on annual wages would miss the fact that most of the growth from 1989 to 1996 was due to more work rather than a higher hourly wage.

The 1979-89 period was also characterized by growing annual hours of work (up 78, from 1,745 to 1,823), while real hourly wage growth was modest — growing $0.59 over 10 years, or 0.4% annually. The 0.4% yearly growth in hours worked was driven by the increase in the average work year to 45.4 weeks from 43.8 weeks, a 0.4% annual growth, and a slight increase in the hours of the average workweek, to 39.3 hours. In the 1973-79 period, when hourly wages were essentially flat (falling 0.1% annually) and annual hours grew slowly (0.2% annually), the annual wage grew only 0.1% annually. In contrast, real hourly wages rose 2.9% annually between 1967 and 1973, while annual hours declined 0.4%. Thus, the post-1973 trend of greater work effort coupled with modestly rising or falling hourly wages replaced a trend of strong real annual wage growth based on higher real hourly wages and reduced work time. (Data for earlier years are not available.)

Productivity growth over the last two decades has been less than that of the pre-1973 economy (Table 3.1), but these lower numbers are not sufficient to explain the modest growth in real wages. After all, hourly productivity actually increased by roughly 1.0% annually over the last three business cycles, 1973-79, 1979-89, 1989-96, while hourly wage growth was stagnant.

Since 1979, few groups in the labor force have been able to enjoy even the modest growth in the "average wage" because of the large and continuing growth of wage inequality: high-wage workers received real wage gains while the remainder of the wage structure fell. Understanding and explaining this growth in wage inequality is a major focus of this chapter.

TABLE 3.1 Trends in average wages and average hours, 1967-96

Year	Productivity per hour (1992=100)	Wage levels ($1997)			Hours worked		
		Annual wages	Weekly wages	Hourly wages	Annual hours	Weeks per year	Hours per week
1967	69.2	$21,830	$501.78	$12.76	1,758	43.5	39.3
1973	80.7	25,393	585.22	15.17	1,720	43.4	38.6
1979	86.3	25,580	584.02	15.05	1,745	43.8	38.8
1989	95.7	27,905	614.65	15.64	1,823	45.4	39.3
1992	100.0	27,065	597.47	15.24	1,818	45.3	39.2
1996	102.0	28,222	613.52	15.45	1,868	46.0	39.7
*Annual growth rate**							
1967-73	2.6%	2.5%	2.6%	2.9%	-0.4%	0.0%	-0.3%
1973-79	1.1	0.1	0.0	-0.1	0.2	0.2	0.1
1979-89	1.0	0.9	0.5	0.4	0.4	0.4	0.1
1989-96	0.9	0.2	0.0	-0.2	0.3	0.2	0.1

* Log growth rates.

Source: Authors' analysis of CPS data and Murphy and Welch (1989). For detailed information on table sources, see Table Notes.

Contrasting compensation and wage growth

There has been increased attention to the fact that "wages" do not make up the total pay package received by workers. It is possible that nonwage payments, sometimes referred to as "fringe benefits," have been growing rapidly, thereby driving total compensation to grow far faster than wages. Though widely believed, this characterization of the growth of workers' pay — disappointing wage growth but fast fringe-benefit and significant compensation growth — is an inaccurate characterization of pay trends, especially over the last few years when benefits grew more slowly than wages. This section examines the growth of compensation using the only two available data series and finds that hourly compensation grew slightly faster than wages in the 1980s but not in the 1990s. One implication of compensation and wages growing in tandem is that analyses, such as ours below, that focus on wage trends are using an appropriate proxy for compensation. If anything, analyses of wage growth overstate the corresponding growth of compensation in the 1990s.

Table 3.2 examines the wage and compensation data that are developed as a major part of the Commerce Department's effort — the National Income and

TABLE 3.2 Growth of average hourly wages, benefits, and compensation, 1959-96 (1997 dollars)

Year	Wages & salaries	Benefits*	Total compensation	Benefit share of compensation
*Hourly pay***				
1959	$11.35	$1.10	$12.45	8.9%
1967	13.65	1.67	15.32	10.9
1973	15.81	2.59	18.40	14.1
1979	15.94	3.46	19.39	17.8
1989	16.82	3.74	20.55	18.2
1992	17.15	3.98	21.13	18.8
1996	17.40	3.80	21.21	17.9
Annual dollar change				
1959-73	$0.32	$0.11	$0.42	
1973-79	0.02	0.14	0.17	
1979-89	0.09	0.03	0.12	
1989-96	0.08	0.01	0.09	
1979-96	0.09	0.02	0.11	
Annual percent change				
1959-73	2.4%	6.3%	2.8%	
1973-79	0.1	4.9	0.9	
1979-89	0.5	0.8	0.6	
1989-96	0.5	0.2	0.4	
1979-96	0.5	0.6	0.5	

* Includes payroll taxes, health, pension, and other nonwage benefits.
** Deflated by personal consumption expenditure (PCE) index for all items, except health, which is deflated by PCE medical index.

Source: Authors' analysis of BEA NIPA data.

Product Accounts (NIPA) — to measure gross domestic product, the size of the national economy. Compensation levels exceed wage levels because they include employer payments for health insurance, pensions, and payroll taxes (primarily payments toward Social Security and unemployment insurance).

It is true that benefits grew faster, if not far faster, than wages in the 1960s, 1970s, and 1980s. For instance, over the 1979-89 period benefits grew 0.8% annually while wages grew only 0.5%. Yet total compensation (wages and benefits) grew at relatively the same rate as wages, 0.6% versus 0.5% per year. This apparent contradiction is readily explained: nonwage compensation in 1979 totaled just 17.8% of total compensation. Thus, even a fast growth of a small part of compensation (benefits) did not lead to a growth in total compensation much greater than in wages.

Another way of portraying the limited role of benefits growth is to note that a 0.8% annual growth over the 1979-89 period translated to a $0.03 per year growth in hourly benefits, boosting benefits from $3.46 in 1979 to $3.74 in 1989.

Over the 1989-96 period the growth of benefits slowed to 0.2% (or $0.01) per year. In contrast, the annual growth in average hourly wages maintained its 0.5% pace. Consequently, the benefits share of compensation fell slightly, from 18.2% to 17.9%, and compensation grew more slowly than wages, 0.4% versus 0.5%. As Table 3.2 shows, the slowdown in benefits in the 1989-96 period as a whole was driven by a *reduction* in benefits over the 1992-96 period. Over the entire 1979-96 period the growth of hourly compensation, 0.5% per year, equaled that of wages.

Why is it that some analysts have presumed that fringe benefit growth in recent years has balanced declining wages, thus leaving overall compensation to grow at its historical rate? This reasoning seems plausible, since health care costs have been rising rapidly and since most people assume that fringe benefits make up a large share of total compensation, perhaps as high as 40-45%.

However, the data presented in Table 3.2 show that benefits are not as important in the overall compensation package as is commonly believed, nor did compensation increase rapidly in recent years. Part of the confusion about the role of fringe benefits is definitional. In surveys of employers by trade associations and by the Bureau of Labor Statistics, fringe benefits are broadly defined (following standard corporate accounting procedures) to include paid leave (holidays and vacations), supplemental pay (overtime and shift premiums), as well as payroll taxes (the employer portion of Social Security and unemployment taxes), pensions, and insurance. Under this broad definition, benefits make up about 28% of total compensation costs. However, wage-related items that are received by workers in their regular paychecks, such as paid leave and supplemental pay, are already reported as wages when workers report their wages in government surveys and to the Internal Revenue Service.

The data in **Table 3.3** take a different look at the role of benefit growth in driving total compensation growth. These data are drawn from the Bureau of Labor Statistics' Employment Cost Index (ECI) program, which provides the value of wages and employer-provided benefits for each year since 1987. These ECI data corroborate our earlier finding that benefits, defined as pension, insurance (health and life), and payroll taxes make up an 18-20% share of total compensation that has not changed much since 1987. In fact, these ECI data are somewhat more pessimistic than those in Table 3.2, since they show a nontrivial 7.6% *decline* in compensation and a 9.2% *decline* in benefits from 1989 to 1997.

TABLE 3.3 Growth in private-sector average hourly wages, benefits, and compensation, 1987-97 (1997 dollars)

Year*	Wages & salaries	Benefits**	Total compensation***	Benefit share of compensation
Hourly pay				
1987	$15.87	$3.59	$19.46	18.4%
1988	15.59	3.64	19.23	18.9
1989	15.40	3.58	18.98	18.9
1990	15.27	3.60	18.87	19.1
1991	14.87	3.54	18.41	19.2
1992	15.05	3.62	18.67	19.4
1993	15.08	3.62	18.69	19.3
1994	14.93	3.68	18.62	19.8
1995	14.64	3.46	18.10	19.1
1996	14.62	3.37	17.99	18.8
1997	14.72	3.26	17.98	18.1
Change 1989-97				
Dollars	-$1.15	-$0.33	-$1.48	
Percent	-7.3%	-9.2%	-7.6%	

*   Data are for March.
**   Includes payroll taxes, health, pension, and other nonwage benefits.
***   Deflated by CPI-U-X1, except health deflated by CPI-U-X1 medical care index.

Source: Authors' analysis of BLS ECI levels data.

These numbers vary from the ones presented earlier because they describe only the private sector (government employment is excluded), and the definition of "hours worked" is different. Nevertheless, neither source of data provides much support for the view that, although wage growth may be disappointing, increased benefits are making up the difference. We return to a discussion of benefit growth below when we examine the growth of specific benefits, such as health insurance and pensions.

Although studies of labor market trends should examine both wage and benefit trends, those that focus on wage trends alone (usually because of a lack of benefit data) are not misleading. Taking account of payroll taxes or pension and insurance costs (including both health and life insurance), given their small size and slow growth, would not substantively alter the picture emerging from analyses, such as this one, of the government wage data frequently used to track labor market trends.

TABLE 3.4 Hourly and weekly earnings of production and nonsupervisory workers,* 1947-97 (1997 dollars)

Year	Real average hourly earnings	Real average weekly earnings
1947	$ 7.50	$302.30
1967	11.85	450.28
1973	13.40	494.39
1979	13.36	476.97
1982	12.89	448.69
1989	12.50	432.63
1992	12.09	415.96
1997	12.26	424.20
Business cycles	Annual Growth Rate	
1947-67	2.3	2.0
1967-73	2.1	1.6
1973-79	0.0	-0.6
1979-89	-0.7	-1.0
1989-97	-0.2	-0.2
Recoveries		
1982-89	-0.4	-0.5
1992-97	0.3	0.4

* Production and nonsupervisory workers account for more than 80% of wage and salary employment.

Source: Authors' analysis.

Wages by occupation

We now turn to the growth or decline in wages of the various segments of the workforce since 1973. In general, the workers who experienced the greatest fall in real wages were those who initially had lower wages, were without a college degree, were in blue-collar or service occupations, or were younger. In the 1990s, however, there has also been real wage erosion among male white-collar and college-educated workers.

The data in **Table 3.4** and **Figure 3A** show wage trends for the 80% of the workforce who are "production and nonsupervisory workers." This category includes factory workers, construction workers, and a wide variety of service sector workers ranging from restaurant and clerical workers to nurses and teachers; it leaves out higher-paid managers and supervisors. Between 1989 and 1997,

FIGURE 3A Hourly wage and compensation growth of production/nonsupervisory workers, 1959-97

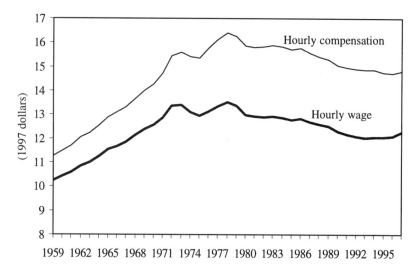

Source: Authors' analysis.

average hourly earnings for these workers fell $0.24, or 0.2% annually, despite positive wage growth over the 1992-97 recovery. Over the entire 1979-97 period, wages for these workers fell from $13.36 to $12.26, a decline of $1.10 per hour. In contrast, hourly earnings were flat in the 1973-79 period and grew 2.1-2.3% per year from 1947 to 1973.

Weekly earnings fell at a rate of 1.0% each year from 1979 until 1989 because of reductions in both weekly hours and hourly earnings. Real hourly and weekly earnings fell in tandem over the 1989-97 period, implying that weekly hours remained stable. The earnings of production and nonsupervisory workers in 1997 were $424.20 per week (in 1997 dollars), $26 less than what they were in 1967.

Table 3.5 presents post-1973 wage trends by occupation for men and women. The decline in hourly wages from 1989 to 1997 among men was evident in every occupation category except professionals, although greater among blue-collar (-6.4%) than managers (-2.7%). For blue-collar men, who made up 41.0% of male employment in 1997, these recent wage setbacks follow the deep, 9.2% real wage declines of the 1979-89 period. Men in the higher-paid white-collar occupations, on the other hand, enjoyed real wage growth in the 1980s, so their

TABLE 3.5 Changes in hourly wages by occupation, 1973-97

Occupation*	Percent of employment 1997	Hourly wage ($1997)				Percent change		
		1973	1979	1989	1997	1973-79	1979-89	1989-97
Males								
White collar	45.8%	$19.18	$19.18	$19.29	$19.24	-0.0%	0.6%	-0.3%
Managers	13.2	21.24	21.36	22.86	22.25	0.5	7.1	-2.7
Professional	12.8	21.28	20.79	21.89	22.56	-2.3	5.3	3.1
Technical	3.4	18.09	17.84	18.33	18.26	-1.4	2.8	-0.4
Sales	10.0	16.67	16.88	15.80	15.47	1.3	-6.5	-2.1
Admin., clerk	6.4	14.58	14.67	13.47	12.82	0.6	-8.2	-4.8
Service	10.7%	$12.01	$11.03	$10.05	$9.66	-8.2%	-8.9%	-3.8%
Protective	3.1	15.51	14.01	14.06	13.91	-9.7	0.4	-1.0
Other	7.6	10.29	9.65	8.31	7.96	-6.2	-13.9	-4.3
Blue collar	41.0%	$14.45	$14.52	$13.18	$12.34	0.5%	-9.2%	-6.4%
Craft	18.9	16.53	16.21	14.94	14.09	-1.9	-7.9	-5.7
Operatives	8.3	12.96	13.41	12.27	11.22	3.5	-8.5	-8.5
Trans. op.	7.5	13.61	13.90	12.36	11.83	2.2	-11.1	-4.3
Laborers	6.3	11.88	11.77	10.04	9.17	-0.9	-14.7	-8.6
Females								
White collar	73.0%	$11.64	$11.47	$12.52	$13.21	-1.5%	9.2%	5.5%
Managers	13.6	13.41	13.16	15.24	16.02	-1.9	15.8	5.1
Professional	17.8	15.56	14.53	16.47	17.29	-6.6	13.3	5.0
Technical	4.1	12.27	12.83	13.74	13.66	4.6	7.1	-0.6
Sales	12.0	8.01	9.27	9.24	9.71	15.6	-0.3	5.1
Admin., clerk	25.5	10.45	10.19	10.61	10.44	-2.4	4.0	-1.6
Service	15.6%	$7.59	$7.83	$7.33	$7.30	3.2%	-6.4%	-0.5%
Protective	0.7	n.a.	n.a.	n.a.	11.40	n.a.	n.a.	n.a.
Other	14.9	7.54	7.79	7.18	7.16	3.2	-7.8	-0.3
Blue collar	10.2%	$8.83	$9.39	$9.02	$8.83	6.3%	-3.9%	-2.1%
Craft	2.1	10.14	10.62	10.77	10.52	4.7	1.4	-2.2
Operatives	5.4	8.66	9.14	8.48	8.37	5.6	-7.2	-1.3
Trans. cp.	0.9	n.a.	n.a.	n.a.	n.a.	n.a.	n.a.	n.a.
Laborers	1.8	n.a.	n.a.	n.a.	n.a.	n.a.	n.a.	n.a.

* Data for private household and farming, forestry, and fishing occupations not shown and not included in wage calculations.

Source: Authors' analysis.

recent experiences represent a turnaround. White-collar men in 1997 earned essentially the same as their counterparts did in 1973 or 1979, about $19.20.

Nearly three-fourths (73%) of women workers were white-collar workers in 1997, and their wage growth of 5.5% in the recent period from 1989 to 1997 was slower relative to the 9.2% growth of the prior decade, even after taking the different lengths of these time periods into account. The wages of women in blue-collar and service occupations fell in both the 1980s and 1990s.

Wage trends by wage level

For any given trend in average wages, there will be different outcomes for particular groups of workers if wage inequality rises, as it has in recent years. Wage trends can be described by examining groups of workers by occupation, education level, and so on, but doing so omits the impact of changes such as increasing inequality within groups. The advantage of an analysis of wage trends by percentile (or wage level), as in **Table 3.6**, is that it captures all of the changes in the wage structure. Table 3.6 provides data on wage trends for workers at different points (or levels) in the wage distribution, thus allowing us to characterize wage growth for low-, middle-, and high-wage earners. The data, presented for the cyclical peak years 1973, 1979, and 1989 and for the most recent full year for which we have data, 1997, show that the deterioration in real wages since 1979 was both broad and uneven. The breadth of recent wage problems is clear from the fact that real wages fell for the bottom 70% of wage earners over the 1979-89 period, while wages were flat or falling for the bottom 80% over the 1989-97 period. That is, only workers in the upper 20% of the wage scale obtained real wage growth in the 1990s, including the 1992-97 recovery period.

Over the longer term, the lower the wage, the greater the decline. Over the 1979-97 period, wages were flat at the 80th percentile (up 0.4%) but were down 8.0% and 14.9% at the 20th and 10th percentiles, respectively. The wage of the median worker, who earned more than half of the workforce but also less than half of the workforce, fell 2.4% from 1979 to 1989 and another 3.1% from 1989 to 1997.

This overall picture, however, masks somewhat different outcomes for men and women. Among men, wages have fallen more and at nearly all parts of the wage distribution (**Table 3.7** and **Figure 3B**). In the middle, the median male hourly wage fell 9.1% between 1979 and 1989 and another 6.7% between 1989 and 1997, for a total fall of 15.3%. Even high-wage men (those at the 80th percentile) experienced a decline in wages of 2.0% over the 1979-89 period,

TABLE 3.6 Wages for all workers by wage percentile, 1973-97

	Wage by percentile*								
Year	10	20	30	40	50	60	70	80	90
Real									
hourly wage ($1997)									
1973	$6.07	$7.33	$8.70	$10.13	$11.61	$13.32	$15.46	$17.68	$22.22
1979	6.42	7.33	8.61	10.13	11.46	13.27	15.69	18.29	22.46
1989	5.39	6.71	8.05	9.62	11.18	13.05	15.53	18.57	23.46
1992	5.49	6.68	7.99	9.34	11.16	12.75	15.10	18.24	23.07
1997	5.46	6.74	7.94	9.25	10.82	12.69	15.08	18.37	23.90
Dollar change									
1973-79	$0.35	$0.00	-$0.10	$0.00	-$0.15	-$0.04	$0.23	$0.61	$0.24
1979-89	-1.03	-0.62	-0.56	-0.51	-0.28	-0.22	-0.16	0.28	1.00
1989-97	0.07	0.03	-0.11	-0.36	-0.35	-0.36	-0.45	-0.20	0.44
1979-97	-0.96	-0.59	-0.67	-0.87	-0.63	-0.58	-0.61	0.08	1.44
Percent change									
1973-79	5.8%	0.1%	-1.1%	0.0%	-1.3%	-0.3%	1.5%	3.5%	1.1%
1979-89	-16.1	-8.5	-6.5	-5.0	-2.4	-1.7	-1.0	1.5	4.5
1989-97	1.4	0.5	-1.4	-3.8	-3.1	-2.7	-2.9	-1.1	1.9
1979-97	-14.9	-8.0	-7.8	-8.6	-5.5	-4.4	-3.9	0.4	6.4

* Wage at which x% of the wage earners earn less and (100-x)% earn more.

Source: Authors' analysis.

followed by an even faster 3.2% drop after 1989. Wages among low-wage men fell the most — about 18% — from 1979 to 1997. These data thus show significant wage deterioration for nearly all men, with the bottom 60% suffering between a 12% and 18% wage reduction from 1979 to 1997. Since 1979, the median male hourly wage has fallen $2.20, or about 0.9% per year. Even the high-wage men at the 90th percentile, who earn about $26 per hour, have done well only in relative terms, since their wage was just 2% higher in 1997 than in 1979.

The pattern of male wage deterioration shifted between the 1980s and 1990s. In the 1980s, wages fell most the lower the wage, while in the 1990s there was somewhat greater wage erosion in the middle than at the bottom. Thus, the wage gap between middle- and low-wage men fell slightly in the 1990s, although the gap between high-wage men (at the 90th percentile) and middle- and low-wage men continued to grow.

The only significant wage growth between 1989 and 1997 appears to have

TABLE 3.7 Wages for male workers by wage percentile, 1973-97

Year	Wage by percentile*								
	10	20	30	40	50	60	70	80	90
Real hourly wage ($1997)									
1973	$7.16	$9.19	$10.84	$12.42	$14.08	$15.96	$17.56	$20.21	$25.74
1979	7.07	8.98	10.80	12.56	14.39	16.33	18.32	21.27	25.93
1989	6.17	7.73	9.49	11.23	13.07	15.38	17.79	20.85	26.12
1992	5.79	7.31	9.02	10.81	12.54	14.63	17.22	20.44	26.16
1997	5.92	7.36	8.86	10.29	12.19	14.44	17.02	20.18	26.44
Dollar change									
1973-79	-$0.09	-$0.21	-$0.04	$0.15	$0.31	$0.37	$0.75	$1.06	$0.19
1979-89	-0.90	-1.25	-1.31	-1.33	-1.32	-0.94	-0.52	-0.42	0.18
1989-97	-0.25	-0.37	-0.63	-0.94	-0.88	-0.94	-0.77	-0.67	0.32
1979-97	-1.15	-1.62	-1.94	-2.27	-2.20	-1.89	-1.30	-1.09	0.51
Percent change									
1973-79	-1.3%	-2.3%	-0.3%	1.2%	2.2%	2.3%	4.3%	5.2%	0.7%
1979-89	-12.7	-13.9	-12.1	-10.6	-9.1	-5.8	-2.9	-2.0	0.7
1989-97	-4.1	-4.8	-6.6	-8.4	-6.7	-6.1	-4.4	-3.2	1.2
1979-97	-16.2	-18.1	-17.9	-18.1	-15.3	-11.5	-7.1	-5.1	2.0

* Wage at which x% of wage earners earn less and (100-x)% earn more.

Source: Authors' analysis.

been among the highest-wage women (**Table 3.8** and **Figure 3C**). For instance, wages grew 6.6%, or $1.28 per hour, for women at the 90th percentile. Among the bottom 60% of women wage earners, however, there was very little wage growth over the 1989-97 period.

The pattern of wage growth among women in the 1989-97 period differs markedly from the pattern in the 1980s in two crucial respects. The first is that low-wage women's wages held steady (or grew a bit) in the 1990s, whereas they fell significantly in the 1980s (a shift related to changes in minimum wage policies, as shown below). The second distinction between the 1980s and 1990s is that the wage trends for middle- and upper-middle-wage (80th percentile) women have been far less favorable in the 1990s: wages grew modestly in the 1980s but were stagnant in the 1990s.

FIGURE 3B Real hourly wages for men by wage percentile, 1973-97

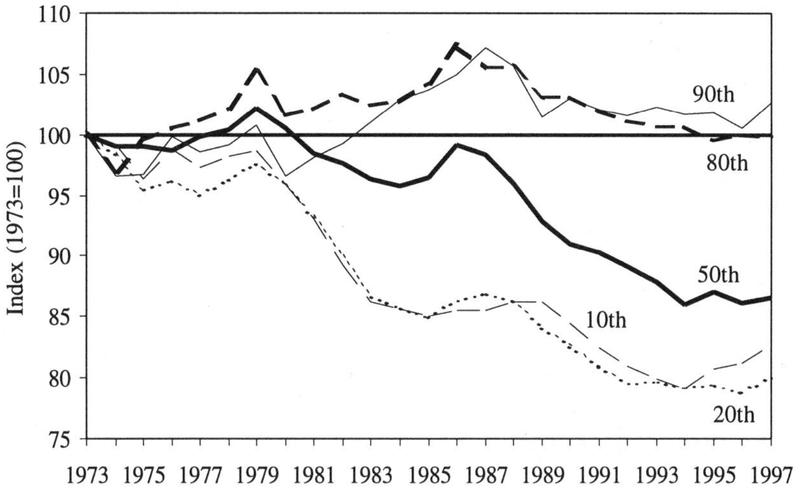

Source: Authors' analysis.

TABLE 3.8 Wages for female workers by wage percentile, 1973-97 (1997 dollars)

Year	Wage by percentile*								
	10	20	30	40	50	60	70	80	90
Real hourly wage ($1997)									
1973	$5.05	$6.27	$7.05	$7.89	$8.89	$10.01	$11.27	$13.00	$16.07
1979	6.13	6.64	7.22	8.05	9.03	10.27	11.46	13.32	16.62
1989	5.02	6.18	7.15	8.22	9.55	10.91	12.85	15.40	19.33
1992	5.20	6.06	7.13	8.35	9.55	11.21	12.82	15.50	20.00
1997	5.15	6.14	7.16	8.25	9.63	11.08	13.07	15.91	20.61
Dollar change									
1973-79	$1.08	$0.37	$0.16	$0.16	$0.14	$0.27	$0.18	$0.32	$0.55
1979-89	-1.11	-0.46	-0.07	0.17	0.52	0.64	1.39	2.09	2.71
1989-97	0.13	-0.04	0.01	0.03	0.08	0.16	0.21	0.51	1.28
1979-97	-0.98	-0.50	-0.06	0.20	0.60	0.80	1.61	2.60	3.99
Percent change									
1973-79	21.3%	5.9%	2.3%	2.0%	1.6%	2.7%	1.6%	2.5%	3.4%
1979-89	-18.2	-7.0	-0.9	2.1	5.7	6.2	12.2	15.7	16.3
1989-97	2.7	-0.7	0.1	0.3	0.8	1.5	1.7	3.3	6.6
1979-97	-16.0	-7.6	-0.8	2.5	6.6	7.8	14.0	19.5	24.0

* Wage at which x% of wage earners earn less and (100-x)% earn more.

Source: Authors' analysis.

FIGURE 3C Real hourly wages for women by wage percentile, 1973-97

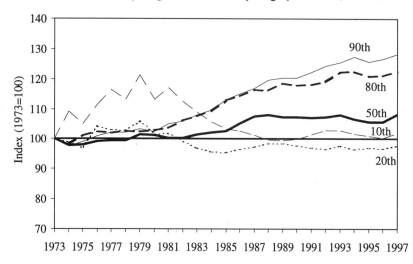

Source: Authors' analysis.

The male-female wage gap

From 1979 to 1989, the median hourly wage fell $1.32 for men and rose $0.52 for women (**Table 3.9**). Consequently, the ratio of men's to women's hourly wages grew by 10.3 percentage points, from 62.8% in 1979 to 73.1% in 1989, representing a sizable reduction in gender wage inequality. The gender–wage gap closed further, but more slowly, in the 1990s, rising to 79.0% in 1997. However, women still earned one-fifth less than men in 1997.

This narrowing of the male/female wage gap since 1979 was the result of both improvements in real hourly wages for women and real wage reductions for men. Table 3.9 provides an assessment of how much the narrowing of this male-female wage differential was due to rising real wages for women and how much to the real wage loss for men. If real wages among men had not fallen by 1989 but had remained at their 1979 level (at $14.39), the wage gap would have been 66.4%, a drop of just 3.6 rather than the actual 10.3 percentage points. Thus, falling real wages among men can explain 64.9% of the closing of the gender–wage gap between 1979 and 1989; correspondingly, only 35.1% (3.6% divided by 10.3%) was due to women's rising real wages.

Between 1989 and 1997, the median wage of men fell ($0.88) and the median wage of women grew by only $0.08. Not surprisingly, therefore, the less-

TABLE 3.9 Changes in the gender wage differential,
1973-97

| Year | Median hourly wage ($1997) | | | Women's share of employment |
	Male	Female	Ratio	
1973	$14.08	$8.89	63.1%	38.5%
1979	14.39	9.03	62.8	41.7
1989	13.07	9.55	73.1	45.2
1997	12.19	9.63	79.0	46.2
1989 (alt.)*	14.39	9.55	66.4	
1997 (alt.)*	14.39	9.63	66.9	
Change				
1979-89	-$1.32	$0.52	10.3	
1989-97	-0.88	0.08	5.9	

*Contribution to narrowing of gender wage gap:***

Period	Male wage decline	Female wage growth	Total
1979-89	64.9%	35.1%	100.0%
1989-97	74.4	25.6	100.0

* Alternative scenario if male wages did not decline in real terms since 1979.
** The contribution of "female wage growth" is the growth of the gender differential assuming male real wages did not fall (the alternative scenario), relative to the actual change in the differential.

Source: Authors' analysis.

ening of gender inequality in the 1990s was driven by male wage decline to a greater extent than in the 1980s; it accounted for 74.4% of the reduction in the gender–wage gap.

The expansion of low-wage jobs

Another useful way of characterizing changes in the wage structure is to examine the trend in the proportion of workers earning low, middle, and high wages. These trends are presented in **Table 3.10** for all workers and for men and women. The workforce is divided into six wage groups based on multiples of the "poverty-wage level," or the hourly wage that a full-time, year-round worker must

TABLE 3.10 Share of all workers earning poverty level hourly wages and multiples, 1973-97

	Share of employment by wage multiple of poverty wage*							
	Poverty level wages:							
Year	0-75	75-100	Total**	100-125	125-200	200-300	300+	Total
Total								
1973	8.0%	15.6%	23.5%	13.3%	34.7%	19.9%	8.6%	100.0%
1979	4.2	19.4	23.7	15.3	31.4	21.0	8.7	100.0
1989	13.4	15.1	28.5	13.5	29.2	19.1	9.7	100.0
1997	12.1	16.5	28.6	14.1	29.6	17.3	10.3	100.0
Change								
1973-79	-3.7	3.9	0.1	2.0	-3.3	1.1	0.0	
1979-89	9.2	-4.3	4.9	-1.8	-2.2	-1.9	1.0	
1989-97	-1.3	1.3	0.1	0.6	0.4	-1.7	0.7	
Men								
1973	3.8%	9.0%	12.8%	9.7%	36.7%	27.9%	12.9%	100.0%
1979	2.4	11.0	13.4	11.3	32.1	29.6	13.6	100.0
1989	9.1	12.1	21.2	11.3	29.7	23.7	14.1	100.0
1997	8.8	13.7	22.5	12.6	30.6	20.5	13.8	100.0
Change								
1973-79	-1.5	2.1	0.6	1.6	-4.6	1.7	0.6	
1979-89	6.8	1.1	7.8	0.0	-2.5	-5.9	0.5	
1989-97	-0.3	1.6	1.3	1.3	0.9	-3.2	-0.3	
Women								
1973	14.0%	25.1%	39.1%	18.6%	31.7%	8.3%	2.3%	100.0%
1979	6.7	30.4	37.0	20.5	30.4	9.8	2.3	100.0
1989	18.2	18.6	36.8	16.0	28.6	13.8	4.7	100.0
1997	15.7	19.5	35.3	15.8	28.5	13.9	6.6	100.0
Change								
1973-79	-7.3	5.3	-2.1	1.9	-1.2	1.5	0.0	
1979-89	11.6	-11.8	-0.3	-4.5	-1.8	4.1	2.5	
1989-97	-2.5	1.0	-1.5	-0.3	-0.1	0.0	1.8	

* The wage ranges are equivalent in 1996 dollars to: $5.78 and below (0-75), $5.79-$7.71 (75-100), $7.72-$9.64 (100-125), $9.65-$15.42 (125-200), $15.43-$23.13 (200-300), and $23.14 and above (300+).

** Combines lowest two categories and represents the share of wage earners earning poverty-level wages.

Source: Authors' analysis.

FIGURE 3D Share of workers earning poverty-level wages, 1973-97

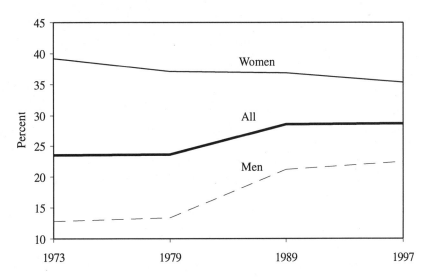

Source: Authors' analysis.

earn to sustain a family of four at the poverty threshold, which was $7.71 in 1997 (in 1996 dollars). Thus, workers are assigned to a wage group according to the degree to which they earned more (or less) than poverty-level wages.

Table 3.10 and **Figure 3D** show a significant expansion of workers earning far less than poverty-level wages since 1979, primarily in the 1980s. In 1979, only 4.2% of the workforce were "very low earners," with wages at least 25% below the poverty-level wage (labeled "0-75"). By 1989, 13.4% of the workforce earned such wages, a shift of 9.2% of the workforce into this low-wage group. This group declined by 1.3% between 1989 and 1997, however. Looking at the total group earning poverty-level wages, Table 3.10 shows that, in 1997, 28.6% of the workforce earned poverty-level wages, a rise from 23.7% in 1979. There was no change over the 1989-97 period. Over the 1979-89 period, there was not only a sizable growth (4.8% of the workforce) in the proportion of workers earning poverty-level wages, but also a shift within this group to those earning very low wages.

Over the 1979-89 period, there was a general downward shift in the entire wage structure, with proportionately fewer workers in the middle- and high-wage groups in 1989 than in 1979. The only exception is the modest expansion

137

of the share of the workforce at the very highest earnings level (exceeding three times the poverty-level wage). In the 1989-97 period there was a similar slight shift to the highest-wage jobs but a larger shift from higher-wage (200-300 percent of poverty wage) to middle-wage jobs.

Among women, there was a larger shift to the "bottom" during the 1979-89 period — an additional 11.6% earned very low wages — and a larger shift upward — the two highest-wage groups grew by 6.6 percentage points. The shift downward among women appears to be an enlargement of the workforce earning very low wages, while the proportion earning poverty-level wages was stable, remaining at about 37%. In the 1989-97 period, the very bottom of the wage structure shrank and the proportion of women earning poverty-level wages diminished. However, there was also a more modest shift to the top two wage categories among women in the 1990s relative to the 1980s.

Among men, the overall changes in the wage structure between 1979 and 1997 meant proportionately fewer middle-wage workers and more low-wage workers, with essentially no growth of very high earners (up in the 1980s but reversed in the 1990s). For instance, there was an increased proportion of men earning less than the poverty-level wage — a 7.8% and then a 1.3% shift — and a shrinking proportion of men in the second- and third-highest wage groups.

Women are much more likely to earn low wages than men. In 1997, 35.3% of women earned poverty-level wages or less, significantly more than the share of men (22.5%). Women are also much less likely to earn very high wages. In 1997, only 6.6% of women, but 13.8% of men, earned at least three times the poverty-level wage.

Tables 3.11, 3.12, and 3.13 (and **Figure 3E**) present an analysis similar to the one in Table 3.10 for white, black, and Hispanic employment. For instance, **Table 3.11** shows that there was a modest shift downward in the wage structure for whites in the 1970s, followed by a larger downward shift in the 1979-89 period. In the 1989-97 period, however, whites moved from low- to middle- and from high- to very-high-wage jobs. Over the entire period from 1973 to 1997, however, there was a significant shift toward proportionately fewer white men in the middle and higher wage groups and an equivalent growth of the share of men earning poverty-level wages, which grew from 10.7% in 1973 to 17.6% in 1997. Among white women, there was a simultaneous shift toward very-low-wage work (at least until 1989) but an overall expansion of women at the highest wage levels.

Among blacks (**Table 3.12**), there was a general downward shift out of better-paying and middle-wage employment into low-wage employment from 1979 to 1989, with modest growth of very high earners. In the 1989-97 period, however, the very lowest wage group declined, shifting upward among those

FIGURE 3E Share of workers earning poverty-level wages, by race/ethnicity, 1973-97

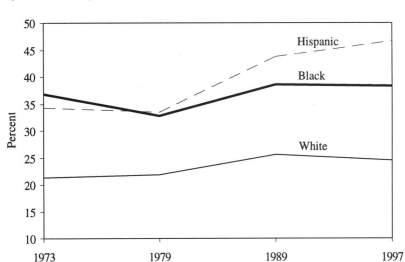

Source: Authors' analysis.

earning poverty-level wages. The shift from high-wage jobs continued in the 1990s.

By 1997, 38.2% of black workers (33.2% of black men and 42.6% of black women) were in jobs paying less than poverty-level wages. The post-1979 shift toward the very lowest-paying jobs (the "0-75" category) — an additional 8.5% of black men and 10.9% of black women — was much larger than among whites. However, the share of black women earning poverty-level wages has fallen considerably since 1973 (from 50.7% to 42.6%), while poverty wages became more commonplace among black men (up from 24.8% to 33.2%).

Since 1979, there has been a general downshifting of the Hispanic wage structure, for both men and women, with a very modest growth in the highest-wage jobs among women (**Table 3.13**). Among Hispanic women, however, there was a large shift into the lowest-wage jobs between 1979 and 1997 (up 19.3 percentage points) driven by changes in the 1980s. The growth in the percentage of Hispanic males earning poverty-level wages was substantial, up from 23.3% in 1979 to 42.4% in 1997.

TABLE 3.11 Share of white workers earning poverty-level hourly wages and multiples, 1973-97

| | Share of employment by wage multiple of poverty wage* | | | | | | | |
| | Poverty-level wages: | | | | | | | |
Year	0-75	75-100	Total**	100-125	125-200	200-300	300+	Total
All whites								
1973	6.9%	14.4%	21.3%	12.9%	35.0%	21.2%	9.5%	100.0%
1979	3.9	17.9	21.8	14.8	31.8	22.1	9.6	100.0
1989	11.9	13.8	25.6	13.1	29.8	20.5	10.9	100.0
1997	10.0	14.4	24.5	13.5	30.8	19.3	12.0	100.0
Change								
1973-79	-3.0	3.5	0.5	1.8	-3.2	0.9	0.0	
1979-89	8.0	-4.2	3.8	-1.6	-1.9	-1.6	1.4	
1989-97	-1.8	0.7	-1.2	0.3	1.0	-1.2	1.1	
White men								
1973	3.1%	7.6%	10.7%	8.9%	36.3%	29.6%	14.4%	100.0%
1979	2.0	9.4	11.4	10.3	32.0	31.3	15.0	100.0
1989	7.4	10.2	17.6	10.5	30.0	25.7	16.2	100.0
1997	6.6	11.0	17.6	11.4	31.7	23.1	16.2	100.0
Change								
1973-79	-1.1	1.8	0.7	1.3	-4.2	1.6	0.6	
1979-89	5.4	0.8	6.2	0.2	-2.0	-5.6	1.2	
1989-97	-0.8	0.8	0.0	0.9	1.7	-2.6	0.0	
White women								
1973	12.5%	24.5%	37.1%	18.9%	33.0%	8.7%	2.3%	100.0%
1979	6.3	29.2	35.6	20.7	31.4	10.0	2.3	100.0
1989	16.9	17.8	34.7	16.1	29.6	14.6	5.0	100.0
1997	13.7	18.2	31.9	15.7	29.9	15.1	7.4	100.0
Change								
1973-79	-6.2	4.7	-1.5	1.8	-1.6	1.3	0.0	
1979-89	10.6	-11.5	-0.9	-4.6	-1.8	4.6	2.7	
1989-97	-3.2	0.4	-2.7	-0.4	0.2	0.5	2.4	

*   The wage ranges are equivalent in 1996 dollars to: $5.78 and below (0-75), $5.79-$7.71 (75-100), $7.72-$9.64 (100-125), $9.65-$15.42 (125-200), $15.43-$23.13 (200-300), and $23.14 and above (300+).

** Combines lowest two categories and represents the share of wage earners earning poverty-level wages.

Source: Authors' analysis.

TABLE 3.12 Share of black workers earning poverty-level hourly wages and multiples, 1973-97

	Share of employment by wage multiple of poverty wage*							
	Poverty-level wages:							
Year	0-75	75-100	Total**	100-125	125-200	200-300	300+	Total
All blacks								
1973	14.8%	22.0%	36.8%	14.8%	32.9%	12.3%	3.2%	100.0%
1979	6.3	26.5	32.8	17.9	29.9	15.7	3.8	100.0
1989	19.1	19.4	38.5	15.7	27.0	14.4	4.3	100.0
1997	16.3	21.9	38.2	17.2	28.1	12.0	4.6	100.0
Change								
1973-79	-8.5	4.5	-4.0	3.0	-3.0	3.4	0.6	
1979-89	12.8	-7.1	5.7	-2.2	-2.9	-1.2	0.6	
1989-97	-2.8	2.5	-0.3	1.5	1.0	-2.4	0.2	
Black men								
1973	7.4%	17.4%	24.8%	13.9%	39.7%	17.6%	4.1%	100.0%
1979	4.3	19.1	23.4	16.2	32.9	21.8	5.7	100.0
1989	15.0	18.2	33.2	15.3	28.9	17.4	5.3	100.0
1997	12.8	20.4	33.2	17.1	30.6	13.4	5.8	100.0
Change								
1973-79	-3.2	1.8	-1.4	2.3	-6.8	4.2	1.6	
1979-89	10.7	-0.9	9.8	-0.9	-4.0	-4.4	-0.4	
1989-97	-2.2	2.2	0.0	1.9	1.7	-4.0	0.5	
Black women								
1973	23.3%	27.3%	50.7%	16.0%	25.0%	6.1%	2.2%	100.0%
1979	8.5	34.3	42.8	19.6	26.7	9.2	1.7	100.0
1989	23.1	20.5	43.6	16.1	25.3	11.6	3.5	100.0
1997	19.4	23.2	42.6	17.2	25.9	10.8	3.6	100.0
Change								
1973-79	-14.9	7.0	-7.9	3.7	1.6	3.0	-0.5	
1979-89	14.6	-13.8	0.8	-3.6	-1.4	2.4	1.7	
1989-97	-3.7	2.6	-1.0	1.1	0.6	-0.8	0.1	

* The wage ranges are equivalent in 1996 dollars to: $5.78 and below (0-75), $5.79-$7.71 (75-100), $7.72-$9.64 (100-125), $9.65-$15.42 (125-200), $15.43-$23.13 (200-300), and $23.14 and above (300+).

** Combines lowest two categories and represents the share of wage earners earning poverty-level wages.

Source: Authors' analysis.

TABLE 3.13 Share of Hispanic workers earning poverty-level hourly wages and multiples, 1973-97

	Share of employment by wage multiple of poverty wage*							
	Poverty-level wages:							
Year	0-75	75-100	Total**	100-125	125-200	200-300	300+	Total
All Hispanics								
1973	12.2%	22.2%	34.3%	16.8%	34.1%	11.5%	3.2%	100.0%
1979	5.3	28.2	33.5	18.0	29.8	14.8	3.8	100.0
1989	20.9	22.9	43.8	14.7	26.1	11.6	3.9	100.0
1997	21.9	24.8	46.7	15.8	24.0	9.4	4.0	100.0
Change								
1973-79	-6.8	6.0	-0.8	0.0	-4.3	3.3	0.6	
1979-89	15.5	-5.2	10.3	-3.4	-3.8	-3.2	0.0	
1989-97	1.0	1.9	2.9	1.2	-2.1	-2.2	0.2	
Hispanic men								
1973	8.9%	16.1%	25.0%	14.1%	40.6%	15.8%	4.4%	100.0%
1979	3.5	19.8	23.3	17.2	33.8	20.3	5.4	100.0
1989	17.4	21.6	39.0	14.3	27.7	14.1	4.9	100.0
1997	18.2	24.2	42.4	16.4	25.7	10.8	4.8	100.0
Change								
1973-79	-5.4	3.7	-1.7	3.1	-6.8	4.5	1.0	
1979-89	13.9	1.8	15.7	-2.8	-6.2	-6.2	-0.5	
1989-97	0.8	2.6	3.4	2.0	-2.0	-3.3	-0.2	
Hispanic women								
1973	17.8%	32.6%	50.4%	21.6%	22.7%	4.0%	1.2%	100.0%
1979	8.2	41.0	49.1	19.4	23.7	6.4	1.5	100.0
1989	26.0	24.9	50.9	15.2	23.8	7.9	2.3	100.0
1997	27.5	25.8	53.3	15.0	21.3	7.4	3.0	100.0
Change								
1973-79	-9.7	8.3	-1.3	-2.2	0.9	2.3	0.3	
1979-89	17.9	-16.1	1.8	-4.2	0.1	1.5	0.8	
1989-97	1.4	1.0	2.4	-0.2	-2.4	-0.5	0.7	

*   The wage ranges are equivalent in 1996 dollars to: $5.78 and below (0-75), $5.79-$7.71 (75-100), $7.72-$9.64 (100-125), $9.65-$15.42 (125-200), $15.43-$23.13 (200-300), and $23.14 and above (300+).

** Combines lowest two categories and represents the share of wage earners earning poverty-level wages.

Source: Authors' analysis.

Trends in benefit growth and inequality

The data already reviewed show that real wages have declined for a wide array of workers over both the 1980s and the 1990s. We have also seen, in Tables 3.2 and 3.3, that total compensation, the real value of both wages and fringe benefits, grew at the same pace as wages over the same time period. Benefits grew modestly until recently, but since they make up a small (18-20%) share of compensation, their growth did not generate fast compensation growth. In this section we examine changes in benefits by type of benefit and examine changes in health and pension coverage for different groups of workers, allowing us to describe the growing inequality of benefits.

Table 3.14 provides a breakdown of growth in nonwage compensation, or benefits, using the two available data series (the "aggregates" were shown already in Tables 3.2 and 3.3). The NIPA data provide a long-term perspective. In the 1959-73 and 1973-79 periods, the inflation-adjusted value of benefits grew by $0.11 and $0.14 each year, respectively, translating into annual growth rates of 6.3% and 4.9%. In contrast, the average value of benefits, including employer-provided health insurance, pension plans, and payroll taxes, grew just $0.02 per year over the 1979-96 period. Benefit growth decelerated from its 0.8% pace in the 1979-89 period to a stagnant 0.2% annual pace from 1989 to 1996. The ECI data in the bottom panel of Table 3.14 confirm this slow annual growth of benefits since 1989. In fact, the ECI data show an actual decline in benefits, from $3.58 in 1989 to $3.26 in 1997.

How can it be that benefits grew so slowly when health insurance costs rose rapidly (relative to other products) for many years and there was a sizable hike in the payroll tax for Social Security in the 1980s? One reason is that health insurance costs are converted to "real" dollars by a medical care price index and reflect the degree to which more health care was being bought (e.g., if medical care prices rise by 10% and health insurance expenditures rise 10%, then health care purchases did not rise). Even if health costs were adjusted by the general consumer price index, however, the results would not change significantly. More important, health care costs have been contained because many workers (about a third of the workforce) receive no health insurance coverage from their employers and the share of workers covered has been falling (as discussed below). Thus, even rapid increases in health costs among a small group of workers with excellent health plans does not necessarily mean that health costs for the workforce as a whole rose rapidly. Last, the efforts of employers to shift the costs of health care onto employees has probably helped to contain the growth of benefits paid by employers. Overall, health care costs per hour worked rose from $1.05 in 1979 to $1.28 in 1989 and to just $1.30 in

TABLE 3.14 Growth of specific fringe benefits, 1959-97 (1997 dollars)

Year	Voluntary benefits			Payroll taxes	Total benefits and nonwage compensation
	Pension	Health*	Subtotal		
Hourly pay, BEA NIPA**					
1959	$0.21	$0.34	$0.63	$0.47	$1.10
1967	0.30	0.47	0.88	0.79	1.67
1973	0.47	0.76	1.36	1.23	2.59
1979	0.63	1.05	1.89	1.56	3.46
1989	0.39	1.28	1.92	1.81	3.74
1992	0.42	1.44	2.12	1.86	3.98
1996	0.45	1.30	1.96	1.85	3.80
Annual dollar change					
1959-73	$0.02	$0.03	$0.05	$0.05	$0.11
1973-79	0.03	0.05	0.09	0.06	0.14
1979-89	-0.02	0.02	0.00	0.03	0.03
1989-96	0.01	0.00	0.00	0.00	0.01
1979-96	-0.01	0.01	0.00	0.02	0.02
Annual percent change					
1959-73	5.9%	5.8%	5.6%	7.1%	6.3%
1973-79	5.2	5.7	5.6	4.0	4.9
1979-89	-4.7	2.0	0.2	1.5	0.8
1989-96	2.1	0.2	0.2	0.3	0.2
1979-96	-1.9	1.2	0.2	1.0	0.6
Hourly pay, BLS ECI levels***					
1987	$0.69	$1.29	$1.97	$1.62	$3.59
1989	0.55	1.36	1.91	1.67	3.58
1992	0.53	1.40	1.93	1.69	3.62
1997	0.55	1.09	1.64	1.62	3.26
Annual percent change					
1992-97	0.8%	-4.9%	-3.2%	-0.9%	-2.1%
1989-97	0.0	-2.8	-1.9	-0.3	-1.2

*   Deflated by medical care price index.
** National Income and Product Accounts (NIPA).
*** Employment cost index (ECI) levels data for March of each year.

Source: Authors' analysis of BLS and BEA data.

1996. In fact, employer health care costs actually dropped over the recovery years of 1992-96.

The drop in pension costs since 1979 has partially offset the rise in health care costs. In 1979, employers paid $0.63 an hour for various pension and retirement schemes; by 1996 hourly pension costs were down to $0.45. In the 1979-89 period this drop in pension costs nearly fully offset higher health costs, as reflected in the minimal rise in total "voluntary benefits" from $1.89 to $1.92.

Employers pay payroll taxes for their employees into a variety of social insurance programs: unemployment insurance, Medicare, Social Security, and workers compensation insurance. These costs grew 1.5% annually in the 1980s but grew minimally in the post-1989 period. There was much more rapid growth of payroll taxes over the 1959-79 period, when such costs more than tripled, from $0.47 to $1.56.

The data in Table 3.14 reflect "average" benefit costs. Given the rapid growth of wage inequality in recent years, it should not be surprising to find a growing inequality of benefits. Tables 3.15 and 3.16 examine changes in health and pension insurance coverage for different demographic groups between 1979, 1989, and 1996. The share of workers covered by employer-provided health care plans dropped a steep 7.6 percentage points, from 70.2% to 62.6%, with most of the decline occurring in the 1980s (**Table 3.15**). Unfortunately, there are no data available to show the degree to which the quality of coverage has changed — whether health plans are more inclusive or more restricted.

Over the 1979-96 period, health care coverage has declined more among men than women but similarly among both whites and blacks, with Hispanics suffering by far the largest drop. The drop in health care coverage by education level repeats the pattern we already saw in wages — dramatic declines among the least educated but a broad-based erosion, including among those with a college degree. The pattern in the erosion of health insurance coverage by wage level shows a similar growth in inequality in the 1980s, with erosion greater the lower the wage. In the 1990s, however, there were modest extensions of coverage for the bottom 40% (including a 2.6 percentage-point expansion for the bottom 20%) while erosion continued for middle- and high-wage workers.

Pension plan coverage (**Table 3.16**) declined as quickly as health care coverage in the 1980s: it dropped from 51.1% in 1979 to 44.3% in 1989. This decline is perhaps one of the reasons for the lessening of pension costs for employers over that period. In the 1989-96 period, however, pension coverage expanded, easing back to 47% in 1996, still 4.1% below the 1979 coverage rate. Over the 1979-96 period, lower pension coverage occurred primarily among men, whose coverage fell from 56.2% to 48.3%. Women's pension coverage, on the other hand, rose slightly, from 42.8% to 45.3%. Women workers by 1996

TABLE 3.15 Change in private sector employer-provided health insurance coverage, 1979-96

Group*	Health insurance coverage (%)			Change		
	1979	1989	1996	1979-89	1989-96	1979-96
All workers	70.2%	63.1%	62.6%	-7.1%	-0.5%	-7.6%
Sex						
Men	75.1%	66.8%	65.2%	-8.3%	-1.6%	-9.9%
Women	62.2	57.9	59.1	-4.3	1.2	-3.1
Race						
White	71.6%	65.8%	65.6%	-5.7%	-0.3%	-6.0%
Black	64.1	56.9	59.7	-7.2	2.8	-4.4
Hispanic	60.9	46.3	45.2	-14.5	-1.1	-15.6
Education						
Less than high school	62.2%	46.2%	43.8%	-16.0%	-2.4%	-18.4%
High school graduate	70.2	61.7	59.5	-8.5	-2.3	-10.7
Some college	71.8	64.3	63.4	-7.5	-0.9	-8.4
College	79.4	75.1	74.8	-4.2	-0.3	-4.6
More than college	79.5	78.4	79.5	-1.1	1.1	0.0
Wage fifth						
Lowest	40.7%	29.4%	32.0%	-11.3%	2.6%	-8.8%
Second	62.8	54.7	55.1	-8.1	0.5	-7.6
Middle	75.9	69.4	67.5	-6.5	-1.9	-8.4
Fourth	84.0	78.6	77.6	-5.5	-1.0	-6.4
Top	87.9	83.7	82.4	-4.2	-1.2	-5.5

* Private sector, wage and salary workers, ages 18-64, who worked at least 20 hours per week and 26 weeks per year.

Source: Authors' analysis.

were only slightly less likely than men to be covered by an employer's pension plan. Both black and white workers saw pension coverage erode, but Hispanics experienced the largest decline, with a 10.4 percentage-point drop in pension coverage from 1979 to 1996. Pension coverage was stable among college graduates over the 1979-96 period because the expanded coverage in the 1990s offset the declines in the 1980s. Pension coverage among those with less than a college degree, however, dropped over the 1979-96 period, especially among those with a high school degree or less.

TABLE 3.16 Change in private sector employer-provided
pension coverage, 1979-96

Group*	Pension coverage (%)			Change		
	1979	1989	1996	1979-89	1989-96	1979-96
All workers	51.1%	44.3%	47.0%	-6.8%	2.8%	-4.1%
Sex						
Men	56.2%	46.4%	48.3%	-9.7%	1.9%	-7.9%
Women	42.8	41.2	45.3	-1.5	4.1	2.5
Race						
White	52.6%	46.7%	50.6%	-5.9%	3.9%	-2.0%
Black	46.4	41.3	42.3	-5.0	0.9	-4.1
Hispanic	38.3	26.5	27.9	-11.8	1.4	-10.4
Education						
Less than high school	44.4%	28.7%	25.4%	-15.7%	-3.3%	-19.0%
High school graduate	51.0	42.6	43.9	-8.4	1.2	-7.1
Some college	51.4	45.8	47.9	-5.6	2.0	-3.5
College	59.3	54.5	59.7	-4.8	5.2	0.4
More than college	62.2	62.0	67.3	-0.2	5.3	5.1
Wage fifth						
Lowest	19.5%	14.0%	16.0%	-5.5%	2.1%	-3.4%
Second	38.0	30.8	34.4	-7.2	3.6	-3.6
Middle	53.3	46.4	49.9	-6.9	3.5	-3.4
Fourth	68.9	60.2	63.6	-8.7	3.3	-5.4
Top	76.5	70.2	73.0	-6.3	2.8	-3.5

* Private sector, wage and salary workers, ages 18-64, who worked at least 20 hours per week and 26 weeks per year.

Source: Authors' analysis.

The pattern of decline in pension coverage by wage level shows coverage dropping relatively evenly across wage groups in the 1980s and an across-the-board broadening of coverage in the 1990s. All wage groups experienced a similar drop in coverage over the entire period. Nevertheless, lower-wage workers are very unlikely to have jobs with employer-provided pension plans (just 16% were covered in 1996), and only about half of all workers have pension coverage.

The widening coverage of employer-provided pension plans is most likely

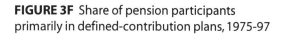

FIGURE 3F Share of pension participants
primarily in defined-contribution plans, 1975-97

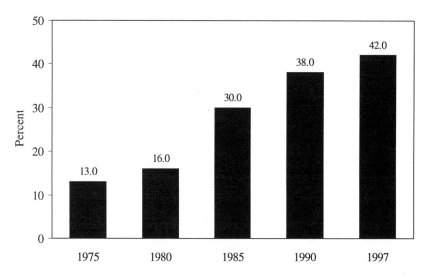

Source: Authors' analysis.

due to the expansion of 401(k) and other "defined-contribution" pension plans. Defined-benefit plans guarantee a worker a fixed payment in retirement based on pre-retirement wages and years of service and are generally considered the best plans from a worker's perspective. In contrast (as shown in **Figure 3F**), a larger share of workers are now covered by defined-contribution plans, in which employers make contributions (to which employees often can add) each year. With this type of plan, a worker's retirement income depends on his or her success in investing these funds, and investment risks are borne by the employee rather than the employer. Therefore, the shift from traditional defined-benefit plans to defined-contribution plans represents an erosion of pension quality. The expenditures data from Table 3.14 suggests a long-term cutback in pension costs, mirroring other indicators of lessened pension quality.

Figure 3F shows the share of active participants (workers and retirees) in pension plans that are in defined-contribution plans as their primary plan (meaning they are not also in a defined-benefit plan). Whereas in 1975 13% of plan participants were in defined-contribution plans, that share rose to 42% in 1997. These data show the erosion of pension plan quality over time, especially when coupled with data showing lower employer pension contributions.

Dimensions of inequality

In this section we shift the discussion from a presentation of wage and benefit trends overall, and for subgroups, to an examination of explanations for the pattern of recent wage growth. The items to be explained include stagnant average wages since 1973 and the continuous growth in wage inequality in the 1980s and 1990s. More specifically, it is important to understand both the average performance of wage growth and why particular groups fared well or poorly.

The data presented above have shown the stagnation of wages and overall compensation since 1973. **Table 3.17** presents indicators of the variety of dimensions (excluding race and gender differentials) of the wage structure that have grown more unequal over the 1973-97 period. Any explanation of growing wage inequality must be able to explain the movement of these indicators. These inequality indicators are computed from our analysis of the Current Population Survey (CPS) Outgoing Rotation Group (ORG) data series. These trends, however, parallel those in the other major data series (the March CPS).

The top panel shows the trends in the 90/10 wage differential and its two components, the 90/50 and 50/10 wage differential (which are also shown in Figures 3G and 3H), over the 1973-97 period. These differentials reflect the growth in overall wage inequality that we are attempting to explain. The 90/10 wage gap, for instance, shows the degree to which the 90th percentile worker — a "high-wage" worker who makes more than 90% but less than 10% of the workforce — fared better than the low-wage worker at the 10th percentile. The growth in the 90/10 differential is frequently broken down into two components: the 90/50 wage gap shows how high earners fared relative to middle earners, and the 50/10 wage gap shows how middle earners fared relative to low earners.

Among men, there was a dramatic growth in wage inequality at the top and bottom in the 1979-89 period that has continued, in terms of the 90/50 differential, as quickly through the 1989-97 period (**Figure 3G**). The character of this growing male wage inequality shifted in the most recent period. In the 1980s there was a growing separation between both the top and the middle and the middle and the bottom (seen in the 50/10 differential). However, in the 1989-97 period, all of the growing wage inequality was generated by a divergence between the top and everyone else: the 90/50 differential grew while the 50/10 differential actually fell.

Among women, the wage inequality trends across time periods are sensitive to the "endpoints," or years selected for the analysis. The data on the 90/10 differential for women in Table 3.17 suggests a large decline in women's wage inequality in the 1970s and a larger growth in the 1980s. However, the year-by-year pattern, shown in **Figure 3H**, shows a large dip in wage inequality between

TABLE 3.17 Dimensions of wage inequality, 1973-97

Differential	Wage differential				Change		
	1973	1979	1989	1997	1973-79	1979-89	1989-97
Total wage inequality (logx100)							
90/10							
Men	127.9	130.0	144.3	149.6	2.1	14.3	5.4
Women	115.7	99.8	134.9	138.7	-16.0	35.2	3.7
90/50							
Men	60.3	58.9	69.2	77.4	-1.4	10.3	8.2
Women	59.2	59.2	70.5	76.1	0.0	11.3	5.6
50/10							
Men	67.6	71.1	75.0	72.2	3.5	4.0	-2.8
Women	56.5	38.8	64.4	62.6	-17.8	25.6	-1.8
Between-group inequality							
College/high school*							
Men	32.5%	27.3%	41.8%	44.1%	-5.2	14.5	2.3
Women	43.0	30.8	46.0	51.1	-12.2	15.2	5.1
Experience							
Middle/young**							
Men	25.8%	25.2%	29.1%	28.9%	-0.6	3.9	-0.1
Women	11.8	12.2	19.7	22.5	0.4	7.4	2.9
Old/middle**							
Men	4.2%	6.9%	10.6%	9.1%	2.6	3.8	-1.5
Women	-3.5	-1.6	1.8	4.4	2.0	3.4	2.6
Within-group inequality							
Men							
90/50	40.4%	41.2%	42.9%	45.7%	0.8	1.7	2.8
50/10	39.1	42.2	46.8	41.8	3.1	4.6	-5.0
Women							
90/50	38.6%	45.9%	45.5%	47.4%	7.3	-0.4	1.9
50/10	36.2	28.7	44.0	38.1	-7.5	15.4	-5.9

* Estimated log differential between college-only and high school graduates, controlling for experience, marital status, race, and four regions.

** Estimated log differential with experience specified as a quartic with controls for education levels,
marital status, race, and four regions. Young, middle, and old reflect workers with 5, 15, and 30
years' experience.

Source: Authors' analysis.

FIGURE 3G Men's wage inequality, 1973-97

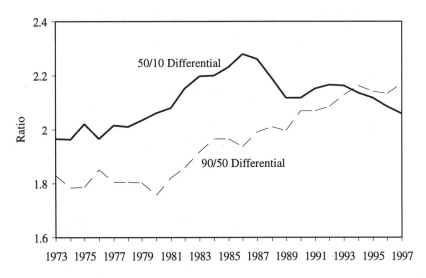

Source: Authors' analysis.

FIGURE 3H Women's wage inequality, 1973-97

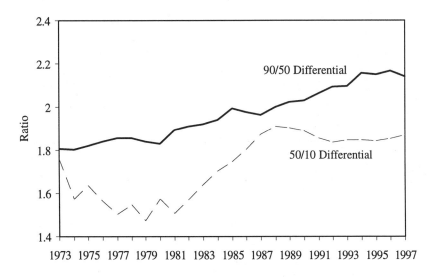

Source: Authors' analysis.

1978 and 1979 and an equal rise between 1979 and 1980. This "jumpiness" in the data reflects the movement of the 10th percentile wage, which grew a lot in 1979 but then fell back to its 1978 level in 1980. A better description of the trends in women's wage inequality might be that wage inequality fell between 1973 and the late 1970s (1978-80) and then rose in the 1980s. Among women, the growth of the 90/50 differential was slightly stronger than among men in the 1980s but weaker than among men in the 1990s. There was, however, a stronger growth of inequality at the bottom (reflected in the 50/10 differential) among women in the 1980s and, as with men, an actual decline in the 1990s.

Analysts have tended to "decompose," or break down, growing wage inequality into two types of inequality — "between group" and "within group." The former is illustrated in Table 3.17 in two ways: the growing wage differentials between groups of workers defined by their education levels and by their labor market experience. The "college wage premium" — the wage gap between college and high school graduates — fell in the 1970s among both men and women but exploded in the 1980s, growing about 15% for each. The growth of the college wage premium in the post-1989 period, however, has differed between men and women. Among men there has been only modest growth in this education premium since 1989, which year-by-year trends (discussed below) show to be flat between 1990 and 1997. Among women, however, there has been a relatively steady, modest growth of the college wage premium in the post-1989 period.

The growth of experience differentials, reflecting the wage gap between older and middle-age and younger workers, runs parallel to that of education differentials, although the changes are smaller. The wage gap between middle-age and younger workers grew in the 1980s and continued to grow after 1989, but only among women. Likewise, the wage gap between older and middle-age workers grew over the entire 1973-89 period and continued to do so among women in the 1990s.

Within-group wage inequality — wage dispersion among workers with comparable education and experience — has been a major dimension of growing wage inequality. The growth of within-group wage inequality, according to Table 3.17, has differed across time periods, across segments of the wage structure (the top versus the bottom), and by gender. For instance, the growth of within-group wage inequality among men in the upper half of the wage structure (the 90/50 gap) has been growing over the entire 1973-97 period, but at an accelerated pace in the 1980s and again in the 1990s. In contrast, within-group wage inequality at the bottom among men grew similarly in the 1970s and the 1980s and then declined in the 1990s.

Within-group inequality grew the most at the bottom of the female wage structure in the 1980s, up 15.4 percentage points (though some of this change may reflect the jumpiness of the data, as discussed earlier), but fell in both the 1970s and 1990s. Among higher-wage women the growth of within-group wage inequality was only a small factor in both the 1980s and the 1990s.

Since growing or shrinking within-group wage inequality has been a significant factor in various periods, it is important to be able to explain and interpret these trends. Unfortunately, the interpretation of growing wage inequality among workers with similar "human capital" has not been the subject of much research. Some analysts suggest it reflects growing premiums for skills of workers that are not captured by traditional human capital measures available in government surveys. Others suggest that changing "wage norms," employer practices, and institutions are responsible. We turn to these trends next.

Productivity and the compensation–productivity gap

The most commonly mentioned reason for recent wage problems is slow productivity growth (i.e., changes in output per hour worked) since 1973. As the data in Table 3.1 showed, productivity has been growing 1.0% annually over the entire 1973-97 period. This is a slower growth in productivity than occurred in the pre-1973 period, and so recent decades are considered to be suffering from a "productivity slowdown."

Slow productivity growth has been a major problem, but it provides only a partial explanation for average wage trends, since productivity has grown significantly more than wages or compensation.

The relationship between hourly productivity and compensation growth is portrayed in **Figure 3I**, which shows the growth of each relative to 1973 (i.e., each is indexed so that 1973 equals 100). As Figure 3I shows, there has been a 29% growth in productivity since 1973, enough to generate broadly shared growth in living standards and wages. Also, there is a gap between the growth of average compensation and productivity as well as between both median hourly compensation (for either men or all workers) and average compensation. The latter gap, between average and median compensation, is the larger gap and reflects growing wage and benefit inequality. Thus, the most important reason why median compensation (or wages) lags behind productivity is that growing inequality creates a "wedge" that prevents the typical worker from enjoying the average growth of national output or income.

There are several possible interpretations of the gap between average compensation and productivity. One explanation is that prices for national output have grown more slowly than prices for consumer purchases. Therefore, the

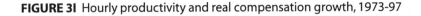

FIGURE 31 Hourly productivity and real compensation growth, 1973-97

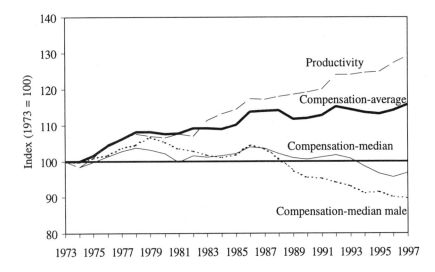

Source: Authors' analysis.

same growth in nominal, or current dollar, wages and output yields faster growth in real (inflation-adjusted) output (which is adjusted for changes in the prices of investment goods, exports, and consumer purchases) than in real wages (adjusted for changes in consumer purchases only). That is, workers have suffered a worsening "terms of trade," in which the prices of things they buy (i.e., consumer goods) have risen faster than the items they produce (consumer goods but also capital goods).

This "terms of trade" explanation is actually more of a description than an explanation. A growing gap between output and consumer prices has not been a persistent characteristic of our economy, and the emergence of this gap requires an exploration of what economic forces are driving it. Once the causes of the price gap are known (not simply accounted for), it can be interpreted. In the meantime, there are two ways to look at the divergence of compensation and productivity created by the "terms of trade" shift of prices. One is to note that, regardless of cause, the implication is that the "average" worker is not benefiting fully from productivity growth. Another is to note that the price divergence does not simply reflect a redistribution from labor to capital; the gap between compensation and productivity growth reflects, at least in part, differences in price trends rather than a larger share of productivity growth going to capital incomes.

This leaves open the question of whether wages are being squeezed by higher profits. In other words, has the growth in rates of profit (defined broadly as profits and interest per dollar of assets) meant that wages have grown less? As discussed in Chapter 1, there has been significant growth in the share of income going to capital driven by a large increase in "profitability," or the return to capital per dollar of plant and equipment. There has been a corresponding decline in labor's share of corporate sector income. This provides evidence of a redistribution of wages to capital incomes. As discussed in Chapter 1, had growth in profitability been more modest, hourly compensation would have been 7.7% higher in 1997.

Rising education–wage differentials

Changes in the economic returns to education affect the structure of wages by changing the wage gaps between different educational groups. The growth in "education–wage differentials" has led to greater wage inequality in the 1980s and 1990s (see Table 3.17) and helps explain the relatively faster wage growth among high-wage workers. This section examines wage trends among workers at different levels of education and begins the discussion, carried on through the remainder of the chapter, of the causes of rising education wage differentials.

Table 3.18 presents the wage trends and employment shares (percentage of the workforce) for workers at various education levels over the 1973-97 period. It is common to point out that the wages of "more-educated" workers have grown faster than the wages of "less-educated" workers since 1979, with the real wages of "less-educated" workers falling sharply. This pattern of wage growth is sometimes described in terms of a rising differential, or "premium," between the wages of the college-educated and high-school-educated workforces (as shown earlier in Table 3.17).

The usual terminology of the "less educated" and "more educated" is misleading. Given that workers with some college education (from one to three years) also experienced falling real wages (down 8.6% from 1979 to 1997), it is apparent that the "less-educated" group with falling wages makes up about three-fourths of the workforce. The last column of Table 3.18 shows the average non-college wage falling 12.0% over the 1979-97 period. Moreover, the "college-educated" group consists of two groups: one, with just four years of college, enjoyed a minimal 5.6% wage gain over the 1979-97 period, while the other, the more-educated ("advanced degree") but smaller (6.9% of the workforce in 1989) group, enjoyed 12.4% wage growth.

TABLE 3.18 Change in real hourly wage for all by education, 1973-97

Year	Less than high school	High school	Some college	College	Advanced degree	Memo: Non-college educated*
Hourly wage ($1997)						
1973	$11.21	$12.82	$14.16	$18.60	$22.67	$12.52
1979	11.15	12.49	13.61	17.43	21.42	12.42
1989	9.38	11.36	13.19	17.88	23.24	11.54
1997	8.23	11.03	12.44	18.41	24.09	10.94
Percent change						
1973-79	-0.6%	-2.6%	-3.9%	-6.3%	-5.5%	-0.8%
1979-89	-15.9	-9.0	-3.1	2.6	8.5	-7.1
1989-97	-12.3	-2.9	-5.7	2.9	3.6	-5.2
1979-97	-26.2	-11.7	-8.6	5.6	12.4	-12.0
*Share of employment***						
1973	28.5%	41.7%	15.1%	8.8%	3.6%	85.4%
1979	20.1	42.1	19.2	11.0	5.0	81.3
1989	13.7	40.5	22.3	14.0	6.9	76.5

*   Those with less than four years of college.
** Since the shares of those with one year of schooling beyond college are not shown, the presented shares do not sum to 100. There are no reliable data for 1997 using the same definitions.

Source: Authors' analysis.

This increased differential between college-educated and other workers is frequently ascribed to a relative increase in employer demand for workers with greater skills and education. This interpretation follows from the fact that the wages of college-educated workers increased relative to others despite an increase in their relative supply, from 11.0% of the workforce in 1979 to 14.0% in 1989. That is, given the increased supply of college-educated workers, the fact that their relative wages were bid up implies a strong growth in employer demand for more-educated workers, presumably reflecting technological and other workplace trends.

Yet an increased relative demand for educated workers is only a partial explanation, especially if ascribed to a benign process of technology or other factors leading to a higher value for education, thus bidding up the wages of

TABLE 3.19 Change in real hourly wage for men by education,
1973-97

Year	Less than high school	High school	Some college	College	Advanced degree	Memo: Non-college educated*	College-H.S. wage differential**
Hourly wage ($1997)							
1973	$13.11	$15.43	$16.25	$21.40	$23.82	$14.74	32.5%
1979	12.87	15.01	15.94	20.46	23.32	14.63	27.3
1989	10.63	13.18	15.03	20.58	25.73	13.15	41.8
1997	9.02	12.49	14.00	20.82	26.65	12.18	44.1
Percent change							
1973-79	-1.9%	-2.7%	-1.9%	-4.4%	-2.1%	-0.7%	
1979-89	-17.4	-12.2	-5.7	0.6	10.3	-10.1	
1989-97	-15.1	-5.2	-6.9	1.2	3.6	-7.4	
1979-97	-29.9	-16.8	-12.2	1.8	14.2	-16.8	
*Share of employment***							
1973	30.6%	38.1%	15.6%	8.9%	4.5%	84.3%	
1979	22.3	38.6	18.8	11.5	6.1	79.7	
1989	15.9	38.7	21.0	14.2	7.8	75.5	

*   Those with less than four years of college.
**   Estimated with controls for education, experience as a quartic, four regions, marital status, and
      race.
*** Since the shares of those with one year of schooling beyond college are not shown, the presented
      shares do not sum to 100. There are no reliable data for 1997 using the same definitions.

Source: Authors' analysis.

more-educated workers. Note, for instance, that the primary reason for an increased wage gap between college-educated and other workers is the precipi-
tous decline of wages among the non-college-educated workforce and not any
strong growth of the college wage. Moreover, as discussed below, there are many
important factors (that may not reflect changes in demand for skill), such as the
shift to low-wage industries, deunionization, a falling minimum wage, and import competition, that can also lead to a wage gap between workers with more
and less education. Below, we present direct evidence that technological change
has not been the driving force behind growing wage inequality.

Tables 3.19 and **3.20** present trends in wage and employment shares for the
various education groups for men and women. Among men, the wages of non-
college-educated workers have been falling steadily since 1979: they fell 10.1%

TABLE 3.20 Change in real hourly wage for women by education, 1973-97

Year	Less than high school	High school	Some college	College	Advanced degree	Memo: Non-college educated*	College-H.S. wage differential**
Hourly wage ($1997)							
1973	$7.91	$9.75	$10.86	$14.43	$19.40	$9.39	43.0%
1979	8.26	9.77	10.70	13.08	17.05	9.68	30.8
1989	7.38	9.50	11.37	14.76	19.50	9.77	46.0
1997	6.94	9.44	10.93	15.90	20.89	9.54	51.1
Percent change							
1973-79	4.5%	0.2%	-1.5%	-9.4%	-12.1%	3.0%	
1979-89	-10.7	-2.8	6.3	12.9	14.3	0.9	
1989-97	-5.9	-0.6	-3.9	7.7	7.2	-2.3	
1979-97	-16.0	-3.4	2.1	21.6	22.5	-1.4	
*Share of employment***							
1973	25.6%	47.7%	14.4%	8.7%	2.3%	87.1%	
1979	17.2	46.7	19.6	10.4	3.5	83.6	
1989	11.2	42.6	23.9	13.8	5.8	77.8	

*   Those with less than four years of college.
**   Estimated with controls for education, experience as a quartic, four regions, marital status, and race.
*** Since the shares of those with one year of schooling beyond college are not shown, the presented shares do not sum to 100. There are no reliable data for 1997 using the same definitions.

Source: Authors' analysis.

over the 1979-89 period and another 7.4% between 1989 and 1997. The decline in wages was sizable even among men with "some college" — 12.2% from 1979 to 1997. The wage of the average high-school-educated male fell somewhat more, 16.8% from 1979 to 1997, while the wages of those without a high school degree fell 29.9%. In contrast, the wages of male college graduates rose just 0.6% from 1979 to 1989 and just 1.2% over the 1989-97 period. Year-by-year data show male college wages peaked in 1985.

This pattern of stagnant wages for college men and declining wages for non-college-educated men has meant a rise in the relative wage or premium for male college graduates. As shown in the last column, the estimated college/high school wage premium (where experience, race, and other characteristics are "controlled" for) grew from 27.3% in 1979 to 41.8% in 1989 and to 44.1% in

FIGURE 3J College/high school wage premium, 1973-97

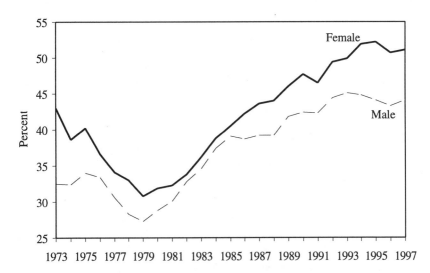

Source: Authors' analysis.

1997. As **Figure 3J** shows, however, there has been a flattening of the college/ high school premium in the 1990s. Since there has not been an acceleration of the supply of college-educated men (as shown in a later section), this implies, within a conventional demand-supply framework, that there was a slowdown in the growth of relative demand for college workers.

A somewhat different pattern has prevailed among women (Table 3.20). In the 1979-89 period wages fell modestly (2.8%) among high-school-educated women but significantly among those without a high school degree (10.7%). Women with some college, unlike their male counterparts, saw wage gains in the 1980s (6.3%), but not as much as college-educated women (12.9%). This pattern of wage growth, however, still resulted in an equivalent growth of the college/high school wage differential from 30.8% in 1979 to 46.0% in 1989. Thus, the education–wage gap grew as quickly among women as among men but the relative losers — non-college-educated women — saw stagnant, not declining, wages.

The pattern of wage growth among women shifted in the 1990s; wages were stagnant or fell among women without a four-year college degree, including women with some college. In 1997, wages for women with less than a college degree were slightly lower (1.4%) than they were in 1979. Wages among

159

TABLE 3.21 Educational attainment of workforce, 1997

Highest degree attained	Percent of workforce		
	Men	Women	All
Less than high school	13.2%	8.9%	11.1%
High school/GED	33.0	33.3	33.2
Some college	20.3	21.9	21.0
Assoc. college	7.4	9.6	8.5
College B.A.	17.6	18.6	18.1
Advanced degree*	8.4	7.7	8.1
Total	100.0	100.0	100.0
Memo			
High school or less	46.2%	42.2%	44.3%
Less than college degree	74.0	73.7	73.8
College only	17.6	18.6	18.1
More than college	8.4	7.7	8.1

* Includes law degrees, Ph.D.s, M.B.A.s, and similar degrees.

Source: Authors' analysis.

college-educated women continued to grow strongly in the 1989-97 period. In contrast with men, the college/high school differential among women continued to grow in the 1990s (Figure 3J).

Even though the wages of college-educated women have grown rapidly since 1979, a female college graduate in 1997 still earned about what a male with only some college earned in 1979 ($15.90 versus $15.94) and about what a high-school-educated male earned in 1973 ($15.43).

Table 3.21 shows a breakdown of the workforce in 1997 by the highest degree attained. Only about one-fourth (26.2%) of the workforce has at least a four-year college degree (18.1% have no more than a college degree and 8.1% also have a graduate or professional degree). Roughly two-thirds (65.3%) of the workforce has no more than a high school degree, with 11.1% never completing high school, 33.2% completing high school, and another 21.0% having attended college but earning no degree beyond high school. An additional 4.0% hold associate degrees. These data reinforce our earlier discussion that the wage reductions experienced by the "less educated" (frequently defined by economists as those without a college degree) since 1979 have affected roughly 75% of the workforce.

TABLE 3.22 Hourly wages of entry level and experienced workers by education, 1973-97

Education/ experience	Hourly wage ($1997)				Percent change			
	1973	1979	1989	1997	1973-79	1979-89	1989-97	1979-97
High school								
Men								
Entry level*	$11.10	$10.98	$8.58	$7.95	-1.0%	-21.8%	-7.4%	-27.6%
16-20	16.81	16.84	14.27	13.29	0.1	-15.2	-6.9	-21.1
31-35	17.82	18.11	16.34	14.98	1.6	-9.8	-8.3	-17.3
Women								
Entry level*	$8.36	$8.34	$7.25	$6.81	-0.2%	-13.0%	-6.1%	-18.3%
16-20	10.15	10.20	9.96	9.81	0.5	-2.4	-1.5	-3.8
31-35	10.57	10.43	10.51	10.60	-1.3	0.7	0.9	1.6
College								
Men								
Entry level*	$14.82	$14.79	$14.60	$13.65	-0.2%	-1.3%	-6.5%	-7.7%
16-20	26.17	23.78	22.68	23.53	-9.2	-4.6	3.7	-1.1
31-35	26.56	26.92	25.95	26.31	1.3	-3.6	1.4	-2.3
Women								
Entry level*	$12.95	$11.84	$13.17	$12.20	-8.6%	11.2%	-7.4%	3.0%
16-20	16.46	14.16	15.55	17.84	-14.0	9.8	14.7	26.0
31-35	15.66	14.16	15.28	17.20	-9.6	7.9	12.6	21.5

* Entry-level wage measured as wage of those with 1-5 years experience.

Source: Authors' analysis.

Young workers have been hurt most

Since 1973, the wages of younger workers have been falling faster than the wages of older workers. As a result, there have been significant changes in the wage differentials between younger and older workers, as shown earlier in Table 3.17. Since the wages of both younger and non-college-educated workers have fallen most rapidly, it follows that the wages of workers who are both young and non–college educated have fallen dramatically.

These adverse wage trends were strongest among men. **Table 3.22** presents trends in "entry-level" wages for high school and college graduates as reflected in the wages of workers with one to five years of experience. The entry-level hourly wage of a young, male high school graduate in 1989 was 21.8% less than that for the equivalent worker in 1979, a drop of $2.40 per hour, and another 7.4% less by

FIGURE 3K Entry-level wages of male and female high school graduates, 1973-97

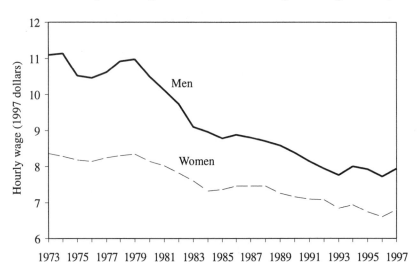

Source: Authors' analysis.

1997. The accumulated wage declines from 1979 forward left entry-level wages for male high school graduates 27.6% lower in 1997 than in 1979; among women, the entry-level high school wage fell 18.3% in this period. This dramatic decline in entry-level wages among high school graduates is shown in **Figure 3K**.

Entry-level wages among male college graduates were stagnant over the 1973-89 period and fell 6.5% from 1989 to 1997, as shown in **Figure 3L**. Thus, new male college graduates earned $1.17 less per hour in 1997 than their counterparts did in 1973. This sharp decline in entry-level wages of college graduates also took place among women in the 1990s (see Figure 3L), when the wage fell 7.4%. The fact that entry-level wages for college graduates remain higher than for high school graduates means that it still makes economic sense for individuals to complete college. Nevertheless, men who obtain a college degree will have a lower wage than that obtained by an earlier generation of male college graduates. For instance, the wage of a college-educated male with 16-20 years' experience (in his late 30s) was $23.53 per hour in 1997, $2.64 less than what an equivalent worker in his late 30s earned in 1973.

As already noted above, there is not only a growing inequality between groups of workers characterized by education or experience levels but also a growing inequality among workers with similar education and experience, a

FIGURE 3L Entry-level wages of male and female college graduates, 1973-97

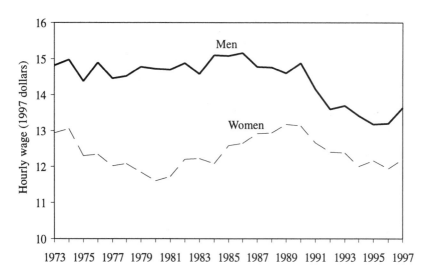

Source: Authors' analysis.

dimension of wage inequality referred to as "within-group" wage inequality. This growth in within-group wage inequality was shown earlier in Table 3.17. The analysis in **Table 3.23** goes a step further by presenting wage trends of high-, middle-, and low-wage workers among high school and college graduates. In other words, the data track the wages of 90th, 50th (median), and 10th percentile high-school-educated and college-educated workers by gender.

Because of rising within-group inequality, the wage growth of the median, or "typical," worker within each group has been less than that of the "average" worker. For instance, the wage of the median male high school graduate fell 21.2% over the 1979-97 period, compared to the 16.8% wage drop of the "average" male high school graduate (Table 3.19). Similarly, the wage growth of male college graduates in the 1979-97 period was 1.8% at the average (Table 3.19), but down 0.9% at the median.

The growing disparity of wages within groups is amply demonstrated in Table 3.23. While the high (90th percentile) wage among female college graduates grew 28.6% from 1979 to 1997, the low (10th percentile) wage in this group rose just 2.9%, a 26 percentage-point divergence. Similarly, there was a large divergence between wage growth at the top of the college male wage ladder (5.4%) relative to the bottom (a 12.1% drop) over the 1979-97 period.

TABLE 3.23 Hourly wages by decile within education groups, 1973-97

Education/	Hourly wage ($1997)				Percent change			
gender decile	1973	1979	1989	1997	1973-79	1979-89	1989-97	1979-97
High school								
Men								
Low*	$7.75	$7.20	$6.11	$5.94	-7.2%	-15.1%	-2.7%	-17.4%
Median	14.21	13.91	11.92	10.97	-2.1	-14.3	-8.0	-21.2
High	23.27	22.96	21.30	20.13	-1.3	-7.2	-5.5	-12.3
Women								
Low	$5.33	$6.14	$4.91	$5.04	15.2%	-20.0%	2.6%	-17.9%
Median	8.83	8.67	8.48	8.20	-1.8	-2.3	-3.3	-5.5
High	14.67	14.99	15.38	15.02	2.1	2.6	-2.3	0.2
College								
Men								
Low	$9.86	$9.49	$8.82	$8.35	-3.8%	-7.1%	-5.4%	-12.1%
Median	18.45	17.88	18.28	17.73	-3.1	2.2	-3.0	-0.9
High	34.42	32.86	33.18	34.62	-4.5	1.0	4.3	5.4
Women								
Low	$7.65	$6.83	$6.96	$7.03	-10.7%	1.9%	1.0%	2.9%
Median	13.08	11.85	13.44	14.05	-9.5	13.4	4.5	18.6
High	20.74	20.18	23.40	25.96	-2.7	16.0	10.9	28.6

* "Low," "median," and "high" earners refers to, respectively, the 10th, 50th, and 90th percentile wage.

Source: Authors' analysis.

Decomposing the growth in wage inequality

The data presented so far illustrate the various dimensions of wage inequality. There has been a growing gap between workers by both education and experience (or age). This "between-group" inequality can also be characterized as a growth in education and experience differentials, as increases in the "returns to education and experience," or as a shift in the rewards or price of "skill." We have also seen that wage inequality has grown among workers with similar education and experience ("within group"), as illustrated by a growing wage gap among college graduates and high school graduates.

The question remains, however, as to how much the growth in overall wage inequality in particular time periods has been driven by changes in between-group versus within-group wage inequality. Plus, it is useful to know the role of the growth of between- and within-group inequality on growing wage inequality at the top (the 90/50 differential) versus the bottom (the 50/10 differential).

Unfortunately, there is no analysis available that completely "decomposes" the growth of wage inequality into the contribution of between- and within-group inequality over the 1973-97 period. Such an analysis would allow us to state, for instance, what percentage share of the growth of inequality is due to the growing returns to education, experience, and other factors, with the role of all contributing factors summing to 100%.

Tables 3.24 and 3.25 present a "partial" decomposition that isolates the impact of the growth of between-group inequality — changing education and experience differentials — on total wage inequality. This is done by imposing a series of counterfactuals. For instance, one can determine the wages of workers in 1997 as if the wage differentials by education and experience (returns to "skill") that prevailed in 1989 were also present in 1997. The difference between the counterfactual measures of inequality in 1997 relative to the actual measures of inequality (such as the 90/10 wage differential) captures the effect of the 1989-97 change in between-group differentials (returns to "skill") on wage inequality in this period. This change in the returns to skill can then be compared to the actual growth of wage inequality to gauge its proportionate contribution.

The estimates in Tables 3.24 and 3.25 of the role of between-group inequality are an "upper-bound," meaning that the contribution may be less but is not greater than that presented. These are upper-bound estimates because there has been no direct quantification of the "other" components of wage inequality, which include the impact of changes in the distribution of "skills" (i.e., more college graduates or older workers) and within-group wage inequality. Because changes in the composition of the workforce may have an equalizing effect, it is possible that two forces for inequality, between- and within-group, can have "contributions" totaling more than 100%. It is also an upper-bound estimate because not all changes in wage differentials between education and experience groups is driven by "skill," as deunionization and an eroded minimum wage affect these differentials as well (as shown below).

The partial decomposition of the growth of male wage inequality in **Table 3.24** yields the following results:

- Overall wage inequality (the 90/10 differential) grew marginally (2.1 percentage points) in the earliest (1973-79) period. Inequality at the top (the 90/50 differential) diminished, but inequality at the bottom (the 50/10 differential) grew.

TABLE 3.24 Decomposing the change in
overall wage inequality among men, 1973-97

Period	Log point change in differential*			Percent of overall change		
	90-10	90-50	50-10	90-10	90-50	50-10
1973-79						
Overall	2.1	-1.4	3.5	100.0%	100.0%	100.0%
Returns to "skill"**	-2.1	-0.4	-1.6	-100.0	30.5	-46.7
Other***	4.1	-1.0	5.1	200.0	69.5	146.7
1979-89						
Overall	14.3	10.3	4.0	100.0%	100.0%	100.0%
Returns to "skill"**	8.7	5.4	3.3	61.0	52.7	82.5
Other***	5.6	4.9	0.7	39.0	47.3	17.5
1989-97						
Overall	5.4	8.2	-2.8	100.0%	100.0%	100.0%
Returns to "skill"**	2.8	2.1	0.7	52.3	25.9	24.4
Other***	2.6	6.1	-3.5	47.7	74.1	-124.4
1973-97						
Overall	21.7	17.1	4.6	100.0%	100.0%	100.0%
Returns to "skill"**	9.4	7.1	2.3	43.5	41.7	50.5
Other***	12.3	10.0	2.3	56.5	58.3	49.5

*   In logs multiplied by 100, approximately equal to percentage change.
**   Change in between-group inequality, i.e., change in returns to education and experience.
*** Changes in within-group inequality and change in levels of education and experience.

Source: Authors' analysis of the Outgoing Rotation Group of the CPS.

- The large growth of wage inequality in the 1979-89 period resulted from a widening at the top — the 90/50 differential grew 10.3 percentage points. The change in the returns to education and experience (between-group inequality) had more impact in the 1980s on the 90/50 than on the 50/10 differential. Education and experience differentials explain, at most, about half (52.7%) of the growth of the 90/50 differential during this period. The growth of between-group inequality accounts for as much as 61% of the growth of the male 90/10 differential in the 1980s.

- The character of inequality growth shifted in the 1990s as widening between-group inequality became a less important determinant of the growth in the 90/10 differential; its role shrank, from an 8.7 percentage-point contribution over the 1979-89 period to a modest 2.8-point contribution in 1989-97. Also in the 1990s, the 50/10 wage differential declined among men, although the 90/50 differential grew as quickly in the 1990s as in the 1980s (8.2 and 10.3 percentage points, respectively, over the 1989-97 and 1979-89 periods). Only a small portion of the growth in the 90/50 differential in the 1990s, 2.1 of an 8.2 percentage-point growth, can be attributed to changes in the returns to education and experience. This result corresponds to the earlier discussion of the small growth of education (and no growth in experience differentials) among men in the 1990s (Table 3.17).

- When one looks over the entire 1973-97 period, the growth of between-group wage inequality can account for 43.5% of the total growth of wage inequality. This suggests that any explanation of growing male wage inequality over the long term must focus at least as much on explaining within-group as between-group inequality.

It is more difficult to identify the percentage contribution of between-group wage inequality to the growth of total women's wage inequality in specific time periods over the 1970s and 1980s because of the "jumpiness" of the data describing the 50/10 differential in the 1978-80 period (as discussed along with Table 3.17). The decomposition in **Table 3.25**, however, provides a reliable indicator of the effect of growing between-group inequality. The effect of between-group inequality on the 90/10 differential fell more in the 1970s (down 6.5 percentage points) and grew more in the 1980s (up 13.0 percentage points) among women than among men. Nevertheless, the effect of growing between-group inequality over the entire 1973-89 period was comparable among men and women at about 6.5 percentage points, which amounts to less than a third of the growth of the 90/10 differential of 19.2 percentage points from 1973 to 1989.

In the 1989-97 period, the 50/10 differential declined and between-group inequality rose modestly. In contrast, the 90/50 differential grew at three-fourths the pace as in the 1980s, but only 37.9% of the growth could be attributed to changes in the returns to education and experience. Thus, as with men, the importance of between-group inequality in driving the continuing growth of the 90/50 differential has diminished in the 1990s. Over the entire 1973-97 period, between-group inequality can explain only about 30% of the 16.9 percentage-point growth in the 90/50 differential but can explain all of the small 6.0 percentage-point growth in the 50/10 differential.

TABLE 3.25 Decomposing the change in
overall wage inequality among women, 1973-97

Period	Log point change in differential*			Percent of overall change		
	90-10	90-50	50-10	90-10	90-50	50-10
1973-79						
Overall	-16.0	1.8	-17.8	100.0%	100.0%	100.0%
Returns to "skill"**	-6.5	-3.0	-3.5	40.8	-166.9	19.8
Other***	-9.5	4.8	-14.2	59.2	266.9	80.2
1979-89						
Overall	35.2	9.5	25.6	100.0%	100.0%	100.0%
Returns to "skill"**	13.0	6.2	6.8	37.0	64.5	26.7
Other***	22.2	3.4	18.8	63.0	35.5	73.3
1989-97						
Overall	3.7	5.6	-1.8	100.0%	100.0%	100.0%
Returns to "skill"**	5.6	2.1	3.5	150.1	37.9	192.7
Other***	-1.9	3.5	-5.3	-50.1	62.1	-292.7
1973-97						
Overall	22.9	16.9	6.0	100.0%	100.0%	100.0%
Returns to "skill"**	12.1	5.3	6.8	52.8	31.2	113.1
Other***	10.8	11.6	-0.8	47.2	68.8	-13.1

*   In logs multiplied by 100, approximately equal to percentage change.
**   Change in between-group inequality, i.e., change in returns to education and experience.
*** Changes in within-group inequality and change in levels of education and experience.

Source: Authors' analysis of the Outgoing Rotation Group of the CPS.

School quality and tests

One potential explanation for the poor performance of wages for the non-college-educated workforce is a deterioration in school quality. That is, if schools have worsened, then the lower wages of high school graduates might simply reflect that they are less knowledgeable. Several studies have rejected this explanation on the grounds that a significant growth in wage inequality and in education premiums has occurred in every age group. If "school deterioration" were the driving force behind wage inequality, then one would expect these wage developments to be limited to recent entrants to the workforce and not affect the graduates of the 1970s, 1960s, and 1950s. The data in Table 3.22, for instance, show that wages for high school men fell over the 1980s and 1990s not only among recent high school graduates but also for those who had graduated roughly 20 to 35 years earlier.

Another reason for skepticism is that there is not much evidence of a deterioration in school quality, although there is not much evidence of overall improvement either, as evidenced by the historical trends in mathematics and reading test scores for 17-year-olds shown in **Figure 3M**. Among whites, test scores have been fairly constant since the early 1970s. In contrast, black and Hispanic 17-year-olds in 1994 scored higher in math and reading than their counterparts did in the early 1970s.

Wage growth by race and ethnicity

Race and ethnicity have long played a role in shaping employment opportunities and labor market outcomes. As the United States has become more diverse, it becomes useful to review trends among more race/ethnic subgroups. Tables 3.26 and 3.27 present the wage trends for key indicators of the wage structure for four populations: white, black, Hispanic, and Asian. A finer breakdown of groups was not possible in the 1990s because of sample size limitations and, for the same reason, the trends for the 1980s are not available.

The median wage trends show that all groups, except Asians, experienced declining wages for the median male worker over the 1989-97 period, with blacks and Hispanics having a drop in such wages over the 1992-97 recovery (**Table 3.26**). All college-educated male workers within each racial/ethnic group, with the exception of Asian male college graduates, who benefited from healthy 6.7% growth, experienced modest or stagnant wage growth in the recovery years and over the business cycle, 1989-97. In contrast, high-school-educated male workers suffered significant wage declines over the 1989-97 period, with Asians having the largest losses, an 8.8% drop. This suggests a large increase in the education–wage gap among Asian males.

Among women, the typical (or median) black and Hispanic worker lost ground in the 1989-97 period, including the recovery years. White and Asian women's median wages grew slowly in the recovery but by 1997 were barely ahead of their 1989 levels. Wage growth among high-school-educated women showed a similar pattern, with blacks and Hispanics having persistent wage erosion but whites and Asians having modest wage gains. As we saw in an earlier table, college-educated women have been the group with the fastest wage growth. As **Table 3.27** shows, the wage gains among college-educated women have been strong among whites and Asians but very modest (1.0%) among blacks over the 1989-97 period. Black and Hispanic women college graduates actually saw their wages decline over the 1992-97 recovery.

FIGURE 3M Reading and mathematics proficiency by race, 1971-94

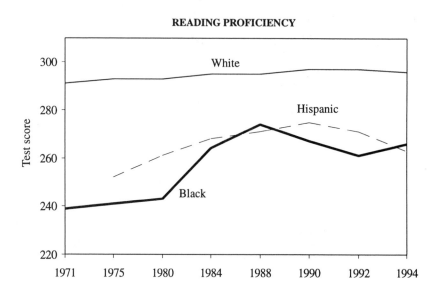

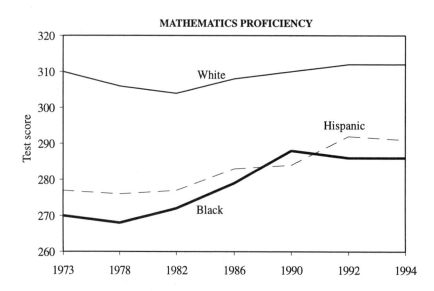

Source: Authors' analysis.

TABLE 3.26 Hourly wage growth among men
by race/ethnicity, 1989-97

	Hourly wage ($1997)			Changes	
	1989	1992	1997	1992-97	1989-97
Medians					
White	$18.95	$18.17	$18.20	0.2%	-4.0%
Black	13.71	13.45	12.92	-3.9	-5.7
Hispanic	12.93	12.43	11.53	-7.2	-10.8
Asian	18.42	18.40	18.66	1.4	1.3
By education					
High school*					
White	$13.69	$13.10	$13.12	0.2%	-4.1%
Black	10.98	10.37	10.56	1.9	-3.8
Hispanic	11.31	10.88	10.62	-2.4	-6.1
Asian	11.83	11.64	10.79	-7.3	-8.8
College*					
White	$21.18	$20.93	$21.45	2.5%	1.3%
Black	16.11	16.51	16.53	0.1	2.6
Hispanic	17.22	17.07	17.37	1.7	0.9
Asian	18.61	19.32	19.86	2.8	6.7

* Average wage.

Source: Authors' analysis.

The shift to low-paying industries

There was a large employment shift to low-wage sectors in the 1980s and 1990s, a consequence of trade deficits and deindustrialization as well as stagnant or falling productivity growth in service sector industries. This section examines the significant erosion of wages and compensation for non-college-educated workers that results from an employment shift to low-paying industries. This "industry-shift" effect is not the consequence of some natural evolution from an agricultural to a manufacturing to a service economy. For one thing, a significant part of the shrinkage of manufacturing is trade related. More important, industry shifts would not provide a downward pressure on wages if service sector wages were more closely aligned with manufacturing wages, as is the case in other countries. Moreover, since health coverage, vacations, and pensions in this country are related to the specific job or sector in which a worker is em-

TABLE 3.27 Hourly wage growth among women
by race/ethnicity, 1989-97

	Hourly wage ($1997)			Changes	
	1989	1992	1997	1992-97	1989-97
Medians					
White	$9.84	$9.88	$10.02	1.4%	1.9%
Black	8.76	8.67	8.49	-2.1	-3.1
Hispanic	7.82	7.95	7.43	-6.5	-5.0
Asian	10.18	10.04	10.26	2.2	0.7
By education					
*High school**					
White	$9.64	$9.67	$9.67	0.1%	0.3%
Black	8.92	8.83	8.73	-1.1	-2.1
Hispanic	8.96	8.82	8.62	-2.2	-3.8
Asian	9.18	9.20	9.58	4.2	4.4
*College**					
White	$14.78	$15.41	$16.09	4.4%	8.9%
Black	14.51	15.15	14.66	-3.2	1.0
Hispanic	14.13	14.84	14.69	-1.0	3.9
Asian	15.03	15.96	16.03	0.5	6.7

* Average wage.

Source: Authors' analysis.

ployed, the sectoral distribution of employment matters more in the United States than in other countries. An alternative institutional arrangement found in other advanced countries sets health, pensions, vacation, and other benefits through legislation in a universal manner regardless of sector or firm. Therefore, the downward pressure of industry shifts on pay can be said to be the consequence of the absence of institutional structures that lessen inter-industry pay differences.

Trends in employment growth by major industry sector are presented in **Table 3.28**. The 18.1 million (net) jobs created between 1979 and 1989 involved a loss of roughly 1.2 million manufacturing and mining jobs and an increase of 19.3 million jobs in the service sector. The largest amount of job growth (14.2 million) was in the two lowest-paying service sector industries — retail trade and services (business, personnel, and health). In fact, these two industries accounted for 79% of all the net new jobs over the 1979-89 period.

The shift toward low-paying industries has continued in the 1990s, although

TABLE 3.28 Employment growth by sector, 1979-97

Industry sector	Employment (000)			Job growth		Industry share of job growth		Average hourly comp.
	1979	1989	1997	1979-89	1989-97	1979-89	1989-97	($1997)
Goods producing	26,461	25,254	24,739	-1,207	-515	-6.7%	-3.6%	$21.86
Mining	958	692	574	-266	-118	-1.5	-0.8	n.a.
Construction	4,463	5,171	5,629	708	458	3.9	3.2	21.47
Manufacturing	21,040	19,391	18,537	-1,649	-854	-9.1	-5.9	21.84
Durable goods	12,760	11,394	10,916	-1,366	-478	-7.6	-3.3	23.49
Nondurable goods	8,280	7,997	7,623	-283	-374	-1.6	-2.6	19.48
Service producing	63,363	82,642	97,520	19,279	14,878	106.7%	103.6%	$16.73
Trans., comm., util.	5,136	5,625	6,425	489	800	2.7	5.6	n.a.
Wholesale	5,204	6,187	6,657	983	470	5.4	3.3	19.98
Retail	14,989	19,475	22,136	4,486	2,661	24.8	18.5	9.92
Fin., ins., real est.	4,975	6,668	7,053	1,693	385	9.4	2.7	23.01
Services	17,112	26,907	35,595	9,795	8,688	54.2	60.5	17.84
Government	15,947	17,779	19,655	1,832	1,876	10.1	13.1	n.a.
Total	89,823	107,895	122,259	18,072	14,364	100.0%	100.0%	$17.97

Source: Authors' analysis.

at a slower pace. Low-wage retail jobs have played a smaller role in overall job creation, contributing 18.5% of the new jobs, but the services industry (primarily health and temporary services) became more important, supplying 60.5% of the net new jobs. Together, these low-wage industries accounted for 79.0% of all new jobs in 1989-97, as they did in the 1979-89 period.

The extent of the shift to low-wage industries in the 1980s is more evident in an analysis of changes in the shares of the workforce in various sectors (**Table 3.29**). Several high-wage sectors, such as construction, transportation, wholesale, communications, and government, increased employment in the 1980s or 1990s but ended up providing a smaller or similar share of overall employment over time. A lower share of employment in these high-wage sectors puts downward pressure on wages. Overall, the share of the workforce in low-paying services and in retail trade was 7.3 percentage points higher in 1989 than in 1979. The parallel trend was the 8.0 percentage-point drop in the share of the workforce in high-paying industries, such as manufacturing, construction, mining, government, transportation, communications, and utilities. In the 1990s, the only private sector industry to significantly expand its employment share was services, which (as shown in Table 3.28) is the second-lowest-paying industry.

TABLE 3.29 Changes in employment share by sector, 1979-97

Industry sector	Share of employment			Change in employment share	
	1979	1989	1997	1979-89	1989-97
Goods producing	29.5%	23.4%	20.2%	-6.1%	-3.2%
Mining	1.1	0.6	0.5	-0.4	-0.2
Construction	5.0	4.8	4.6	-0.2	-0.2
Manufacturing	23.4	18.0	15.2	-5.5	-2.8
Durable goods	14.2	10.6	8.9	-3.6	-1.6
Nondurable goods	9.2	7.4	6.2	-1.8	-1.2
Service producing	70.5%	76.6%	79.8%	6.1%	3.2%
Trans., comm., util.	5.7	5.2	5.3	-0.5	0.0
Wholesale	5.8	5.7	5.4	-0.1	-0.3
Retail	16.7	18.0	18.1	1.4	0.1
Fin., ins., real est.	5.5	6.2	5.8	0.6	-0.4
Services	19.1	24.9	29.1	5.9	4.2
Government	0.2	16.5	16.1	-1.3	-0.4
Total	100.0%	100.0%	100.0%	0.0%	0.0%

Source: Authors' analysis.

Table 3.30 presents an analysis of the impact of the shift in the industry mix of employment on the growth of the college–high school wage premium, providing evidence of how "industry shifts" affect the growth of wage inequality. This analysis suggests that the employment shift to low-wage industries can account for almost 20% of the growth of education premiums over the 1979-89 period among men and women but only had an effect on men in the 1990s. The analysis uses wage data on individuals (the ORG CPS) to determine the growth of the college–high school wage premium when one does and does not control for industry shifts — labeled respectively "industry composition constant" and "industry composition actual." Comparing the growth of the education premium in the first two columns provides information on the impact of changes in the industry composition of employment, or "industry shifts." Among men, for instance, the college–high school wage premium grew 16.8 percentage points from 1979 to 1997, but would have grown 13.8 percentage points had industry composition not changed. Therefore, 3.0 percentage points (16.8 less 13.8) of the 16.8 percentage-point growth, equivalent to 17.5% of the total growth, in the college–high school differential can be accounted for by industry shifts.

TABLE 3.30 The effect of industry shifts on the
growth of the college/high school differential, 1973-97

| | College/high school wage differential | | Industry shift effect*** |
| | Industry composition: | | |
	Actual*	Constant**	
Men			
1973	32.5%	35.9%	
1979	27.3	30.5	
1989	41.8	42.4	
1997	44.1	44.4	
Change			
1979-89	14.5	11.9	17.6%
1989-97*	2.3	1.9	17.2
1979-97*	16.8	13.8	17.5
Women			
1973	43.0%	39.6%	
1979	30.8	28.6	
1989	46.0	40.8	
1997	51.1	46.1	
Change			
1979-89	15.2	12.2	19.6%
1989-97*	5.1	5.3	-2.6
1979-97*	20.3	17.5	14.0

* Estimated with controls for experience as a quartic,
marital status, race, and four regions.
** Adds 12 industry controls to the regression reported in first col-
umn, thereby holding industry "constant."
*** Share of the rise in "actual" that is explained by industry shifts,
calculated from the difference between "actual" and "constant"
relative to "actual."

Source: Authors' analysis.

Trade and wages

The process of "globalization" in the 1980s and 1990s has been an important
factor both in slowing the growth rate of average wages and in reducing the
wage levels of workers with less than a college degree. The increase in international trade and investment flows affects wages through several channels. First,

increases in imports of finished manufactured goods, especially from countries where workers earn only a fraction of what U.S. workers earn, reduces manufacturing employment in the United States. While increases in exports create employment opportunities for some domestic workers, imports mean job losses for many others. Large, chronic trade deficits over the last 17 years suggest that the jobs lost to import competition have outnumbered the jobs gained from increasing exports. Given that export industries tend to be less labor intensive than import-competing industries, even growth in "balanced trade" (where exports and imports both increase by the same dollar amount) would lead to a decline in manufacturing jobs.

Second, imports of intermediate manufactured goods (used as inputs in the production of final goods) also help to lower domestic manufacturing employment, especially for production workers and others with less than a college education. The expansion of export "platforms" in low-wage countries has induced many U.S. manufacturing firms to outsource part of their production processes to low-wage countries. Since firms generally find it most profitable to outsource the most labor-intensive processes, the increase in outsourcing has hit non-college-educated production workers hardest.

Third, low wages and greater world capacity for producing manufactured goods can lower the prices of many international goods. Since workers' pay is tied to the value of the goods they produce, lower prices internationally can lead to a reduction in the earnings of U.S. workers, even if imports themselves do not increase.

Fourth, in many cases the mere threat of direct foreign competition or of the relocation of part or all of a production facility can lead workers to grant wage concessions to their employers.

Fifth, the very large increases in direct investment (i.e., plant and equipment) flows to other countries have meant reduced investment in the domestic manufacturing base and significant growth in the foreign manufacturing capacity capable of competing directly with U.S.-based manufacturers.

Finally, the effects of globalization go beyond those workers exposed directly to foreign competition. As trade drives workers out of manufacturing and into lower-paying service jobs, not only do their own wages fall, but the new supply of workers to the service sector (from displaced workers plus young workers not able to find manufacturing jobs) also helps to lower the wages of those already employed in service jobs.

This section briefly examines the role of international trade and investment in recent changes in the U.S. wage structure. Since even the preceding list of channels through which globalization affects wages is not complete and not yet quantified, this analysis will *understate* the impact of globalization on wages in the 1980s and 1990s. This topic is a relatively new area of inquiry in empirical labor economics and international trade; as befits a new area of investigation, there is considerable controversy and confusion.

Table 3.31 provides information on the growth of the manufacturing trade deficit (the excess of imports over exports) from 1973 to 1993 by region and by type of industry — industries that heavily use "unskilled" labor, "skilled" labor, or capital. The trade deficit grew to $130.7 billion in 1993 (and has grown further since) whereas our manufacturing trade was balanced in 1973 and mildly unbalanced in the late 1970s. This growing trade deficit reflects the fast growth of imports in the 1980s and 1990s and the much slower growth of exports.

The trade deficit has increased because of a sizable deterioration with Asian developing countries (Singapore, Taiwan, Korea, and Hong Kong), China (in "other Asia"), and Japan. In contrast, the trade deficit with other advanced (and higher-wage countries) grew less than $15 billion over this period.

Much of the growth in the trade deficit from 1973 to 1993 occurred in industries that intensively use "unskilled labor," about $70 billion of the $130 billion growth. However, there was also a roughly $45 billion deterioration (from $7.5 to -$37.3 billion) in skill-intensive industries and a $14 billion erosion in capital-intensive industries. More recent data would show a large deterioration with China, Canada, and Mexico fueling a historically high trade deficit.

These data suggest not only a large increase in the trade deficit but a growing exposure of a broad range of industries to foreign competition from the most advanced, developing countries. This growth in the trade deficit and increased global competition can, and would be expected to, adversely affect the wages of non-college-educated workers relative to others. In fact, any potential gains from trade would be created precisely through such a mechanism — a redeployment of workers and capital into more highly skilled or capital-intensive industries, which lessens the need for non-college-educated workers.

We now turn to an examination of the types of jobs that were lost as the trade deficit grew, as job losses in import-sensitive industries exceeded job gains in export industries. In periods of low unemployment, it may be the case that a trade deficit does not cause actual job loss because workers displaced by rising imports have found employment in nontraded sectors such as services. Nevertheless, even at low unemployment a trade deficit will affect the composition of jobs (less manufacturing, more services), thereby affecting wage inequality. In this light, **Table 3.32** indicates how trade flows affect the composition of employment by wage level and education relative to a situation where the ratios of imports and exports to output remained at 1979 levels.

Of the 2,366,000 jobs lost over the 1979-94 period, there were jobs lost to both college-educated (290,00) and high-wage (230,000) workers. The impact

TABLE 3.31 Net trade in U.S. manufactures by skill intensity and trading partner, 1973-93 ($ millions)

Country/Region	Skilled-intensive manufactures			Unskilled-intensive manufactures			Capital-intensive manufactures			Total		
	1973	1984	1993	1973	1984	1993	1973	1984	1993	1973	1984	1993
Advanced	$2,648	-$8,249	-$27,531	-$5,863	-$26,078	-$18,728	-$3,941	-$36,550	-$45,746	-$7,156	-$70,877	-$92,006
Japan	-2,088	-19,999	-45,284	-1,903	-10,772	-4,703	-2,005	-17,596	-26,076	-5,997	-48,367	-76,063
Other	4,736	11,750	17,753	-3,960	-15,306	-14,026	-1,936	-18,955	-19,671	-1,159	-22,510	-15,943
OPEC	1,207	5,029	6,070	206	79	-2,044	718	2,921	5,847	2,131	8,030	9,872
Eastern Europe	285	174	1,587	-236	-469	-1,355	101	19	496	149	-276	728
Developing	3,375	337	-17,407	-2,713	-24,971	-57,812	3,594	8,643	25,918	4,256	-15,991	-49,301
Latin America	2,422	4,420	6,136	-41	-2,656	-872	2,091	4,178	8,981	4,472	5,942	14,245
Asia-Four Tigers	-311	-8,699	-23,431	-2,322	-18,640	-33,013	354	788	7,900	-2,278	-26,551	-48,545
Other Asia	464	2,167	-2,603	-244	-3,148	-20,854	344	1,773	6,148	564	792	-17,309
Other	799	2,449	2,491	-106	-527	-3,073	804	1,904	2,889	1,498	3,826	2,308
Total	7,515	-2,709	-37,281	-8,606	-51,438	-79,940	471	-24,968	-13,486	-620	-79,114	-130,708

Source: Cline (1997).

TABLE 3.32 Trade-deficit-induced job loss by wage and education level, 1979-94

Job characteristic	Share of total employment, 1989	Trade-deficit-related job loss (000)		
		1979-89	1989-94	1979-94
Education level				
College graduate*	18.6%	-215	-31	-290
Non-college graduate	81.4	-1,550	-356	-2,076
Some college	31.3	-403	-55	-519
High school	31.2	-653	-148	-867
Less than high school	<u>18.9</u>	-495	-153	-690
	100.0			
Wage level**				
Highest wage	9.7%	-163	-34	-230
High wage	11.2	-186	-27	-244
Upper-middle	16.6	-269	-36	-345
Lower-middle	26.4	-478	-96	-631
Lowest wage	<u>36.1</u>	-670	-194	-916
	100.0			
Total		-1,765	-387	-2,366

*   Four years of college or more.
** Corresponding to jobs that paid in the following wage percentile ranges in 1979: 90-99; 75-89; 50-74; 21-49; 0-20.

Source: Scott et al. (1997), Tables 1 and 2.

of the growing trade deficit, nevertheless, was disproportionately borne by non-college-educated workers, especially those with no more than a high school degree. Likewise, trade-deficit-related job losses fell disproportionately on the lowest-wage workers and lower-middle-wage workers, the 62.5% of the workforce with the lowest pay. Consequently, it can be seen that non-college-educated and middle- and lower-wage workers disproportionately bear the costs and pressures due to trade deficits and the global competition they reflect.

Taken together, Tables 3.31 and 3.32 suggest that trade, particularly with low-wage developing countries, accelerated the long-term decline in manufacturing employment. The data also suggest that the fall in employment opportunities was especially severe for non-college-educated manufacturing production workers. Since production workers in manufacturing on average earn substantially more than workers with similar skills in nonmanufacturing jobs, these trade-induced job losses contributed directly to the deterioration in the wage structure. Since millions of trade-displaced workers sought jobs in nonmanufacturing sectors, trade also worked to depress wages outside manufacturing.

As discussed earlier, international trade can also affect U.S. wages through the prices of internationally traded manufactured goods without any change in the quantity of exports or imports. The expansion of manufacturing capacity in low-wage countries since the 1970s has significantly increased the supply of less-skill-intensive manufactured goods, inducing a reduction in the U.S. price of these goods. Since workers' earnings reflect changes in the prices of the goods they produce, a lower price for less-skill-intensive goods drives down the wages of less-skilled workers. **Table 3.33** presents results from some simple calculations designed to estimate the effect of trade-induced price changes on U.S. wages. It examines whether prices grew more slowly in the manufacturing industries most reliant on non-college-educated or unskilled and semi-skilled workers — the industries most affected by low-wage imports. Two measures of "skill intensity" are shown. The first panel shows that between 1979 and 1989 the price of college-worker-intensive industries increased by 2.9% relative to non-college-worker-intensive industries. The second panel shows that the price of non-production-intensive industries rose by 5.4% relative to production-worker-intensive industries over the same period.

These relative price changes require wages of non-college-educated and production workers to fall. The size of the wage declines depend on the importance of labor costs in overall manufacturing costs. If labor were a small share of total manufacturing costs, say 10%, then a 1% decline in the relative prices of less-skill-intensive goods would require a large fall (10%) in the less-skilled workers' wage in order to leave the overall industry costs unchanged (a 10% fall in something that is 10% of total costs represents a 1% savings on overall costs). If labor were a large share of total manufacturing costs, or value-added (say, 100%), then a 1% decline in the relative prices of less-skill-intensive industries would require a much smaller (1%) decline in the costs of less-skilled labor (a 1% fall in the costs of something that is 100% of total costs represents a 1% savings on overall costs). Since labor costs are, on average, 70% of total manufacturing value-added, then a 1% fall in the relative less-skill-intensive industry price requires about a 1.4% fall in the wage of the relatively less-skilled worker. If we assume that the average real wage for college-educated and nonproduction workers was unchanged between 1979 and 1989 (as was generally the case), then the 2.9% fall in the relative prices in non-college-educated-intensive industries should have lowered the noncollege wage by 4.1% over the period. The 5.4% relative fall in production-worker-intensive prices should have lowered production worker wages by 7.7%. Since the wages of non-college-educated relative to college-educated workers actually fell

TABLE 3.33 Effect of changes in prices of internationally traded manufactured goods on wage inequality

Industry price changes*	1959-69	1969-79	1979-89
College weighted	12.9%	159.5%	61.4%
Noncollege weighted	15.1	142.8	58.5
Difference	-2.2	16.7	2.9
Nonproduction weighted	16.1%	13.7%	62.0%
Production weighted	16.2	137.5	56.6
Difference	-0.1	-0.5	5.4
Labor share in value-added			70.0%
Implied decline in wages**			
Noncollege			4.1%
Production			7.7
Actual change in relative wages			
College/noncollege***			13.9%
Nonproduction/production			7.7
Share of change in relative wages **caused by change in relative prices**			
College/noncollege			29.8%
Nonproduction/production			110.2

*   Change in value-added producer price indexes over the period.
** Assuming no change in the real wage of nonproduction and college workers.
*** Change between 1979 and 1989 in regression-based college-noncollege wage differential, controlling for workers' experience and region of residence.

Source: Authors' analysis of Schmitt and Mishel (1996).

14% over the period, trade appears to have contributed about 30% of the decline in the college–non-college wage over the 1979-89 period. By this measure, trade was entirely responsible for the 7.7% fall in production worker wages relative to those of nonproduction workers.

The preceding tables document the rise in trade deficits and the decline in prices of less-skill-intensive, internationally traded manufactured goods. These channels have contributed to the long-term decline in manufacturing employment and directly and indirectly to the deterioration in the U.S. wage structure. Little concrete evidence is available on the other channels discussed at the beginning of this section — the "threat effect" of imports and plant relocation on U.S. manufacturing wages and the reality of large-scale international direct in-

TABLE 3.34 Legal immigrant flow to the United States, 1881-1996

Decade	Number (000s) Total	Number (000s) Annual	As percentage of change in population	Foreign-born as share of population*
1881-1890	5,246.6	524.7	41.0%	14.7%
1891-1900	3,687.6	368.8	28.3	13.6
1901-1910	8,795.4	879.5	53.9	14.6
1911-1920	5,735.8	573.6	40.8	13.2
1921-1930	4,107.2	410.7	24.6	11.6
1931-1940	528.4	52.8	5.9	8.8
1941-1950	1,350.0	135.0	5.3	6.9
1951-1960	2,515.5	251.6	8.7	5.4
1961-1970	3,321.7	332.2	13.7	4.7
1971-1980	4,493.3	449.3	20.7	6.2
1981-1990	7,338.1	733.8	33.1	7.9
1991-1996	6,146.2	1,024.4	39.4	9.3

* At end of period.

Source: Borjas (1994) and Camarota (1998).

vestment flows. Nevertheless, these effects are likely to be as large or larger than those that are more readily quantifiable.

Another aspect of globalization is immigration. After six decades of decline in the percentage of immigrants in the total population of the United States, the immigrant share began to grow in the 1970s (**Table 3.34**).

The annual increase in legal immigrants (no data are available on "undocumented," or "illegal," immigrants) has grown significantly, now more than 1 million each year in the 1990s, up from less than half that much in the 1970s (449,000 annually). As a result, the foreign-born share of the population rose to 9.3% in 1996, with legal immigrants comprising 39.4% of the population growth in the 1990s.

Holding all else constant, a rise in immigration increases the available labor supply in the United States and thus tends to reduce wages. **Table 3.35** shows that a large share of recent immigrants have less than the equivalent of a high school education (although immigrants, at least until 1990, also were more likely than natives to have a college degree). These numbers suggest that immigrants compete disproportionately with the least-skilled U.S. workers and therefore have contributed to lower wages for those without a high school degree since the end of the 1970s.

TABLE 3.35 Educational attainment of immigrant
and native men, 1970-96

	Less than high school		College educated	
Year	Native	Immigrants	Native	Immigrants
1970	39.6%	48.2%	15.4%	18.9%
1980	23.1	37.4	22.9	25.3
1990	14.8	36.9	26.6	26.6
1996	9.7	35.8	28.3	26.9

Source: Authors' analysis of Borjas (1994) and Camarota (1998).

The union dimension

The percentage of the workforce represented by unions fell rapidly in the 1980s and continued to fall in the 1990s after having been stable in the 1970s, as shown in **Figure 3N**. This falling rate of unionization has lowered wages, not only because some workers no longer receive the higher union wage but also because there is less pressure on nonunion employers to raise wages (a "spillover" or "threat effect" of unionism). There are also reasons to believe that there has been a weakening of union bargaining power, a qualitative shift beyond the quantitative decline. This erosion of bargaining power is partially related to a harsher economic context for unions because of trade pressures, the shift to services, and ongoing technological change. However, analysts have also pointed to other factors, such as employer militancy and changes in the application and administration of labor law, that have helped to weaken unions.

Table 3.36 shows the union wage premium — the degree to which union wages exceed nonunion wages — by type of pay (benefits or wages) for all workers and for blue-collar workers in 1997. The union premium is larger for total compensation (35.9%) than for wages alone (23.2%), reflecting the fact that unionized workers are provided insurance and pension benefits that are more than double those of nonunion workers. For blue-collar workers (where the comparison is more of an "apples to apples" one), the union premium in insurance and benefits is even larger: union blue-collar workers receive 158.2% and 362.5% more in health and pensions than do their nonunion counterparts.

The bottom panel provides a more refined analysis of the union wage premium through a comparison of the pay in unionized occupations compared to nonunion pay in comparable occupations and establishments (factories or of-

FIGURE 3N Union coverage in the United States, 1973-97

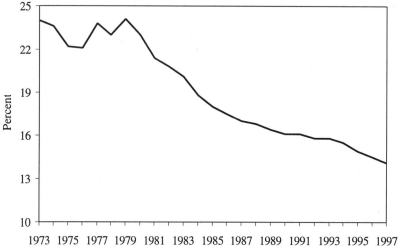

Source: Hirsch and Macpherson (1997).

fices). Specifically, the estimated union premium controls for whether an establishment is in the public sector, for its size, whether workers are full time, and for its detailed industry and region. In this analysis, the union wage premium is 21%, while the union compensation premium (combining the effect on wages and benefits) is 27.8%. Similarly, the employers of unionized workers pay 51.3% more in insurance costs (health and life) per hour and 20.3% more for retirement/savings/pension plans

This analysis also shows that unionized workers are 16% more likely to be in an employer-provided insurance plan (the "incidence" effect), and, among workers who are in employer-provided insurance plans, unionized employers pay 44.2% more per hour for the plan (the "expenditure" effect). Similarly, unionized workers are 26.7% more likely to be in a pension plan, and unionized employers pay 16% more into these plans than do comparable nonunion employers who provide pension plans.

Table 3.37, using a different data source and methodology (and year), presents another set of estimates of the union wage premium. Specifically, the union wage premium is computed so as to reflect differences in hourly wages between union and nonunion workers who are otherwise comparable in experience, edu-

TABLE 3.36 Union wage and benefit premium, 1997

| | Hourly pay ($1997) | | | |
	Wages	Insurance	Pension	Compensation
All workers				
Union	$17.60	$2.19	$1.33	$23.48
Nonunion	14.29	0.94	0.44	17.28
Union premium				
Dollars	$3.31	$1.25	$0.89	$6.20
Percent	23.2%	133.0%	202.3%	35.9%
Blue collar				
Union	$17.73	$2.35	$1.48	$24.07
Nonunion	11.84	0.91	0.32	14.75
Union premium				
Dollars	$5.89	$1.44	$1.16	$9.32
Percent	49.7%	158.2%	362.5%	63.2%
Regression-adjusted union effect*				
Union effect, total	21.0%	51.3%	20.3%	27.8%
Incidence		16.0	26.7	
Expenditure		44.2	16.0	

* Controlling for full-time, industry (74), occupation (47), public sector, region (9), establishment size in 1994.

Source: Authors' analysis of BLS data and Pierce (1998).

cation, region, industry, occupation, and marital status. This methodology yields a lower but still sizable union premium of 15.1% overall — 15.7% for men and 12.8% for women. The differences in union wage premiums across demographic groups are relatively small, ranging from 12.8% to 21.0%. Hispanic and black union members tend to reap the greatest wage advantage from unionism.

The effect of the erosion of unionization on the wages of a segment of the workforce depends on the degree to which deunionization has taken place and the degree to which the union wage premium among that segment of the workforce has declined. **Table 3.38** shows both the degree to which unionization and the union wage premium have declined by occupation and education level over the 1978-97 period (1979 data were not available). These data, which are for men only (some data on women are in a later table), are used to calculate

TABLE 3.37 Union wage premium by demographic group, 1997

Demographic group	Percent union*	Union premium**	
		Dollars	Percent
Total	16.1%	$1.42	15.1%
Men	18.3	1.59	15.7
Women	13.8	1.24	12.8
Whites	15.9%	$1.41	14.9%
Men	18.6	1.54	15.0
Women	13.1	1.28	12.8
Blacks	20.5%	$1.57	15.1%
Men	22.5	1.74	17.0
Women	18.7	1.48	13.1
Hispanics	13.8%	$1.73	18.7%
Men	14.5	2.20	21.0
Women	12.6	0.87	13.1

* Union member or covered by a collective bargaining agreement.

** Regression-adjusted union wage premium controlling for experience, education, region, industry, occupation, and marital status.

Source: Authors' analysis.

the effect of weakened unions (less representation and a weaker wage effect) over the 1978-97 period on the wages of particular groups and how deunionization affected occupation and education wage differentials — the contribution of a weaker union effect to the growth of the wage gaps between particular occupation and education groups.

Union representation fell dramatically among blue-collar and high-school-educated male workers from 1978 to 1997. Among the high-school-graduate workforce, unionization fell from 37.9% in 1978 to 20.8% in 1997, almost by half. This obviously weakened the effect of unions on the wages of both union and nonunion high-school-educated workers. Because unionized high school graduates earned about 21% more than equivalent nonunion workers (a premium that did not change over the 1978-97 period), unionization raised the wage of the average high school graduate by 8.2% in 1978 (the "union effect"). Unions had a 0.9% impact on male college graduate wages in 1978, leaving the

TABLE 3.38 Effect of deunionization on male wage differentials, 1978-97

A. Effect of union decline on wages

	Percent union			Union wage premium*			Union effect**		
	1978	1989	1997	1978	1989	1997	1978	1989	1997
By occupation									
White collar	14.7%	12.1%	10.4%	1.1%	-0.3%	2.2%	0.2%	0.0%	0.2%
Blue collar	43.1	28.9	23.6	26.6	23.3	22.2	11.5	6.7	5.3
Difference	-28.4	-16.7	-13.2	-25.6	-23.6	-20.1	-11.3	-6.8	-5.0
By education									
College	14.3%	11.9%	11.6%	6.3%	4.2%	5.1%	0.9%	0.5%	0.6%
High school	37.9	25.5	20.8	21.7	21.5	20.8	8.2	5.5	4.3
Difference	-23.6	-13.6	-9.2	-15.3	-17.3	-15.8	-7.3	-5.0	-3.8

B. Contribution of union decline on wage differentials

	Change in wage differential***			Change in union effect			Contribution of lower union effect		
Differential	1978-89	1989-97	1978-97	1978-89	1989-97	1978-97	1978-89	1989-97	1978-97
White collar/ blue collar	9.3%	2.4%	11.6%	4.6%	1.7%	6.3%	49.2%	74.3%	54.3%
College/ high school	13.4	2.3	15.8	2.3	1.2	3.5	17.2	52.8	22.5

*   Estimated with a simple human capital model plus industry and occupation controls.
**   Calculated as the product of percent union and the union wage premium.
*** Estimated with a simple human capital model.

Source: Authors' update of Freeman (1991).

net effect of unions to narrow the college–high school gap by 7.3 percentage points in that year. The decline in union representation from 1978 to 1997, however, reduced the union effect on high school male workers to 4.3% in 1997, and hardly affected college graduates, so unions closed the college–high school wage gap by only 3.8 percentage points in 1997. The lessened ability of unions to narrow the college–high school wage gap (from a 7.3% to a 3.8% narrowing effect) contributed to a 3.5 percentage-point rise in the college–high school wage differential, an amount equal to 22.5% of the total rise in this wage gap.

The weakening of unionism's wage impact had an even larger effect on blue-collar workers and the wage gap between blue-collar and white-collar workers. As a result of blue-collar men being unionized at a 43.1% rate in 1978

TABLE 3.39 Effect of unions on wages, by wage fifth, 1973-87

	Lowest fifth	Second fifth	Middle fifth	Fourth fifth	Top fifth	Average
Percent union						
1973	39.9%	43.7%	38.3%	33.5%	12.5%	33.7%
1987	23.5	30.3	33.1	24.7	17.7	26.4
Change, 1973-87	-15.4	-13.4	-5.2	-8.8	7.2	-7.3
Effect of union on:						
Union wage, 1987	27.9%	16.2%	18.0%	0.9%	10.5%	15.9%
Average wage, 1987	6.6	4.9	6.0	2.1	2.1	4.2
Wage effect of: **deunionization**						
1973-87	-4.3%	-2.2%	-0.9%	-0.1%	0.8%	-1.1%

Source: Card (1991).

and a 26.6% union wage premium, blue-collar men earned 11.5% more, thereby closing the blue-collar/white-collar wage gap by 11.3 percentage points in that year. The union impact on this differential declined as unionization and the union wage premium declined, such that unionism reduced the blue-collar/white-collar differential by 5.0 rather than 11.3 percentage points in 1997, a 6.3 percentage-point weakening. This lessened effect of unionism can account for about half (54.3%) of the 11.6 percentage-point growth of the blue-collar/white-collar wage gap over the 1978-97 period.

Table 3.39 presents the results of a study that examines the effect of lower unionization on workers at various wage levels and thus analyzes the impact of deunionization on overall wage inequality (between low-, middle- and high-wage workers), not just between groups (e.g., high school versus college educated). The data show that unions have their largest effect on the wages of lower-wage workers, raising the wages of union members in the lowest and second-lowest fifths by 27.9% and 16.2%, respectively. Because workers in the bottom three-fifths have higher unionization rates and higher union wage premiums, the effect of unions on average wages for these groups is largest, increasing the average wage from 4.9% to 6.6%.

Unionization declined more among low-wage than high-wage workers from 1973 to 1987, with unionization actually increasing among the top fifth. The wage impact of changes in unionization was to increase the wage gap between high- and low-wage workers. For instance, an increase in union representation

TABLE 3.40 Effect of deunionization on male wage inequality

	Wage inequality		
Item	1973-87*	1978-88**	1979-88***
Early year	0.227	0.235	n.a.
Later year	0.284	0.269	n.a.
Change in inequality	0.057	0.034	0.066
Change due to lower unionization	0.012	0.007	0.014
Deunionization contribution to total rise in inequality	21%	21%	21%

*   Change in variance of log earnings among men age 25-64.
**   Change in variance of log earnings among men age 25-65.
***   Change in standard deviation of log earnings among men age 25-65.

Sources: Card (1991); DiNardo, Fortin, and Lemieux (1994); Freeman (1991).

lifted the wages of the top fifth by 0.8%, but deunionization lowered the wages in the bottom fifth by 4.3%, creating a roughly 5 percentage-point divergence between high- and low-wage earners.

The data in **Table 3.40** report the results of three studies of the effect of the drop in unionization on overall male wage inequality. These data show that there was sizable growth in wage inequality between the 1970s and the late 1980s. Remarkably, all three studies found that lower unionization can account for the same proportion of overall higher wage inequality — 21% — even though they employ radically different methodologies. Unfortunately, these studies do not examine women's wages. Another study, discussed below (Table 3.45), shows deunionization playing a smaller role among women than men.

An eroded minimum wage

The real value of the minimum wage has fallen considerably since its high point in the late 1960s (**Figure 3O**). The decline was particularly steep and steady between 1979 and 1989, when inflation whittled down the real minimum wage (in 1997 dollars) from $6.29 to $4.34, a fall of 31.1% (**Table 3.41**). Despite the legislated increases in the minimum wage in 1990 and 1991, and again in 1996 and 1997, the value of the minimum wage in 1997 was still 18.1% less than in

FIGURE 30 Real value of the minimum wage, 1960-97

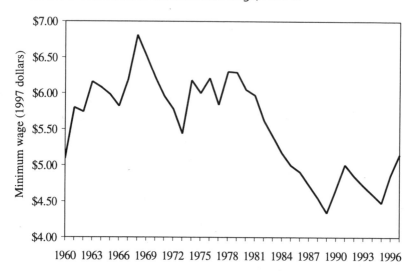

Source: Authors' analysis.

1979. Recent increases in the minimum wage, however, did raise its real value by 18.8% over the 1989-97 period.

It has been argued that the minimum wage primarily affects teenagers and others with no family responsibilities. **Table 3.42** examines the demographic composition of the workforce that benefited from the recent increases in the minimum wage. In fact, only 28.6% of the affected 9,886,158 minimum wage workers were teenagers, suggesting that many minimum wage workers have economic responsibilities. The information at the bottom of the table shows that minimum wage earners contribute 54% of their family's weekly earnings. Although the majority work part time (less than 35 hours weekly), 46.0% in 1993 worked full time and another 33.3% worked more than 20 hours each week. While minorities are disproportionately represented among minimum wage workers, almost two-thirds are white. These workers also tend to be women (58.2% of the total). Table 3.42 also shows that minimum wage and "other" low-wage workers are heavily concentrated in the retail trade industry but are underrepresented in manufacturing industries and among unionized employers.

An analysis of only those earning between the old and the new minimum wage would be too narrow, however, since a higher minimum wage affects workers who earn more than but close to the minimum — they receive increases

TABLE 3.41 Value of the minimum wage, 1960-97

Year	Minimum wage Current $	$1997
1960	$1.00	$4.99
1967	1.40	6.19
1973	1.60	5.44
1979	2.90	6.29
1989	3.35	4.34
1990	3.80	4.67
1991	4.25	5.01
1996	4.75	4.86
1997	5.15	5.15
Period averages		
1960s	$1.29	$5.94
1970s	2.07	6.02
1980s	3.33	5.17
1990-97	4.10	4.79
Percent change		
1979-89		-31.1%
1989-97		18.8
1979-97		-18.1
1967-97		-16.8

Source: Authors' analysis.

when the minimum wage rises. For these reasons, Table 3.42 also presents the demographic breakdown of those workers who earned within a dollar of the new minimum wage level ($5.15-$6.14), a group labeled "other low-wage workers." This more broadly defined minimum wage workforce includes an additional 9.6 million workers, or an additional 8.7% of the total workforce. Thus, any significant change in the minimum wage would affect a substantial group, amounting to as much as 18% of the workforce. The demographic breakdown of "other low-wage workers" is more inclusive of full-time and adult workers but has proportionately fewer minority workers compared to the group of directly affected minimum wage earners.

Table 3.43 assesses the impact of the lowering of the real value of the minimum wage on key wage differentials. The analysis is limited to women, where the impact of the minimum wage is concentrated. This can be seen by examin-

TABLE 3.42 Characteristics of minimum wage and other workers, Oct.'95-Sep.'96

Characteristic	Workers directly affected by new minimum ($4.25-$5.14)	Other low-wage workers ($5.15-$6.14)	Workers above minimum wage ($6.15+)	All workers
Average wage	$4.73	$5.72	$14.64	$12.73
Employment	9,886,158	9,610,926	89,079,931	110,999,085
Share of total	8.9%	8.7%	80.3%	100.0%
Demographics				
Male	41.8%	41.9%	54.9%	52.3%
16-19	13.7	8.1	1.0	2.9
20+	28.2	33.8	53.9	49.4
Female	58.2	58.1	45.1	47.7
16-19	14.9	7.9	0.7	2.8
20+	43.2	50.2	44.4	44.9
White	62.8	67.7	77.9	75.4
Male	24.6	26.2	42.8	39.4
Female	38.2	41.5	35.1	36.0
Black	16.1	13.8	10.4	11.3
Male	6.4	5.5	5.1	5.3
Female	9.8	8.3	5.3	6.0
Hispanic	17.5	14.8	7.9	9.5
Male	9.3	8.6	4.9	5.7
Female	8.2	6.2	3.0	3.8
Teens (16-19)	28.6%	16.0%	1.7%	5.6%
Work hours				
Full time (35+)	46.0%	62.7%	87.7%	81.1%
Part time				
20-34 hours	33.3%	25.4%	9.0%	13.0%
1-19 hours	20.7	11.9	3.3	5.9
Industry				
Manufacturing	8.8%	12.7%	19.7%	17.8%
Retail trade	42.6	35.8	12.2	17.3
Union*				
Union	4.4%	6.3%	19.1%	16.4%
Nonunion	95.6	93.7	80.9	83.6

Addendum: The share of weekly earnings contributed by minimum wage workers, 1997

	Average	Median
All families with affected workers	54%	41%
excluding one-person families	44	27

* Includes both union members and nonmembers covered by union contracts.

Source: Bernstein and Schmitt (1998).

TABLE 3.43 Impact of lower minimum wage on key wage differentials among women, 1979-97

Wage differential	Actual wage differentials			Simulated wage differentials at 1979 minimum wage		1979-89				1979-97			
						Change in wage differential			Minimum wage effect	Change in wage differential			Minimum wage effect
	1979	1989	1997	1989	1997	Actual	Simulated	Difference		Actual	Simulated	Difference	
Wage ratios (logs)													
50/10	0.39	0.64	0.63	0.41	0.41	0.26	0.02	0.23	91.1%	0.24	0.02	0.21	89.5%
90/10	1.00	1.35	1.39	1.12	1.18	0.35	0.12	0.23	66.4	0.39	0.18	0.21	54.3
Education differentials													
College/high school	0.31	0.46	0.51	0.42	0.48	0.15	0.11	0.04	28.1%	0.20	0.17	0.03	15.8%
College/less than high school	0.49	0.69	0.75	0.60	0.67	0.20	0.11	0.09	44.2%	0.26	0.18	0.08	29.4%
Memo:													
Percent earning less than 1979 minimum													
Less than high school		43.4%	53.7%										
High school		23.6	26.2										
College		6.1	7.0										
All		20.1	21.5										

Source: Authors' analysis.

ing the extent to which workers in recent years earn less than the inflation-adjusted equivalent of the 1979 minimum wage, a measure that directly captures the size of the group affected by the post-1979 erosion of the minimum wage's value. As the bottom of Table 3.43 shows, 20.1% of women workers in 1989 earned less than the real value of the minimum wage in 1979. Women without a high school degree were the group most affected by the lowering of the minimum wage, with 43.4% and 53.7% earning below the 1979 minimum wage level in 1989 and 1997, respectively.

The analysis of the impact of a lower minimum wage on the wage structure in Table 3.43 is based on a simple simulation. Data on individual workers' wages in recent years are used to construct what the wage structure would have been in 1989 and 1997 if the 1979 minimum wage (again, inflation-adjusted) had still prevailed. Drawing on these simulated "counterfactuals," the analysis compares the actual growth in wage differentials to the growth that would have occurred if the 1979 minimum wage had been maintained. The difference between "actual" and "simulated" is a measure of the impact of the lowering of the minimum wage on particular wage differentials.

The minimum wage most affects women at the 10th percentile and women with the least education, so it should not be surprising that wage differentials between middle- and low-wage women (the 50/10 differential) and college/less-than-high-school wage differentials are greatly affected by a decline in the minimum wage. For instance, the 50/10 differentials (in logs, which approximate percentage differences) would have grown from 0.39 in 1979 to only 0.41, rather than to 0.64, in 1989 if the minimum wage had been maintained. Thus, 0.23 of the 0.26 rise in the 50/10 differential in the 1980s among women, or 91% of the rise, can be attributed to a change in minimum wage policy. Similarly, the devaluing of the minimum wage can explain 44% of the growth in the college/less-than-high-school wage gap among women in the 1980s. A lower minimum wage also greatly affected the college/high school wage gap, explaining 28% of its growth in the 1980s. This analysis confirms the importance of the erosion of a key labor market institution, the minimum wage, on the growth of women's wage inequality at the bottom of the wage scale.

Because there is substantial evidence (with some controversy, of course) that a moderately higher minimum wage does not significantly lower employment (or reduce it at all), there has been an increased focus on who benefits from a higher minimum wage. In other words, because a higher minimum may not have much of an effect on efficiency or output, the merit of such a policy will depend greatly on its fairness or, in other words, who benefits.

Table 3.44 presents a computation of which families benefited from the higher minimum wage legislated over the 1996-97 period. The analysis calcu-

TABLE 3.44 Distribution of minimum wage gains and income shares by fifth for various household types

Income fifth	Share of gain from increase	Share of income	Average income
Prime-age working households,* 1997			
Lowest	35.3%	5.4%	$15,728
Second	22.8	11.0	32,547
Middle	15.2	15.9	47,699
Fourth	14.5	22.3	66,104
Highest	12.2	45.3	134,128
All prime-age households (including nonworking), 1997			
Lowest	28.0%	3.8%	$10,518
Second	22.8	9.8	26,965
Middle	20.2	15.6	42,848
Fourth	15.8	22.7	62,502
Highest	13.3	48.0	131,991

* Prime-age households are headed by a person age 25-54. One-person households are included. Top panel excludes households with no earners.

Source: Bernstein and Schmitt (1998).

lates the annual gain to each worker based on the amount of his or her wage increase (i.e., based on the distance to the new minimum) and annual hours worked. Given this information, it is possible to calculate the share of the aggregate wage gain generated from the higher minimum wage that accrues to each household income fifth. As shown in Table 3.44, 35.3% of the gains generated by the higher minimum wage were received by the poorest 20% of working households; 58.1% of the gains were received by the poorest 40% of working households.

The minimum wage generates the most help to those with the least income and the least help to those with the most income. For instance, as Table 3.44 also shows, the poorest fifth of working households had 5.4% of all income but received 35% of the gains from the higher minimum wage. In contrast, the best-off families received 45.3% of all income but received only 12.2% of the benefits of the higher minimum wage. The results are comparable when the analysis is repeated for all households, including those with no workers.

Summarizing the role of labor market institutions

The analysis in **Table 3.45**, which examines the impact of changes in labor market institutions on wage differentials, adds several new dimensions to our discussion. First, it looks at the effect of specific factors (increases and decreases in the minimum wage, deunionization) on different dimensions of the overall wage structure — the 90/50 and 50/10 differentials. The analysis, therefore, permits a more refined discussion that allows some factors to affect the bottom of the wage structure while other factors might affect the top. Second, the analysis covers several subperiods (1973-79, 1979-88, 1988-92), so one can observe how a factor's impact can shift over time.

Over the 1973-79 period there was a growth in the minimum wage and stability of union representation. The result of the strong minimum wage was a sizable lowering of the 50/10 differential among women (4.6 percentage points) and a slight lowering of the wage gap at the bottom among men (0.3 percentage points). Changes in unionism in this period were equalizing among men but disequalizing among women.

The results for the 1979-88 period make clear that deunionization was an important factor in the growth of male wage inequality at the top, contributing 4.0 of the 11.9-percentage-point growth in the 90/50 differential. The reduction of the minimum wage over the 1979-88 period, on the other hand, generated 15.0 of the 24.3 percentage-point growth in the 50/10 differential among women and a large part (5.0) of the 7.6 percentage-point growth in the male 50/10 differential. Thus, a lower minimum wage was a major factor in lowering the wages of low-wage men and women relative to the median. Deunionization, in contrast, primarily lowered the wages of middle-wage men relative to high-wage men.

In the 1988-92 period, a modest rise in the minimum wage tightened the wage structure at the bottom, and continued deunionization helped to widen the male wage structure at the top.

Looking at the 1979-92 period as a whole, deunionization was a major factor driving wage inequality at the top of the wage structure, responsible for 5.0 of the 14.4 percentage-point rise of the 90/50 differential (contributing 35% of the total growth). The erosion of the minimum wage, on the other hand, was the major factor generating inequality at the bottom among women (contributing 66% of the growth) and men (69% of the growth). Together, the shifts in labor market institutions — deunionization and a lower minimum wage — over the 1979-92 period can explain 36% and 44% of the growth of overall wage inequality (the 90/10 differential), respectively, among men and women.

TABLE 3.45 The impact of labor market institutions
on wage differentials, 1973-92

	Men			Women		
Period	90/10	90/50	50/10	90/10	90/50	50/10
1973-79						
Total change	-0.4	-1.8	1.5	-1.7	-1.6	-0.1
Change in minimum wage	-0.2	0.1	-0.3	-4.4	0.3	-4.6
Deunionization	-0.9	-1.0	0.2	0.7	0.1	-0.5
1979-88						
Total change	19.5	11.9	7.6	32.8	8.5	24.3
Change in minimum wage	4.9	0.0	5.0	14.8	-0.2	15.0
Deunionization	2.1	4.0	-1.9	0.4	1.4	-1.0
1988-92						
Total change	2.0	2.5	-0.5	1.9	3.7	-1.9
Change in minimum wage	-0.1	0.0	-0.1	-0.4	-0.1	-0.3
Deunionization	0.9	1.0	-0.1	0.2	0.2	0.0
Contribution to growing wage inequality						
1979-92						
Total change	100%	100%	100%	100%	100%	100%
Change in minimum wage	22	0	69	42	-2	66
Deunionization	14	35	-28	2	13	-5

Source: Fortin and Lemieux (1996).

The technology story of wage inequality

Technological change can affect the wage structure by displacing some types of workers and by increasing demand for others. Given the seemingly rapid diffusion of microelectronic technologies in recent years, many analysts have considered technological change a major factor in the recent increase in wage inequality. Unfortunately, because it is difficult to measure the extent of technological change and its overall character (whether it is generally "deskilling" or "up-skilling" and by how much), it is difficult to identify the role of technological change on recent wage trends. More than a few analysts, in fact, have simply assumed that whatever portion of wage inequality is unexplained by measurable factors can be considered to be the consequence of technological change. This type of analysis, however, only puts a name to our ignorance.

It is easy to understand why people might consider technology to be a major factor explaining recent wage and employment trends. We are often told that the pace of change in the workplace is accelerating, and there is a widespread visibility of automation and robotics; computers and microelectronics provide a visible dimension evident in workplaces, such as offices, not usually affected by technology. Perhaps even more important is that technology has provided advances in products used by consumers, including the availability of CD players, VCRs, microwaves, electronic game systems, advanced televisions, portable phones, and so on. Given these advances, it is not surprising for noneconomists to readily accept that technology is transforming the wage structure. It needs to be noted, however, that technological advances in consumer products are not related to changes in labor market outcomes — it is the way goods and services are produced and changes in the relative demand for different types of workers that affect wage trends. Since many high-tech products are made with low-tech methods, there is no close correspondence of advanced consumer products with an increased need for skilled workers.

The economic intuition for a large role for technology in the growth of wage inequality is that the growth of wage inequality and the employment shift to more-educated workers has occurred within industries and has not been caused primarily by shifts across industries (i.e., more service jobs, fewer manufacturing jobs). Research has also shown that technological change has traditionally been associated with an increased demand for more-educated or "skilled" workers. This pattern of change suggests, to some analysts, an increase in "skill-biased technological change" driving large changes within industries.

Because wages have risen the most for groups whose supply expanded the fastest (e.g., college graduates), most economists have concluded that nonsupply factors (i.e., shifts in demand or institutional factors, such as those discussed in earlier sections) are the driving force behind growing wage inequality. They reason that those groups with the relatively fastest growth in supply would be expected to see their wages depressed relative to other groups unless there were other factors working very strongly in their favor, such as a rapid expansion in demand. Rapid technological change favoring more-educated groups could logically explain demand side shifts leading to wider wage differences.

There are many reasons to be skeptical of a technology-led increase in demand for "skill" as an explanation for growing wage inequality. First, note that there has been little or no growth in multifactor productivity (a commonly used proxy for technological change) for decades, nor has there been any greater growth in labor productivity in recent years (see the Introduction). However, the technology explanation assumes that there was a large technology-led transformation of the workplace that substantially decreased the need for "unskilled" workers and thereby led to a large shift in wage differentials. It is implausible that there has been a technology shock that has transformed workplaces but has not boosted productivity growth.

Second, the experience since the mid- to late 1980s does not accord with the conventional technology story, whose imagery is of computer-driven technology bidding up the wages of "more-skilled" and "more-educated" workers, leaving behind a small group of "unskilled" workers with inadequate skills. The facts are hard to reconcile with the notion that technological change grew as fast or faster in the 1990s than in earlier periods. If technology were adverse for unskilled or less-educated workers, then we would expect a continued expansion of the wage differential between middle-wage and low-wage workers (the 50/10 differential). Yet, the 50/10 differential has been stable or declining among both men and women from 1986 or 1987 to 1997. Instead, we are seeing the top earners pulling away from nearly all other earners. Therefore, there seem to be factors driving a wedge between the top 10% and everyone else, rather than a skill-biased technological change aiding the vast majority but leaving a small group of unskilled workers behind. Further confirmation of the breadth of those left behind is that wages have been stable or in decline for the bottom 80% of men and the bottom 70% of women over the 1989-97 period, with wages falling for the entire non-college-educated workforce (roughly 75% of workers). Of course, even high-wage, white-collar, or college-graduate men have failed to see real wage growth in 10 years.

The flattening of the growth of male education differentials (as seen in Figure 3J) in the late 1980s and 1990s also does not easily fit a technology story. Since the wages of college-graduate men are not being bid up relative to others at the same pace as in the early and mid-1980s, one can only conclude that there has been a deceleration of the relative demand for education (given that the supply of college workers did not accelerate). This would not be the case if technology were being introduced into workplaces at the same or a faster pace in the late 1980s or in the 1990s. Moreover, the late 1980s to mid-1990s period has been one of continued growth of wage inequality as the top pulls away from the middle and bottom; since this growing gap is not being driven by wider education differentials (the primary mechanism by which technology is said to lead to greater wage inequality), it is hard to believe that technology is playing a major role. As shown earlier, only a small portion of the growth of wage inequality in the 1990s can be attributed to a change in the "returns to skill."

Third, there is no evidence that the growth of wage inequality over the entire 1973-97 period has been primarily driven by changes in the economic return to education or experience, the most easily measured dimensions of skill. Rather, wage inequality has been largely driven by the growth of within-group wage inequality — the growing gap among workers with similar education and experience. The growth of within-group inequality may be related to technological change if it is interpreted as a reflection of growing economic returns to worker skills that are not easily measured (motivation, aptitudes for math, etc). However, there are no signs that the growth of within-group wage inequality has been fastest in those industries where the use of technology grew the most (as discussed below). It is also unclear why the economic returns for measurable skills (e.g., education) and unmeasured skills (e.g., motivation) should not grow in tandem. In fact, between-group and within-group inequality have not moved together in the various subperiods since 1973.

Finally, the notion that technology has been bidding up the wages of the skilled relative to the unskilled does not accord with the basic facts presented earlier. Or, it holds true in a relative but not an absolute sense. The wages of skilled men, defined as white-collar, college-educated, or 90th percentile workers, have been flat or declining since the mid-1980s. As described in Chapter 4, white-collar men have increasingly become displaced and beset by employment problems. High-wage women have continued to see their wages grow, but it does not seem likely that technology is primarily affecting skilled women but not skilled men. Moreover, as discussed below, the wages of new college graduates working in information technology occupations were stagnant or falling through most of the 1990s until the last year or so.

We now turn to other challenges to the technology story, examining which occupations are driving up education differentials and whether there has been an acceleration of technology's impact on the labor market.

One way of gaining insight into the role of technology in generating a widening of the education wage gap is to examine which occupations, in terms of their employment expansion and relative wage improvements, have contributed to the growth of education differentials. Such an analysis is presented in Tables 3.46 and 3.47 for, respectively, men and women. In these analyses, the workforce is divided into 11 specific white-collar occupations (from among the aggregate managerial, professional, technical, and sales groups) and three more aggregate, lower-paid occupations (blue-collar, service, and clerical). This breakdown permits an examination of which occupations within the white-collar workforce experienced the greatest growth in demand in the 1980s and 1990s, as reflected by their fast growth in employment and wages.

As **Table 3.46** shows, the wage premium of college-educated male workers (excluding those with degrees beyond college) relative to non-college-educated males (including those with some college, a high school degree, or less) rose 7.9 percentage points from 1979 to 1989. This wage premium grew because of a 6.3 percentage-point "relative wage" effect (the wages of college grads within

TABLE 3.46 Decomposition of growth of male college/noncollege wage premium by occupation, 1979-97

| | 1979-89 | | | | 1989-97 | | | | 1979-97 | | | |
| | Growth due to: | | | | Growth due to: | | | | Growth due to: | | | |
Occupation	Higher relative wage*	Increased relative employment**	Combined effect	Share of aggregate change	Higher relative wage*	Increased relative employment**	Combined effect	Share of aggregate change	Higher relative wage*	Increased relative employment**	Combined effect	Share of aggregate change
Managers	2.9	1.7	4.6	58.3%	1.2	-0.2	0.9	27.6%	4.1	1.5	5.6	49.2%
Engineers	1.0	-0.1	0.8	10.5	0.1	-0.4	-0.3	-7.6	1.1	-0.5	0.6	5.1
Math/computer	0.5	-0.4	0.1	1.5	0.2	1.0	1.2	34.9	0.6	0.6	1.3	11.5
Natural science	0.1	0.0	0.0	0.5	0.0	0.1	0.1	2.8	0.1	0.1	0.1	1.2
Health professional	0.2	0.0	0.2	3.1	0.2	0.3	0.5	14.1	0.4	0.3	0.7	6.3
Soc. science/law	0.0	0.0	0.0	-0.6	0.0	0.0	0.0	-0.5	0.0	0.0	-0.1	-0.5
Other professional	-0.4	-2.5	-2.9	-36.2	1.0	0.4	1.4	42.6	0.6	-2.0	-1.4	-12.7
Hlth., eng., sci. tech.	0.1	0.0	0.1	1.4	0.1	0.0	0.1	4.2	0.2	0.0	0.3	2.2
Other technician	-0.1	1.4	1.3	16.7	0.3	-0.2	0.1	3.4	0.2	1.2	1.4	12.7
Other sales	1.1	1.5	2.6	32.7	0.1	-0.3	-0.1	-3.5	1.3	1.2	2.5	21.9
Sales, finance	0.6	0.1	0.7	9.4	-0.2	-0.2	-0.4	-11.3	0.4	-0.1	0.4	3.2
Clerks	0.1	0.0	0.1	0.9	0.2	-0.1	0.1	4.4	0.3	-0.1	0.2	2.0
Service	0.1	0.0	0.1	1.2	0.2	-0.1	0.2	4.5	0.3	-0.1	0.2	2.2
Blue collar, farm	0.1	-0.1	0.1	0.7	-0.4	-0.1	-0.5	-15.7	-0.3	-0.2	-0.5	-4.2
Growth of college/noncollege Wage premium***	6.3	1.6	7.9	100.0%	3.1	0.2	3.4	100.0%	9.4	1.9	11.3	100.0%

* Measures whether college grads (four-year only) in this occupation had a greater (than other college grads) increase in wages relative to non-college-educated workers, controlling for other human capital characteristics.

** Measures whether college graduates in this occupation had a greater growth in employment relative to other college graduates.

*** Sample excludes those with more than four years of college.

Source: Authors' analysis.

particular occupations growing relatively faster than those of non-college-edu-cated workers) and a 1.6 percentage-point "relative employment" effect (the occupations in which college grads worked expanded employment relatively faster). The analysis in Table 3.46 identifies the "relative wage" effect and "rela-tive employment" effect overall and for specific occupations, allowing a com-putation of the "share of the aggregate change" in the premium associated with trends in each occupation.

The results show that it was the fast growth in the wages and employment of managers and sales workers ("other sales" and "financial sales") that drove up the education wage differential among men, accounting for more than all of the increase. In contrast, engineers, scientists, mathematicians, and computer science professionals (and associated technical workers) played a very small role in driving up education differentials.

As we have noted, the college wage premium grew only modestly over the 1989-97 period (and hardly at all in 1990-97). Table 3.46 suggests this was because white-collar occupations increased employment relative to other occu-pations only slightly, and white-collar wage gains were smaller as well.

Over the entire 1979-97 period, managers were responsible for half (49.2%) of the entire 11.3 percentage-point rise in the college/non-college wage pre-mium among men, with another fourth (25.1%) associated with sales workers.

Table 3.47, which presents the occupational decomposition of the growth of the education wage gap among women, generally shows the same pattern as among men, increased wages and employment of managers and sales workers accounting for more than 80% of the 13.8 percentage-point growth in the edu-cation–wage premium, with very little role for scientists, engineers, or com-puter professionals or for technical workers. Again, this pattern seems hard to reconcile with the conventional technology story.

What does this analysis tell us about a technology story of wage inequality? Basically, if technology is responsible for bidding up the education–wage gap by increasing the demand for skilled or educated workers, then the particular skills associated with technological change in this period were those of manag-ers and sales workers. Such a portrait of technology's role is at odds with the conventional one, which tends to focus on the role of computers and microelec-tronics. It may be that information-age technology transforms workplaces by generating fast wage and employment growth for managers and sales workers. Nevertheless, managers and sales workers are not the usual occupations associ-ated with the mastery of the new skills associated with an information technol-ogy era.

We now turn to the issue of whether technology's impact accelerated in the 1980s and 1990s so as to increase the demand for skills much faster than the

TABLE 3.47 Decomposition of growth of female college/noncollege wage premium by occupation, 1979-97

| | 1979-89 | | | | 1989-97 | | | | 1979-97 | | | |
| | Growth due to: | | | | Growth due to: | | | | Growth due to: | | | |
Occupation	Higher relative wage*	Increased relative employment**	Combined effect	Share of aggregate change	Higher relative wage*	Increased relative employment**	Combined effect	Share of aggregate change	Higher relative wage*	Increased relative employment**	Combined effect	Share of aggregate change
Managers	1.6	4.0	5.6	67.7%	1.6	1.4	3.0	53.8%	3.2	5.4	8.6	62.1%
Engineers	0.1	0.6	0.7	8.4	-0.1	0.0	-0.1	-1.9	0.0	0.6	0.6	4.2
Math/computer	0.1	-0.1	0.0	-0.1	0.2	0.4	0.5	9.4	0.2	0.3	0.5	3.7
Nat. science	0.1	0.0	0.1	1.4	0.0	0.0	0.0	0.6	0.1	0.0	0.1	1.1
Health professional	1.9	0.5	2.4	29.2	0.6	-0.3	0.3	4.6	2.4	0.2	2.7	19.3
Soc. science/law	0.0	0.0	0.0	0.5	0.0	0.1	0.1	1.7	0.1	0.1	0.1	1.0
Other professional	0.2	-4.8	-4.6	-55.5	1.8	0.2	2.0	35.0	2.0	-4.6	-2.6	-18.9
Hlth, eng., sci. tech.	0.1	0.1	0.3	3.1	0.0	-0.2	-0.2	-3.6	0.1	-0.1	0.1	0.4
Other technical	0.1	1.0	1.2	14.1	0.1	-0.3	-0.2	-4.0	0.2	0.7	0.9	6.8
Other sales	0.8	1.1	1.8	22.2	0.5	0.0	0.5	9.5	1.3	1.0	2.4	17.0
Sales, finance	0.1	0.0	0.0	0.5	0.3	0.0	0.3	5.7	0.4	0.0	0.4	2.6
Clerks	0.8	-0.3	0.5	5.7	-0.1	-0.3	-0.4	-7.8	0.7	-0.7	0.0	0.2
Service	0.0	0.1	0.1	1.0	-0.1	0.1	0.0	-0.9	-0.1	0.2	0.0	0.3
Blue collar, farm	0.2	0.0	0.2	1.8	-0.1	0.0	-0.1	-2.1	0.1	0.0	0.0	0.2
Growth of college/noncollege Wage premium***	5.9	2.3	8.2	100.0%	4.7	0.9	5.6	100.0%	10.6	3.2	13.8	100.0%

* Measures whether college grads (four-year only) in this occupation had a greater (than other college grads) increase in wages relative to non-college-educated workers, controlling for other human capital characteristics.

** Measures whether college graduates in this occupation had a greater growth in employment relative to other college graduates.

*** Sample excludes those with more than four years of college.

Source: Authors' analysis.

ongoing expansion of college grads in the workforce. The rhetoric in the discussion of technology's role in growing wage inequality presumes that we have entered a new era of technological change, signified by the computer revolution. In this scenario, either the rate of introduction of new technologies or the types of technologies being introduced is creating a new situation in today's workplace, along with an enhanced demand for cognitive skills. Some analysts have explicitly talked in terms of a "technology shock." This widely expressed view assumes an *acceleration* of technology's impact on relative demand, suggesting that one test of the technology hypothesis is whether technology had a greater impact on skill demand in the 1980s or 1990s than in the 1970s or earlier periods.

That a technology explanation requires an acceleration of technology's impact on workplace skills is implicit in the conventional demand-and-supply framework used to explain wage differentials. As discussed earlier, most analysts have concluded that the growth of wage inequality since 1979 must be primarily explained by demand side factors (or non-supply side factors, including institutional shifts) rather than supply side factors (i.e., fewer college graduates). This is why there has been such a focus on trade, industry shifts, and technological change, all factors that could explain shifts in "relative demand." However, it would not make sense to be seeking the source of relative-demand shifts in the 1980s and 1990s if demand trends were essentially the same over the last few decades. Similarly, demand side shifts seem relevant to explaining a wage inequality originating in the 1980s only if there were something new and different about recent demand trends. In fact, if the relative demand for skill grew at the same pace over the last three decades — at a smooth, secular, or historic rate — then the only factors that could be different in the 1980s and 1990s and explain growing wage inequality are those affecting the supply of "skills," a context with no possible special role for trade, technology, or other factors shaping relative demand.

In this light, a technology explanation makes sense only if there is a greater growth in the demand for skills in the 1980s and 1990s than in earlier periods and if these demand side changes can be attributed to technological change. This motivates our efforts to test for an acceleration of technology's impact on the use of more-educated and higher-paid workers.

It is also useful to distinguish between the role of technology in the growth of wage inequality and the issue of "skill complementarity," the concept that there is a positive relationship between capital (e.g., computers) and worker skill. The existence of skill complementarity is one of the main explanations of the growing need for workers with more education and skills: as investment or capital per worker has grown, the need for more skills has grown commensurately. The explanation of growing wage inequality, on the other hand, requires an analysis that separates out the *growth* of the relative supply and demand for education/skill. To show that relative demand for skill is accelerating (as is necessary, as argued above), it is not enough to simply cite the existence of skill complementarities, since such complementarities have long been associated with the need for greater skills and education. That is, technological change has been a force for increasing employers' demand for more-skilled and more-educated workers for a long time. The issue regarding wage inequality is whether technological change has increased demand for skill faster than the supply of skill has been growing.

We do not question that technological change and capital accumulation have been historically associated with the need for greater skills and education. Technology and investment have been major forces driving the long-term growth of demands for skill.

But, is there reason to believe that technology's impact *accelerated* in the 1980s or 1990s? Technological change is inherently difficult to quantify. The analysis in **Table 3.48** examines technology's impact on the utilization of different types of workers, such as high-wage (therefore, presumably high-skill) or college-educated workers. Specifically, Table 3.48 presents quantitative estimates of the impact of technological change on the rate at which there were within-industry shifts toward the use of more-educated workers (i.e., the effect of technology on relative demand within industries in different time periods). These estimates reflect whether there was a faster rate of introduction of new technology (proxied by increased equipment investment, computerization, and research and development) and changes in the degree to which new technology was associated with higher skill requirements (a tighter complementarity of skill and technology). The estimate of technology's impact on utilization, therefore, reflects new investment, R&D innovations, and any associated technical, work organization, or work-process changes.

Table 3.48 presents estimates in four periods, 1963-73, 1973-79, 1979-89, and 1989-94. Estimates of the differences in technology's impact across time periods are also presented. The critical issue to be addressed is whether technology's impact was greater in the 1980s or 1990s than in the 1970s.

Consider, first, technology's impact on the increased utilization of college-educated workers, as shown in the bottom panel. The data show that in the 1970s, 1980s, and 1990s technology was indeed associated with an increased utilization of college-educated workers, as seen by the positive estimates (e.g., technology led to a 0.217 annual change in the male employment share of workers with a college degree in the 1973-79 period). However, there was no sizable (and statistically significant) growth, or acceleration, of technology's impact on

TABLE 3.48 Utilization* of workers by technology's impact on wage and education level, 1963-94

Within-industry change in use of:	Technology's impact on utilization of:	
	Men	Women
Low-wage workers		
1963-73	-.088	-.135
1973-79	-.498***	-.362***
1979-89	-.152	-.176***
1989-94	.237	.221***
Differences		
1970s Less 1960s	-.411***	-.228**
1980s Less 1970s	.346***	.187**
1990s Less 1970s	.735***	.583***
1990s Less 1980s	.389***	.396***
Highest-wage workers		
1963-73	.185	.107
1973-79	.603***	.148***
1979-89	.227***	.061
1989-94	-.187**	-.098***
Differences		
1970s Less 1960s	.418***	.041
1980s Less 1970s	-.376***	-.087
1990s Less 1970s	-.790***	-.246***
1990s Less 1980s	-.414***	-.159***
College-educated workers		
1963-73	-.032	.046
1973-79	.217***	.050
1979-89	.220***	.117***
1989-94	.359***	.181***
Differences		
1970s Less 1960s	.249**	.003
1980s Less 1970s	.004	.067
1990s Less 1970s	.142	.131***
1990s Less 1980s	.138	.064

* Utilization refers to annual increase in the employment share of particular type of worker.
** Statistically significant change at the 10% level.
*** Statistically significant change at the 5% level.

Source: Mishel, Bernstein, and Schmitt (1997).

the utilization of more-educated workers in the 1980s and 1990s relative to the 1970s (e.g., the difference between the 1980s and 1970s was 0.004, a statistically insignificant change). Therefore, although technology may have played an important role in each period, its impact did not grow in such a way as to be able to explain why wage inequality (or education differentials) began to grow after 1979. These estimates do show an acceleration of technology's impact on the use of college-educated men in the 1970s relative to the 1960s, but this hardly corresponds to the onset of information-age technology.

Table 3.48 also examines a broader measure of technology's impact by estimating the effect on the utilization of high-wage workers (earning in the upper 25% of the wage distribution) or low-wage workers (earning in the bottom half of the wage distribution). These estimates are extremely inhospitable to a technology story of wage inequality, since technology is associated with a declining use of high-wage workers both in the 1980s relative to the 1970s and in the 1990s relative to the 1980s (most of the declines being statistically significant). Correspondingly, technology was associated with a declining utilization of low-wage men and women in the 1970s, but less so in the 1980s and 1990s. In fact, these estimates show that technology was less adverse for low-wage workers in the 1980s and 1990s relative to the 1970s. These estimates using the broadest measure of skill (a worker's wage level), therefore, run directly counter to a technology story of an ever-accelerating technology-driven growth in demand for skill.

Information technology workers

There has been much attention paid recently to the assertions of high-technology companies that they are facing a labor shortage of "information technology" workers. This has raised a series of issues such as whether these firms should be able to recruit more information technology workers via immigration or whether these firms need to reform their own human resource systems by raising pay, ending age discrimination, and offering more regular, full-time positions (rather than temporary ones). Such issues are beyond the scope of our inquiry. We do address, however, whether employment and wage trends indicate that there is an information technology worker shortage and, if so, its character. To do so, Tables 3.49 and 3.50 present the employment shares and hourly wages by occupation in the 1989-97 period for two groups of workers, all workers and young college graduates, the latter presumably being the chief beneficiaries of any shortage.

The employment shares presented in **Table 3.49** show a steady rise in rela-

TABLE 3.49 Changes in employment shares by occupation for all workers and young college graduates, 1989-97

Occupation	Shares of employment by occupation									Change
	1989	1990	1991	1992	1993	1994	1995	1996	1997	1989-97
All workers										
Managers	11.9%	11.6%	11.9%	11.9%	12.1%	12.4%	12.9%	13.0%	13.4%	1.5%
Engineers	1.8	1.9	1.9	1.7	1.6	1.8	1.9	1.8	1.9	0.0
Math/computer science	0.8	0.8	0.9	0.9	1.0	1.1	1.0	1.2	1.3	0.5
Natural scientists	0.4	0.4	0.4	0.4	0.5	0.5	0.5	0.5	0.5	0.1
Health professionals	2.4	2.5	2.6	2.8	2.8	2.9	3.0	3.0	3.0	0.5
Other professionals	7.9	8.0	8.2	8.2	8.4	8.3	8.5	8.8	8.6	0.8
Technicians	3.5	3.7	3.7	4.1	3.9	3.6	3.6	3.5	3.7	0.2
Sales	10.5	10.7	10.6	10.6	10.6	10.7	10.9	10.8	11.0	0.4
Other occupations	60.8	60.2	59.8	59.4	59.1	58.6	57.8	57.3	56.8	-4.0
Total	100.0%	100.0%	100.0%	100.0%	100.0%	100.0%	100.0%	100.0%	100.0%	0.0%
*Young college graduates**										
Managers	22.6%	22.6%	21.9%	21.4%	21.2%	21.7%	22.6%	22.8%	23.3%	0.7%
Engineers	6.3	6.1	5.6	5.6	5.1	5.4	5.1	4.9	5.4	-0.9
Math/computer science	2.8	3.0	3.0	3.0	2.8	3.1	3.0	3.5	4.0	1.2
Natural scientists	0.9	0.9	1.0	1.2	1.1	1.5	1.5	1.3	1.3	0.5
Health professionals	5.5	5.2	5.4	5.4	5.7	5.4	5.0	5.1	5.2	-0.4
Other professionals	15.5	15.7	15.8	17.2	18.7	18.2	19.5	20.3	19.7	4.3
Technicians	6.5	6.5	6.6	6.3	6.1	6.1	5.4	5.1	5.1	-1.4
Sales	15.4	15.6	15.2	14.8	14.5	14.1	14.0	13.6	13.8	-1.6
Other occupations	24.6	24.5	25.5	25.1	24.8	24.4	23.7	23.5	22.2	-2.3
Total	100.0%	100.0%	100.0%	100.0%	100.0%	100.0%	100.0%	100.0%	100.0%	0.0%

* College graduates (four-year) with 1-10 years' experience.

Source: Authors' analysis.

tive employment among math and computer science professionals but not among engineers. Among young college graduates there has been a shrinkage of engineering employment but an upward movement of mathematics and computer science employment. Thus, there does seem to be an increased growth in relative demand for some segments of information technology workers (computer science) but not among others. Whatever growth there has been, however, seems to be of very recent vintage, since most of the expansion of employment is in the 1995-97 period. The overall significance of this increased relative demand for computer workers is also unclear, since there is a nearly comparable, or greater, expansion of employment among other professional or white-collar occupations, as there has been for decades. All in all, therefore, nothing spectacular seems to be taking place, although the last few years may anticipate large changes ahead.

Do wage trends show information technology workers having their wages bid up, as one would expect if a shortage exists? **Table 3.50** suggests that wages have risen for computer science professionals but not for engineers, relative to other workers. Nevertheless, the wage improvements have come only in the last year, 1996-97, following six years of wage stagnation, and have been modest (less than 1% annually over the 1989-97 period). This suggests that there has been no long-term growing shortage but perhaps a short-term temporary shortage in a very low unemployment economy.

It is also instructive to note that the workers who should most benefit from an information technology era, the young college graduates working in the computer/mathematics occupation, are only making a few percent more than their counterparts did in 1989.

Executive pay soars

Another cause of greater wage inequality has been the enormous pay increases received by top executives and the spillover effects (the pay of other executives and managers rising in tandem with CEO pay) of these increases. These large pay raises go far beyond those received by other white-collar workers.

The 1980s and 1990s have been prosperous times for top U.S. executives. **Table 3.51** presents the trends in CEO pay over the 1989-97 period. CEO wages (cash payments including bonuses) grew 44.6% from 1989 to 1997, far exceeding the growth in any other occupation. These CEO wages grew 36.6% just in the recovery years from 1992 to 1997.

Nevertheless, the growth in CEO pay has been even larger when one includes all of the components of direct compensation: salaries, bonuses, incentive awards, stock options exercised, stock granted, and so on. The full compen-

TABLE 3.50 Hourly wages by occupation for all workers and young college graduates, 1989-97

Selected occupation	Hourly wage ($1997)*									Change
	1989	1990	1991	1992	1993	1994	1995	1996	1997	1989-97
All workers										
Managers	$19.07	$19.09	$19.09	$19.09	$18.72	$18.79	$18.84	$18.50	$18.80	-1.4%
Engineers, architects, surveyors	23.87	24.18	23.83	23.77	23.95	23.31	22.88	23.10	23.53	-1.4
Math/computer science	21.96	22.68	22.31	22.33	22.62	21.72	22.05	22.01	23.01	4.8
Natural scientists	21.94	21.20	20.24	20.44	21.23	20.06	20.08	20.44	21.41	-2.4
Sales	12.12	12.12	12.09	11.93	12.03	12.12	11.90	11.98	12.17	0.5
Blue collar	12.11	11.92	11.74	11.63	11.51	11.52	11.36	11.33	11.43	-5.6
All	$13.13	$13.09	$13.05	$13.00	$13.02	$13.14	$13.03	$12.98	$13.21	0.6
Young college graduates*										
Managers	$17.07	$16.90	$16.70	$17.03	$16.74	$16.47	$15.91	$16.10	$16.39	-3.9%
Engineers, architects, surveyors	20.90	21.04	21.02	20.39	20.42	19.51	18.90	18.38	18.65	-10.8
Math/computer science	19.22	20.34	19.56	20.97	19.15	19.28	20.13	19.04	20.19	5.1
Natural scientists	16.55	16.09	16.09	15.01	14.91	14.79	15.01	14.44	15.24	-7.9
Sales	16.76	15.83	15.21	15.33	15.26	15.18	15.14	14.66	15.37	-8.3
Blue collar	13.57	13.08	12.38	12.66	12.08	11.87	12.17	12.42	12.16	-10.4
All	$15.48	$15.42	$15.00	$14.97	$14.95	$14.71	$14.51	$14.43	$14.78	-4.5

*   Wages and salaries per hour worked.

**   Clerical, service, technician, farm, and some professional occupations not shown.

***   College graduates (four-year) with 1-10 years' experience.

Source: Authors' analysis.

TABLE 3.51 Executive pay growth, 1989-97 (1997 dollars)

Pay category and percentile	($000)							Change 1992-97 ($000)	Change 1992-97 %	Change 1989-97 %
	1989	1992	1993	1994	1995	1996	1997			
*Realized direct compensation**										
25th percentile	n.a.	$1,099	$1,175	$1,159	$1,279	$1,423	$1,636	$537	48.8%	n.a.
Median	n.a.	1,773	1,973	1,928	2,098	2,431	3,093	1,320	74.4	n.a.
75th percentile	n.a.	3,382	3,133	3,198	3,764	4,728	5,967	2,585	76.5	n.a.
Average	$1,783	2,085	2,094	2,095	2,380	2,860	3,565	1,481	71.0	100.0%
*Cash compensation*** Index, 1989=100										
Median	100.0	105.9	111.2	120.8	129.6	132.5	144.6		36.6%	44.6%

* Sum of salary, bonus, gains from options exercised, value of restricted stock at grant, and other long-term incentive award payments.
** Salary and cash bonuses.

Source: Authors' analysis of *Wall Street Journal*/Mercer Survey.

sation of CEOs actually doubled over the 1989-97 period, growing 71% in the 1992-97 recovery. Even lesser-paid CEOs at the 25th percentile saw a 48.8% compensation growth in the recovery.

The increased divergence between the growth of CEO pay and an average worker's pay is captured in the growth of the ratio of CEO to worker pay, shown in **Figure 3P**. In 1978, U.S. CEOs in major companies earned 28.5 times more than an average worker; this ratio grew to 56.1 in 1989 and to 115.7 by 1995. This contrasts even more sharply with the 20.3 ratio prevailing in 1965. In other words, in 1997, a CEO worked half a week to earn what an average worker earned in 52 weeks. In 1965, in contrast, it took a CEO two and a half weeks to earn a worker's annual pay.

Not only are U.S. executives paid far better than U.S. workers, they also earn substantially more than CEOs in other advanced countries. **Table 3.52** presents CEO pay in 12 other countries in 1997 (the U.S. data differ from the numbers in Table 3.51 and Figure 3P because the survey covers a different sample of firms) and an index that sets U.S. compensation equal to 100 (any index value less than 100 implies that that country's CEOs earn less than U.S. CEOs). The index shows that U.S. CEOs earn double the average of the 12 other advanced countries for which there are comparable data. In fact, there is no country listed whose CEOs are paid even as much as 60% that of U.S. CEOs. This interna-

FIGURE 3P Ratio of CEO to average worker pay, 1965-97

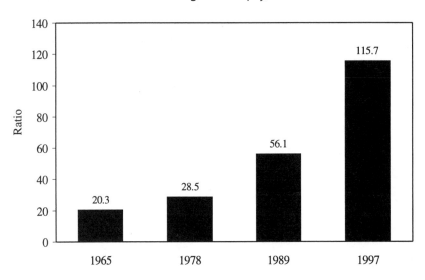

Source: Authors' analysis.

tional pattern does not hold true for the pay of manufacturing workers (Table 3.52). Workers in other advanced countries earn, on average, more than U.S. workers, with workers in nine of the 12 other countries earning at least 90% of what U.S. workers earn. Not surprisingly, the ratio of CEO to worker pay was far larger in the United States in 1997 than in other countries, 24.0 versus 13.8. Last, Table 3.52 shows that CEO pay in other countries has tended to grow rapidly over the 1988-97 period.

What does the future hold?

This section examines future trends in wages and job quality by analyzing the projected trends of the key forces that will shape the wage structure — demand (skill requirements), labor supply factors (education, age, immigration), and various institutional factors. We do not attempt to predict wages in the future, but our assessment of wage trends over the current business cycle and the forces at work over the next decade lead us to believe that wage inequality will continue to grow, although perhaps not as quickly as it has over the last 20 years. Unless there is a sizable improvement in productivity growth, as some optimists

TABLE 3.52 CEO pay in advanced countries, 1988-97

Country	CEO compensation ($000) 1988	1997	Percent change 1988-97	Ratio of CEO to worker pay, 1997	U.S. pay relative to foreign pay, 1997, U.S. = 100 CEO	Worker
Australia	$154.7	$476.7	208.2%	19.0	52.9	79.9
Belgium	328.3	470.7	43.4	13.0	52.2	134.3
Canada	362.2	440.9	21.7	13.0	48.9	91.7
France	346.0	523.5	51.3	15.0	58.1	99.6
Germany	352.7	423.9	20.2	11.0	47.0	159.7
Italy	293.1	450.3	53.7	16.0	50.0	94.5
Japan	430.1	397.7	-7.5	10.0	44.1	125.3
Netherlands	339.2	442.9	30.6	14.0	49.1	122.3
Spain	301.2	333.6	10.7	15.0	37.0	67.0
Sweden	200.8	340.7	69.7	11.0	37.8	110.0
Switzerland	436.9	465.2	6.5	10.0	51.6	145.2
United Kingdom	388.0	489.7	26.2	18.0	54.3	79.6
United States	689.2	901.2	30.8	24.0	100.0	100.0
Non-U.S. Average	$327.8	$438.0	33.6%	13.8	48.6	109.1

Source: Authors' analysis of Towers Perrin (1988 and 1997).

predict, it is reasonable to expect that real wages for typical male and female workers will continue to stagnate or decline, as they have, for most men and many women in the 1990s.

The first dimension of change we consider are shifts in demand for skills. The greater the increase in employer demand for workers with more skill and education, the greater is the economy's ability to shift people into better-paying jobs (although there is not necessarily a one-to-one relationship between skill and pay).

Some analyses in the late 1980s contended that there would be an explosive growth in the demand for skill in the 1990s. In fact, an analysis of recent trends and future projections suggests that the jobs of the future will not be markedly different from the jobs available today. Future jobs will have somewhat greater educational and skill requirements, primarily the need for basic literacy and numeracy, but the job structure will not shift markedly toward higher-paying jobs. Most important, the skill and education requirements of jobs are expected to grow more slowly than they did in the 1970s, 1980s, and early 1990s. Despite the widely held assumption that higher-paying white-collar jobs are the wave of the future, there is little evidence that the deterioration of job quality and wages that took place in the 1980s and 1990s will be reversed in the late 1990s, unless current trends change dramatically.

This view of future jobs is based on an analysis of labor market trends anticipated by the Bureau of Labor Statistics in its employment projections to the year 2006. The data in **Table 3.53** allow us to assess the effect of occupational upgrading (e.g., the rising importance of white-collar professional/technical jobs) on education requirements. Specifically, the data show the effect of changes in the distribution of employment among occupations on the education levels required and on the pay received for jobs. The analysis examines trends over the last three decades to provide a point of comparison.

The analysis shows that job education requirements have been increasing since 1973 and are projected to increase over the late 1990s and into the next century. Rather than the skills explosion projected by some analysts, however, future growth in education requirements will be historically modest. For instance, the new distribution of jobs across occupations in 2006 will require a worker's average years of schooling to grow at a 0.6% rate over the 1996-2006 period, slower than in any of the three periods since 1973. Thus, occupation shifts are not expected to generate a large growth in the demand for education, at least by historical standards. This can also be seen in the analysis of the effects of occupation shifts on the need for workers at various education levels. For instance, projected changes in the occupational composition of employment imply an extra growth of 0.62% of the workforce needing a college degree every 10 years, a growth less than half of that generated by the actual employment shifts in the 1970s, 1980s, or 1990s. This analysis corroborates one of our conclusions drawn from the recent declines in the pay of white-collar and college-educated workers and the flattening of education premiums among men—the expansion of demand for "more-skilled" and "more-educated" workers is slowing down. The ultimate conclusion to be drawn from these analyses is that demand shifts in the future will not be a powerful force for improving overall job quality and pay, absent some change in government policies and employer strategies.

Table 3.54 presents data on future labor supply trends that affect the wage structure. One major factor is how fast the supply of more-educated workers, or college graduates, will expand. If the supply outpaces the demand for college graduates, then the college premium will fall, creating a tendency toward less wage inequality. The data in Table 3.54 show that college enrollment rates are expected to rise by 2008, but only among women and only slightly. This suggests that the supply of college-educated workers may expand somewhat, although maybe not as fast as in the last few decades.

TABLE 3.53 Demand shifts: changes in pay
and education requirements, 1973-2006*

Job characteristic	1973-79	1979-89	1989-97	BLS projections 1996-2006
Pay	Annual growth			
Hourly compensation	1.6%	2.3%	1.7%	0.6%
Hourly wages	2.0	2.9	2.1	0.8
Education requirements				
Years of schooling	0.9%	1.4%	0.9%	0.4%
Shares of employment Requiring:	Percentage-point change per decade			
Less than high school	-1.57	-1.33	-0.66	-0.38
High school**	-1.03	-1.51	-1.67	-0.94
Associate college	0.33	0.26	0.10	0.06
College (4-year)	1.21	1.69	1.27	0.62
Advanced degree	0.73	0.99	0.96	0.54

* Based on a shift-share analysis using the shares of employment by occupation and the 1995 education distributions of 13 occupation groups and their relative pay structure over the 1979-93 period.
** Includes those with "some college" but no degree beyond high school.

Source: Authors' update of Mishel and Teixeira (1991).

What matters, however, is not how many attend college but how many people
earn degrees. As Table 3.54 shows, the number of bachelor's degrees awarded
annually is not expected to rise among men but to increase by 16.6%, or 105,000,
among women. This expected growth in the numbers completing college, however, is less than the expected growth rate of the labor force, as seen in the trend
of degrees awarded as a share of employment. For instance, nearly 6.5 million
more men will be employed in 2008 but only 5,000 more bachelor's degrees
will be awarded to men. The 16.6% expected growth among women is comparable to the 16.8% expected growth in women's employment. Thus, new entrants will not be driving up the relative supply of "educated workers." In fact, as
Table 3.54 and **Figure 3Q** show, the amount of new college degrees relative to
the size of adult employment is expected to be stable or falling over the 1996-
2008 period (down for men, stable for women). A surge in the supply of college
graduates is not likely to be a strong force for restoring a lesser college wage
premium.

TABLE 3.54 Future labor supply trends

Characteristic	1979	1989	1995	2008
College education				
College full-time enrollment rate				
Men	n.a.	n.a.	22.3%	22.1%
Women	n.a.	n.a.	25.7	28.6
College-age population (000)				
18-24 years	30,048	27,378	25,283	29,368
Bachelor's degrees awarded (000)				
Men	477	483	526	530
Women	444	535	634	739
Degrees awarded as share of employment				
Men	0.90%	0.79%	0.82%	0.75%
Women	1.08	1.01	1.17	1.14

Immigrant share of labor force	1979	1988	2005
Men	7.0%	9.9%	13.3-14.8%
Women	6.8	8.6	10.9-13.4

	1980	1990	1994	2006
Labor force age (median)	34.6	36.6	37.6	40.6

Source: Authors' analysis.

Immigration trends imply a further growth of immigrants as a share of the labor force. If future immigrants are proportionately less educated, in accordance with recent trends, then future immigration will also serve to depress low-end wages and be a force for a further widening of wage inequality.

The workforce is expected to have a significantly higher age in 2005 than in recent years. The move by the youngest of the baby boomers into their forties and fifties should put upward pressure on average wages (wage trajectories are relatively rapid for these age groups) and may serve to narrow the wage gap between younger and older workers. How powerful a force this will be is uncertain. Note that the age of the workforce grew considerably over the 1980-90

FIGURE 3Q Bachelor's degrees as share of employment, 1961-2008*

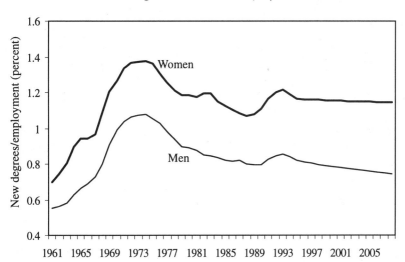

* 1996-2008 projected.

Source: Authors' analysis.

period (from 34.6 to 36.6 years), when experience differentials actually widened.

Other trends will also affect the wage structure. The continued expansion of international trade's role in the economy and the continued shrinkage of employment in goods production will act to depress wages for the non-college-educated workforce, as they have in recent years. If union coverage rates stabilize and grow (in response to a renewed union effort at organizing), some of the pressure for greater inequality may lessen or reverse itself. Likewise, if the minimum wage rises relative to inflation in the next few years (a further increase has been proposed in Congress as of this writing), then there will be less pressure for wage inequality at the bottom to grow, especially among women. This mix of trends suggests some continuation of the growth of wage inequality, but perhaps not as quickly as in the recent past.

The most optimistic trend is the possibility of higher productivity growth in the future. To the extent that higher productivity leads to higher average wage growth (they are closely related but, as we have shown, less so than in the past), wages can be expected to grow more for every type of worker. Put another way, a productivity-related acceleration of average wage growth can partially offset any further growth of wage inequality. However, it is uncertain whether a faster pace of productivity can be counted on in the future, as discussed in the Introduction.

To conclude, the forces that drove wage inequality in the past can be expected to have a similar, although possibly lesser, effect in the future. And if productivity growth persists in its recent (1980s and 1990s) trajectory, then wages over the long term will continue to deteriorate for most men, rise modestly only among high-wage women, and stagnate for women at the median. However, if low unemployment persists (i.e., the business cycle is repealed) and/or productivity growth accelerates, then future wage trends can continue in the positive vein of the last few years.

Conclusion

There have been dramatic changes in the wage structure over the last 18 years. The real hourly wages of most workers have fallen, and the group experiencing the greatest wage decline has been non-college-educated workers, especially new entrants to the labor force. Given that three-fourths of the workforce has not earned a four-year college degree, the continuing deterioration of the wages of high school graduates (whose wages fell somewhat less than those of high school dropouts but somewhat more than those of workers with some college) means that the vast majority of men and many women are working at far lower wages than their counterparts did a generation earlier. More recently (i.e., since the mid-1980s), wages have been falling or stagnant among college graduates and white-collar workers, especially men. New college graduates earn less than their counterparts did in the late 1980s.

The wage trends of the 1989-97 period mirror those of the 1980s in that wage inequality at the top of the wage scale has continued to grow and median male wages have continued their 1% annual decline (except the last few years). The difference between the 1980s and 1990s is that there is a broader decline of wages among women, including a decline at the median, and there has been no growth and even a decline in the last few years in inequality at the bottom. As discussed in the Introduction, low and falling unemployment coupled with a higher minimum wage and an unexpected slowdown in inflation have combined to generate broad-based real wage gains since 1996. These increases may prove short-lived and evaporate as unemployment rises in the next recession.

CHAPTER 4

Jobs: falling unemployment, but increasing insecurity

UNEMPLOYMENT IN MID-1998 WAS AT ITS LOWEST LEVEL SINCE THE 1960s. AS ARGUED IN the Introduction and Chapter 3, the relatively low unemployment rates of 1996-98 have been a major reason for the improved wage performance during the late-1990s expansion. Nevertheless, job problems persist. The unemployment rate for black workers in 1997 stood at 10.0%, a level that we would associate with a deep recession if it applied to the overall workforce. Broader measures of "underemployment" suggest that close to 9.0% of potential workers would like a job but can't find one or can't find as many hours of work as they would like.

In what historians may view as one of the most emblematic features of the 1990s economy, the underlying level of job security appears to have been falling throughout much of the decade, despite consistent improvements in the unemployment rate. Between the 1980s and the 1990s, the number of years that the typical worker has been at his or her current job has fallen. So has the share of workers who have been on their current job for at least 10 years. Workers appear less and less likely to be able to count on the long-term employment attachments that in the past provided opportunities for steady wage growth, fringe benefits, and long-term job security. Involuntary job loss (layoffs, "downsizing," and other job displacements not for cause) actually *increased* between the recession of 1992 and the recovery through 1995. These objective measures of job stability have contributed to workers' subjective perceptions that jobs are less secure now than in the past. Survey data show workers feeling less optimistic that their jobs will last and more pessimistic about their employment prospects if they lose their jobs.

Given that the unemployment rate is relatively low, we should probably look elsewhere for the source of workers' insecurity. One of the prime suspects is the increasingly "contingent" nature of much of the work available in the 1990s. Almost 30% of workers in 1997 were employed in situations that were *not* regular full-time jobs. This "nonstandard" work ranged from independent contracting and other self-employment arrangements to work in temporary agencies or as day labor. While many of these workers appreciate the flexibility of their current arrangements, nonstandard workers generally earn less than workers with comparable skills and backgrounds who work in regular full-time jobs. Nonstandard workers are also far less likely than regular full-time workers to have health or pension benefits.

This chapter first examines developments in unemployment and underemployment, relating changes in the entire postwar period to developments in several dimensions of job creation. Next, we look at a variety of objective and subjective evidence on job security. Finally, we analyze the growth and current state of nonstandard work arrangements.

Unemployment and underemployment

Table 4.1 gives a broad overview of unemployment rates by sex and race during the various peak years in the business cycles since World War II and for 1997, the most recent year for which data are available. The economy is at its strongest in peak years, and therefore unemployment is at its lowest. In 1989, the most recent cyclical peak year, unemployment in every category was less than or roughly equal to that in 1979, the prior cyclical peak. Relative to 1973 and earlier peak years, however, 1989 unemployment rates were generally above average. The early-1990s recession caused unemployment to rise to as high as 7.7% in mid-1992 (not shown). By mid-1998 unemployment was 4.3%, well below the level at cyclical peaks in the 1970s and 1980s, though still above rates achieved in the earlier postwar period.

Workers' experiences with unemployment differ markedly by race (or ethnicity) and sex. Unemployment rates for black workers, for example, are consistently more than double the rates for white workers. This is true even with the relatively bright unemployment picture in 1997: the black unemployment rate was 10.0%, compared to a 4.2% rate for whites. Unemployment rates for Hispanic workers tend to lie between those for whites and blacks, but even in 1997 the Hispanic unemployment rate of 7.7% was at a level that the overall unemployment rate reaches only during economic recessions. During the period 1947-79, women workers generally had an unemployment rate substantially higher than the rate for males. Since 1979, however, women have seen their unemployment rate converge on the male rate.

TABLE 4.1 Unemployment rates, 1947-97

	Total	Male	Female	White	Black	Hispanic*
1947	3.9%	4.0%	3.7%	n.a.	n.a.	n.a.
1967	3.8	3.1	5.2	3.4%	n.a.	n.a.
1973	4.9	4.2	6.0	4.3	9.4%	7.7%
1979	5.8	5.1	6.8	5.1	12.3	8.3
1989	5.3	5.2	5.4	4.5	11.4	8.0
1997**	4.9	4.9	5.0	4.2	10.0	7.7
Annual averages						
1947-67	4.7%	4.5%	5.0%	n.a.	n.a.	n.a.
1967-73	4.6	4.0	5.7	4.1%	n.a.	n.a.
1973-79	6.5	5.8	7.5	5.8	12.5%	9.5%
1979-89	7.1	7.0	7.3	6.2	14.7	10.3
1989-97**	6.0	6.1	5.8	5.2	11.7	9.4

* Hispanic category includes blacks and whites.
** Changes to the Current Population Survey in 1990, 1994, and 1997 mean that data are not strictly comparable with earlier years.

Source: Authors' analysis of BLS data. For detailed explanation on table sources, see Table Notes.

Table 4.2 presents data on "underemployment," a broader measure of the lack of employment success in the labor market. This alternative measure includes unemployed workers as well as: (1) those working part time but who want to work full time ("involuntary" part-timers); (2) those who want to work but have been discouraged from searching by their lack of success ("discouraged" workers); and (3) others who are neither working nor seeking work at the moment but who indicate that they want and are available to work and have looked for a job in the last 12 months. (The second and third categories together are described as "marginally attached" workers.) At 8.9%, the 1997 underemployment rate (see Table 4.2 and **Figure 4A**) was substantially higher than the 4.9% unemployment rate, primarily because of the more than 4 million involuntary part-time workers. Discouraged and other marginally attached workers added another 1.4 million to the number underemployed.

Unemployment and the earnings distribution
Any slowing of the economy, which inevitably brings a rise in unemployment, will disproportionately affect the bottom 60% of families. **Table 4.3** shows the

TABLE 4.2 Underemployment, 1997

Category	Thousands
Civilian labor force	136,297
Unemployed	6,739
Discouraged*	343
Other marginally attached*	1,073
Involuntary part time	4,068
Total underemployed	12,223
Underemployment rate**	8.9%
Unemployment rate	4.9%

*   Marginally attached workers are persons who currently are neither working nor looking for work, but who indicate that they want and are available for a job and have looked for work in the last 12 months. Discouraged workers are the subset of the marginally attached who have given a job-market-related reason for not currently looking for a job.

**   Total underemployed workers divided by the sum of the labor force plus discouraged and other marginally attached workers.

Source: Authors' analysis of BLS data.

effect of a 1% increase in unemployment on the number of weeks unemployed and employed in a year and on the annual earnings for families in each income group (estimated over the 1967-91 period). The last column shows the effect of a 1% rise in the unemployment rate on the "average" family; among all persons, an extra 0.46 weeks of unemployment means 0.62 fewer weeks of work and $457 (1991 dollars), or 1.7%, less in annual earnings. (Weeks worked in a year falls by a greater amount than weeks spent unemployed as a consequence of people withdrawing from the labor force.)

The disparate impact of unemployment among different income groups is most apparent for weeks unemployed among household heads: an overall 1% increase in unemployment leads to a half a week (0.49) more unemployment among household heads in the lowest-income group, but it barely affects households in the highest fifth (0.06 weeks per year).

The total impact of unemployment on families depends not just on the effect on the head of household but also on the effect on other earners in the

FIGURE 4A Underemployment, 1997

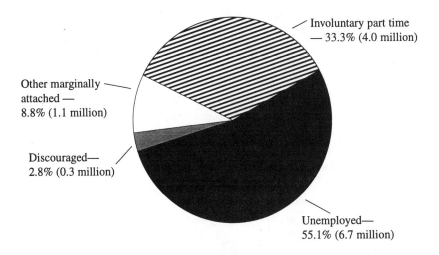

Source: Authors' analysis.

TABLE 4.3 Effect of 1% higher unemployment rate on weeks unemployed and employed and on annual earnings, 1967-91

	Lowest fifth	Second fifth	Middle fifth	Fourth fifth	Highest fifth	All
Weeks unemployed						
Household head	0.49	0.33	0.23	0.15	0.06	0.25
Other adults	0.13	0.16	0.22	0.27	0.25	0.21
All persons	0.63	0.50	0.45	0.42	0.31	0.46
Weeks employed						
All persons	-0.51	-0.89	-0.61	-0.57	-0.46	-0.62
Annual earnings ($1991)						
Household head	-$75	-$334	-$292	-$278	-$435	-$288
Other adults	-5	-29	-89	-232	-488	-169
All persons	-80	-362	-381	-511	-924	-457
Annual earnings (%)						
All persons	-3.7%	-3.7%	-1.8%	-1.4%	-1.4%	-1.7%

Source: Blank and Card (1993).

family. Since low-income households tend to have fewer earners, the impact of rising unemployment on "other adult workers" is not as great as it is for upper-income groups, where two-earner families are more prevalent. Thus, the effect of higher unemployment on "all persons" is not as unequal as for heads of households. Nevertheless, unemployment more adversely affects middle- and low-income families relative to the best-off families.

Finally, Table 4.3 shows the earnings lost to each income group as unemployment grows. Although better-off families lose more money than middle- or lower-income families, on a percentage basis the reduction in earnings is disproportionately greater in lower-income families.

Job growth slows since the 1970s

Table 4.4 looks at employment growth over the last three business cycles (1973-79, 1979-89, and the period since 1989) relative to the earlier postwar period. The table presents four measures of employment growth. The first two examine job creation — nonfarm payroll employment (from a national survey of business establishments) and civilian employment (from a national survey of households). The second two indicators track the total "volume" of work — measured as the total number of hours worked in the economy in a year and the total number of full-time equivalent jobs (which combines part-time and full-time according to practices in each industry).

The 1990s business cycle differs in important ways from the earlier postwar period. Job creation rates, whether measured using nonfarm payrolls or counts of civilian employment based on household surveys, have been slower in the 1989-97 period than during any earlier, comparable period in the data presented here. Nonfarm payrolls grew at a 1.6% annual rate between 1989 and 1997, just below the annual rate for 1979-89 but well below the rates for 1967-73 and 1973-79 (both 2.6% per year). Civilian employment grew only 1.2% per year in the 1990s, just two-thirds the rate for 1979-89 and only about half the rates achieved in 1967-73 (2.3%) and 1973-79 (2.5%).

Despite these lower job creation rates in the 1990s, the growth in the "volume" (total hours) of work has been almost as rapid in the current business cycle as it was during the 1960s, 1970s, and 1980s. The average growth in annual hours worked was 1.6% per year in the period 1989-96, almost identical to the rates in the three earlier business cycles reported here. Between 1989 and 1996, full-time-equivalent employment grew 1.8% per year, close to its recent historical rates of 1.7% for 1979-89, 2.4% for 1973-79, and 1.9% for 1967-73. Given the deceleration in job creation rates, the relatively constant growth rate in total hours worked implies that, on average, Americans are working more hours per year. This is consistent with our finding in Chapter 1 that families' total hours

TABLE 4.4 Employment growth, 1947-97 (annual percentage rates of growth)

	Measures of employment			Working-age population	Labor-force participation rate*
	Nonfarm payroll	Civilian employment	Hours of work	Full-time equivalent employment		
1947-67	2.0%	1.3%	n.a.	n.a.	1.2%	0.07%
1967-73	2.6	2.3	1.6%	1.9%	2.1	0.20
1973-79	2.6	2.5	1.8	2.4	1.9	0.48
1979-89	1.8	1.7	1.6	1.7	1.2	0.28
1989-97**	1.6	1.2	1.6	1.8	1.1	0.07

* Average annual percentage-point change.
** Figures for hours of work and full-time equivalent employment cover 1989-96.

Source: Authors' analysis of BLS and NIPA data.

worked have been rising in the 1980s and 1990s, and our finding in Chapter 3 that annual hours per worker have been growing. In the earlier postwar period, American workers and their families appear to have taken some of the benefits of higher productivity growth in the form of more hours of leisure. Slower growth and rising inequality since the mid-1970s, however, seem to have pushed more workers to work longer hours.

The data on decelerating job growth rates in the 1990s raise an important question: how can unemployment rates be falling below those of the 1970s and 1980s if job creation rates in the 1990s are below those achieved in the earlier two decades? The last two columns of Table 4.4 provide the answer. Slower job creation rates can still produce lower unemployment rates because the portion of the population seeking employment is growing much more slowly than before. The first reason is that, in the 1990s, the working-age population (see the next-to-last column) is growing at only about half the rate of the 1960s and 1970s. The two principal determinants of the working-age population are native population growth and immigration. The current generation entering the labor force is smaller in numbers than the baby boomers that preceded them. While immigration rates grew in the 1980s and again in the 1990s, they were not sufficient to offset a deceleration in the growth of the native working-age population.

The second factor affecting the supply of available workers is the slow-down in the rate at which women join the paid labor force. The last column of Table 4.4 shows the change in the overall labor force participation rate (the share of the population that is in work or seeking work) over the postwar period. Since the labor force participation rate for men was falling over much of this period (in part because of increased schooling and early retirement), the strong rise in the labor force participation rate in the 1960s, 1970s, and 1980s reflects the large increase in women's work outside the home. The U.S. economy had to produce many more jobs in the 1960s, 1970s, and 1980s to accommodate the large influx of women. With much slower rates of growth in labor force participation, the U.S. economy can achieve lower unemployment rates in the 1990s despite the deceleration in job creation rates.

The evidence on the number of jobs created in the 1980s and 1990s, however, tells us nothing about the changing characteristics of new and existing jobs. In Chapter 3, we saw that the hourly wages for most men and many women have been declining over most of the last two decades. In the remainder of this chapter, we look at other aspects of job quality: job stability and security, "nonstandard" or "contingent" work arrangements, and multiple job holding.

Job stability and job security

The widespread anxiety expressed about living standards has often been linked to the feeling that job security and long-term employment prospects have declined considerably in the 1980s and 1990s. In this section, we examine the available data on job stability and job security. First, we look at data from the 1970s and 1980s on changes in male workers' attachment to their jobs. In many respects this first set of data is ideal because it tracks the employment and earnings of sets of the same workers over the two decades, allowing us to measure changes in job stability as well as the earnings costs associated with diminished long-term attachments. Unfortunately, no comparable data cover women's job stability over the same period, and more recent data for men are not yet available. We, therefore, next turn to a broader set of measures of job stability. These include data on the duration of a typical job, the share of workers in "long-term jobs," the tendency of workers to stay in a particular job once they have established a relationship with an employer, the rate of involuntary job loss (not for cause), and workers' perceptions of job security. Each measure has its problems, but, taken together, they paint a comprehensive picture of the changing nature of job stability and security over the last two decades.

Throughout the review of these data, we should keep in mind the distinction between *job stability* — what economists Daniel Aaronson and Daniel Sullivan have called "the tendency of workers and employers to form long-term bonds" — and *job security* — "workers' ability to remain in an employment relationship for as long as their job performance is satisfactory." From a social perspective, our primary concern should be with job security. We would not be worried, for example, if job stability had declined primarily because workers found that they could improve wages, benefits, and working conditions by frequently changing jobs.

Unfortunately, much of the available evidence — the number of job changes in a period of time, the duration of the typical job, and the share of workers in long-term jobs — deals more directly with job stability than job security. The data on job stability, however, are still potentially instructive. Given the well-documented tendency of wages to rise with a worker's tenure (the time spent with a particular employer), and given the apparently widespread anxiety over the perceived decline in long-term jobs, any evidence of declining job stability would tend to support the view that job security is falling. Moreover, in some cases, we can link declining job stability with falling earnings for affected groups. While workers could be trading their old, better-paying jobs for new, lower-paying jobs that these workers prefer for other reasons, we believe that these kinds of job changes are the exception, not the rule. We, therefore, feel comfortable interpreting declining job stability in the presence of falling earnings as evidence of diminished job security. Finally, we note that job stability need not fall for job security to decline. When job insecurity rises, workers may become less likely to quit their current jobs to look for new ones or to leave their current jobs for new ones. This reluctance to change would contribute to rising job stability even as job security was falling.

Declining job stability

Table 4.5 reports the results of an analysis of employment stability for a large group of men whose job situations were tracked yearly over the 1970s and 1980s. (Women were also interviewed, but the sample was too small to produce reliable estimates.) In each year, the survey noted the occupation, industry, and specific employer of each member of the sample. At the end of the two decades, the men were sorted into groups according to "strong," "medium," or "weak" attachment to their occupation, industry, and employer in each of the two decades. In this study, workers with "strong" occupation and industry stability were in the same broad occupation or industry category in eight or more years out of 10. Those with "strong employer attachment" had at most one year in 10 in which their employer changed. Workers with "medium" occupation and industry stability were in the same broad category in five to seven years out of 10. Those with "medium employer attachment" changed employer in only two to three years of the 10-year period. Workers with "weak" occupation and industry stability were in the same category for fewer than

TABLE 4.5 Employment stability for men, 1970s versus 1980s

	Percent of all workers		Percentage-point change
	1970s	1980s	
Occupational attachment			
Strong	68%	68%	0
Medium	28	27	-1
Weak	4	5	1
Industry attachment			
Strong	63%	59%	-4
Medium	29	31	2
Weak	8	10	2
Employer attachment			
Strong	67%	52%	-15
Medium	21	24	3
Weak	12	24	12

Source: Authors' analysis of Rose (1995).

five years. Those with "weak employer attachment" had four or more employers in the decade.

The last column of Table 4.5 shows the change in job stability between the 1970s and 1980s. Occupational stability changed little: the share of workers with strong attachment to their occupations was roughly constant across the two decades. Industry attachment changed slightly more. Those with strong ties fell by 4 percentage points, with increases of 2 percentage points for both those with medium and weak stability. Employer stability, however, appears to have eroded significantly between the 1970s and the 1980s. The share of workers with the same employer for nine years in each decade fell 15 percentage points, from 67% to 52%. At the same time, workers with weak ties to their employers increased by 12 percentage points.

As job instability increased, so too did its costs to workers. **Table 4.6** examines earnings growth by workers' level of job stability in both of the decades. During the 1970s, those with strong occupation, industry, and employer stability experienced, on average, about a 25% increase in their inflation-adjusted earnings. Over the same period, those with weak occupation and employer stability saw small declines in their real earnings, while those with weak industry ties managed a small increase. In the 1980s, strong job stability yielded even

TABLE 4.6 Employment stability and earnings for men,
1970s versus 1980s (1997 dollars)

	1970s			1980s		
	Start*	End*	Change	Start*	End*	Change
Occupational attachment						
Strong	$42,066	$51,783	23.1%	$44,042	$56,280	27.8%
Medium	34,370	39,759	15.7	33,625	33,267	-1.1
Weak	34,545	34,106	-1.3	28,961	22,538	-22.2
Industry attachment						
Strong	$40,474	$50,682	25.2%	$42,687	$55,362	29.7%
Medium	39,414	44,809	13.7	39,413	42,134	6.9
Weak	33,876	35,458	4.7	31,736	28,832	-9.1
Employer attachment						
Strong	$42,316	$52,688	24.5%	$44,431	$57,478	29.4%
Medium	37,221	43,214	16.1	40,200	49,311	22.7
Weak	28,732	27,745	-3.4	32,639	28,320	-13.2

*The starting and ending periods are three-year averages: for the 1970s, of 1967-69 and 1977-79; for the 1980s, of 1977-79 and 1987-89.

Source: Authors' analysis of Rose (1995).

larger increases in average real earnings than in the 1970s, but weak stability had far worse consequences than in the earlier period. Workers with weak industry ties suffered an average 9.1% decline in real earnings; weak employer stability was associated with an average earnings drop of 13.2% (recall from the previous table that the share of workers with weak employer stability doubled between the 1970s and 1980s); and weak occupational stability led to an average 22.2% fall in annual earnings over the decade.

As mentioned above, no comparable data exist for women over the same period, and comparable data for men in the 1990s are still not yet available. For a more comprehensive and more up-to-date picture of job stability, therefore, we now turn to a broader set of measures. Unlike the data in Table 4.6, which followed the same workers over time, the data we now present are "snapshots" of the employment circumstances of different workers at different points in time.

Table 4.7 and **Figure 4B** provide the most basic information on job sta-

TABLE 4.7 Median job tenure by age, 1963-96

					Change	
Group	1963	1981	1987	1996	1963-96	1987-96
Age 25-34						
All	3.0	3.1	2.9	2.8	-0.2	-0.1
Men	3.5	3.1	3.1	3.0	-0.5	-0.1
Women	2.0	3.0	2.6	2.7	0.7	0.1
Age 35-44						
All	6.0	5.1	5.5	5.3	-0.7	-0.2
Men	7.6	7.1	7.0	6.1	-1.5	-0.9
Women	3.6	4.1	4.4	4.8	1.2	0.4
Age 45-54						
All	9.0	9.1	8.8	8.3	-0.7	-0.5
Men	11.4	11.1	11.8	10.1	-1.3	-1.7
Women	6.1	6.1	6.8	7.0	0.9	0.2

Source: Aaronson and Sullivan (1998).

bility — the median number of years of tenure for men and women from the early 1960s through 1996 (tenure data are not available for our standard years, so we use those closest to them). Since the tenure distribution is sensitive to the age distribution in the population (young workers can't have long job tenure no matter how stable underlying employment relationships are at a particular time), we present the data separately for 25-34-year-olds, 35-44-year-olds, and 45-54-year-olds. Several features of the tenure distribution stand out. First, tenure for men in all age groups fell between 1963 and 1996, with much of the decline between 1987 and 1996. Declines in male tenure were largest for the middle and older age groups. For 35-44-year-old men, median tenure dropped 1.5 years, from 7.6 years in 1963 to 6.1 years in 1996; most of the decline (nine-tenths of a year) occurred between 1987 and 1996. The pattern is similar for 45-54-year-old men, who saw median tenure fall 1.3 years between 1963 and 1996, with an even steeper decline between 1987 and 1996. Tenure fell only slightly for the youngest group of men, about half a year (0.5) between 1963 and 1996, with a minimal one-tenth of a year fall between 1987 and 1996.

Second, women consistently have lower tenure than men of the same age. In 1996, for example, 35-44-year-old women had a median tenure of 4.8 years, while median man in the same age range had 6.1 years with their current em-

FIGURE 4B Median job tenure by age, 1963-96

AGES 25-34

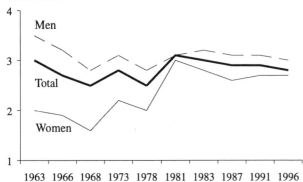

AGES 35-44

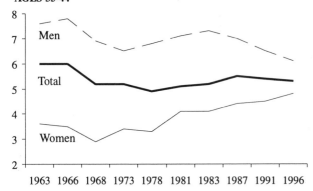

AGES 45-54

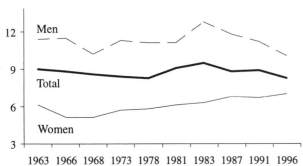

Source: Aaronson and Sullivan (1998).

ployer. Third, while women still have lower tenure than men, a combination of rising tenure for women and declining tenure for men allowed women to narrow the tenure gap between 1963 and 1996. Finally, the declining tenure for men and the rising tenure for women have come close to canceling each other out. The overall distribution at all three age levels generally changes much less than either of the corresponding male or female distributions.

The median job tenure sheds important light on job stability, but the share of jobs that are "long-term" may be more relevant to workers' perceptions of job security. "Long-term" jobs (ones that last, say, at least 10 years) typically are the kinds of employment situations that provide workers with the best potential for sustained wage growth, good fringe benefits, and a feeling of employment security. **Table 4.8** reports the share of workers in 1979, 1988, and 1996 who had been in their jobs for 10 or more and 20 or more years. The data show a significant decline during the 1980s and 1990s in the share of men in long-term jobs and little change in the share of women in such jobs. In 1979, just under half (49.8%) of all men had been in their jobs for 10 years or longer; by 1996, the share had fallen 9.8 percentage points to 40.0%. In 1979, far fewer women (29.1%) than men had tenure of 10 years or more. The share increased only slightly by 1996 (to 30.3%). The data for men and women with 20 years on the job tell a similar story. The share of men with these very-long-tenure jobs fell 6.8 percentage points between 1979 and 1996, from 33.8% to 27.0%. Meanwhile, the share of women in the same situation rose 1.2 percentage points, from 13.1% to 14.3%. The data by education level, which include both men and women, suggest that the declines in job tenure cut across all education levels. Declines in 10-year-tenure jobs between 1979 and 1996, for example, were almost as large among college-educated workers (-6.9 percentage points) as they were for those with less than a high school degree (-7.3 percentage points).

Another important feature of job stability is the probability that a worker's current job will continue into the future. **Table 4.9** shows the results of an analysis that asks how likely it is that a worker with a given number of years on his or her current job will be holding the same job in four years' time (the time period is forced by the nature of the underlying data). The data presented here allow us to look separately at men, women, whites, and blacks, and, within each of these groups, at workers with zero to two, two to nine, nine to 15, and 15 or more years of tenure. The time period covered begins in the mid-1980s (1983-87) and ends in the first half of the 1990s (1991-95).

The data for men show that, on average, the probability that a worker's current job will continue for four more years changed relatively little between the mid-1980s and the first half of the 1990s. In 1983-87, 58.5% of current

TABLE 4.8 Share of employed workers in long-term jobs, 1979-96

| | 1979 | 1988 | 1996 | Change | | |
				1979-88	1988-96	1979-96
More than 10 years on current job						
All	41.0%	39.1%	35.4%	-1.9	-3.7	-5.6
Male	49.8	45.7	40.0	-4.1	-5.7	-9.8
Female	29.1	31.2	30.3	2.1	-0.9	1.2
Less than high school	38.6	39.8	31.3	1.2	-8.5	-7.3
High school	41.9	40.2	37.2	-1.7	-3.0	-4.7
Some college	38.8	34.8	33.3	-4.0	-1.5	-5.5
College and beyond	43.6	40.4	36.7	-3.2	-3.7	-6.9
More than 20 years on current job						
All	25.1%	23.7%	20.9%	-1.4	-2.8	-4.2
Male	33.8	31.4	27.0	-2.4	-4.4	-6.8
Female	13.1	14.5	14.3	1.4	-0.2	1.2
Less than high school	22.5	21.8	19.8	-0.7	-2.0	-2.7
High school	26.3	23.8	22.0	-2.5	-1.8	-4.3
Some college	25.5	21.5	19.2	-4.0	-2.3	-6.3
College and beyond	26.6	26.7	21.7	0.1	-5.0	-4.9

Source: Farber (1997).

male jobs lasted at least four more years. By 1991-95, the share of male jobs lasting at least four more years fell only 2.1 percentage points to 56.4%. The average figure, however, masks two offsetting trends in the data. The share of short-tenure jobs (up to two years) that lasted at least four more years rose from 35.2% in 1983-87 to 39.4% in 1991-95. Over the same period, however, the share of longer-tenure jobs that survived for four or more years fell: 5.3 percentage points in the case of two-to-nine-year jobs; 7.5 percentage points for nine-to-15-year jobs; and 2.7 percentage points for 15-or-more-year jobs. Since the share of employment in jobs lasting up to two years is larger than the other four categories, the 4.2 percentage-point rise in four-year retention rates for this group counteracted much of the larger decline in retention rates for longer-tenure workers. Since workers' perceptions of job security probably weigh the fate of longer-tenure jobs more heavily than shorter-tenure jobs, the relatively large decline in job retention rates for longer-tenure jobs may have a

TABLE 4.9 Four-year job retention* rates, 1983-95

Years of Tenure	Mid-1980s (1983-87)	Late 1980s (1987-91)	Early 1990s (1991-95)	Change Mid-80s to late 80s	Late 80s to early 90s	Mid-80s to early 90s
Male	58.5%	56.5%	56.4%	-2.0	-0.1	-2.1
0-2	35.2	36.1	39.4	0.9	3.3	4.2
2-9	63.7	56.6	58.4	-7.1	1.8	-5.3
9-15	86.1	84.6	78.6	-1.5	-6.0	-7.5
15+	66.0	70.5	63.3	4.5	-7.2	-2.7
Female	48.4%	50.3%	52.1%	1.9	1.8	3.7
0-2	30.5	33.1	38.8	2.6	5.7	8.3
2-9	53.4	52.9	54.4	-0.5	1.5	1.0
9-15	78.2	78.0	70.5	-0.2	-7.5	-7.7
15+	55.7	69.7	63.3	14.0	-6.4	7.6
White	53.2%	53.5%	54.2%	0.3	0.7	1.0
0-2	32.2	34.7	38.4	2.5	3.7	6.2
2-9	57.9	54.6	56.4	-3.3	1.8	-1.5
9-15	81.8	81.9	74.0	0.1	-7.9	-7.8
15+	62.8	69.5	64.0	6.7	-5.5	1.2
Black	60.5%	55.4%	55.3%	-5.1	-0.1	-5.2
0-2	38.3	34.2	41.8	-4.1	7.6	3.5
2-9	64.4	56.9	54.9	-7.5	-2.0	-9.5
9-15	89.2	79.9	85.2	-9.3	5.3	-4.0
15+	66.1	75.7	59.4	9.6	-16.3	-6.7

*Share of workers with given characteristics who work with same employer for the four-year period beginning and ending in the years indicated.

Source: Neumark, Polsky, and Hansen (1997).

bigger influence on workers' perceptions of job security than the smaller de-cline in average retention rates, which includes the effects of improvements on the shortest-tenure jobs.

The job retention rates for women generally show a steady convergence toward those of men. Retention rates for women are all below those of men in 1983-87, but are on the whole much closer in 1991-95. For example, the 10 percentage-point gap between the male and female average four-year retention rates in 1983-87 (58.5% for men compared to 48.4% for women) fell to only a little over 4 percentage points by 1991-95 (56.4% compared to 52.1%). The convergence reflects both the decline in most male retention rates and the in-crease in most female retention rates.

TABLE 4.10 Rate of job loss by reason,* 1981-95

					Change		
Reason	1981-83	1987-89	1991-93	1993-95	1981-83–1991-93	1987-89–1993-95	1991-93–1993-95
Plant closing	4.5%	3.6%	3.6%	3.2%	-0.9	-0.4	-0.4
Slack work	5.4	2.4	3.7	3.8	-1.7	1.4	0.1
Position abolished	1.4	1.1	2.2	2.4	0.8	1.3	0.2
Other	1.0	0.8	1.4	2.0	0.4	1.2	0.6
All reasons	12.3%	7.9%	10.9%	11.4%	-1.4	3.5	0.5
Unemployment rate	9.1%	5.7%	7.3%	6.2%	-1.8	0.5	-1.1

* Data are adjusted for change in recall period, and the "other" response has been discounted in all years.

Source: Farber (1998).

Displacement

Job stability can decline because workers change jobs more frequently in order to take advantage of other opportunities, or it can fall because employers lay off or fire workers in greater numbers. The evidence on the poor wage-growth prospects of those with weak job stability (see Table 4.6) argues that much of the increase in job instability was probably involuntary. This section focuses special attention on involuntary job loss.

Table 4.10 reports data for the 1980s and 1990s on the share of workers that have experienced involuntary job loss during four different three-year periods. The data show that, in any given three-year period over the last two decades, 8-12% of workers suffered at least one involuntary job loss. The 12.3% job loss rate for 1981-83 was the highest level over the last two decades. The 1981-83 period, which included the 1982 recession, had an average unemployment rate of 9.1%. The job loss rate fell to 7.9% during the economic recovery years of 1987-89, when the average unemployment rate was a much lower 5.7%. Job displacement rates rose in the 1990s, to 10.9% in 1991-93 (the average unemployment rate was 7.3%) and then increased again to 11.4% in 1993-95, despite the economic recovery that lowered the average unemployment rate during these years to 6.2%. The rise in the job loss rate between 1991-93, a period of relatively high unemployment, and 1993-95, a period of relatively low unemployment, suggests that the underlying structural rate of job loss (that is, the component of job loss that is independent of the rise and fall of the business cycle) accelerated in the 1990s.

Table 4.10 also summarizes how the reasons for job loss have changed over time. Plant closings and "slack work" both declined between the two recessionary periods, 1981-83 and 1991-93, reflecting in part the much lower unemployment rates in the second recession and the steeper manufacturing downturn in the 1980s recession. Over the same period, however, "position abolished," a term that may reflect the "downsizing" phenomenon, rose sharply, from 1.4% to 2.2%. Displacements due to "position abolished" continued to rise through 1993-95 (to 2.4%), despite the economic recovery.

Table 4.11 examines differences in job loss by occupation. The data presented here examine only the three principal reasons for involuntary job loss because the survey that generated these data did not ask workers about their occupation if they lost their job for "other" reasons. The first striking feature is the high rate of job loss for blue-collar workers (craftsmen, operatives, and laborers) relative to workers in other professions. The job loss rate for blue-collar workers over the 1981-83 period was 21.2%, almost three times higher than the next most heavily affected group (sales and administration workers, with 8.5%). By 1993-95, the job loss rate for blue collars had fallen to 13.5%, but it still exceeded the rates for all other broad occupational categories.

The second feature of the displacement data is the significant increase during the 1990s in the risk of job loss for white-collar workers (managers, professional and technical workers, and sales and administrative workers). Between the two recessionary periods, 1981-83 and 1991-93, the share of managers whose positions were abolished more than doubled, from 1.4% to 3.0%; over the same period, the proportion of professional and technical workers whose positions were abolished increased from 1.1% to 1.7%; for sales and administrative workers the share grew from 1.3% to 2.4%. Between the two periods of economic recovery, 1987-89 and 1993-95, the incidence of job loss from "position abolished" was just as dramatic: from 1.3% to 2.4% for managers; from 1.0% to 2.2% for professional and technical workers; and from 1.3% to 2.7% for sales and administrative workers.

When workers leave their jobs voluntarily, they generally move on to better circumstances in a new job with better pay or working conditions. (They may also choose to leave work to pursue other activities such as studying, raising children, or retirement.) When workers lose their jobs involuntarily, however, they typically pay a large economic price. **Table 4.12** provides estimates of some of the principal economic costs associated with involuntary job loss. The first obvious cost of job loss is that displaced workers often experience difficulty finding a new job. Among all workers who reported losing their jobs in the previous three years (the data cover the period 1981-95), 35.1% (see last column) were out of work at the time they were interviewed about their experience of job loss. While not all of these displaced, out-of-work workers were looking

TABLE 4.11 Rate of job loss by occupation and reason,* 1981-95

					Change		
Occupation/reason	1981-83	1987-89	1991-93	1993-95	1981-83–1991-93	1987-89–1993-95	1991-93–1993-95
Managers							
All reasons	8.%2	6.4%	9.7%	7.8%	1.5	1.4	-1.9
Plant closing	4.2	3.9	3.9	3.4	-0.3	-0.5	-0.5
Slack work	2.6	1.2	2.7	2.0	0.1	0.8	-0.7
Position abolished	1.4	1.3	3.0	2.4	1.6	1.1	-0.6
Professional, technical workers							
All reasons	5.1%	3.5%	5.5%	5.8%	0.4	2.3	0.3
Plant closing	1.8	1.4	1.6	1.7	-0.2	0.3	0.1
Slack work	2.3	1.1	2.1	1.9	-0.2	0.8	-0.2
Position abolished	1.1	1.0	1.7	2.2	0.6	1.2	0.5
Sales, administrative workers							
All reasons	8.5%	6.9%	9.1%	9.3%	0.6	2.4	0.2
Plant closing	4.1	3.8	3.8	3.9	-0.3	0.1	0.1
Slack work	3.1	1.8	3.0	2.8	-0.1	1.0	-0.2
Position abolished	1.3	1.3	2.4	2.7	1.1	1.4	0.3
Service workers							
All reasons	5.9%	4.8%	6.5%	7.3%	0.6	2.5	0.8
Plant closing	3.0	3.0	3.1	3.4	0.1	0.4	0.3
Slack work	2.3	1.3	2.4	2.8	0.1	1.5	0.4
Position abolished	0.6	0.5	1.0	1.1	0.4	0.6	0.1
Crafts, operatives, and laborers							
All reasons	21.2%	11.1%	13.7%	13.5%	-7.5	2.4	-0.2
Plant closing	7.7	5.1	5.2	4.2	-2.5	-0.9	-1.0
Slack work	12.1	5.1	7.0	7.6	-5.1	2.5	0.6
Position abolished	1.5	0.9	1.5	1.7	0.0	0.8	0.2
Unemployment rate	9.1%	5.7%	7.3%	6.2%	-1.8	0.5	-1.1

*Data are adjusted for change in recall period and exclude "other" category.

Source: Farber (1997).

for a job at the time they were interviewed, if they were, then the 35.1% out-of-work rate would translate to an unemployment rate that was five times the average unemployment rate for the 1981-95 period (6.9%). Among the 65% or so of workers that did manage to find new jobs, the new job paid on average less than the old one. Specifically among the workers who moved from full-time to full-time work, their new positions paid, on average, 9.2% less than the old jobs.

TABLE 4.12 The costs of job loss, averages for 1980s and 1990s

Post-loss outcome	Reason for job loss				
	Plant closing	Slack work	Position abolished	Other	All
Out of work* (%)	30.2%	40.9%	29.7%	37.2%	35.1%
Average wage change (%)					
Full time to full time	-9.3%	-8.7%	-12.0%	-6.5%	-9.2%
All job changes	-13.0	-14.3	-19.2	-11.4	-14.2
Average wage loss, compared to continuously employed (%)**	-13.2%	-13.0%	-16.3%	-9.2%	-13.0%
Health benefits before loss, no health benefits after loss (%)	n.a.	n.a.	n.a.	n.a.	28.7%
No health benefits after loss, including those with no coverage at lost job	n.a.	n.a.	n.a.	n.a.	14.0%

* Of those who lost job in the last three years, the share out of work at time of interview.
** Full-time to full-time job changes only.

Sources: Authors' analysis of Farber (1997) and Gardner (1995).

Many previous full-timers, however, were not able to find full-time work (though some displaced part-timers did manage to find new full-time positions). Therefore, the average decline in hourly wages for all workers, including those who went from full-time to part-time work and vice versa, was even steeper (-14.2%). With both lower wages and fewer hours, workers who lost full-time jobs and managed only to find part-time replacement jobs were especially badly off.

The preceding figures for wage loss compare displaced workers' wages on their new jobs with those earned on their old jobs. These estimates of the wage costs of job loss, however, almost certainly underestimate the true wage loss. Some of these workers lost their jobs as many as three years before they were asked about the wages at their new job. If they had not lost their old jobs and had been able to continue at that same job for one to three years longer, many would have received further nominal pay increases. When we compare displaced workers with similar workers who did not lose their jobs, the average decline in wages for those who went from full-time to full-time jobs grows from -9.2% to -13.0% (see row 4).

FIGURE 4C Job leavers, 1967-97

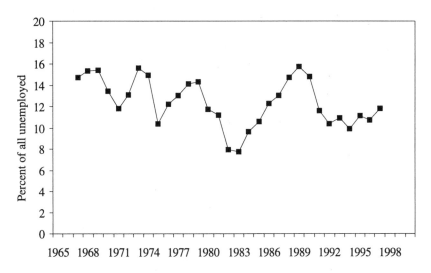

Source: Authors' analysis of BLS data.

Wages are only part of the story. Many displaced workers also lose the nonwage benefits provided through their previous employers. Of those workers who had health benefits on the job they lost, 28.7% (see row 5) had no employer-provided health benefits on their new jobs. Some displaced workers, of course, had no health insurance coverage at their old jobs but found new jobs that did provide insurance. When we include these workers in the calculation, job displacement reduced health insurance coverage by 14.0 percentage points (see row 6). Both health insurance figures paint an overly rosy picture, however, because, as we noted above, many displaced workers have difficulty finding new work.

Figure 4C takes a different look at the connection between job stability, job security, and job changes. Rather than examining the incidence and reasons for involuntary job loss, the data here show the share of all unemployed workers who are unemployed because they quit their previous jobs to look for new ones. Until the mid-1990s, the share of voluntary job "leavers" among the total unemployed followed the business cycle. When times were good and unemployment fell, the share of job leavers rose, reflecting both lower levels of layoffs and workers' greater confidence about their ability to find new, better jobs. When times were bad and the unemployment rate rose, the share of leavers in total unemployment fell, reflecting both an influx of involuntarily displaced workers and the general unwillingness of workers to give up their jobs in hand to search for new ones. During the economic recovery in the 1990s, however, the share of job leavers has not recovered along with the rest of the economy. The relatively constant share of job leavers over the recovery is a clear break with a longstanding economic relationship. It may reflect the continued high level of job displacement in the 1990s recovery as well as workers' ongoing anxieties about job security.

Job security

The preceding sections on job stability and job displacement examined statistical measures of the economy's tendency to create and destroy long-term employment relationships. We began that discussion by emphasizing the importance of differentiating between objective measures of job stability and more subjective, and probably more important, measures of "job security" — workers' perceptions of their ability to remain in their current job as long as they perform satisfactorily. Much of the evidence presented on job stability and displacement suggests that the underlying level of employment instability is higher in the 1990s than it was in the 1980s and earlier periods. Since the decline in job stability and the rise in job displacement appear to be linked to worsening economic circumstances for affected workers, we believe that this evidence on instability supports the conclusion that job insecurity has also increased in the 1990s. In this section, we turn to direct evidence on job security, based on workers' reported evaluation of the security of their current jobs.

Table 4.13 presents results on reported levels of job security from a nationally representative survey of workers in the years 1978, 1989, and 1996 (no survey data exist for 1979, our normal comparison year). The share of workers who said that they thought they were very or fairly likely to lose their jobs in the next 12 months was 8.0% in both 1978 and 1989 (despite a slight decline in the national unemployment rate between the two years). Between 1989 and 1996, however, the share of workers who thought they faced a significant chance of losing their jobs in the next year rose 3.2 percentage points to 11.2%. Perceived job security fell over the period even though the national unemployment rate was essentially identical in the two years (5.3% in 1989 compared to 5.4% in 1996). The same polling data also show a large drop between 1978 and 1996 in the share of workers who thought that they were not at all likely to lose their job in the next 12 months. In 1978, 71.0% of workers thought that they faced very little chance of losing their job; by 1996, the figure had fallen 10.7 percentage

TABLE 4.13 Perceptions of job security, 1978-96

	1978*	1989	1996	Change 1978-89	1989-96
How likely to lose your job or be laid off in next 12 months?					
Very or fairly likely	8.0%	8.0%	11.2%	0.0	3.2
Not at all likely	71.0	69.2	60.3	-1.8	-8.9
How easy to find a job with another employer with about the same income and benefits?					
Not easy at all	38.7%	37.8%	39.4%	-0.9	1.6
Very easy	28.1	34.2	27.1	6.1	-7.1
National unemployment rate	6.1%	5.3%	5.4%	-0.8	0.1

* No data available for 1979.

Source: Aaronson and Sullivan (1998) analysis of GSS data.

points to 60.3%. As before, most of the decline in perceived job security took place in the 1990s, with 8.9 percentage points of the decline occurring between 1989 and 1996, compared to only a 1.8 percentage-point drop between 1978 and 1989.

Workers also appear less optimistic about their employment prospects in the event that they do lose their jobs. In all three years, just under 40% of workers thought that it would not be at all easy to find another job with the same pay and benefits as their current job. The share of pessimists increased slightly (1.6 percentage points) between 1989 and 1996, from 37.8% to 39.4% of all workers. Over the same period, the share of optimists — those who thought it would be very easy to find a new job with the same pay and benefits — fell sharply (7.1 percentage points), from 34.2% to 27.1% of all workers.

The data on workers' perceptions show a high and growing level of job insecurity in the 1990s. These subjective impressions are consistent with the increases in job instability over the last two decades. They also support the conclusion that rising job instability does not respond to workers' desires to enter more "flexible" employment relationships, but rather represents an additional psychological and financial burden on workers.

The contingent workforce

The preceding analysis of job stability, job displacement, and direct measures of job security suggests that underlying job security fell markedly between the 1970s and the 1980s, appeared to be relatively stable through the 1980s, and deteriorated further in the 1990s. One important reason that workers may feel less secure in their jobs in the middle of the 1990s than they did in earlier periods with comparable or even higher unemployment rates is that a large and growing part of the workforce holds "nonstandard" or "contingent" jobs.

Broadly defined, nonstandard employment arrangements are all jobs that are not regular, full-time employment. These include temporary, part-time, on-call, and self-employed workers. Businesses hire contingent workers on a temporary basis in a variety of ways. Some firms put workers directly on their payrolls but assign them to an internal temporary worker pool. Others hire on-call workers and day laborers. Employers also use temporary help agencies and contracting firms to obtain workers on a temporary basis, sometimes for long periods. Some businesses hire independent contractors to perform work that would otherwise be done by employees.

In this section, we report results from two special analyses of nonstandard work arrangements, the 1995 and 1997 Contingent Work Supplements to the Current Population Survey (the monthly government household survey that has provided much of the information on wages and employment presented in this book). These data allow us to examine the different types of nonstandard work, their prevalence, and their associated pay and working conditions. While the two surveys provide a comprehensive look at nonstandard work arrangements in the mid-1990s, no comparable, earlier surveys exist. After reviewing the most recent data, therefore, we will turn to other, less comprehensive data that can give some indication of longer-term trends in the growth of nonstandard work arrangements.

Nonstandard work: widespread and often substandard
Table 4.14 and **Figure 4D** show the distribution of employment in 1997 by type of work arrangement. About 70% of all workers held regular full-time jobs, leaving almost 30% in different nonstandard work arrangements. The largest nonstandard category was regular part-time work (13.6%), followed by various types of self-employment including regular self-employment (4.8%), independent contracting (5.8%), and independent contracting on a wage and salary basis (0.7%). Some workers held nonstandard jobs through temporary help agencies (1.0%) and contract companies (1.4%). Others were "on call" with their regular employers (1.4%).

TABLE 4.14 Workers by work arrangement, 1997 (percent of all workers)

Work arrangement	All 1995	All 1997	Women	Men	White	Black	Hispanic
All nonstandard	29.3%	28.7%	33.8%	24.2%	30.3%	21.3%	24.0%
Regular part time	13.6	13.6	21.3	6.9	14.0	12.0	12.2
Temporary help agency	1.0	1.0	1.3	0.8	0.9	2.1	1.4
On call	1.3	1.4	1.5	1.2	1.3	1.0	2.1
Day labor	0.1	0.0	0.0	0.0	0.0	0.0	0.1
Self-employed	5.5	4.8	4.1	5.5	5.6	1.5	2.3
Indep. contracting-WS*	0.9	0.7	0.8	0.7	0.8	0.6	0.7
Indep. contracting-SE*	5.6	5.8	3.9	7.3	6.3	2.6	4.3
Contract company	1.3	1.4	0.9	1.8	1.4	1.5	0.9
Regular full-time	70.5%	71.3%	66.2%	75.8%	69.7%	78.7%	76.0%

* WS: Wage and Salary; SE: Self-employed.

Source: EPI analysis of CPS-CWS data.

Table Note: Column percentages may not sum to 100.0 because of rounding and the exclusion of category for day laborers (which account for less than 0.1% of all workers).

Women were three times more likely to hold regular part-time work than men (21.3% compared to 6.9%). Men were more likely than women to be self-employed (5.5% compared to 4.1%) or work as self-employed independent contractors (7.3% compared to 3.9%). Black workers were twice as likely as white workers to be temps (2.1% of black workers compared to 0.9% of whites), but were much less likely than whites to be self-employed (1.5% of blacks compared to 5.6% of whites) or work as self-employed independent contractors (2.6% of blacks, 6.3% of whites). Hispanic workers had a larger share of "on call" workers (2.1%) than blacks (1.0%) or whites (1.3%).

While many nonstandard workers prefer their work arrangements to regular full-time jobs, nonstandard workers generally earn less and receive fewer fringe benefits than workers with similar skills in regular full-time jobs. **Table 4.15** reports the results of a statistical analysis of wages of workers in different work arrangements in 1995. The findings presented in the top panel control for key worker characteristics such as the level of education and years of work experience. The analysis demonstrates that women and men in nonstandard work arrangements earn substantially less than their counterparts with similar skills and backgrounds but who are in regular full-time jobs. For example, regular part-time women workers — who make up about one-fifth of the female workforce— on average, earned 20% less than similar women in full-time employment. The

FIGURE 4D Workers, by work arrangement, 1997

ALL WORKERS

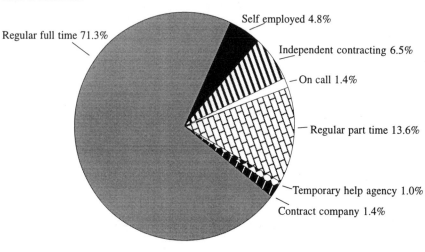

Regular full time 71.3%

Self employed 4.8%

Independent contracting 6.5%

On call 1.4%

Regular part time 13.6%

Temporary help agency 1.0%

Contract company 1.4%

NONSTANDARD WORKERS

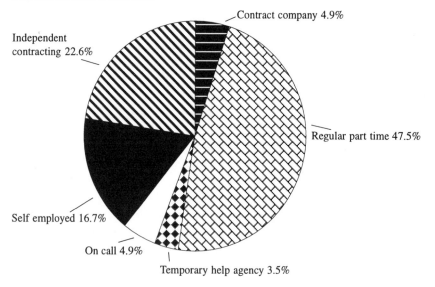

Contract company 4.9%

Independent contracting 22.6%

Regular part time 47.5%

Self employed 16.7%

On call 4.9%

Temporary help agency 3.5%

Source: EPI analysis of CPS-CWS data.

TABLE 4.15 Wages of nonstandard workers, compared to regular full-time workers, by sex and work arrangement, 1995

Work arrangement	Women	Men
Controlling for personal characteristics		
Regular part time	-20%	-24%
Temporary help agency	-17	-21
On call	-21	-9
Self-employed	-25	-13
Independent contracting	-14	-5
Contract company	—	7
Controlling for personal and job characteristics		
Regular part time	-5%	-10%
Temporary help agency	—	-8
On call	-6	—
Self-employed	-6	8
Independent contracting	7	12
Contract company	11	9

— Indicates that the difference is not statistically significant. All other differences are statistically significant.

Source: Kalleberg et al. (1997) analysis of CWS data.

gap between men and women who worked as temps and their regular part-time counterparts was also about 20%. Not all nonstandard workers, however, earn less than regular full-timers. Men working with contract companies, for example, earn about 7% more than comparable standard workers.

One reason that the nonstandard wages in the top panel of Table 4.15 are so much lower than those for regular full-time work is that nonstandard workers tend to be concentrated in low-paying industries and occupations. In the second panel of the table, we present further results that control for both workers' personal characteristics and the characteristics of the jobs they perform. In this analysis, the wage "penalty" for working in nonstandard jobs is smaller than when we ignore job characteristics. In half the cases, nonstandard workers appear to earn more than "standard" workers with similar personal skills in the same kinds of jobs. This evidence supports the view that nonstandard workers tend to work in less-well-paid industries and occupations.

TABLE 4.16 Percentage share of workers with employer-provided health and pension benefits by work arrangement, 1997

	Women	Men
Health benefits	20.5%	35.3%
Regular part time	18.1	15.4
Temporary help agency	5.0	6.0
On call	8.2	36.5
Self-employed*	34.4	53.6
Indep. contracting-WS*	14.1	26.8
Indep. contracting-SE*	27.0	39.7
Contract company	34.0	53.1
Regular full time	64.7%	68.5%
Pension benefits	23.6%	29.8%
Regular part time	20.9	11.8
Temporary help agency	3.9	3.7
On call	16.2	24.6
Self-employed	36.4	45.8
Indep. contracting-WS*	10.5	16.2
Indep. contracting-SE*	37.5	37.0
Contract company	23.1	40.8
Regular full time	57.7%	57.1%

*WS: Wage and Salary; SE: Self-employed.

Source: EPI analysis of CPS CWS data.

One reason that some nonstandard workers may earn wages above those of comparable full-timers in similar jobs is that nonstandard workers are much less likely to receive fringe benefits. Employers may have to pay a slightly higher cash wage to compensate for the lack of health or pension benefits. (Employers may also have to pay a slightly higher hourly wage to help offset the higher level of job insecurity associated with nonstandard work.) **Table 4.16** shows the share of workers, by work arrangement, with health and pension coverage through their employer. About two-thirds of regular full-time workers (64.7% of women, 68.5% of men) had employer-provided health benefits in 1997. Among nonstandard workers, the average health coverage rates were far lower: less than one-third the regular full-time rate for women (20.5%) and about one-half the regular full-time rate for men (35.3%). In every case, the share of nonstandard workers with benefits was substantially lower for regular full-time workers. Self-employed and contract workers enjoyed the highest level of health insurance coverage among nonstandard workers (34.4% of women and 53.6% of men). Temporary workers had the lowest health-coverage rates for both women (5.0%) and men (6.0%). A similar pattern holds for pension benefits (see the bottom panel), with about 57% of both male and female standard workers receiving pension benefits compared to much smaller shares of nonstandard workers (23.6% of women, 29.8% of men).

The most recent evidence on nonstandard work shows that such arrangements are widespread, varied, and generally substandard. Nonstandard work pays less, is much less likely to provide health or pension benefits, and typically provides far less job security than regular full-time employment. Unfortunately, the kind of detailed survey that has allowed us to sketch the main features of nonstandard work in the mid-1990s does not exist for earlier periods. As a result, we have some difficulty gauging the growth in nonstandard work over the last two decades of substantial economic change. In the remainder of this chapter, we look at the data that do exist on the growth of some kinds of nonstandard work: regular part-time employment, temporary work, self-employment, and multiple job holding.

Long-term growth in part-time work

As we saw earlier, one important reason for the high level of underemployment in 1997 was the 4 million workers who wanted full-time jobs but who were able only to find part-time work. This section examines the growth of part-time work more closely.

The expansion of part-time work is not necessarily a problem. Many workers prefer a part-time schedule because it allows time to pursue education, leisure, or family responsibilities. Nevertheless, large numbers of part-timers would prefer to work full time. Even those who work part time schedules by choice would prefer to receive the same compensation (pay and prorated benefits) for the same work performed by their full-time coworkers. Nevertheless, part-timers generally have lower pay, less-skilled jobs, poor chances of promotion, less job security, inferior benefits (such as vacation, health insurance, and pension), and lower status overall within their places of employment.

Table 4.17 shows that the share of jobs that are part time increased from 16.6% in 1973 to 18.1% in 1989. (The definition of part time used here differs from the earlier analysis of nonstandard work. See the note in the table.) This increase in part-time work from 1973 to 1989 resulted almost entirely from the

TABLE 4.17 Nonagricultural employment by full-time
and part-time status,* 1973-97

Year	Percent part time			Percent full time	Total
	Total	Involuntary	Voluntary		
1973	16.6%	3.1%	13.5%	83.4%	100.0%
1979	17.6	3.8	13.8	82.4	100.0
1989	18.1	4.3	13.8	81.9	100.0
1997**	17.8	3.2	14.5	82.2	100.0

* The definition of part time used here differs from the earlier analysis of nonstandard work. Here, part-time workers include any of the work types in the earlier
table, including temps and the self-employed who work part-time schedules. In
the earlier tables a temp or self-employed worker who generally worked part time
would have been classified as a temp or as self-employed regardless of hours.
This explains the much smaller share of part-timers in Table 4.14.
** Data for 1997 not strictly comparable with earlier years because of survey changes.

Source: Authors' analysis of BLS data.

rise in *involuntary* part-time employment, which expanded from 3.1% to 4.3%
of the total workforce. By 1989, nearly one-fourth of all part-time workers were
involuntary part-timers. The rise in involuntary part-time work, then, clearly
reflected the more widespread use of part-timers by employers and not the pref-
erence of the workforce for shorter hours. The overall rate of part-time employment declined slightly between 1989 and 1997, with the share of involuntary
part-time employment falling by 1997 to 3.2%, only slightly above its 1973
level. (Changes to the Current Population Survey suggest caution in drawing
strong conclusions when comparing these kinds of data before and after 1994,
when the survey underwent important changes. In identical economic circumstances, the new survey appears to yield a higher number of part-time workers
than older versions of the survey.)

Growth in temping

As we saw earlier, temps and workers with contract agencies are an important
part of the nonstandard workforce. **Table 4.18** reports changes in the number
of workers employed in personnel services industries between 1973 and 1997.
The last three columns of the table show the change in employment as a percent of the total labor force. The data show a large increase in the share of
workers employed through such agencies, from 0.3% of the total workforce in
1973 to 2.4% of all workers in 1997. The share of workers in the personnel

TABLE 4.18 Employment in personnel services industry, 1973-97

	Number (thousands)			As share of total employment		
Year	All	Men	Women	All	Men	Women
1973	247	118	128	0.3%	0.2%	0.2%
1979	508	210	298	0.6	0.2	0.3
1989	1,455	581	874	1.3	0.5	0.8
1992	1,629	676	954	1.5	0.6	0.9
1997	2,968	1,322	1,646	2.4	1.1	1.3

Source: Authors' analysis of BLS data.

TABLE 4.19 Employment in temporary help industry, 1982-97

	Number (thousands)			As share of total employment		
Year	All	Men	Women	All	Men	Women
1982*	417	158	259	0.5%	0.2%	0.3%
1989	1,216	494	722	1.1	0.5	0.7
1992	1,411	594	817	1.3	0.5	0.8
1997	2,646	1,203	1,443	2.2	1.0	1.2

* Earliest data available.

Source: Authors' analysis of BLS data.

services industry almost doubled in the 1990s. Government data have tracked employment in the narrower category of temporary help agencies since 1982 (see **Table 4.19** and **Figure 4E**). These data show that employment in temporary agencies doubled between 1982 and 1989 and doubled again between 1989 and 1997.

Self-employment

A significant portion of total employment consists of self-employed workers, those whose primary job is working in their own business, farm, craft, or profession. Individual independent contracting, mentioned earlier, is another form of

FIGURE 4E Employment in temporary help industry, 1982-97

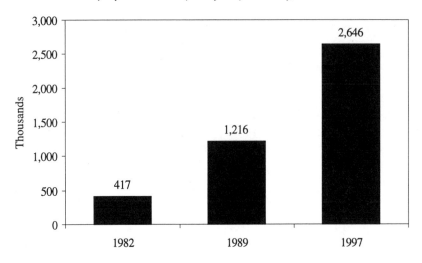

Source: Authors' analysis of BLS data.

self-employment. (The definition used in this section includes all forms of self-employment.)

Over recent business cycle peaks, self-employment has remained relatively constant at just over 7% of the workforce (see **Table 4.20**). As we saw in Table 4.14, men are more likely than women to be self-employed. The share of self-employed women, however, has increased somewhat since the mid-1960s, from 4.4% in 1967 to 6.0% in 1997.

More than one job

A final aspect of nonstandard work, which we have not addressed so far, is the prevalence of multiple job holding — people working in at least two jobs. In part, multiple job holding reflects the deterioration in hourly wages in workers' primary jobs and the rise, at least during the 1980s, in the share of workers working part time because they were not able to find full-time work.

Table 4.21 summarizes the available data on multiple job holding for selected years between 1973 and 1997. The share of multiple job holders in the total workforce has increased steadily, from 4.9% in 1979 to 6.3% in 1997. Most of the increase occurred in the economic recovery years of 1985-89 (0.8

TABLE 4.20 Self-employment, 1948-97
(percent of total employment*)

Year	All	Men	Women
1948	12.1%	n.a.	n.a.
1967	7.3	8.8%	4.4%
1973	6.7	8.2	4.9
1979	7.1	8.8	5.8
1989	7.5	9.0	6.0
1997**	7.2	8.2	6.0

* Nonagricultural industries.
** Not strictly comparable with data for earlier years because of survey changes.

Source: Authors' analysis of BLS data.

percentage points compared to a 0.5 percentage-point increase for 1979-85 and a 0.1 percentage-point increase for 1989-97).

For the 1979-89 period the Current Population Survey, which is the underlying source of the data presented here, also asked multiple job holders why they held more than one job. In 1989, just under half (2.8 percentage points of the 6.2% of multiple job holders) cited economic hardship (to meet regular household expenses or to pay off debts) as the reason they were working more than one job. Moreover, workers citing economic hardship for their multiple jobs accounted for most (1.0 percentage points) of the 1.3 percentage-point increase in multiple job holders between 1979 and 1989. These data support the view that multiple job holding was one method for coping with declining real wages. Unfortunately, no data on the reasons people work multiple jobs exist after 1991, and so we can only speculate about what factors led multiple job holding to level off at just over 6% of the workforce between 1989 and 1997.

Table 4.22 makes clear that the majority of those working multiple jobs do not combine two part-time jobs to create the equivalent of a full-time position. Multiple job holders, on average, work more than the standard 40-hour week, and the majority worked at least 50 hours per week. More than 60% of the men and almost 40% of the women with more than one job worked at least 50 hours per week.

TABLE 4.21 Multiple job holding, 1973-95

Year	Number of multiple job holders (000)	Multiple-job-holding rate	Percent of workforce who hold multiple jobs because of:	
			Economic hardship*	Other reasons**
1973	4,262	5.1%	n.a.	n.a.
1979	4,724	4.9	1.8%	3.1%
1985	5,730	5.4	2.2	3.2
1989	7,225	6.2	2.8	3.4
1997	8,197	6.3	n.a.	n.a.
Change				
1973-79	462	-0.2	n.a.	n.a.
1979-85	1,006	0.5	0.4	0.1
1985-89	1,495	0.8	0.6	0.2
1989-97***	972	0.1	n.a.	n.a.

*   To meet regular household expenses or pay off debts.
**   Includes savings for the future, getting experience, helping a friend or relative, buying something special, enjoying the work, and so on.
*** Data for 1997 not strictly comparable with data for earlier years because of survey design changes.

Source: Authors' analysis of BLS data.

TABLE 4.22 Hours worked by multiple job holders, by sex, 1997

Sex	Average weekly hours	Percent of multiple job holders working:				
		0-39 Hours	40-49 Hours	50-69 Hours	70+ Hours	Total
All	48.3	24.3%	24.6%	39.6%	11.5%	100.0%
Men	52.6	16.2	22.1	45.5	16.2	100.0
Women	43.5	33.6	27.5	32.8	6.2	100.0

Source: Authors' analysis of unpublished BLS data.

Conclusion

While the overall unemployment rate is at its lowest levels in three decades, many workers have still not felt the full benefits. Black and Hispanic unemployment rates are well above the national average, and underemployment rates are roughly double the rosier unemployment figure. Overwhelming evidence supports the view that underlying levels of job stability and job security are lower in the 1990s than they were in the 1980s or the 1970s. The rise in insecurity is probably not too surprising given that almost 30% of the jobs in the current economy are "nonstandard" positions, which typically offer lower wages, fewer benefits, and far less security than regular full-time work.

Wealth: concentration at the top intensifies

STAGNANT INCOMES AND FALLING WAGES ARE ONLY PART OF THE DECLINE IN THE well being of working Americans. A family's standard of living, as well as its ability to cope with financial emergencies, are affected by its wealth. For example, financial assets such as money in a bank account or stocks and bonds can help a family make ends meet during periods of illness or unemployment. Tangible assets such as a home or a car can directly affect a family's quality of life and the ease with which it meets its needs for housing and transportation. Families also need to accumulate wealth for their future needs, such as retirement income or college expenses for children.

The distribution of wealth is even more concentrated at the top than is the distribution of income, with the top 1% of households controlling 38.5% of all wealth compared to 14.4% of household income. As with the income distribution, the wealth distribution has become more uneven since 1983. While average wealth per household has grown about 2.1% per year in the 1990s, the growth has not been evenly distributed. The real value of financial assets, which are held in highly concentrated form by a relatively small share of the population, increased 3.8% per year between 1989 and 1997, largely reflecting the prolonged increase in the value of the stock market. Over the same period, the value of nonfinancial assets, which include real estate and which are generally more widely held, *fell* at a 1.9% annual rate. As a result, the inflation-adjusted value of the wealth held by the middle fifth of the population declined about $1,600 between 1989 and 1997. Over roughly the same period, the share of households with zero or negative wealth (families with negative wealth owe more than they own in assets) increased from 15.5% to 18.5% of all households. Almost one-third (31.3%) of black households had zero or negative wealth in 1995.

The stock market boom of the 1980s and 1990s has not enriched working families for the simple reason that most working families do not own much stock. While the share of households owning stock has risen in the 1990s, by 1995 almost 60% of households still owned no stock in any form, including mutual funds. Moreover, many of those new to the stock market have only small investments there. Fewer than one-third of all households, for example, had stock holdings greater than $5,000. In the same year, almost 90% of the value of all stock was in the hands of the best-off 10% of households. Not surprisingly, then, wealth projections through 1997 suggest that 85.8% of the benefits of the increase in the stock market between 1989 and 1997 went to the richest 10% of households. As we saw earlier, the conditions that have created stock market growth have not generated widely shared wage or income growth. In this section, we see that these same conditions have also contributed to a worsening of the distribution of wealth.

Aggregate household wealth:
financial assets boomed, tangibles failed to grow

We have seen in earlier chapters that income growth in recent years has been slow by historical standards, increasingly unequal, and, for many, characterized by more work at lower wages. In this section, we examine the change in the overall growth of wealth. In the next section, we turn our attention to trends in the distribution of wealth.

A basic measure of aggregate wealth is *household net worth*, which is the total assets of all households minus their debts. **Table 5.1** and **Figure 5A** trace the growth of household net worth over the postwar period between cyclical peak years through 1997. Household net worth increased at a rate of 4.1% per year between 1989 and 1997, a rate well above that of the 1980s (2.6%). The solid growth in wealth since 1979 follows a period of declining household wealth in 1967-73 (-1.0%) and 1973-79 (-1.3%). The recent performance is also above the growth rates achieved in the early postwar period from 1949 through 1967 (3.0%).

Not all household assets, however, grew at the same rate. Table 5.1 also distinguishes between "tangible assets" — consumer durables (cars, refrigerators, and so on) and housing, which are the most widely held form of wealth — and "financial assets" — stocks, bonds, mutual funds, and so on, which are owned mostly by the wealthy (as discussed below). The breakdown between the two forms of wealth demonstrates that all of the growth in wealth during the 1990s has been a consequence of the increase in financial assets (as we shall see

TABLE 5.1 Growth of household wealth, 1949-97

	Annual growth of average household net worth				
Type of wealth	1949-67	1967-73	1973-79	1979-89	1989-97
Total net worth*	3.0%	-1.0%	-1.3%	2.6%	4.1%
Net tangible assets**	2.5	3.9	1.7	1.4	-1.9
Net financial assets***	3.3	-0.7	-0.7	2.8	3.8
Stock	7.6	-8.7	-7.8	4.2	9.6
Mutual funds	12.3	-8.3	-9.4	20.2	14.5
Stock and mutual funds	7.8	-8.7	-7.9	5.9	10.6

*   Includes all households, personal trusts, and nonprofit organizations.
** Consumer durables, housing, and land assets less home mortgages.
***Financial assets less nonmortgage debt.

Source: Authors' analysis of Federal Reserve Board and other data. For detailed information on table sources, see Table Notes.

FIGURE 5A Growth of household wealth per household, 1947-97

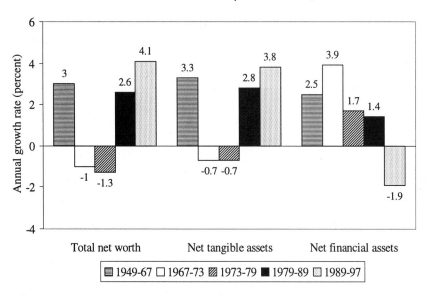

Source: Authors' analysis of Federal Reserve Board and other data.

TABLE 5.2 Distribution of income and wealth, 1995

	Distribution of:		
Wealth class	Net worth	Net financial assets	Household income
All	100.0%	100.0%	100.0%
Top 1%	38.5	47.2	14.4
Next 9%	33.3	35.8	24.9
Bottom 90%	28.2	17.1	60.8

Source: Authors' analysis of Wolff (1998).

later, primarily the long-term rise in the value of stocks), a form of wealth that is concentrated in a small portion of the population. Wealth held in tangible assets, which is much more widely held, actually declined over the 1989-97 period. The pattern in the 1990s is broadly consistent with that of the 1980s, when the value of financial assets per household grew at twice the rate of tangible assets. This disappointing growth of tangible assets since 1979 is especially impressive because there had been strong tangible asset growth throughout the 1950s, 1960s, and 1970s. Since tangible assets are distributed more evenly than financial assets, their stagnation indicates that the bulk of the population was unable to accumulate possessions in the post-1979 period. The pattern of wealth growth shown in Table 5.1 — higher growth in financial than tangible assets — thus previews the growing wealth inequality detailed in the next section.

Wealth inequality exceeds income gap

The distribution of wealth is considerably less equal than the distribution of income. The concentration of wealth among very high income households is dramatic. **Table 5.2** shows that in 1995 the top 1% of households earned 14.4% of total income, yet owned 38.5% of total net worth (the value of one's assets minus one's debts) and a remarkable 47.2% of net financial assets. (These income data are from a different source than that used in Chapters 1 and 2.) For a typical family, net worth reflects the value of its house, car, other consumer goods, and bank accounts less the amount owed on its mortgage and credit cards. Net financial assets are financial assets minus debts. For the same family, this would be the bank account balance minus mortgage and credit card debts. The value of pension plans is included in this analysis only if the assets are in defined-contribution plans.

TABLE 5.3 Households with low net wealth, 1962-95
(as percent of all households)

	1962	1983	1989	1995	Percentage-point change	
					1962-95	1983-95
Zero or negative	23.6	15.5	17.9	18.5	-5.1	3.0
Less than $10,000*	34.3	29.7	31.8	31.9	-2.4	2.2

*Constant 1995 dollars.

Source: Unpublished analysis of SCF data by Wolff.

In contrast to the top 1%, the bottom 90% of households received 60.8% of all income but held just 28.2% of total net worth and just 17.1% of net financial assets. Many of the households at the bottom of the income distribution have no assets to fall back on. **Table 5.3** shows that, in 1995, 18.5% of households had zero or negative net wealth, while 31.9% had net wealth totaling less than $10,000. Though most of these households with little, no, or negative wealth are not poor, their lack of financial assets indicates that many American families are living from paycheck to paycheck, with little or nothing in the bank in case of job loss or another serious financial emergency.

The concentration of financial assets at the top implies that American businesses are owned and financed primarily by the richest families. In 1995, for example, the wealthiest 1% owned 51.4% of all corporate stocks, while the bottom 90% owned only 11.6% (**Table 5.4**). The top 1% also owned 65.9% of bonds and 69.5% of private business equity (ownership of firms that do not sell stock to the public), while the bottom 90% owned only 10.2% of bonds and 8.3% of business equity. Overall, Table 5.4 demonstrates that the types of wealth that generate income, such as bonds, businesses, stocks, and other financial assets, tend to be held almost exclusively by the richest 10%, with the majority held by the top 1%, of families.

The types of wealth held by the bottom 90% of families are primarily homes and life insurance. Nonwealthy families also own "deposits" (primarily cash in checking, savings, and money market accounts), which are used to meet regular expenses. The bottom 90% of families also owe 71.7% of all debt, consisting primarily of mortgages on their homes.

TABLE 5.4 Percent of total assets held by wealth class, 1995

Asset type	Top 1%	Next 9%	Bottom 90%	Total	Share of top 10% 1989	Share of top 10% 1995
Assets held primarily by the wealthy						
Stocks and mutual funds	51.4%	37.0%	11.6%	100.0%	86.0%	88.4%
Bonds	65.9	23.9	10.2	100.0	87.1	89.8
Trusts	49.6	38.9	11.5	100.0	87.9	88.5
Business equity	69.5	22.2	8.3	100.0	89.8	91.7
Non-home real estate	35.1	43.6	21.3	100.0	79.6	78.7
Total for group	55.5	32.1	12.5	100.0	85.7	87.5
Assets held primarily by the nonwealthy						
Principal residence	7.1%	24.6%	68.3%	100.0%	34.0%	31.7%
Deposits*	29.4	32.9	37.7	100.0	61.5	62.3
Life insurance	16.4	28.5	55.1	100.0	44.6	44.9
Pension accounts**	17.7	44.7	37.6	100.0	50.5	62.3
Total for group	12.8	29.7	57.5	100.0	43.9	42.5
Total debt	9.4%	18.9%	71.7%	100.0%	29.4%	28.3%

* Includes demand deposits, savings deposits, time deposits, money market funds, and certificates of deposit.

**Includes IRAs, Keough plans, 401(k) plans, the accumulated value of defined contribution pension plans, and other retirement accounts.

Source: Wolff (1998).

Growing wealth inequality

As we shall see, there was a dramatic growth in wealth inequality during the late 1980s that has persisted through the 1990s. It is important to note, however, that the long-term trend prior to the 1980s was toward a lesser concentration of wealth. **Figure 5B** shows the share of total wealth (both excluding and including retirement wealth) over the 1922-81 period for years in which data are available. In general, wealth was more concentrated in the 1920s and 1930s than in any period after World War II. The concentration of wealth (excluding retirement wealth) held by the wealthiest 1% remained fairly steady over the 1940s, 1950s, and 1960s, ranging from a low of 25.7% in 1949 to a high of 31.9% in 1965, with no discernible trend up or down. The data for 1976 and 1981, however, suggest that wealth became less concentrated during the 1970s.

FIGURE 5B Share of total household wealth held
by richest 1% of individuals, 1922-81

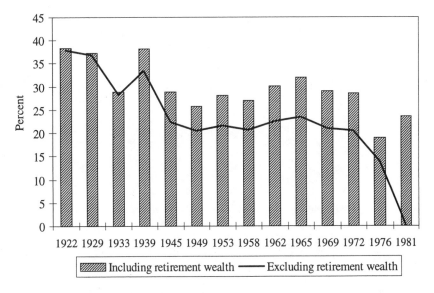

Source: Wolff (1992).

Surveys by the Federal Reserve Board in 1962, 1983, 1989, 1992, and 1995, summarized in **Table 5.5**, allow a direct examination of changes in the distribution of wealth. Table 5.5 also includes projections for the wealth distribution in 1997 that use data from the 1995 survey and available information on the change between 1995 and 1997 in the value of different types of assets and debt. Between 1962 and 1983, the distribution of wealth changed only slightly. The percentage of total wealth held by each fifth of families remained roughly equal between these years, with a modest redistribution to the bottom 40% and to the upper 5%.

Between 1983 and 1989, however, a major upward redistribution of wealth took place. In 1989, the richest 1% of families owned 37.4% of household net worth, up 3.6 percentage points from the 33.8% share in 1983. No group other than the richest 1% increased its share of wealth over the same period. Two comparisons help to put into perspective the magnitude of this shift in wealth toward the top. First, the share of wealth held by the top 1% grew by just 0.3 percentage points over the entire 21-year period between 1962 and 1983, then grew 12 times as much in only six years between 1983 and 1989. Second, the 3.6% increase in the share of wealth held by the top 1% was almost as large as

TABLE 5.5 Changes in the distribution of wealth,* 1962-97**

Wealth class	Share of wealth*					Change			
	1962	1983	1989	1995	1997**	1962-83	1983-89	1989-95	1989-97**
Top fifth	81.0%	81.3%	83.5%	83.7%	84.3%	0.4	2.2	0.2	0.8
Top 1%	33.4	33.8	37.4	37.6	39.1	0.3	3.6	0.2	1.8
Next 4%	21.2	22.3	21.6	22.3	22.3	1.2	-0.8	0.7	0.7
Next 5%	12.4	12.1	11.6	11.7	11.4	-0.2	-0.5	0.1	-0.2
Next 10%	14.0	13.1	13.0	12.1	11.5	-0.9	-0.1	-0.8	-1.5
Bottom four-fifths	19.0%	18.7%	16.5%	16.3%	15.7%	-0.4	-2.2	-0.2	-0.8
Fourth	13.4	12.6	12.3	11.5	10.8	-0.8	-0.2	-0.8	-1.5
Middle	5.4	5.2	4.8	4.5	4.4	-0.2	-0.4	-0.3	-0.4
Second	0.9	1.2	0.8	0.9	1.0	0.2	-0.3	0.0	0.1
Lowest	-0.7	-0.3	-1.5	-0.7	-0.5	0.4	-1.2	0.8	1.0
Total	100.0%	100.0%	100.0%	100.0%	100.0%				

* Wealth defined as net worth (household assets minus debts).
** 1997 figures are estimates.

Source: Authors' analysis of Wolff (1998).

the *total* value of wealth holdings of the bottom 60% in 1989 (about 4.1%). One of the most startling developments of the 1983-89 period was the erosion of the wealth shares of the bottom 40% of families. The poorest fifth of families had more debt than assets in 1983 and fell further in debt by 1989. The second fifth saw its share of wealth reduced by a third, shrinking from a negligible 1.2% in 1983 to just 0.8% in 1989.

After a decade that witnessed spectacular upward redistribution, the distribution of wealth was relatively stable between 1989 and 1995. The share of wealth held by the top 1% grew only 0.2 percentage points, while the share of wealth owned by the bottom 20% increased 0.8 percentage points (the net debt of the group fell from -1.5% of all wealth to -0.7% of all wealth). At the same time, some reshuffling of the distribution of wealth occurred in the middle categories.

Figure 5C summarizes the changes in the wealth distribution over the full 1983-95 period. The Survey of Consumer Finance data show the large shift in wealth toward the top 1% (from 33.8% to 37.6% of all wealth) at the expense of the bottom 95% of the wealth distribution.

The stock market boom probably contributed to a further concentration in wealth between 1995 and 1997. The projections for 1997 in Table 5.5 suggest

FIGURE 5C Distribution of wealth, 1983-95

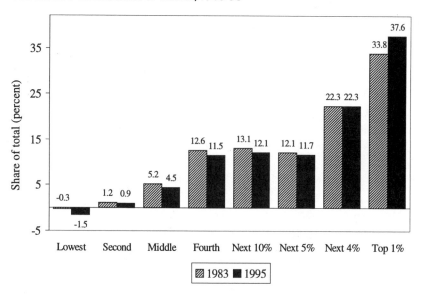

Source: Authors' analysis of Wolff (1998).

that during the 1989-97 period the share of wealth controlled by the top 1% increased by 1.8 percentage points. The next wealthiest 4% of households are also projected to receive a larger share of wealth (up 0.7 percentage points). The next 55% of households, however, probably saw their share in total wealth fall. The same projections suggest that the bottom 20% experienced a significant improvement in wealth (up about 1.0 percentage points), though still not enough to give them positive net wealth.

Table 5.6 shows the changes in wealth in dollar terms rather than as shares of total wealth, as in Table 5.5. To understand the usefulness of this alternative representation of the data, consider the case of the top 1% of households. In Table 5.5, we saw that in 1995 the top 1% of households controlled 37.6% of all wealth; in Table 5.6, we can see that this 37.6% share of total wealth translated into an average wealth of about $8.0 million per household for this group. Since the wealth figures in Table 5.6 have been adjusted for inflation, we can also use the table to examine how the value of wealth has changed over time for households at different points in the wealth distribution.

The level of wealth has undergone a series of dramatic changes since 1962. Between 1962 and 1983, average and median wealth rose substantially, with increases of roughly equal proportions at all wealth levels. In the 1983-89 pe-

TABLE 5.6 Change in wealth* by wealth class, 1962-97**
(thousands of 1997 dollars)

						Percent change		
Wealth class	1962	1983	1989	1995	1997**	1983-89	1989-95	1989-97**
Top fifth	$578.4	$851.3	$1,001.4	$903.7	$1,088.4	17.6%	-9.8%	8.7%
Top 1%	4,777.4	7,065.1	8,962.1	8,012.7	9,977.9	26.9	-10.6	11.3
Next 4%	756.4	1,168.6	1,293.3	1,185.8	1,422.0	10.7	-8.3	10.0
Next 5%	353.5	508.3	556.9	500.6	579.8	9.6	-10.1	4.1
Next 10%	199.8	274.5	311.1	258.9	292.0	13.4	-16.8	-6.1
Bottom								
four-fifths	$34.0	$48.8	$49.4	$43.3	$50.1	1.2%	-12.4%	1.3%
Fourth	95.7	131.5	147.8	122.9	137.6	12.3	-16.8	-6.8
Middle	38.8	54.7	57.9	48.3	56.2	6.0	-16.5	-2.9
Second	6.7	12.3	10.1	9.5	12.3	-17.9	-6.2	21.9
Lowest	-5.3	-3.2	-18.1	-7.5	-5.9	n.a.	n.a.	n.a.
Average	$142.9	$209.4	$239.8	$215.4	$257.7	14.5%	-10.2%	7.5%
Median	35.2	51.1	54.6	45.6	n.a.	6.8	-16.5	n.a.

* Wealth defined by net worth.
**Projections.

Source: Authors' analysis of Wolff (1998) and unpublished data from Wolff.

riod, average and median wealth continued to grow, but the growth was un-equally distributed. The average wealth of the top 1%, for example, increased from $7.1 million per household to $9.0 million. At the same time, wealth *fell* for the bottom 20% (from -$3,200 to -$18,100) and for the next 20% (from $12,300 to $10,100). The bottom 40% of families, therefore, not only saw their *share* of wealth decline in 1983-89, as shown above, but also experienced significant losses in the *value* of their wealth.

During the 1989-95 period, average household wealth declined 10.2% and median household wealth fell 16.5%. In fact, wealth fell at all levels except the bottom fifth, where net indebtedness was reduced about $10,600 per household (from -$18,100 to -$7,500). As we shall see later, despite the rise between 1983 and 1995 in the value of stockholdings across the whole wealth distribution, stock market gains were not enough to counteract the declines in the values of other assets plus the rise in household indebtedness.

The projections for 1997 suggest that developments between 1995 and 1997 — including rapid stock price increases and a small decline in debt levels — have been sufficiently strong to reverse much of the 1989-95 decline

TABLE 5.7 Change in wealth* by income class, 1983-95 (thousands of 1997 dollars)

Income level	1983	1989	1995	Percent change 1983-89	1989-95
$75,000 or more	$869.8	$870.7	$815.5	0.1%	-6.3%
$50,000-74,999	173.0	180.8	178.5	4.5	-1.3
$25,000-49,999	91.6	109.1	81.4	19.1	-25.4
$15,000-24,999	52.3	75.2	52.9	43.7	-29.7
Under $15,000	33.2	21.9	33.6	-34.0	53.4
Average	$179.1	$208.9	$182.9	16.6%	-12.4%

* Wealth defined by net worth.

Source: Authors' analysis of Wolff (1998).

in wealth. According to the projections for 1997, wealth gains in 1995-97 at all levels of the wealth distribution will raise the average wealth 7.5% above its 1989 level. The largest increases (in percent terms) will take place at the top and bottom. For the top 1%, wealth in the 1989-97 period will grow an estimated 11.3% (a $1 million average increase). Meanwhile, the bottom 20% will move closer to the breakeven point — from a net wealth of -$18,100 to -$5,900 — and the second 20% will see a 21.9% increase in average household wealth (from $10,100 to $12,300). The projections also demonstrate, however, the relatively small impact that the stock market boom has had on families in the middle of the wealth distribution. Even after factoring in stock market growth between 1995 and 1997, households in the middle fifth of the wealth distribution had a lower level of wealth in 1997 than they did in 1989.

The data in **Table 5.7** examine changes in wealth by household income level rather than by household wealth level. The distribution of wealth by income level shows many of the same features as the distribution by wealth level. Wealth is very unequally distributed across income levels. Households earning more than $75,000 per year had an average wealth of $815,500 in 1995, compared to $33,600 for households with less than $15,000 in annual income. (The data here exclude households where the head is 65 years or older. Retired households can frequently have low annual incomes and significant net wealth.) The level of wealth also underwent significant changes over the economic recovery of 1983-89 and the ongoing business cycle of 1989-95. Average wealth increased in the 1983-89 period, with strong gains in the middle-income categories and a steep decline for those below $15,000 in annual income. Average wealth fell in the 1989-95 period, with middle-income households experiencing the largest declines and the lowest-income households seeing a strong recovery.

Table 5.8 examines another dimension of the wealth distribution — the highly unequal distribution by race. In 1995, average wealth in black households was $43,000, just 16.8% of the average for white households ($255,300). The difference at the median was even more striking. The median black household had wealth equal to $7,800, or about 12.1% of the $64,200 in median wealth for whites. In the same year, black households were twice as likely to have zero or negative net wealth (31.3%) as white households (15.0%). Two factors account for most of the differences in wealth across the two racial groups. The first is that black households have far less financial wealth than white households. In 1995, average financial wealth in black households was $22,300, compared to $198,400 in white households; median financial wealth in black households was just $200, compared to median white financial wealth of $18,100. The second factor is that blacks are far less likely than whites to own the houses in which they live. In 1995, the homeownership rate for blacks was 46.8%, about two-thirds the rate for white households (69.4%).

Who gains from the stock market boom?

As **Figure 5D** shows, stock prices, measured using the inflation-adjusted value of the broad-based Standard & Poors 500 composite index, rose substantially over the 1980s and 1990s. Stock price gains were especially strong in 1994-97. For the stock market boom to have had a significant impact on family well-being, however, stock ownership would have to be widespread, and the value of shares held by low- and middle-income families would have had to be large enough to allow stock appreciation to offset declines in labor income. This section examines the distribution of stock held directly and indirectly in order to determine who has benefited from the run-up in the stock market since the early 1980s.

Table 5.9 presents the available information on the extent of direct and indirect holdings of stock among U.S. households for the period 1962-95. The top panel shows that the share of households directly holding publicly traded stock has increased over the last three decades, from 10.7% in 1962 to 15.2% in 1995, with much of the increase taking place in the 1990s. While information on indirect stock holdings (ownership of stock through mutual funds, defined-contribution pension plans, and individual retirement accounts (IRAs), for example) is harder to come by, the data in Table 5.9 establish that many more households

TABLE 5.8 Wealth by race, 1983-95
(thousands of 1997 dollars)

	1983	1989	1995
Average wealth			
Black	46.0	48.6	43.0
White	244.6	289.4	255.3
Black/white (%)	18.8	16.8	16.8
Median wealth			
Black	4.6	2.1	7.8
White	70.5	83.6	64.2
Black/white (%)	6.6	2.5	12.1
Average financial wealth			
Black	23.2	23.7	22.3
White	180.2	218.7	198.4
Black/white (%)	12.9	10.8	11.3
Median financial wealth			
Black	0.0	0.0	0.2
White	19.6	26.4	19.1
Black/white (%)	0.0	0.0	1.1
Homeownership rate (%)			
Black	44.3	41.7	46.8
White	68.1	69.3	69.4
Black/white (%)	65.1	60.2	67.4
Households with zero or negative net wealth (%)			
Black	34.1	40.7	31.3
White	11.3	12.1	15.0
Black/white (%)	301.8	336.4	208.7

Source: Wolff (1998).

hold stock indirectly (30.2% in 1995) than do so directly. The data also indicate that the share of households with indirect stock holdings (up 5.5 percentage points) increased more in the period 1989-95 than did the share with direct holdings (up 2.1 percentage points).

Thus, some support exists for the notion that stock ownership has become more widespread. But even by 1995, almost 60% of households held no stock whatsoever. Moreover, if we examine the share of households with more than $5,000 worth of stock (in 1995 dollars), as does the second panel of Table 5.9,

FIGURE 5D Growth of U.S. stock market, 1959-97 (1997 dollars)

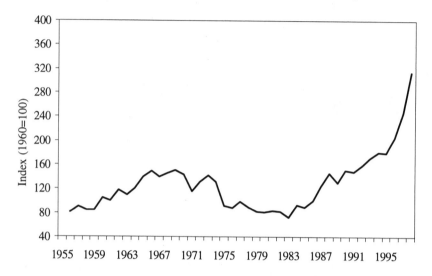

Source: Authors' analysis of data from ERP.

TABLE 5.9 Share of households owning stock

	1962	1983	1989	1995	Percentage-point change 1989-95
Any stock holdings			31.7%	40.4%	8.7
Direct holdings	10.7%	13.7%	13.1	15.2	2.1
Indirect holdings			24.7	30.2	5.5
Stock holdings, $5,000*+			22.6%	28.8%	6.2
Direct holdings			10.0	12.3	2.3
Indirect holdings			16.9	22.7	5.8

* Constant 1995 dollars.

Source: Unpublished analysis of SCF data by Wolff.

we see that only 28.8% of households have more than a minimal ownership of stock. These data do not support the notion that pension fund or mutual fund managers have a primarily "middle-class constituency" or that the gains of the stock market are widely shared, since any significant stock gain goes to, at most, about 29% of households. Also, recall that Table 5.4 showed that, in 1995, 51.4% of stocks (by value) were owned by the wealthiest 1% of households, compared to only 11.6% of stock owned by the least wealthy 90%. Finally, whatever gains the middle class made from the recent stock market boom were not enough to allow these households to accumulate wealth: the total wealth of the median household (the median of the middle-fifth) actually *fell* over the 1983-95 in the Federal Reserve Board surveys (Table 5.6).

Table 5.10 takes a closer look at the impact of the stock market on the distribution and growth of total wealth over the full 1962-95 period and includes projections through 1997. The top panel shows the value of stock holdings by the level of overall household wealth. The second panel presents the value of all other household assets such as bonds, real estate, checking accounts, and so on. The third panel displays the level of household debt (primarily mortgages, but also including credit card and other forms of debt). The bottom panel adds both stock and nonstock assets from the first two panels and subtracts debt from the third panel to produce household "net worth," or wealth. (Note that the figures in this last panel match the wealth numbers in Table 5.6.)

As we saw earlier, stock ownership is heavily concentrated at the top. Projections for 1997, for example, suggest that the top 1% of households held stock worth, on average, $2.5 million and that the next wealthiest 9% of households had average stock holdings of about $276,000. Projections for the same year suggest that the average stock holdings of the middle 20% of households were just $7,900, while the bottom 40% held, on average, only $1,600 in stocks. The stock value data do show large increases after 1983 in the average value of stock holdings across all levels of wealth. Even after the increases, however, the vast majority of households have stock holdings whose returns would add little to their current household income.

Table 5.10 illustrates that the rise in stock wealth is only part of the story of the 1990s. Between 1989 and 1997, at the same time that the average value of stock holdings per household increased from $28,800 to $61,200, the average value of other assets *fell* from $253,100 to $236,300. Average household debt levels over the same period declined only marginally, from $42,000 to $39,800. As we have seen before, however, these average figures are sensitive to changes in the assets and liabilities of the wealthiest households. Therefore, we also examine changes over the 1989-97 period for the middle fifth and the bottom two-fifths of the wealth distribution. Households in the middle fifth saw their

TABLE 5.10 Household assets and liabilities by wealth class, 1962-97*
(thousands of 1997 dollars)

Assets and liabilities	Top 1.0%	Next 9%	Next 10%	Next 20%	Middle 20%	Bottom 40%	Average
Stocks**							
1962	$2,372.1	$121.3	$13.5	$4.3	$1.2	$0.3	$37.7
1983	1,540.1	99.4	11.9	4.5	1.6	0.4	27.3
1989	1,162.6	127.7	25.1	8.7	3.7	0.6	28.8
1995	1,745.0	194.8	36.6	13.9	5.6	1.1	43.3
1997*	2,470.9	275.9	34.6	19.6	7.9	1.6	61.2
All other assets							
1962	$2,580.5	$445.6	$211.7	$117.7	$63.7	$15.1	$128.7
1983	5,927.8	769.4	311.0	160.1	78.8	16.5	213.7
1989	8,238.8	845.8	334.4	182.6	87.7	19.0	253.1
1995	6,648.5	699.1	271.0	150.9	86.7	20.3	214.0
1997*	7,868.8	759.8	286.0	157.8	90.0	21.0	236.3
Total debt							
1962	$175.1	$34.3	$25.4	$26.2	$26.0	$14.6	$23.5
1983	402.8	67.0	48.4	33.0	25.7	12.3	31.6
1989	439.3	89.5	48.3	43.7	33.5	23.6	42.0
1995	380.8	88.8	46.8	41.8	43.9	20.4	41.9
1997*	361.8	81.6	43.1	39.7	41.7	19.3	39.8
Net worth							
1962	$4,777.4	$532.6	$199.8	$95.7	$38.8	$0.7	$142.9
1983	7,065.1	801.7	274.5	131.5	54.7	4.6	209.4
1989	8,962.1	884.2	311.1	147.8	57.9	-4.0	239.8
1995	8,012.7	805.1	258.9	122.9	48.3	1.0	215.4
1997*	9,977.9	954.1	292.0	137.6	56.2	3.2	257.7

* Projections.
** All direct and indirect stock holdings.

Source: Unpublished analysis of SCF data by Wolff.

stock holdings (projected for 1997) more than double in value between 1989 and 1997 (from $3,700 to $7,900). The value of other assets also increased over the period (from $87,700 to $90,000). Nevertheless, a large rise in indebtedness (from $33,500 to $41,700) offset the gains in stock and other assets, leaving the projected net wealth of the middle group lower in 1997 ($56,200) than it was in 1989 ($57,900). The bottom two-fifths of households did see their wealth increase over the 1989-97 period, from -$4,000 to $3,200, but the rise in wealth had little to do with the stock holdings (up from $600 to $1,600). The improve-

FIGURE 5E Share of total stock market gains, 1989-97, by wealth class

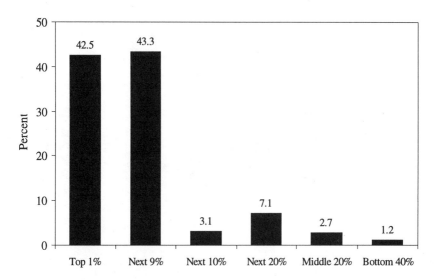

Source: Authors' calculations based on Wolff (1998).

ment, instead, reflected both a growth in the value of other assets (from $19,000 to $21,000) and a decline in debt (from $23,600 to $19,300).

Figure 5E uses the stock distribution data from Table 5.10 to show who has benefited from the stock market boom during the period 1989-97. The 1997 figures are projections based on the 1995 distribution and the growth in the overall value of the stock market between 1995 and 1997. The figure shows that 42.5% of the benefits of the recent growth in the stock market went to the richest 1% of households. The next wealthiest 9% captured 43.3% of the growth, leaving the bottom 90% of households with only 14.2% of the benefits. The middle 20% of households, for example, received just 2.7% of the proceeds from the stock market boom; the bottom 40% split 1.2% of the total increase.

The data in **Table 5.11** and **Figure 5F** provide greater detail on the concentration of the value of stocks, including direct and indirect holdings. These data describe the distribution of stock across income groups, both the share of each income group that owns any stock ("percent who own") and the share of the total value of stock owned by each income group ("percent of stock owned"). Three categories of stock are analyzed: (1) publicly traded stock directly held by households; (2) stock in pension plans, including 401(k) and defined-contribution plans, where the employer puts in a fixed amount or share of salary each

TABLE 5.11 Concentration of stock ownership by income level, 1995 (percent)

Income	Share of	Percent	Percent of stock owned	
level* (in thousands)	households	who own	Shares	Cumulative
Publicly traded stock				
Over 250	1.0	56.6	41.9	41.9
100-250	5.4	41.4	23.2	65.1
75-100	5.8	33.9	9.1	74.2
50-75	13.7	24.4	11.2	85.4
25-50	31.1	14.0	8.7	94.1
15-25	19.1	10.4	3.7	97.8
Under 15	23.9	3.4	2.3	100.0
Total	100.0	15.2	100.0	
Stock in pension plans**				
Over 250	1.0	65.0	17.5	17.5
100-250	5.4	61.7	31.3	48.8
75-100	5.8	58.9	14.8	63.6
50-75	13.7	50.8	18.1	81.7
25-50	31.1	35.1	14.3	96.0
15-25	19.1	16.8	3.1	99.1
Under 15	23.9	3.2	0.9	100.0
Total	100.0	29.2	100.0	
All stock***				
Over 250	1.0	84.6	28.0	28.0
100-250	5.4	80.7	26.2	54.2
75-100	5.8	75.6	11.9	66.1
50-75	13.7	63.7	14.6	80.7
25-50	31.1	47.7	13.0	93.7
15-25	19.1	28.1	4.6	98.3
Under 15	23.9	7.9	1.7	100.0
Total	100.0	40.4	100.0	

*   Constant 1995 dollars.
**   All defined contribution stock plans including 401(k) plans.
*** All stock directly or indirectly held in mutual funds, IRAs, or Keogh plans and defined-contribution pension plans.

Source: Unpublished analyis of SCF data by Wolff.

FIGURE 5F Concentration of stock ownership, 1995

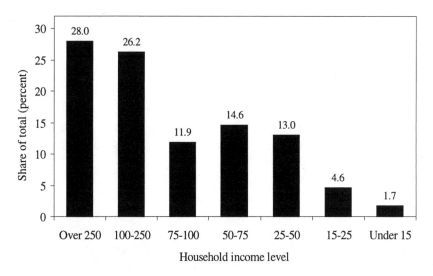

Source: Unpublished analysis of SCF data by Wolff (1998).

year; and (3) all stock, whether held directly or indirectly (such as through a pension or savings plan).

Not surprisingly, households with higher incomes are more likely to own stock. Almost 57% of households with incomes over $250,000 in 1995 held some publicly traded stock, compared to only 14.0% of households with incomes in the $25,000-$50,000 range. Even in the broadest measure of stock ownership (last panel), less than half (47.7%) of households in the $25,000-$50,000 income group held any stock, compared to 84.6% for the best-off group.

Table 5.11 also demonstrates that stock ownership, no matter how defined, is highly concentrated. The three highest income groups, which make up 12.2% of all households, controlled 74.2% of publicly traded stock, 63.6% of pension plan stock, and 66.1% of all stock. In contrast, the three lowest income groups (these with less than $50,000 of income), which make up 74.1% of all households, owned 14.7% of publicly traded stock, 18.3% of pension stock, and 19.3% of all stock.

Pension assets, as reflected by stock ownership, are highly concentrated even though they are more evenly distributed than many other types of assets, including all stock. The main difference between stock holdings in pension plans and other stock holdings is that pension assets are more evenly distributed *among the top fifth of households*. That is, while the highest income group controls 28.0%

of all stock, it controls only 17.5% of stock in pension plans. Nevertheless, the bottom three-fourths of households (with less than $50,000 of income) own 18.3% of the stock in pension plans, a lower share than their holding of all stock.

Growing debt

Household debt grew rapidly between 1973 and 1989. More recently, household debt has grown more slowly by some measures and even fallen by others. By any measure, however, debt levels remain high, and debt continues to represent an important financial burden for most households.

Table 5.12 presents aggregate data from the Federal Reserve Board on two measures of household debt — debt as a percent of assets and debt as a percent of personal income. Debt as a percentage of personal income grew steadily after 1973, though the rate of growth declined somewhat in the 1990s. In 1997, household debt levels stood at 84.8% of personal income. Debt as a percentage of household assets grew continuously over the business cycle peaks since the end of World War II. The most rapid increase in debt as a percent of assets took place in the early postwar period. Debt measured as a percent of assets continued to grow in the 1990s, but at a slower rate than in earlier periods, reaching 14.8% of the value of all household assets. However, the data from the Survey of Consumer Finance, the household survey that has provided much of the information on the distribution presented in this chapter, tell a slightly different story. The SCF data in Figure 5.10 show a large increase in the average dollar value of household debt between 1962 and 1989. Between 1989 and 1995, the level of household debt did not change significantly, and the projections for 1997 suggest a slight decline in average debt levels since 1989. Even using these projections, however, average debt levels in 1997 remain well above those of 1983.

These measures of debt burden do not reflect changes in debt service payments as interest rates change. Such fluctuations can make paying down any debt either more or less difficult. For instance, when interest rates fall, the burden of paying off new debt eases. The estimates of debt service payments presented in the last three columns of Table 5.12 take changes in interest rates and repayment schedules (i.e., more 30-year versus fewer 15-year mortgages) into account. These data show a sizable growth in the debt burden over the period 1979-89 because of a greater burden of home mortgages. Between 1989 and 1997, however, the overall debt burden fell, from 17.3% to 17.0% of disposable income. The decline reflected the benefits of falling home mortgage interest rates that were large enough to offset an increase in the burden of consumer debt.

TABLE 5.12 Household debt burden, 1949-97

	Debt as percent of:		Debt service as percent of disposable income		
	Personal income	Assets*	Total debt	Consumer debt	Mortgage
1949	29.5%	6.0%	n.a.	n.a.	n.a.
1967	59.1	11.7	15.7%	11.8%	3.9%
1973	57.6	12.4	15.5	11.5	4.0
1979	63.3	13.6	15.6	10.7	4.9
1989	75.8	14.5	17.3	10.7	6.7
1997**	84.8	14.8	17.0	11.2	5.8
Annual percentage-point change					
1949-67	1.6	0.3	n.a.	n.a.	n.a.
1967-73	-0.2	0.1	-0.1	-0.2	0.1
1973-79	0.9	0.2	0.1	-0.8	0.9
1979-89	1.3	0.1	1.7	-0.1	1.8
1989-97**	1.1	0.0	-0.3	0.6	-0.9

* Financial assets (including pension funds and insurance), real estate, and consumer durables.
** Figures for personal income are preliminary.

Source: Authors' analysis of Federal Reserve Board and other data.

Conclusion

An examination of changes in the level and distribution of household wealth helps complete the picture of the typical family's economic status. Families need an accumulation of wealth to weather emergencies (health problems, job loss, and so on), to finance retirement, and to pay for large expenditures, such as a child's college expenses or a house downpayment. The available evidence indicates that middle-income families in the mid-1990s had no more wealth, and in many cases less wealth, than they had in 1989 or in 1983. The stock market boom enriched these families neither directly via their stock holdings nor indirectly via their pension or savings plans.

In contrast, the richest 1% of households were able to increase their wealth significantly between 1983 and 1997 (up about 41%, despite setbacks through 1995. Much of the increase stemmed from the stock market boom over the period 1994-97, almost 90% of the benefits of which went to the top 10% of households.

Poverty: increasing inequality undermines connection between growing economy and lower poverty rates

THE THEME OF A GROWING, EVEN BOOMING, ECONOMY LEAVING FAMILIES BEHIND IS perhaps nowhere more relevant than in a discussion of American poverty. The fact that poverty did not fall between 1989 and 1997 (the most recent year for which data are available) poses a stiff challenge to the highly touted recovery of the 1990s.

What determines the poverty rate in the American economy? By definition, poor persons are those who live in families whose pre-tax, post-cash-transfer income leaves them below the poverty line for a family of their size (cash transfers come from various government programs, such as welfare or Social Security). Thus, a family with two parents, two children, and income below $16,276 in 1997 would be considered poor. This threshold is adjusted each year by the growth of inflation.

But this is simply the definition of poverty. The factors that determine poverty rates — which cause them to increase and decline — are also a main theme of this chapter. As in earlier chapters, we find the disconnection between the growing economy and the earnings of many American families to play a central role. This is a key point, because it means that macroeconomic growth in and of itself is not likely to be enough to significantly reduce poverty. Other factors, such as the shift to family types more susceptible to poverty, have also played a role in its growth, but much less so in the 1980s and 1990s than in past decades. A detailed exploration of the competing explanations strongly suggests that the growth of income and wage inequality and the decline in the real wages of low-wage workers have been the key determinants of the growth of poverty in the 1980s and 1990s.

Before turning to poverty's determinants, however, we present a portrait of the poor. Our examination of poverty rates by race/ethnicity and by age shows that minorities and children are the poorest members of our society. The next section examines alternative measures of poverty. While these measures yield different levels (both higher and lower than the official rates), the trends are similar. We then analyze the various factors contributing to the failure of poverty to respond to economic growth, and we document the important role played by increasing inequality. The chapter concludes with an examination of the key wage and employment trends facing low-wage workers. We find that, despite overall labor market tightening, conditions in the low-wage labor market remain weak.

The fact that such weak conditions persist in the low-wage labor market in the late 1990s challenges recent shifts in U.S. antipoverty policy. The welfare-to-work component of welfare reform partially reflects American values regarding the integrity of work as well as voters' distaste for dependence on government support by low-income families. However, the data here show that the wage and employment opportunities facing poor persons will have to expand considerably before we can reasonably expect the poor to work their way out of poverty.

Who are the poor?

Figure 6A shows the trend in the poverty rate for persons (as opposed to families) from 1959 to 1997, the last year for which data of this type are available. **Table 6.1** shows the rates at peaks in the business cycle since 1959 and for 1996. At 22.4%, poverty was exceptionally high in 1959, but it began falling in the 1960s in response to economic growth and more generous government transfers. By 1967 poverty had dropped to 14.2%, and it continued to fall during the early 1970s, hitting a low of 11.1% in 1973, before climbing again. Poverty rose steeply during the recession of the early 1980s, and despite the long recovery afterwards, poverty was higher at the end of the 1980s than in the late 1970s. This pattern was repeated in the 1990s recovery. As Table 6.1 (bottom panel) shows, despite continued economic growth, average poverty rates were higher in the 1990s than in the 1980s.

Given the fact that minority incomes and wages are generally lower than those of whites, we would expect their poverty rates to be higher. As **Table 6.2** shows, this is indeed the case, with minority poverty rates between two and three times those of whites. The rates for blacks were historically the highest, though Hispanic rates (unavailable for 1959 and 1967) have consistently risen since 1979, surpassing the rate for blacks in 1996 (part of this increase is likely due to increased immigration over this period). Note that during the current

FIGURE 6A Poverty rate, 1959-97

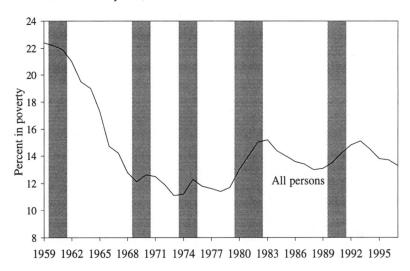

Note: Periods of recssion are shaded.

Source: U.S. Bureau of the Census P60-198.

TABLE 6.1 Percent and number of persons
in poverty, 1959-97

Year	Poverty rates	Number in poverty (000)
1959	22.4%	39,490
1967	14.2	27,769
1973	11.1	22,973
1979	11.7	26,072
1989	12.8	31,528
1997	13.3	35,574
Averages over business cycle peaks		
1959-67	19.1%	
1967-73	12.5	
1973-79	11.6	
1979-89	13.6	
1989-97	14.0	

Source: U.S. Bureau of the Census, P60-201.

TABLE 6.2 Persons in poverty, by race/ethnicity, 1959-97

Year	Total	White	Black	Hispanic
1959	22.4%	18.1%	55.1%	n.a.
1967	14.2	11.0	39.3	n.a.
1973	11.1	8.4	31.4	21.9%
1979	11.7	9.0	31.0	21.8
1989	12.8	10.0	30.7	26.2
1997	13.3	11.0	26.5	27.1

Source: U.S. Bureau of the Census, P60-201.

business cycle (until 1997), black rates have fallen, from 30.7% to 26.5%, while those of whites have increased. Thus, although black poverty rates were double those of whites in 1997, the racial gap had closed somewhat, meaning that poverty's growth in the 1990s has been among whites and Hispanics.

Poverty rates among children are also higher than overall rates, as shown in **Table 6.3**. In 1979, child poverty rates were 16.4%, though here again the rates for black and Hispanic children were many times those of white children. Hispanic child poverty rates grew quickly over the 1980s and continued to increase, though more slowly, over the 1990s. The progress of blacks — both in absolute terms and relative to whites — noted in the last table is accentuated among children, as black child poverty fell at a 10-year rate of 8.1 percentage points in the 1990s.

Poverty rates shown thus far apply to the number and share of persons in a particular group who are poor. Family poverty, shown in **Table 6.4**, shifts the unit of observation to the family, which in Census terminology refers to two or more persons related through blood, marriage, or adoption (i.e., one-person units are excluded). In general, family poverty rates are lower than poverty rates for persons, reflecting both the relatively high number of poor children and unrelated individuals included in the person counts. The patterns over time are similar to those shown in the previous tables, with consistently increasing rates of family poverty at business cycle peaks since 1973. Black families throughout the period had the highest poverty levels; however, they have closed the gaps with both Hispanics and white families and by the end of the period had slightly lower rates than Hispanics.

The last two columns show the poverty rates of two family types with very different probabilities of being poor: married couples with children and female-headed families with children. This latter family type is most vulnerable to pov-

TABLE 6.3 Percent of children in poverty, by race, 1979-96

| Year | Children under 18 | | | |
	Total	White	Black	Hispanic
1979	16.4%	11.8%	41.2%	28.0%
1989	19.6	14.8	43.7	36.2
1997	19.9	16.1	37.2	36.8
Percentage-point change				
1979-89	3.2	3.0	2.5	8.2
1989-97*	0.4	1.6	-8.1	0.7

| Year | Children under 6 | | | |
	Total	White	Black	Hispanic
1979	18.1%	13.3%	43.6%	29.2%
1989	22.5	16.9	49.8	38.8
1997	22.0	18.4	40.2	38.4
Percentage-point change				
1979-89	4.4	3.6	6.2	9.6
1989-97*	-0.6	1.8	-12.0	-0.5

* These changes are converted to 10-year growth rates so as to be comparable with the previous 10-year period.

Source: U.S. Bureau of the Census, various years.

TABLE 6.4 Family poverty, by race/ethnicity of family head and for different family types, 1959-97

| Year | Race/ethnicity of family head | | | | Families with children | |
	All	White	Black	Hispanic	Married couples	Female heads
1959	18.5%	15.2%	n.a.	n.a.	n.a.	59.9%
1967	11.4	9.1	33.9%	n.a.	n.a.	44.5
1973	8.8	6.6	28.1	19.8%	n.a.	43.2
1979	9.2	6.9	27.8	20.3	6.1%	39.6
1989	10.3	7.8	27.8	23.4	7.3	42.8
1997	10.3	8.4	23.6	24.7	7.1	41.0

Source: U.S. Bureau of the Census, P60-201.

TABLE 6.5 High-risk factors for poverty, females 25 and over, 1996

	White	Black	Hispanic*
All	12.6%	31.7%	32.0%
(1) Single heads of households	27.3%	43.7%	50.9%
(2) with less than a high school degree	43.6	58.7	62.1
(1) and (2) with children	63.2	73.6	70.2

* Hispanics can be of any race.

Source: U.S. Bureau of the Census, unpublished tables.

erty: close to three-fifths of such families were poor in 1959. Thanks to the expansion of cash transfers over the 1960s, the increased labor force participation of women (including single mothers), and the expansion of this family type among more affluent women, the female-headed poverty rate fell through 1979 to about two-fifths; it has risen slightly since then. While comparable data on married-couple families with children are not available for the earlier years in the table, their poverty rates are the lowest among all family types examined here.

Race, age, family type, as well as education level of the family head (a factor on which we focus below) all affect the probability of poverty. And, as **Table 6.5** shows, various combinations of minority status, family type, and low educational attainment lead to poverty rates well above the average. The rates in the table refer exclusively to women 25 years and over in 1996.

The first line of Table 6.5 reinforces the importance of race, as black and Hispanic women had poverty rates two and a half times those of white women. The second line reveals that single-head-of-household family type leads to significantly higher poverty rates for women, regardless of race. Note, for example, that in this category alone the poverty rates for white women climb from 12.6% to 27.3%. Lack of a high school degree further drives up poverty rates; well over half of black and Hispanic females meeting these criteria were poor in 1996. Adding children to the mix further strains the scant resources of many families within these categories; the poverty rates here rise to 63.2% for white women, 73.6% for blacks, and 70.2% for Hispanics.

Alternative approaches to measuring poverty

While the rates in Tables 6.1-6.5 are the most commonly cited measures of poverty, there are a variety of alternative ways in which it is measured. The rates presented so far are based on a comparison of each family's pre-tax, post-cash transfer (e.g., unemployment insurance, Social Security, and public assistance payments) income against the official Census poverty thresholds, adjusted for family size and price changes. Although there are a number of potentially important conceptual problems with this definition of poverty (e.g., it ignores the value of noncash benefits such as food and medical care, and it has never been updated to reflect new consumption patterns), the official poverty measures have a long history and are a widely used measure of economic deprivation.

Nevertheless, this section presents some alternative measurements of poverty. The question to be considered in the context of the theme of the chapter — the increasing disconnection between economic growth and declining poverty — is: do any of these alternative measures tell a different story, that poverty has in fact fallen as the economy has expanded? That is, is the supposed disconnect an artifact of conceptual problems with the definition of poverty? In essence, this is a question about the trend of poverty rates over time, as opposed to the level at a point in time. If alternative measures show the same trends as the Census measure, the disconnection theme remains valid. In fact, the following measures show this to be the case.

A common criticism of the official poverty lines is that they no longer reflect even minimal levels of consumption and thus understate the extent of poverty. The original consumption data were collected in 1955, when it was assumed that poor families spent one-third of their income on food (thus assuming that families could purchase all other necessities for twice what they spent on food). The poverty lines were then constructed by multiplying the Department of Agriculture's minimum food budgets for different-sized families by three. However, consumption patterns and the relative prices of goods have changed since 1955. For example, since food costs have fallen relative to the costs of housing, the proportion of income spent on food has fallen over time, with the average family spending a smaller proportion of the family budget on this necessity and, in turn, a larger proportion on other necessities. Therefore, if the poverty lines were recalculated today, they would be higher (as would poverty rates), since the food budget would be multiplied by a number larger than three.

A panel of poverty experts examined these issues and released a study in 1995 under the aegis of the National Research Council (NRC). The panel found that changes in consumption, work patterns, taxes, and government benefits all suggested the need for an updated measure of poverty. Their alternative mea-

TABLE 6.6 1992 poverty rates under official and alternative measures

	Official	Alternative*	Difference
Total	14.5%	18.1%	3.6
Age			
Children under 18	21.9%	26.4%	4.5
Adults 65 and over	12.9	14.6	1.7
Race/ethnicity			
White	11.6%	15.3%	3.7
Black	33.2	35.6	2.4
Hispanic (any race)	29.4	41.0	11.6
Receiving cash benefits**	59.4%	53.4%	-6.0
One or more workers	9.1	13.7	4.6
No health insurance	32.0	44.9	12.9

* Alternative measure updates consumption requirements, includes cash value of near-cash benefits, and subtracts medical and work-related expenses.
** AFDC or SSI (i.e., means-tested benefits).

Source: National Research Council (1995).

sure incorporates these factors. It reflects contemporary consumption patterns, adds the cash value of food stamps and housing benefits, and subtracts out-of-pocket medical, child care, and work-related expenses.

Table 6.6 shows that this alternative measure has the effect of raising poverty rates by 3.6 percentage points in 1992 (the year on which the panel focused). In fact, poverty rates are higher for every group except those receiving cash benefits, who benefit under the alternative measure from the cash value of near-cash benefits such as food stamps. There is a marked increase in poverty rates among Hispanics (due in part to their high housing expenditures relative to other racial groups) and the medically uninsured (due to their out-of-pocket payments for health care). Thus, this more comprehensive measure of poverty would have increased the number of poor persons in 1992 by about 9 million.

Table 6.7 reveals how the NRC's alternative measure affects the distribution of poor persons in 1992. The largest difference is among persons receiving cash benefits (down 11.3 points) and those persons in families with one or more workers (up 10.5 points). These shifts reflect the fact that most recipients of cash benefits also receive in-kind benefits and that the alternative measure includes expenses associated with work (which lowers the income of families with workers). Despite these differences, however, the previous table (Table

TABLE 6.7 Demographic composition of poor persons
under alternative definitions, 1992

	Official	Alternative	Difference
Age			
Children under 18	39.7%	38.4%	-1.4
Adults 65 and over	10.9	9.8	-1.0
Race/ethnicity			
White	66.9%	70.7%	3.8
Black	28.6	24.6	-4.0
Receiving cash benefits*	40.6%	29.2%	-11.3
One or more workers	50.9	61.4	10.5
No health insurance	30.2	34.0	3.8

* AFDC or SSI (i.e., means-tested benefits).

Source: National Research Council (1995).

6.6) shows that persons in families without workers have significantly higher poverty rates than families with at least one worker.

Table 6.8 further explores the issue of noncash benefits by isolating the effects of including the market value of food and housing benefits in recipients' incomes. Medical benefits are omitted from the analysis for two reasons: they are not a common part of everyday consumption, like food and housing, and the inclusion of their full value would have the perverse effect of making the ill appear less poor. Although the inclusion of food and housing benefits lowers the absolute rates in each period, the increase in poverty over both the 1980s and 1990s (bottom panel) is slightly greater using the broader measure. The last column shows that food and housing benefits have been less successful over time at reducing Census poverty levels, a point we return to below.

As noted above, the official poverty lines are indexed for inflation. However, some analysts claim that the price index used to adjust the poverty lines overstated inflation in the 1970s and early 1980s and thereby overestimated real poverty rates. **Figure 6B** tracks poverty rates from 1968 to 1996 using an alternative price index, the CPI-U-X1, which is considered a more conservative measure of inflation (see the Methodology section for a discussion of the differences in these deflators). As would be expected, the more conservative price index leads to lower measured poverty rates. However, Figure 6B also shows that, regardless of the price index chosen to adjust the poverty lines for price

TABLE 6.8 Poverty rates when (nonmedical) noncash benefits are included

Year	Current definition	Plus market value of food and housing benefits	Change	Percent of poverty reduced
1979	11.7%	9.6%	2.1	17.9%
1989	12.8	11.2	1.6	12.5
1997	13.3	11.9	1.4	10.5
Change				
1979-89	1.1	1.6		
1989-97*	0.5	0.7		

* 10-year growth rates.

Source: U.S. Bureau of the Census, P60-182RD and P60-201.

FIGURE 6B Poverty rates by price index, 1968-97

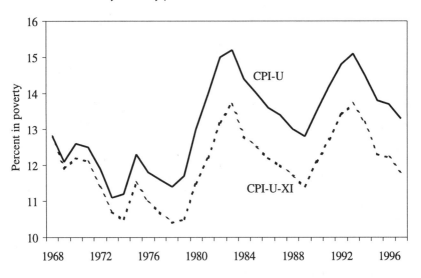

Source: U.S. Bureau of the Census P60-201.

changes, there has been a rise in poverty since 1979 despite overall income growth.

Another important way of measuring poverty is to examine relative economic well being. A conceptual shortcoming of the absolute poverty lines used in the above tables is that they are adjusted only for inflation; they do not reflect overall income growth. The official poverty lines are fixed levels of income that represent a particular standard of living (level of consumption) at a point in time. However, as average income grows over time and standards of living rise, the economic "distance" between the officially poor and the rest of society expands. While the earliest poverty lines were in fact close to 50% of the median family income for a given family size, they have fallen to about 35%. A relative measure of poverty would account for this change by, for example, measuring poverty relative to the median family income (which changes yearly).

Table 6.9 presents such a measure, by race. As would be expected (since median family income grew faster than prices throughout the 1980s), the poverty rates at one-half the median are substantially higher than the official (absolute) rates shown in column 4. For example, whereas 13.3% of the population was poor according to the official poverty measure in 1996, 22.3% of all persons were in families with incomes below one-half of the median family income. As with absolute poverty rates, relative rates increased since 1979, with the bulk of the increase derived from the increased relative poverty of the poorest group: those with incomes less than one-quarter of the median. Thus, as with other alternative measures, the trend in relative rates supports the theme of growing poverty amid overall economic growth.

As seen in Table 6.2, absolute poverty rates for minorities are higher than those of whites. The bottom three panels of Table 6.9 reveal that the same relationship holds for relative poverty rates of minorities (Hispanics in these data can be of any race). In addition, the gap between relative and absolute rates (the last column of Table 6.9) is higher for minorities than whites, suggesting that minorities are, in general, further below the absolute poverty line than whites. In 1997, relative poverty rates for blacks were 39.1% (12.6 points above the absolute rate), and blacks were almost equally divided between zero to one-quarter of the median and one-quarter to one-half. Relative poverty rates for whites in that year were about half those of blacks (19.7%, 8.1 points above the absolute rate) and fell mostly in the one-quarter to one-half category. (Note, however, that black poverty rates fell in the 1989-97 period, while those of whites rose.)

A final comparative measure looks at the relative child poverty in the U.S. compared to that of other advanced economies. **Figure 6C** reveals the high degree of relative deprivation of U.S. children compared to children from these other industrialized countries. This measure, which includes the value of near-

TABLE 6.9 Percent of persons with low relative income, 1969-97, by race, adjusted for family size

	Relative income poverty measures				
	Less than 1/4 the median	1/4 to 1/2 of the median	Less than 1/2 of the median	Official rate	Difference (1/2 median-official rate)
All					
1969	5.5%	12.4%	17.9%	12.1%	5.8
1979	6.7	13.3	20.0	11.7	8.3
1989	8.3	13.7	22.0	12.8	9.2
1997	8.8	13.5	22.3	13.3	9.0
Whites					
1969	4.3%	10.4%	14.7%	9.5%	5.2
1979	5.0	11.7	16.7	9.0	7.7
1989	6.3	12.5	18.8	10.0	8.8
1997	7.1	12.6	19.7	11.0	8.7
Blacks					
1969	15.3%	27.3%	42.6%	32.2%	10.4
1979	18.8	25.3	44.1	31.0	13.1
1989	21.8	22.1	43.9	30.7	13.2
1997	18.6	20.5	39.1	26.5	12.6
Hispanics (any race)					
1969	n.a.	n.a.	n.a.	n.a.	
1979	11.6%	22.6%	34.2%	21.8%	12.4
1989	16.3	23.8	40.1	26.2	13.9
1997	17.4	24.4	41.8	27.1	14.7

Source: U.S. Bureau of the Census (McNeil), various years.

cash transfers (see Table 6.8), shows that close to one-quarter of U.S. children were relatively poor in 1994, while other similar economies had much lower rates. In 1991, child poverty was 18.5% in the United Kingdom and 15.3% in Canada. Child poverty rates were well below 10% in Germany and France, while the Scandinavian countries had almost no relative child poverty. Chapter 8 returns to these measures in the context of international comparisons of poverty and income inequality.

FIGURE 6C Relative poverty rates* for children, mid-1980s to mid-1990s

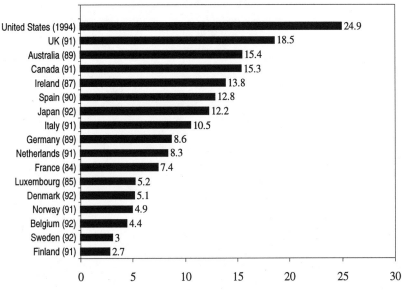

Percent of children in families with less than one-half median income

* Income is post-tax and includes near-cash transfers, such as food stamps and housing assistance.

Source: Smeeding (1997).

The depth of poverty

The depth of poverty at a point in time is another useful gauge of how the poor are faring. Since poverty is a fixed income level, families are considered poor whether they are one dollar or $1,000 below the poverty line. **Table 6.10** examines the poverty gap: the distance in the aggregate or average dollar amounts of a person or family from the poverty line. The results show not only that poverty has risen since the 1970s, but that, despite the growing economy over this period, the poor have actually become poorer. For instance, in 1997 the average poor family had an income $6,602 below the poverty line (in 1997 dollars); in 1973 the mean family poverty gap was $5,694. The aggregate family poverty gap, which is the sum of every poor family's income deficit, was over $48 billion in 1997, up from $21 billion in 1973.

As Figure 6A showed, poverty fell from 1967 to 1973, driving the decline in the aggregate poverty gap, which shrank by 2.6% per year over this period. (The average poverty gap changed little over this period; the smaller number of

TABLE 6.10 Poverty gap: aggregates and means, 1967-97 (1997 dollars)

	Families		Persons not in families	
	Poverty gap, aggregate (millions)	Poverty gap, mean	Poverty gap, aggregate (millions)	Poverty gap, mean
1967	$32,224	$5,685	$17,495	$3,498
1973	27,490	5,694	15,744	3,371
1979	32,557	5,961	18,966	3,303
1989	43,668	6,333	25,005	3,673
1997	48,353	6,602	34,618	3,985
Annual growth rates				
1967-73	-2.6	0.0	-1.7	-0.6
1973-79	2.9	0.8	3.2	-0.3
1979-89	3.0	0.6	2.8	1.1
1989-97	1.3	0.5	4.2	1.0

Source: Center for Budget and Policy Priorities (1997).

poor families led to the lower aggregate gap). In the ensuing periods, however, the aggregate gap for both families and individuals grew around 3% per year, driven by increases in the number of poor families and their deeper levels of poverty (as shown by the increase in the mean gap over the period). In the most recent period, there has been a sharp increase in the growth rate of the aggregate poverty gap of persons not in families, resulting from an increase in this group's poverty rate as well as its population share.

Table 6.11 and **Figure 6D** shows another measure of the depth of poverty: the percentage of the poor below 50% of the poverty line, which in 1997 meant a pre-tax income of about $8,100 for a family of four. In 1979, close to one-third (32.8%) of the poor were in "deep poverty." By 1983, following the deep recession of the early 1980s, this proportion had approached two-fifths (38.5%), where it essentially held throughout the decade. As expected, the share of deeply poor persons expanded in the recession which began in 1990, but it continued to expand in the ensuing recovery and rose in the latest year, 1997 (see Figure 6D).

Thus, while different measures lead to different levels of poverty rates, the trend is similar in all cases. Certain measures, such as those that include the cash value of near-cash benefits such as food stamps, clearly reduce poverty at a point in time, but even by this measure poverty has increased half a percentage point more since 1979 than under the official measure. Other measures of poverty, such as those that incorporate updated consumption needs or those based

TABLE 6.11 Persons below 50% of poverty level

Year	Percent of all poor	Number of persons (000)
1975	29.9%	7,733
1979	32.8	8,553
1983	38.5	13,590
1989	38.0	11,983
1997	41.0	14,594

Source: U.S. Bureau of the Census, various years.

FIGURE 6D Percent of poor persons below 50% of poverty level, 1975-97

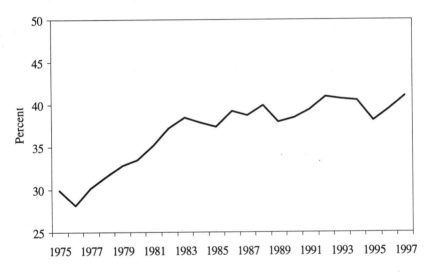

Source: U.S. Bureau of the Census Website.

on relative income, reveal higher poverty rates at a given point in time and, in the latter case (for which we have data over time) generally show a faster increase than do the official rates. In addition, despite the tightening labor market over the current recovery, the share of the deeply poor — those below 50% of poverty — has expanded and was higher in 1997 than at the bottom of the early 1980s recession. The next section examines which factors are most responsible for the failure of poverty rates to decline in the face of overall economic growth.

Poverty, overall growth, and inequality

Several decades ago, economists thought that poverty would continually diminish (and virtually disappear) as the economy expanded. But if economic growth is unequally distributed, as shown in prior chapters, the inverse relationship between growth and poverty is weakened. When the fruits of growth are concentrated at the top of income and wealth distributions, those at the bottom are less likely to benefit from overall growth, and poverty rates are thereby less responsive to the growing economy.

Table 6.12 shows changes in poverty rates along with changes in various indicators of overall growth and inequality. When comparing these relationships over different time periods, the macroeconomic disconnect is evident. During the 1960s, the growing economy appears to have played a notable role in reducing poverty. Between 1959 and 1969, poverty rates fell by 10.3 percentage points, while productivity and per capita income — two broad measures of overall growth — grew by 32.1% and 34.1%, respectively. Unemployment fell by 2% over this 10-year period, and income inequality, as measured by the Gini ratio (see Chapter 1 for an explanation of this measurement method), fell by 1.2 points.

Over the 1970s, productivity and per capita income grew more slowly, and unemployment and inequality both increased. Not surprisingly, therefore, poverty fell only slightly. In the 1980s, however, poverty increased, despite continued growth in productivity (albeit slower than in the previous two decades) and per capita income. Although unemployment fell slightly, the sharp increase in the Gini coefficient is a prime suspect in the explanation for not only the failure of poverty to decline but in its actual increase. The most recent period, 1989-96, shows the same pattern, with poverty and inequality growing, even though the overall economy grew at rates similar to the 1980s.

Figure 6E illustrates the disconnect between overall economic growth and poverty rates. The dotted line in the figure is an update of Rebecca Blank's 1991 model of the relationship between various macroeconomic variables (unemployment, inflation, income, and government transfers; see the figure note for details) and poverty rates for individuals. The model is estimated through 1983, and then projected forward on the basis of those estimates. The model does a good job of tracking poverty rates up until 1983 (the beginning of the 1980s expansion). However, applying the pre-1983 relationship between the macroeconomic variables in the model and post-1983 poverty rates incorrectly forecasts a much steeper fall in poverty rates than actually occurred. In other words, a major shift in the relationship between economic growth and poverty occurred in the 1980s such that the economic recovery in that decade failed to reduce

TABLE 6.12 Changes in poverty rates and growth indicators

	Poverty rates	Productivity*	Per capita income	Unemployment	Gini coefficient
1959-69	-10.3	32.1	34.1	-2.0	-1.2
1969-79	-0.4	20.5	22.9	2.3	1.6
1979-89	1.1	10.9	19.1	-0.5	3.6
1989-96**	1.3	9.5	9.4	0.1	3.4

* Nonfarm business sector.
** 10-year growth rates.

Sources: Columns 1 and 5 from U.S. Bureau of the Census P60-198 and P60-197, respectively. Other data from ERP (1998).

FIGURE 6E Predicted vs. actual poverty rates, 1959-97

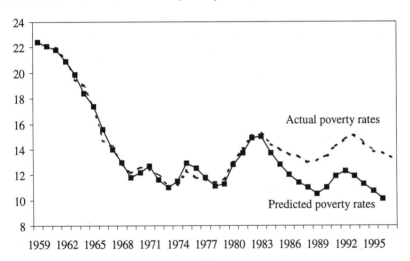

Source: Authors' update of Blank (1991).

poverty as much as occurred in earlier periods of growth (such as the 1960s or 1970s).

Three main explanations have been offered for this phenomenon of unresponsive poverty rates: a decline in government assistance for the poor, changing family demographics, and negative labor market changes such as falling real wages and declining employment opportunities for low-wage workers. While each one of these has played an important role, their respective roles have not been constant over time. For example, while the shift toward family types more susceptible to poverty, like female-headed families, has consistently led to higher poverty rates, this factor was less important in the 1980s and 1990s than in earlier periods. In the next section we examine the relative contributions of these factors.

The role of demographics and inequality

Table 6.13 shows the percent of persons in three different family types in the period 1959-96, along with the poverty rates of persons in those families. Clearly, there has been a shift over time into family types more vulnerable to poverty. For instance, the percentage of persons in married-couple and male-headed families, which have the lowest poverty rates, has consistently fallen, from 85.9% in 1959 to 70.2% in 1996. Conversely, there has been a consistent expansion of female-headed families and an even faster growth of households consisting of single individuals.

By itself, we would expect this pattern of family structure changes to increase poverty rates. However, changes in poverty rates within these groups also play a determinative role. If a vulnerable family type grows as a share of all families, this would put upward pressure on poverty rates. But rising relative incomes concurrent with this growth would be a countervailing factor. In fact, the poverty rates for persons by family type shows that all family types saw their poverty rates fall over the 1960s and 1970s, with single persons showing the largest drop (12 percentage points in both decades). This trend then reversed, and between 1979 and 1989 poverty rates grew comparably for persons in female-headed families (1.0 points) and in married-couple families (0.9 points), while falling more slowly for individuals. Between 1989 and 1996, poverty was unchanged for persons in female-headed families, but rose for persons in other family types.

What does Table 6.13 reveal about the relationship between demographic shifts and changes in poverty rates? The prima facie evidence is mixed. On the one hand, it is clear that there has been a compositional shift to families more vulnerable to poverty. However, when the demographic shifts were occurring most rapidly, in the 1969-79 period, the overall poverty rates declined from 12.1% to 11.7%, with declines occurring for each family type. Conversely, when demographic forces diminished over the 1980s, the poverty trend reversed. Moreover, poverty also grew among the family type least vulnerable to poverty: persons in married-couple families. Thus, while demographic shifts to family types with higher poverty rates have played a role in the high poverty rates of the 1980s, the extent of that role is unclear.

To clarify the role of demographic change, **Table 6.14** uses a decomposi-

TABLE 6.13 Changing family structure and poverty, 1959-96

Year	Percent of persons in:				Poverty rate of persons in:			
	Female-headed families	Married-couple and male-headed families*	Not living in families	Total	Female-headed families	Married-couple and male-headed families*	Not living in families	All persons
1959	8.0%	85.9%	6.1%	100.0%	49.4%	18.2%	46.1%	22.4%
1969	9.0	83.7	7.3	100.0	38.2	7.4	34.0	12.1
1979	12.1	76.2	11.7	100.0	34.9	6.4	21.9	11.7
1989	13.2	72.5	14.3	100.0	35.9	7.3	19.2	12.8
1996	14.5	70.2	15.3	100.0	35.8	7.6	20.8	13.7
Percentage-point changes								
1959-69	1.0	-2.2	1.3	0.0	-11.2	-10.8	-12.1	-10.3
1969-79	3.1	-7.5	4.4	0.0	-3.3	-0.9	-12.0	-0.4
1979-89	1.1	-3.7	2.6	0.0	1.0	0.9	-2.7	1.1
1989-96**	1.8	-3.2	1.4	0.0	-0.2	0.4	2.2	1.3
1959-96	6.5	-15.7	9.2	0.0	-13.6	-10.5	-25.3	-8.6

* From 1979 forward, this group includes a small residual number of persons in unrelated subfamilies.
** 10-year growth rates.

Source: Authors' analysis of U.S. Bureau of the Census, P60-198.

TABLE 6.14 The impact of changes in family structure on poverty rates, 1959-96

	Changes in poverty due to:		
	Family structure*	Other factors**	Total
1959-69	0.7	-10.9	-10.3
1969-79	1.8	-2.2	-0.4
1979-89	0.7	0.4	1.1
1989-96***	0.7	0.6	1.3
1959-96	3.6	-12.3	-8.6

*   Change in poverty rates due to changes in the percent of persons in each of the three family types shown in the previous table.
** Change in poverty rates due to changes in factors other than family structure, most notably, changes in incomes within the various family types.
*** 10-year growth rate so as to be comparable to other rows.

Source: Table 6.13.

tion technique to separate the impact of family structure changes from other factors (the most important of which is economic changes). Column 3 of the table shows the change in the poverty rates over the three periods of interest. Columns 1 and 2 divide these changes into the portions due to demographic change and that due to other factors. The 1989-96 growth rates are adjusted to reflect 10-year growth rates so that they are comparable to the three previous rows.

While the shift to more vulnerable family types has clearly played its expected poverty-increasing role, other than in the 1970s that role has been remarkably consistent. In the 1960s, 1980s, and 1990s, family structure changes added 0.7 percentage points to poverty rates. Only in the 1970s did this value accelerate.

In the 1960s, family structure changes were quite unimportant relative to the other factors (mostly broad-based growth and the expansion of government transfers) that lowered poverty by 10.3 percentage points. In the 1980s and 1990s, family structure changes accounted for similar shares of the increase in poverty, 60% in the 1980s and 53% in the 1990s. Only in the 1970s were family structure changes the key determinant of poverty's growth, accounting for 1.8 percentage points. This contribution, however, was outpaced by other changes, which led to a 2.2 percentage point decline in the 1970s (we focus on the other changes below).

What is the importance of this pattern of the contribution of family structure to changes in poverty rates? If this type of demographic change were to be a reasonable suspect for the question under investigation — what accounts for the post-1979 disconnect between poverty and economic growth? — it would need to have accelerated as a poverty determinant. That is, we would expect to see the family structure component in Table 6.14 growing both numerically and as a share of the total change in poverty. Instead, both the 1980s and 1990s reveal a positive yet decelerating contribution of family structure changes to poverty in the post-1979 period. Thus, we must look beyond family structure changes to explain the uncoupling of poverty and growth in the 1980s and 1990s.

While the shift to more vulnerable family types has led to increases in poverty rates, an often-overlooked countervailing trend is the educational upgrading of heads of families. As Americans from all walks of life become more highly educated, they and their families are less likely to be poor. This relationship can be seen in **Table 6.15**, which shows the family poverty rates for families with children in the 1969-96 period by the education level of the family head, along with the shares of families in each category. Clearly, families headed by persons with higher levels of education are less likely to be poor. Note, for example, that families with children headed by a college graduate have poverty rates between 2% and 3%. The bottom panel of the table shows the persistent shift toward higher levels of educational attainment. For instance, over the full period for which we have these types of data, 1969-96, there was a 24.4 percentage point shift out of the bottom two education categories into the some college and college graduate categories.

So far we have shown that, while family structure changes have played a role in increasing poverty rates, education has played a countervailing role. We have also stressed the role played by other factors, including the increase in economic inequality. While we have lumped the nondemographic factors (such as overall economic growth and growing inequality) together in the above decompositions, we need now to account for these factors separately as well. **Table 6.16** provides a decomposition of poverty's growth that separately accounts for these factors.

This table decomposes, or separates out, the growth in person-level poverty rates into three demographic factors — the race of the family head, the education level of the family head, and family structure — and two economic components — the poverty-reducing effect of overall economic growth and the poverty-increasing effect of growing inequality (these changes are slightly different in some periods than those in previous tables due to rounding). Thus, it highlights the relative importance of these different factors in the growth of poverty in each time period. If the conventional wisdom is correct — that family struc-

TABLE 6.15 Educational level of family heads and poverty, families with children, 1969-96

Educational level of family heads	Poverty rates				Changes			
	1969	1979	1989	1996	1969-79	1979-89	1989-96	1969-96
Less than high school	19.4%	26.8%	38.0%	42.1%	7.3	11.3	5.9	22.7
High school	6.6	10.4	15.4	17.5	3.8	5.0	3.1	10.9
Some college	5.4	6.8	9.0	11.5	1.4	2.2	3.6	6.2
College +	2.0	2.5	2.6	3.0	0.4	0.1	0.6	1.0
Total	10.5	12.5	15.5	16.5	2.0	2.9	1.4	6.0
	Poverty rates				Changes			
Less than high school	37.0%	26.2%	18.9%	16.3%	-10.8	-7.3	-3.6	-20.7
High school	36.4	38.1	38.7	32.7	1.7	0.5	-8.5	-3.7
Some college	12.1	16.3	19.9	27.7	4.2	3.6	11.1	15.6
College +	14.5	19.4	22.6	23.3	4.9	3.2	1.0	8.8
Total	100.0	100.0	100.0	100.0	0.0	0.0	0.0	0.0

Source: Authors' analysis of March CPS data.

TABLE 6.16 Decomposing changes in poverty rates into demographic and economic factors

	1969-79	1979-89	1989-96*	1969-96
Total change	-0.5	1.2	1.3	1.6
Demographic factors	0.5	-0.3	-0.2	0.1
Race/ethnicity	0.3	0.4	0.4	0.9
Education of family head	-1.5	-1.2	-1.1	-3.5
Family structure	1.8	0.7	0.7	3.0
Interaction	-0.2	-0.1	-0.2	-0.4
Economic change	-1.0	1.4	1.5	1.5
Income growth	-1.5	-1.2	-0.9	-3.3
Inequality	0.5	2.6	2.5	4.8

* 10-year growth rates.

Source: Authors' analysis of March CPS data.

ture changes are the key factor driving a wedge between economic growth and poverty — then this decomposition should reveal a consistent increase in this factor's role over time. Similarly, the role of economic factors — such as the overall growth of the economy and especially the increase in inequality — should have diminished.

In fact, as Table 6.16 shows, the opposite is the case. Family structure changes played the largest role in poverty's growth in the 1970s; however, in the 1980s and 1990s, the higher poverty associated with changes in family structure component of demographic change was more than offset by the poverty-reducing impact of educational upgrading. In the 1970s, poverty rates fell by 0.5 percentage points, thanks to economic growth that was only partially offset by increasing income inequality (which grew little in this period relative to later periods) and demographic change. As shown in Table 6.13 above, the 1970s saw an accelerated shift toward female-headed families, leading to a relatively large 1.8 percentage point increase in poverty. However, the educational upgrading described in Table 6.15 was an important countervailing factor (lowering poverty by 1.5 percentage points), and this decomposition shows this effect to almost reverse the poverty-increasing impact of family structure in the 1970s.

Family structure plays a lesser role in the next two time periods, accounting for 0.7 points of poverty's growth in both cases. Education levels of family heads continued to reduce poverty rates, by 1.2 points in the 1980s and 1.1 points in the 1990s. Since the role of race (the racial composition of family heads) accelerated only very slightly, the impact of all demographic change on post-1979 poverty rates was actually slightly negative.

Given that demographic shifts, fully considered, have been relatively neutral in affecting poverty, the factors leading to higher poverty rates must have been economic. In fact, the big change in the post-1970s period was the increased role of inequality, which increased poverty rates by about two-and-a-half points in each period. This, in tandem with the diminished poverty-reducing impact of overall growth (which slowed in the 1980s and 1990s), combined to reverse the post-1970s role of economic change in the growth of poverty. Whereas the combination of economic growth and inequality lowered poverty rates by 1 point over the 1970s, it contributed about one-and-a-half points to poverty's growth over the 1980s and 1990s.

In sum, a full accounting for the scope of demographic change over the last 30 years does not support a simple story where the increased share of female-headed families is the sole, or even the most important, determinant of increased poverty. Family structure changes were most "influential" over the 1970s, when poverty rates actually fell slightly due to strong and fairly balanced economic growth. After that, though such changes continued to put upward pressure on poverty rates, their role decelerated. Also, the usual demographic story fails to take account of the successively higher levels of the education of family heads over time. Over the full period, this factor alone reduced poverty by 3.5 points. Finally, if we examine Table 6.16 for the premier culprit in poverty's post-1979 progress, the growth of income inequality would clearly stand out as playing by far the largest role in both the 1980s and 1990s. We return to a closer examination of this factor below, following a review of the other determinant of poverty's growth — the role of taxes and transfers.

The changing effects of taxes and transfers

Another poverty determinant is the extent to which government transfers reduce poverty rates by providing cash and near-cash resources to persons and families. The impact of this determinant over time is a function of two forces: changes in market-driven poverty rates and changes in the magnitude of benefits. If the pre-tax, pre-transfer distribution delivers up less poverty (say, due to stronger and more equal growth), the transfer system has less work to do to reduce poverty rates. Conversely, when inequality rises and incomes fall, the transfer system must expand if poverty is to be further reduced.

Table 6.17 examines both the changes in market poverty and the impact of taxes and transfers for various family types from 1979 to 1997. Column 1 shows

TABLE 6.17 The poverty-reducing effects of transfers, 1979-97

	(1) Before taxes and transfers	(2) After taxes	(3) Plus nonmeans tested (including Medicare)*	(4) Plus means tested (including Medicaid)*	(5) (1)-(4) Reduction in poverty due to taxes and transfers	(6) (5)/(1) Reduction effectiveness rate
All persons						
1979	19.5%	19.3%	12.4%	8.9%	10.6	54%
1989	20.0	20.3	13.5	10.4	9.6	48
1997	21.0	20.1	12.9	10.0	11.0	52
Persons 65 and over						
1979	54.2%	54.1%	15.4%	12.3%	41.9	77%
1989	47.6	48.1	11.4	8.6	39.0	82
1997	49.1	49.1	10.3	8.4	40.7	83
Persons in female-headed families with children under 18						
1979	53.4%	52.3%	47.3%	28.1%	25.3	47%
1989	51.4	51.1	47.0	34.9	16.5	32
1997	50.5	45.9	41.8	30.3	20.2	40
Persons in married-couple families with children under 18						
1979	9.4%	9.1%	7.3%	5.2%	4.2	45%
1989	10.3	10.5	9.0	6.6	3.7	36
1997	10.1	9.1	7.5	5.5	4.6	46

* Includes fungible value of Medicare and Medicaid benefits; see table note.

Source: EPI analysis of U.S. Bureau of the Census P-60, No. 182-RD and No. 201.

301

the poverty rates before taxes and transfers; these rates represent the degree of poverty that would exist in the absence of any government intervention. Moving left to right, the table introduces different transfers and taxes and shows how poverty would be affected by each. In column 2, for example, the poverty rate for all persons fell slightly in 1979 once taxes (and tax credits) are taken into account, from 19.5% to 19.3%. The addition of non-means-tested benefits, including Medicare (i.e., that portion of Medicare estimated to increase a family's resources), lowered the rate to 12.4% in that year (column 3). Column 5 totals the effects of government tax and transfer policies, showing, for example, that in 1979 they reduced market-generated poverty by 10.6 points. The final column, "reduction effectiveness rate," is the previous column divided by column 1: it represents the share of market poverty reduced by government tax and transfer policy.

Note first that market outcomes worsened slightly for all persons over the 1979-97 period, meaning that the tax and transfer system would have had to work harder to keep poverty from rising. In fact, as seen in column 4, for all persons, poverty rates after taxes and transfers were still higher in 1989 than in 1979. Since transfers reduced poverty less in 1989 than in 1979 (column 5), and market poverty was also slightly higher in the later year, the reduction effectiveness rate (the share of market poverty reduced by taxes and transfers) fell from 54% to 48%.

Between 1989 and 1997, the situation improved somewhat. Although market-driven poverty rates again crept up, from 20.0% to 21.0%, the offsetting effect of taxes and transfers expanded. Note, for example, that while taxes raised market poverty 0.3 points in 1989, in 1997, they lowered market poverty by 0.9 points (mostly due to the expansion of the earned-income tax credit). Thanks in part to this expansion, the reduction effectiveness rate returned to about its 1979 level.

Table 6.17 also shows the importance of transfers for persons over 65, who have the highest rates of poverty reduction by far. Note that market outcomes (column 1) became less poverty inducing over the 1980s and that the reduction effectiveness of transfers increased in each period for the elderly. By 1997, 83% of pre-transfer elderly poverty had been reduced by the tax and transfer system.

Relative to the elderly, taxes and transfers were significantly less effective at reducing the poverty of persons in female-headed families with children. Over the 1979-89 period, market outcomes actually reduced their poverty by 2.0 percentage points, but a fall in benefits led to a post-tax and -transfer poverty rate in 1989 that was 6.8 points higher than that of 1979 (column 4), leading to a 15 percentage point decline in the reduction effectiveness rate, from 47% to 32%. Female-headed families with children had a slightly lower rate of market poverty in 1997 than in 1989 and — as with all persons — an expansion of the poverty-reducing effect of taxes. Nevertheless, by the end of period, the reduction effectiveness rate was nine points less than its 1979 level.

Persons in married-couple families with children have also experienced increasing poverty rates since 1979. Over the 1980s, each category of taxes and transfers led to higher poverty rates; by 1989, the reduction effectiveness rate had fallen by 9 points. Again, this pattern reversed in 1989-97, and poverty among persons in these families fell in 1997 from 10.1% to 5.5%, generating a reduction effectiveness rate (46%) one point higher than that of 1979 (45%).

In terms of identifying the suspects in the disconnect between growth and poverty, the message from this table is that, while market poverty grew somewhat over the post-1979 period, further underscoring the theme of this chapter, taxes and transfers were less effective at reducing poverty in the 1980s than in the 1990s. Over the full period, their role has been fairly constant; thus, we return to the issue of growing income inequality, since this is the poverty-inducing factor that has changed the most since 1979.

Income, wage, and employment trends among the poor

While we have emphasized the growth of inequality as a key factor in poverty's failure to respond to economic growth, we are specifically concerned about the failure of the incomes of low-income families to rise in real terms over the past few business cycles. As discussed in Chapter 1, the character of American income inequality has been increasing real incomes at the top of the income scale and lowering them at the bottom, and this pattern of income growth has meant higher poverty rates for those at the low end of the income scale.

Figure 6F shows the close relationship between the trend in low family incomes and family poverty. The solid line shows the trend in family poverty rates, while the dotted line shows the percentage at which incomes of families in the bottom 20% of the income scale have fallen or risen compared to average incomes (in this figure, a decline in low incomes compared to the average is shown as a positive percentage, and vice versa). The fit is very close, suggesting that, if we can understand the factors driving the trends in low incomes, we can better understand why poverty has failed to respond to economic growth in recent years in the way it did in the 1950s through the 1970s.

Table 6.18 shows the decline in income by component for families headed by a prime-age persons (age 25-54) in the bottom 20% of the income scale. We examine prime-age families since they are most likely to be connected to the labor force and thus most likely to be susceptible to economic changes affecting low incomes. The incomes of these families fell by 1.3% annually over the 1980s and by 1.0% per year over the most recent recovery. By 1996, such families were close to $3,000 (in 1996 dollars) poorer than in 1979. Family earnings,

FIGURE 6F Family poverty and income changes among the lowest 20% of families

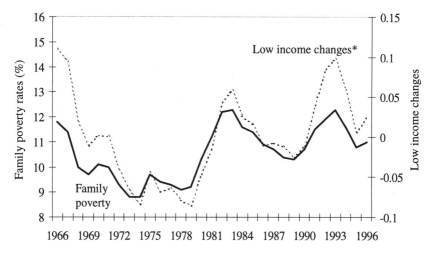

* Negative percent deviation from average income of bottom 20% of families.

Source: Authors' update of Blank and Card (1993).

TABLE 6.18 Family income components of prime-age families in the bottom 20%,* 1979-96 (1996 dollars)

| | 1979 | 1989 | 1996 | Annualized changes | |
				1979-89	1989-96
Total	$15,465	$13,595	$12,628	-1.3%	-1.0%
Earnings	11,490	10,086	9,260	-1.3	-1.2
Unearned income	3,975	3,509	3,368	-1.2	-0.6
Public assistance	1,494	1,259	921	-1.7	-4.4
Other**	2,482	2,250	2,447	-1.0	1.2
Shares of total	100.0%	100.0%	100.0%		
Earnings	74.3	74.2	73.3		
Unearned income	25.7	25.8	26.7		
Public assistance	9.7	9.3	7.3		
Other**	16.0	16.5	19.4		

*   Average values for the bottom 20% of families headed by a prime-age individual.
** Includes income from other cash transfers such as Social Security, as well as a small amount of capital income.

Source: Authors' analysis of March CPS data.

FIGURE 6G Prime-age workers with low earnings and full-time/year-round attachment, 1974-97

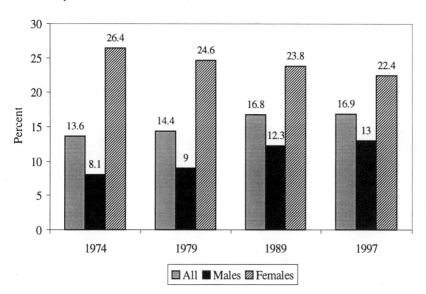

Source: U.S. Bureau of the Census (1992) and unpublished data.

which consistently represent about three-quarters of average family income for these low-income, prime-age families, also fell over both periods. The income component that fell the most in the 1990s was average public assistance (or welfare payments), driven by the real decline in such benefits. Other unearned income sources, such as benefits related to Social Security, increased in the 1990s, but because these families clearly depend on their earnings, which have been falling as the economy has grown, it has become more difficult for them to climb out of poverty.

The next two figures continue this analysis of the earnings of prime-age workers by looking at those with year-round, full-time attachment to the labor force yet with low earnings. These are persons who spent at least 50 weeks of the year at work or looking for work (i.e., in the labor force) and worked full time or else part time but involuntarily, but their annual earnings were not high enough to reach the poverty line for a family of four, which in 1997 was $14,975 (this threshold is based on the CPI-U-X1).

Figure 6G charts the share of these workers, by sex, for the period 1974-97. The trend shows an increased proportion earning poverty-level wages. This

FIGURE 6H Workers in families with children, with low earnings and full-time/year-round attachment 1974-97

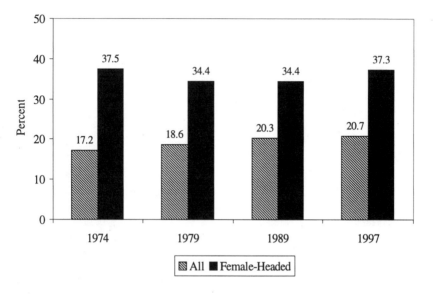

Source: U.S. Bureau of the Census (1992) and unpublished data.

is particularly the case for men, whose share has grown by 4.9 percentage points since 1974. Although the proportion of male low-wage workers grew over the full period, the figure shows that the steepest growth was post-1979, when poverty was least responsive to overall economic growth. For women, the share of low earners hovered around 25% for the full period; by 1997, 22.4% of prime-age female workers (7.6 million) earned poverty-level wages.

Figure 6H focuses on low-earners (again, with full labor-force attachment) in families with children; female-headed families are shown separately. Note that this group of workers is worse off than those shown in the previous figure (compare the levels in the bars marked "All"), suggesting that families with children have a lower standard of living than the population of all prime-age workers. Families with children that are headed by a female are particularly likely to face low earnings; in 1997, close to two-fifths of fully attached workers in these families earned poverty-level wages. Here, too, the pre-1979 trend was toward higher earnings.

As discussed in Chapter 3, the source of these earnings declines is the long-term decline in the real hourly wage rates of low-wage workers. The last few tables in this chapter look at some of the wage and employment trends facing workers with "low-wage" profiles.

Poverty and the low-wage labor market

There are various ways in which poverty trends could be reconnected to economic growth. One way would be to accept the growth of income and wage inequality as a permanent feature on our economic landscape and simply expand the system of transfers from the "winners" to those left behind. Besides the fact that such an expansion of transfer programs is politically unrealistic, this approach consigns the poor to life outside the economic mainstream. Instead, both public sentiment and public policy have stressed the importance of work as a path out of poverty. This sentiment is embodied in welfare reform legislation, the success of which is predicated on former welfare recipients finding gainful employment in the private sector.

But how realistic is this goal? Can we realistically look to the low-wage labor market to reconnect the poor to the growing economy? While the recent tightening in the labor market has led to clear improvements in low-wage labor market conditions, the sector remains economically weak. The high rates of unemployment and underemployment, along with long-term real wage decline among low-wage workers, make it difficult to solve the problem of poverty amidst growth in this segment of the labor market.

We first examine the extent to which the poor actually participate in the labor market. Here again we focus on prime-age workers (age 25-54) and exclude children and the elderly, who are obviously less connected to the labor market. Despite the popular notion that the poor work very little, **Table 6.19** shows that, in 1996, 72.6% of the employable, prime-age poor either worked (67.1%) or sought work (5.5%). The table shows that, of the 12 million prime-age poor persons in 1996, one-quarter were not employable due to illness, disability, school, or retirement. Among the rest of the prime-age poor, termed "employable" in the table, slightly more the one-quarter (27.4%) neither sought nor found work in the most recent year, a share that has continuously fallen since 1979. It is true, however, that while the majority of the prime-age poor work, they are significantly more likely to work part time or part year rather than full time. Here too, though, the trend over time has been toward an increase in the share of full-time, full-year work, from 16.8% in 1979 to 19.7% in 1996.

While Table 6.19 look at the incidence of work among prime-age poor persons, **Table 6.20** extends the analysis by looking at average annual hours of work among low-income families of different family types: all families, all families with a prime-age head of household (25-54), and female-headed and married-couple families with children. The previous table included only the poor; Table 6.20 examines work effort by those in the bottom two-fifths (or quintiles) of the income distribution, which include both the poor and near-poor.

TABLE 6.19 Work experience of the poor, 1979-96

	1979*	1989	1996
Number of poor aged 25-54 (000)	7,659	9,674	11,952
Percent not employable	17.6%	18.4%	25.4%
Ill or disabled	11.7	11.6	17.3
Going to school	5.5	6.3	7.1
Retired	0.4	0.4	1.1
Employable poor aged 25-54	82.4	81.6	74.6
Unable to find work	4.4	6.0	5.5
Percent of employable poor who worked:	64.8	65.0	67.1
Year-round, full time	16.8	18.0	19.7
Part time or part year	48.0	47.0	47.4
Percent of employable poor who either worked or sought work	69.2	71.0	72.6
Percent of employable poor who neither sought nor found work	30.8	29.0	27.4

*Includes persons 22-54.

Source: U.S. Bureau of the Census, various years.

The average hours of work in Table 6.20 represent the pooled work effort of the family. The table shows that, while low-income families predictably have relatively low levels of annual hours of work, particularly in the lowest fifth, they are generally working more now than in 1979 (the one exception is families with prime-age heads of household). In this regard, the table provides no evidence for a shift in labor market participation that would explain the declining incomes of low-income families amidst positive overall economic growth.

Average annual hours of work grew for all family types between 1979 and 1989, with those in the bottom fifth increasing their hours of work by 0.5% per year. Married couples with children have by far the most hours of work; in each year these families supplied an average of well over 2,000 hours of labor. By 1989, the average married-couple family with children in the second fifth worked 3,279 hours, 11.1% more hours than in 1979. Mother-only families with children in the bottom fifth work relatively few hours, on average, over the course of a year, helping to explain their high likelihood of poverty (see Tables 6.4 and 6.5). Nevertheless, their annual hours grew very slightly (0.1% per year) over the 1980s and much more quickly over the 1990s; during that period, their hours of work grew the fastest among the family types examined here.

Given that low-income persons have not generally reduced their work effort, it makes sense to examine the nature of the labor market in which they seek

TABLE 6.20 Annual average of hours worked, low-income families, by family type and income quintile, 1979-96*

	Average annual hours			Annualized percent change		
	1979	1989	1996	1979-89	1989-96	1979-96
All families						
Bottom fifth	1,126	1,185	1,175	0.5%	-0.1%	0.3%
Second fifth	2,267	2,449	2,413	0.8	-0.2	0.4
Families with prime-age head						
Bottom fifth	1,656	1,666	1,540	0.1%	-1.1%	-0.4%
Second fifth	2,820	3,051	2,971	0.8	-0.4	0.3
Female-headed families with children						
Bottom fifth	309	313	366	0.1%	2.3%	1.0%
Second fifth	743	782	952	0.5	2.9	1.5
Married-couple families with children						
Bottom fifth	2,190	2,400	2,333	0.9%	-0.4%	0.4%
Second fifth	2,950	3,279	3,412	1.1	0.6	0.9

* Families exclude unrelated individuals. Fifths are defined separately for each family type.

Source: Authors' analysis of March CPS data.

work. To do this, we first develop a profile of low-wage workers, enabling us to then examine the employment conditions facing persons with those characteristics. **Table 6.21** looks at the demographic characteristics of low-wage workers compared to those of the overall workforce in 1997. Low-wage workers, in column 1, are defined as those whose hourly wage would lift a family of four just up to the poverty line in 1997: $7.89 per hour.

This group's average wage in 1997 was $5.92, 25% below the poverty-level wage. Comparing the percentages in the two columns reveals categories in which low-wage workers are overrepresented. Such workers are disproportionately female, minority, non-college educated, and young. They also are more likely to work in low-wage industries such as retail trade and less likely to work in manufacturing, transportation and utilities, and government. By occupation, low-wage workers are overrepresented in services, where they staff the low-paying jobs in food and health services. They are least likely to be managers and professionals. Finally, they are significantly less likely to either be union members or covered by union contracts.

TABLE 6.21 Characteristics of low-wage workers, 1997

	Low wage*	Total
Share of Total	28.6%	100.0%
Number	31,218,761	109,049,044
Average wage	$5.92	$13.51
Sex		
Male	41.2%	52.3%
Female	58.8	47.7
Race		
White	63.0%	73.6%
Black	15.4	11.5
Hispanic	17.2	10.5
Other	4.4	4.3
Education		
Less than high school	22.9%	11.1%
High school	39.3	33.2
Some college	24.0	21.0
Associate degree	5.5	8.5
College or more	8.3	26.2
Age		
18-25	36.4%	17.1%
26-35	24.3	27.3
35+	39.3	55.6
Industry		
Construction	3.5%	5.5%
Manufacuring	12.9	18.0
Wholesale trade	2.8	3.8
Retail trade	31.7	15.8
Finance	4.0	6.5
Transportation, utilities	3.9	7.7
Services	35.8	35.5
Government	1.9	5.1
Other	3.5	2.1
Occupation		
Managers, professionals	9.4%	28.6%
Technical, sales	17.6	14.7
Clerical	15.0	15.5
Services	28.8	13.4
Blue collar	25.6	26.3
Others	3.6	1.6
Union status		
Union**	6.6%	16.1%
Nonunion	93.4	83.9

* Low wage refers to hourly wage rate necessary to lift a family of four above the poverty line with full-time, full-year work. In 1997, this wage was $7.89.

** Union includes members and workers covered by union contracts.

Source: Authors' analysis of CPS ORG data.

TABLE 6.22 Unemployment and underemployment* rates, 1997, by sex and race

	Males		Females	
	Unemployment	Under-employment	Unemployment	Under-employment
All	4.9%	8.8%	5.1%	10.0%
Less than high school	10.8	18.8	13.1	23.2
16-25	17.8	28.4	19.3	30.1
26-35	9.2	16.9	14.9	26.7
High school	5.3	9.4	5.3	10.8
16-25	10.6	18.4	11.1	21.2
26-35	5.1	8.9	6.1	11.8
White	3.9	7.0	3.8	7.8
Less than high school	9.5	16.5	10.3	18.4
16-25	14.9	24.2	14.6	23.1
High school	4.3	7.7	4.1	8.7
16-25	8.3	15.0	8.4	17.6
Black	10.3	16.7	10.0	17.3
Less than high school	19.4	30.3	21.8	35.2
16-25	36.6	50.9	36.2	51.2
High school	10.7	17.5	10.5	18.3
16-25	23.0	34.2	19.7	31.7
Hispanic	7.1	13.3	9.1	17.5
Less than high school	9.5	17.8	14.2	26.6
16-25	15.7	27.0	23.0	37.2
High school	6.1	11.6	8.3	16.1
16-25	9.2	18.8	14.1	26.1

* Underemployment refers to persons who are either unemployed, discouraged, involuntarily part time, or have sought work in the past year but are not currently looking due to various constraints, such as lack of child care or transportation.

Source: EPI analysis of CPS monthly data.

Table 6.22 examines labor market conditions in 1997 facing workers with "low-wage profiles" identified in the previous table in terms of unemployment and underemployment rates (underemployment adds discouraged workers and marginally connected workers to the unemployed). While overall labor market conditions were positive in 1997, as shown by the unemployment rates in the first row, the unemployment rates of those with the characteristics of low-wage workers were notably higher.

Though overall female unemployment was 5.1% in 1997, women with less

TABLE 6.23 Annualized changes in hourly wages of low-wage workers, 1973-97

	10th	20th	30th
Males			
1973-79	-0.2%	-0.4%	-0.1%
1979-89	-1.3	-1.5	-1.3
1989-97	-0.5	-0.6	-0.9
Females			
1973-79	3.3%	1.0%	0.4%
1979-89	-2.0	-0.7	-0.1
1989-97	0.3	-0.1	0.0

Source: Authors' analysis of CPS ORG data.

than a high school degree (an education level common among long-term welfare recipients) had an unemployment rate of 13.1%; for young women in this education group unemployment was 19.3%. And for young black women with less than a high school education, the unemployment rate was 36.2%, more than seven times the national rate.

As seen in Chapter 4, minority workers have unemployment rates approximately twice the overall rate, and a similar relationship holds for underemployment rates. While overall male underemployment was 8.8% in 1997, for black men it was 16.7% and for Hispanic men, 13.3%. Again, younger males with a high school education or less had relatively high levels of un- and underemployment.

This evidence suggests that, within the tight overall labor market in 1997, there were pockets of weak demand for workers with low-wage characteristics. Further evidence is provided in the next table, which examines the inflation-adjusted wage trends of low-wage workers.

Table 6.23 examines the annualized percentage changes in hourly wage levels of the poorest male and female workers (those in the bottom 30% of the hourly earnings distribution). For low-wage men between 1973 and 1979, there were small negative changes in the bottom three-tenths. For low-wage women, 1973-79 was a period of strong growth, particularly among the lowest-wage female workers, as the 10th percentile female wage grew 3.3% annually. This pattern of gains or small losses reversed, however, between 1979 and 1989, as all groups in the bottom 30% experienced real wage declines. Men in particular (and the lowest-earning women) experienced the steepest losses. Those in the

FIGURE 6I Real hourly wages of low-wage workers (1997 dollars)

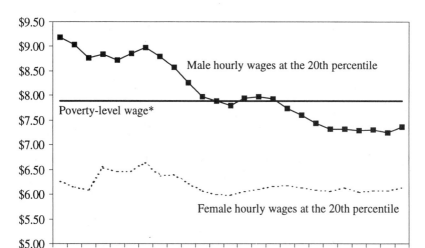

* $7.89 is the wage level that, at full-time, full-year work, would lift a family of four above the poverty line ($16,411 in 1997 dollars).

Source: Authors' analysis of CPS data.

bottom three deciles saw annual declines of 1.3%, 1.5%, and 1.3% in their hourly wages. Between 1989 and 1996, wage rates continued to fall, though at a slower rate, for low-wage men, while things improved slightly for low-wage women, particularly those at the 10th percentile, who benefited from two minimum wage increases over this period. (As Chapter 3 explains, this policy is particularly relevant to low-wage females.)

Figure 6I shows the trend in the 20th percentile wage, in 1997 dollars, relative to the 1997 poverty-level wage ($7.89; see Table 6.21). Clearly, female wages at the 20th percentile have at no time in the period been near the poverty-level wage. Male 20th percentile wages, however, were well above the poverty level wage at the beginning of the period, though their erosion over time has left them below it by the end of the period. Note that labor market tightening and the minimum wage increases led to slight "upticks" in the wage rates of both sexes at the end of period. Nevertheless, the wage and employment conditions shown in these last few tables make it difficult to see how low-wage workers can realistically be expected to work their way out of poverty.

Conclusion

Despite long economic recoveries over the 1980s and 1990s, poverty rates have failed to respond and, at 13.3% in 1997, remain significantly higher than would be expected given the extent of overall economic growth. This chapter has examined the persistent disconnect between growth and poverty in an effort to understand what factors are responsible.

Since there are conceptual problems in the way poverty is measured, we first pointed out that different measures of poverty yield the same trend in poverty rates, showing that the disconnect theme is not an artifact of how poverty is measured. We then turned to a decomposition of the growth of poverty from 1969 to 1996 in order to isolate the roles played by various candidates in the explanation of poverty's failure to fall over the past few recoveries. Contrary to the conventional wisdom, which assigns a large role to changes in family structure, we find that this factor was less important in the 1980s and 1990s than in the 1970s, when poverty fell for all family types. In addition, when we add the poverty-reducing role of educational upgrading by family heads of household, the net effect of demographics is to lower poverty rates in the post-1979 period.

Since the poverty-reducing role of taxes and transfers changed little over the period (the exception is less-effective poverty reduction for families headed by females), we are left with economic explanations. The amount of work, measured either by employment counts or hours of work by low-income families, has changed little over the period. This leads us to suspect that weak conditions in the low-wage labor market must be making it difficult for low-wage workers to generate family income levels that would lift them above the poverty line. We show here that, despite overall tight labor markets in 1997, low-wage workers face pockets of weak demand — with unemployment rates many times that of the national average — in addition to declining real wages.

American antipoverty policy, as embodied in welfare reform, is structured clearly to emphasize the importance of work as a path out of poverty. No doubt, this policy emphasis reflects American values regarding the integrity of work and public distaste for dependence on government support by low-income families. However, the labor market data presented in this chapter pose a stiff challenge to this aspect of current antipoverty policy. Even in the context of the tight labor market of the late 1990s, wages and employment opportunities will have to expand significantly if low-wage workers are to work their way out of poverty.

CHAPTER 7

Regional analysis: tighter labor markets, but income growth stagnant

MOST OF THE ANALYSIS UP TO THIS POINT HAS LOOKED AT THE NATION AS A WHOLE. In this chapter, we shift the focus to regions, divisions (i.e., groups of states within regions), and states. As might be expected, we find that the trends in states and regions often mirror those at the national level: despite positive overall growth, the living standards of many working families have been reduced.

We also depart here from our usual focus on one aspect of the economy per chapter and instead provide an overview of income, employment, wage, poverty, and tax trends at the regional level. One advantage of this approach is that it allows for an examination of economic conditions within a state or region along various dimensions.

A number of overall regional trends stand out. Over the 1980s, most workers in the Northeast did notably better on each indicator (e.g., median wages and incomes rose; poverty and unemployment fell) than did workers in the other regions. However, despite low unemployment, low-wage workers in some Northeastern states (e.g., New York and Pennsylvania) still lost ground. States in the West, particularly California, experienced relatively flat growth rates in terms of employment and median incomes, and wages declined for workers at the median and below.

The 1990s recession, however, was most acutely experienced in California and New York, as incomes and employment contracted and poverty grew. The most recent data (1996 or 1997) show working families in these large states to be worse off than they were at the previous business cycle peak in 1989.

Many other states, however, have clearly benefited from the recent tightening of labor markets. In 1997, unemployment was below 4% in numerous states (e.g., in the Midwest), and, thanks in part to increases in the minimum wage (see

Chapter 3), the real wages of low-wage workers in these states have grown over the recovery.

Due to the limited nature of these regional data, some of these series are presented for time periods that differ from tables in the other chapters. Also, due to lack of sufficient data in some states, it is not possible to accurately show every variable for each state; consequently, in some cases the data are "aggregated up" to the level of division or region.

Median family income declines in most states

As discussed in Chapter 1, the income of the median family (the family at the midpoint of the family income distribution) is a key indicator of the economic well being of the typical family. **Figure 7A** and **Table 7.1** show that, in every region, the income of the median family rose more quickly prior to 1973 than after. While the trends were similar in most regions, the level of the median family's income has been consistently lower in the South. (From 1973 onward this difference has remained roughly constant, with the South about 10% below the national level.)

To some extent, the deregulation of financial markets in the 1980s favored the Northeast, where this sector is most heavily concentrated, and led to a notable deviation from the national trend in this area in the mid- to late 1980s. As the annual changes in Table 7.1 show, while the income of the median family in the other regions was growing at historically moderate rates, the income of families in the Northeast was growing more than three times as fast over the 1980s. By the peak of the 1980s business cycle, the income of the median Northeast family was 29% higher than that of the South and 11% above that of the West.

However, the median family in the Northeast lost ground the fastest in the recession of the early 1990s (although the West was a close second). As noted in Chapter 3, the fact that white-collar workers were uncharacteristically vulnerable in that recession is probably to blame for the sharp Northeastern decline. Thus, in 1996, the last year of available data, the median family in the Northeast was $3,407 dollars below its 1989 peak, representing a larger gap than that of any of the other regions. The median Western family was also worse off in 1996 relative to 1989, by $2,601. (Note that Figure 7A shows a slight downturn in the median income in the West from 1995 to 1996.)

Table 7.2 shows the trend in the median family income for four-person families by state for the period 1974-96. (This series of data is unavailable prior to 1974.) By controlling for family size, the data in this table address the argu-

FIGURE 7A Poverty rates by region, 1971-96

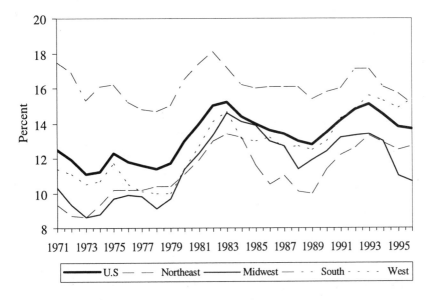

Source: See Table 7.12.

TABLE 7.1 Median family income by region (1996 dollars)

Year	U.S.	Northeast	Midwest	South	West
1953	$22,951	$24,752	$24,801	$17,897	$24,882
1973	40,059	42,715	42,652	35,326	41,452
1979	41,530	43,724	43,616	37,211	43,866
1989	43,290	49,960	43,797	38,591	45,170
1996	42,300	46,553	44,957	38,710	42,569
Annual Growth Rates					
1953-73	2.8%	2.8%	2.7%	3.5%	2.6%
1973-79	0.6	0.4	0.4	0.9	0.9
1979-89	0.4	1.3	0.0	0.4	0.3
1989-96	-0.3	-1.0	0.4	0.0	-0.8

Source: U.S. Bureau of the Census, Income Website.

TABLE 7.2 Median income for four-person families, by state, 1974-96 (1996 dollars)

	1974	1979	1989	1996	Annual growth rates 1974-79	1979-89	1989-96
NORTHEAST							
New England							
Maine	$37,946	$38,322	$48,507	$48,632	0.2%	2.4%	0.0%
New Hampshire	42,281	47,356	60,714	56,497	2.3	2.5	-1.0
Vermont	39,739	40,951	51,115	49,401	0.6	2.2	-0.5
Massachusetts	47,251	50,433	65,542	62,385	1.3	2.7	-0.7
Rhode Island	43,545	45,874	54,761	53,967	1.0	1.8	-0.2
Connecticut	49,809	51,756	67,458	67,380	0.8	2.7	0.0
Middle Atlantic							
New York	$45,858	$44,700	$55,286	$52,799	-0.5%	2.1%	-0.7%
New Jersey	50,568	52,243	67,352	65,586	0.7	2.6	-0.4
Pennsylvania	43,802	47,312	51,124	53,814	1.6	0.8	0.7
MIDWEST							
East North Central							
Ohio	$45,713	$47,765	$52,472	$51,835	0.9%	0.9%	-0.2%
Indiana	43,769	47,948	48,337	52,962	1.8	0.1	1.3
Illinois	49,428	51,448	53,914	55,372	0.8	0.5	0.4
Michigan	48,896	51,781	54,187	56,174	1.2	0.5	0.5
Wisconsin	46,550	49,865	51,318	52,986	1.4	0.3	0.5
West North Central							
Minnesota	$47,741	$51,754	$53,605	$56,200	1.6%	0.4%	0.7%
Iowa	43,445	47,848	46,483	48,167	1.9	-0.3	0.5
Missouri	41,628	45,149	48,687	50,015	1.6	0.8	0.4
North Dakota	45,362	41,388	44,041	45,480	-1.8	0.6	0.5
South Dakota	38,769	40,728	41,539	45,043	1.0	0.2	1.2
Nebraska	40,401	43,993	47,958	46,726	1.7	0.9	-0.4
Kansas	43,518	48,444	48,004	49,034	2.2	-0.1	0.3
SOUTH							
South Atlantic							
Delaware	$46,045	$44,916	$54,143	$56,662	-0.5%	1.9%	0.7%
Maryland	50,335	52,341	63,450	61,860	0.8	1.9	-0.4
DC	45,628	45,183	51,339	53,256	-0.2	1.3	0.5
Virginia	45,740	48,715	57,053	53,394	1.3	1.6	-0.9
West Virginia	37,998	40,022	40,251	41,293	1.0	0.1	0.4
North Carolina	39,854	41,659	48,168	49,272	0.9	1.5	0.3
South Carolina	39,467	42,732	45,695	46,973	1.6	0.7	0.4
Georgia	41,314	45,751	50,637	48,920	2.1	1.0	-0.5
Florida	44,706	44,010	47,322	44,829	-0.3	0.7	-0.8
East South Central							
Kentucky	$37,831	$40,578	$43,514	$44,932	1.4%	0.7%	0.5%
Tennessee	38,660	41,212	44,137	45,245	1.3	0.7	0.4
Alabama	38,711	39,465	44,198	44,879	0.4	1.1	0.2
Mississippi	34,953	37,469	40,870	38,748	1.4	0.9	-0.8

(cont.)

TABLE 7.2 *(cont.)* Median income for four-person families, by state, 1974-96 (1996 dollars)

	1974	1979	1989	1996	Annual growth rates		
					1974-79	1979-89	1989-96
SOUTH *(cont.)*							
West South Central							
Arkansas	$35,945	$39,210	$40,304	$36,828	1.8%	0.3%	-1.3%
Louisiana	38,091	42,757	43,535	41,851	2.3	0.2	-0.6
Oklahoma	38,227	44,212	43,616	43,138	3.0	-0.1	-0.2
Texas	42,094	49,648	44,258	46,757	3.4	-1.1	0.8
WEST							
Mountain							
Montana	$41,374	$42,514	$42,872	$41,462	0.5%	0.1%	-0.5%
Idaho	42,550	43,315	42,557	44,133	0.4	-0.2	0.5
Wyoming	44,842	48,073	45,071	46,830	1.4	-0.6	0.5
Colorado	47,248	53,490	50,948	53,632	2.5	-0.5	0.7
New Mexico	36,710	44,594	39,422	38,143	4.0	-1.2	-0.5
Arizona	46,042	48,766	48,521	45,032	1.2	-0.1	-1.1
Utah	42,333	45,056	46,263	45,775	1.3	0.3	-0.2
Nevada	46,426	53,976	50,280	50,946	3.1	-0.7	0.2
Pacific							
Washington	$46,559	$51,756	$52,799	$53,153	2.1%	0.2%	0.1%
Oregon	45,386	50,952	48,997	46,245	2.3	-0.4	-0.8
California	48,161	53,238	54,172	53,807	2.0	0.2	-0.1
Alaska	58,552	65,807	61,256	62,078	2.4	-0.7	0.2
Hawaii	51,602	52,120	56,924	57,909	0.2	0.9	0.2
TOTAL U.S.	$44,582	$47,483	51,578	$51,518	1.3%	0.8%	0.0%

Source: Authors' analysis of U.S. Bureau of the Census, Income Website.

ment by some analysts that, since family size has declined over time, income trends overstate recent income losses.

Income growth for the median four-person family was fairly uniform across states in the 1970s, although some of the energy-rich states in the Southwest appear to have benefited from the rise in energy prices. Growth was both slower and less uniform in the 1980s: a number of Northeastern states experienced faster-than-average income growth, while some of the Southwestern states saw their fortunes reverse as the growth in energy prices tapered off.

Nationally, the median income of four-person families did not grow at all from 1989 to 1996; by the end of this period, such families in many states were worse off than in 1989. As noted, the recession of the early 1990s led to significant losses for states in the Northeast. The median four-person family income in New Hampshire, for example, fell 1% annually; in New York, the decline was 0.7% annually. In dollar terms, the median four-person family in New York was about $2,500 worse off in 1996 relative to 1989.

Other states with large annual losses (relative to the nation) were Virginia (-0.9%), Arkansas (-1.3%), Arizona (-1.1%), and Oregon (-0.8%). As shown below, some of these states, like Arkansas, enjoyed relatively fast job growth over the period. This disparate pattern of positive job and negative income growth in Arkansas underscores the importance of using various economic criteria to evaluate a state's economic progress.

The growth of income inequality by state

While Chapter 1 focused on the growth of family income inequality at the national level, here we examine the same phenomenon at the state level. The metric we use is the ratio of the average income of the best-off families to that of the least well-off. Thus, we compare the average income of the top fifth to that of the bottom fifth (**Table 7.3**) and, for a subset of states, the top 5% to the bottom fifth (**Table 7.4**; due to sample constraints, we are able to reliably calculate the average income of the top 5% for only 11 states). In order to generate large enough samples to make reliable comparisons, we pooled three years of data together for three time periods: 1978-1980, 1988-1990, and 1994-1996. Thus, we keep to the pattern of comparing economic peaks along with the most recent data available.

As shown in Chapter 1, national family income inequality increased over the 1980s and 1990s. The data in Table 7.3 show that, in the late 1970s, families in the top fifth earned, on average, 7.7 times that of families in the bottom fifth. By the end of the period covered in the table — the mid-1990s — that ratio had increased to 10.7. Comparing the top 5% to the bottom fifth at the national level (Table 7.4), the ratio grew from 12.1 to 18.5.

At the state level, family income inequality increased persistently in both New York and California. Over the 1980s, the top-fifth/bottom-fifth ratio grew 2.4 points in New York and 2.1 points in California. Other states where income inequality grew faster than the national average in the 1980s included Indiana, Michigan, Missouri, West Virginia, Mississippi, Louisiana, and Hawaii. Inequality continued to grow in most states in the 1990s, with faster growth in both New York and California (especially considering the shorter time period). By the end of the period, the average income of the richest fifth of New York families was 13.7 times that of the poorest families in that state. The Southwestern states of

New Mexico and Arizona also saw relatively fast growth in inequality over the 1990s, and ended the period with levels similar to New York (13.0 and 13.8, respectively).

Table 7.4 provides information on the gap between income of the very wealthy in the top 5% and those in the bottom 20%. Even before family inequality began its upward climb over the 1980s and 1990s, the average income of the top 5% was at least 10 times that of the bottom 20%. Over the 1980s, this measure of disparity grew by 3.2 points nationally, led by California (3.6), New York (3.5), and Illinois (3.4). In the 1990s, the growth of inequality accelerated, and by the end of the period the wealthiest families in numerous states had incomes around 20 times that of the lowest-income families.

Job growth, but falling median wages

In this section, we examine employment, unemployment, average wages, and median wages, along with state-level indicators of conditions in the low-wage labor market. Two important findings emerge: (1) growth over the various periods examined was uneven, with a good deal of variation among the states, and (2) the decline of unemployment in the 1990s, in tandem with increases in the minimum wage, led to wage growth for low-wage workers in numerous states. Average and median wages, however, were less likely to respond positively to growing employment and falling unemployment.

Employment and unemployment
Table 7.5 shows nonfarm payroll employment by state for the period 1973-97, along with annual rates of employment growth for various periods. While employment grew by almost 45 million jobs over the full period, growth was uneven by region and time period. Over the 1970s (the fastest period of job growth in the period covered), the Mountain and Pacific states in the West experienced particularly strong growth rates. For example, employment growth in the relatively large Pacific states of California (4.0% per year) and Washington (5.4%) was notably faster than the average national growth rate (2.6%). At the same time, employment growth in some of the large Eastern states, like New York (0.1%), New Jersey (1.6%), and Massachusetts (1.8%), was below average.

During the 1980s employment growth slowed in the West and in the "rust belt" states of the Midwest. Growth in Michigan and Illinois slowed to less than 1%; in Wisconsin, employment grew at about two-thirds the national rate. Growth accelerated, however, in New York and New Jersey as the service sector ex-

TABLE 7.3 Income inequality by state, late 1970s to mid-1980s

	Income ratio, top 20%/lowest 20%			Changes (top 20%/lowest 20%)	
	1978-80	1988-90	1994-96	Late 1970s-late 1980s	Late 1980s-mid-1990s
NORTHEAST					
New England					
Maine	6.7	7.7	7.4	1.0	-0.3
New Hampshire	5.8	7.0	7.6	1.2	0.6
Vermont	6.6	7.4	7.2	0.8	-0.2
Massachusetts	7.4	8.8	10.0	1.4	1.3
Rhode Island	6.5	7.3	8.9	0.8	1.6
Connecticut	6.4	6.4	10.1	0.0	3.7
Middle Atlantic					
New York	8.1	10.5	13.7	2.4	3.2
New Jersey	7.1	8.2	9.6	1.1	1.4
Pennsylvania	6.6	8.0	9.2	1.4	1.2
MIDWEST					
East North Central					
Ohio	6.7	8.5	9.4	1.8	0.9
Indiana	5.9	7.9	8.0	2.0	0.1
Illinois	7.9	9.8	10.3	1.9	0.6
Michigan	6.8	8.9	9.5	2.1	0.5
Wisconsin	6.3	6.6	7.7	0.3	1.2
West North Central					
Minnesota	6.2	7.7	8.2	1.4	0.5
Iowa	5.9	6.6	8.4	0.7	1.9
Missouri	7.1	9.1	7.5	2.0	-1.6
North Dakota	7.5	6.9	7.0	-0.7	0.2
South Dakota	7.6	7.4	7.6	-0.2	0.1
Nebraska	6.8	7.2	7.7	0.4	0.6
Kansas	6.3	7.0	8.8	0.7	1.8
SOUTH					
South Atlantic					
Delaware	6.9	6.8	8.3	-0.1	1.5
Maryland	7.2	8.2	9.4	1.0	1.2
DC	12.5	16.5	21.8	4.0	5.3
Virginia	7.5	9.2	9.7	1.6	0.5
West Virginia	6.5	8.9	10.2	2.4	1.3
North Carolina	7.4	8.5	9.4	1.1	0.9
South Carolina	8.1	9.4	10.0	1.3	0.6
Georgia	8.3	10.4	10.5	2.1	0.1
Florida	8.2	9.2	10.9	1.0	1.7
East South Central					
Kentucky	7.3	9.0	10.6	1.7	1.6
Tennessee	8.5	10.4	10.3	1.9	-0.1
Alabama	9.2	9.9	10.7	0.7	0.9
Mississippi	9.0	11.0	10.5	2.0	-0.6

(cont.)

TABLE 7.3 *(cont.)* Income inequality by state, late 1970s to mid-1980s

	Income ratio, top 20%/lowest 20%			Changes (top 20%/lowest 20%)	
	1978-80	1988-90	1994-96	Late 1970s-late 1980s	Late 1980s-mid-1990s
SOUTH *(cont.)*					
West South Central					
Arkansas	8.7	9.4	8.4	0.7	-1.0
Louisiana	9.5	15.8	13.3	6.3	-2.5
Oklahoma	8.0	9.6	10.5	1.5	1.0
Texas	8.9	10.3	11.7	1.5	1.3
West					
Mountain					
Montana	8.1	7.3	7.9	-0.8	0.6
Idaho	6.5	7.2	8.9	0.7	1.7
Wyoming	5.9	7.2	7.3	1.3	0.0
Colorado	7.1	8.6	8.6	1.6	0.0
New Mexico	8.7	10.6	13.0	1.9	2.4
Arizona	7.5	9.4	13.8	1.9	4.3
Utah	6.2	6.0	7.1	-0.1	1.0
Nevada	6.7	7.0	7.7	0.3	0.6
Pacific					
Washington	7.4	7.1	8.9	-0.3	1.8
Oregon	6.6	7.1	9.4	0.5	2.3
California	7.9	10.0	11.9	2.1	2.0
Alaska	9.9	9.8	8.0	-0.1	-1.8
Hawaii	7.3	9.4	8.9	2.0	-0.5
TOTAL U.S.	7.7	9.5	10.7	1.9	1.2

Source: Authors' analysis of March CPS data.

panded in those states. A number of Southern states also experienced above-average employment growth, but (as we show below) most did not experience corresponding wage growth.

By this measure of employment growth (which differs from the household survey count used in Chapters 4 and 9), the nation added over 14 million jobs between 1989 and 1997 as employment grew by 1.6% per year. Most of this growth occurred at the end of the period, in the most recent years of the 1990s recovery. Employment growth over this period was relatively flat, however, in the Northeast and California, where the effects of the recession tended to linger longer than in other areas. For example, New England as a whole had essentially the same number of jobs in 1989 as in 1997; employment actually fell

TABLE 7.4 Income inequality by selected states,* top 5% to bottom 20%

State (by region)	Income ratio, top 5%/lowest 20%			Changes (top 5%/lowest 20%)	
	1978-80	1988-90	1994-96	Late 1970s- late 1980s	Late 1980s- mid-1990s
Massachusetts	11.4	13.3	16.3	1.9	3.0
New York	12.9	16.4	24.5	3.5	8.0
New Jersey	10.7	12.5	15.5	1.8	3.0
Pennsylvania	10.0	12.5	15.7	2.6	3.2
Ohio	10.4	13.3	15.2	2.9	1.8
Illinois	12.2	15.7	17.4	3.4	1.7
Michigan	10.2	13.2	15.1	3.0	1.8
North Carolina	11.9	13.9	15.7	2.0	1.8
Florida	12.8	14.8	19.9	2.1	5.1
Texas	14.8	16.1	20.4	1.3	4.3
California	12.5	16.1	19.6	3.6	3.6
Total U.S.	12.1	15.3	18.5	3.2	3.2

* These were the states with large enough samples to allow for reliable estimates of the average income of the top 5%.

Source: Authors' analysis of March CPS data.

slightly in New York over this period. Conversely, some of the Mountain states, such as Idaho, Colorado, Utah, and Nevada, enjoyed relatively fast growth.

State unemployment rates for 1979-97 are shown in **Table 7.6**. As noted in Chapter 4, in 1994 the Bureau of Labor Statistics redesigned the survey from which these data are drawn, and thus post-1993 data (from 1994 forward) are not strictly comparable to earlier years. BLS analysis suggests that the new survey led to slightly higher estimates of unemployment, though these differences were insignificant for most groups of job seekers. Nevertheless, given the survey change, we depart from the usual "peak-to-peak" format and present intervening years so that comparisons can be made within consistent surveys.

Unemployment rates fell in most states over the 1980s, particularly in the Northeast region and in the South Atlantic and Pacific states. In many of these states unemployment rates — after reaching postwar highs in the early and mid-1980s (see Chapter 4) — fell to low levels by historical standards (less than 4.0% in some states) by 1989. Other than states in the West South Central area, the increases that occurred were relatively small. Thus, state labor markets were generally "tighter" in 1989 than in 1979. As we show below, however, this tightening was not associated with higher wage growth.

Unemployment rose with the recession in the early 1990s. By 1993, most states remained well above their unemployment rate in the peak year of 1989. The Northeastern states, including the large mid-Atlantic states, were particularly hard hit. For example, by 1993 New Jersey remained 3.3 percentage points above its 1989 level. California suffered as well: its unemployment rate was 4.1 percentage points higher in 1993 than in 1989.

Between 1994 and 1997 — years which rely on a consistent survey — the labor market tightened. Unemployment fell in practically every state, and many states once again had rates below 5% by the end of the period. In the Northeast, declines of between 1 and 2 percentage points occurred in many states; similar labor market tightening occurred in the rust belt states in the Midwest, such as Michigan, Illinois, and Wisconsin. And in the West, California's unemployment rate declined by 2.3 percentage points, the largest drop in the country. The recovery took quite a while to take hold in California, however, and, at 6.3% in 1997, unemployment remained higher there than in most other states.

Wage trends

But was the labor market tightening described above accompanied by real wage gains? As we have seen throughout previous chapters, such aggregate growth indicators as those cited above have not necessarily translated into higher living standards for most working families. The next few tables show that, for many workers, wage growth has been slow to respond to the tightening job market. One important exception is for low-wage workers in the 1990s.

The wage data in **Table 7.7**, average weekly earnings by state, provide a broad measure of earnings, reflecting the effects of both changes in hours worked and changes in hourly wage rates. Trends in average earnings also combine the trends of very highly paid workers with those of low-wage workers. In this regard, weekly earnings trends are not representative of the typical worker's labor-market experience. These data are included, however, because they are frequently cited in the national debate about wages and because they lead to some revealing comparisons with the more representative hourly wage trends presented below.

Between 1979 and 1989, the familiar pattern is repeated: strong growth in the Northeast contrasted with declines in many Southern and Midwestern states. Average weekly earnings in the Northeastern states were relatively high (e.g., weekly earnings grew in Connecticut at six times the national rate). Average earnings were positive in the 1980s in most Southern states, growing relatively quickly in Maryland (1.0% per year) and the District of Columbia (1.1%). Elsewhere, growth was generally negative or flat — with California, at 0.6%, an important exception.

TABLE 7.5 Nonfarm payroll employment, by state, 1989-97 (in thousands)

	1973	1979	1989	1997	Annual growth rates 1973-79	1979-89	1989-97
NORTHEAST	19,150	20,407	23,644	23,734	1.1%	1.5%	0.0%
New England	4,752	5,394	6,569	6,584	2.1	2.0	0.0
Maine	355	416	542	554	2.7	2.7	0.3
New Hampshire	298	379	529	568	4.1	3.4	0.9
Vermont	161	198	262	279	3.5	2.8	0.8
Massachusetts	2,334	2,604	3,109	3,119	1.8	1.8	0.0
Rhode Island	366	400	462	449	1.5	1.4	-0.3
Connecticut	1,239	1,398	1,666	1,616	2.0	1.8	-0.4
Middle Atlantic	14,398	15,013	17,075	17,150	0.7%	1.3%	0.1%
New York	7,132	7,179	8,247	8,027	0.1	1.4	-0.3
New Jersey	2,760	3,027	3,690	3,725	1.6	2.0	0.1
Pennsylvania	4,507	4,806	5,139	5,398	1.1	0.7	0.6
MIDWEST	21,408	24,172	26,580	30,434	2.0%	1.0%	1.7%
East North Central	15,553	17,198	18,669	21,117	1.7	0.8	1.6
Ohio	4,113	4,485	4,817	5,386	1.5	0.7	1.4
Indiana	2,028	2,236	2,479	2,860	1.6	1.0	1.8
Illinois	4,467	4,880	5,214	5,773	1.5	0.7	1.3
Michigan	3,284	3,637	3,922	4,446	1.7	0.8	1.6
Wisconsin	1,661	1,960	2,236	2,653	2.8	1.3	2.2
West North Central	5,856	6,973	7,911	9,317	3.0%	1.3%	2.1%
Minnesota	1,436	1,767	2,087	2,485	3.5	1.7	2.2
Iowa	961	1,132	1,200	1,405	2.8	0.6	2.0
Missouri	1,771	2,011	2,315	2,636	2.1	1.4	1.6
North Dakota	184	244	260	313	4.8	0.6	2.3
South Dakota	199	241	276	354	3.3	1.3	3.1
Nebraska	541	631	708	856	2.6	1.2	2.4
Kansas	763	947	1,064	1,268	3.7	1.2	2.2
SOUTH	23,365	28,571	35,989	42,841	3.4%	2.3%	2.2%
South Atlantic	12,183	14,392	19,433	22,636	2.8	3.0	1.9
Delaware	239	257	345	388	1.2	3.0	1.5
Maryland	1,472	1,691	2,155	2,257	2.3	2.5	0.6
DC	574	613	681	615	1.1	1.1	-1.3
Virginia	1,753	2,115	2,862	3,231	3.2	3.1	1.5
West Virginia	562	659	615	709	2.7	-0.7	1.8
North Carolina	2,018	2,373	3,074	3,667	2.7	2.6	2.2
South Carolina	984	1,176	1,500	1,722	3.0	2.5	1.7
Georgia	1,803	2,128	2,941	3,620	2.8	3.3	2.6
Florida	2,779	3,381	5,261	6,427	3.3	4.5	2.5
East South Central	4,398	5,223	6,121	7,265	2.9%	1.6%	2.2%
Kentucky	1,039	1,245	1,433	1,714	3.1	1.4	2.3
Tennessee	1,531	1,777	2,167	2,582	2.5	2.0	2.2
Alabama	1,136	1,362	1,601	1,863	3.1	1.6	1.9
Mississippi	693	838	919	1,106	3.2	0.9	2.3

(cont.)

326

TABLE 7.5 *(cont.)* Nonfarm payroll employment, by state, 1989-97 (in thousands)

	1973	1979	1989	1997	Annual growth rates		
					1973-79	1979-89	1989-97
SOUTH *(cont.)*							
West South Central	6,784	8,957	10,436	12,939	4.7%	1.5%	2.7%
Arkansas	615	749	893	1,103	3.4	1.8	2.7
Louisiana	1,176	1,517	1,539	1,847	4.3	0.1	2.3
Oklahoma	852	1,088	1,164	1,387	4.2	0.7	2.2
Texas	4,142	5,602	6,840	8,602	5.2	2.0	2.9
WEST	13,286	17,276	21,845	25,648	4.5%	2.4%	2.0%
Mountain	3,258	4,414	5,621	7,644	5.2	2.4	3.9
Montana	224	284	291	366	4.0	0.3	2.9
Idaho	252	338	366	509	5.0	0.8	4.2
Wyoming	126	201	193	224	8.1	-0.4	1.9
Colorado	936	1,218	1,482	1,977	4.5	2.0	3.7
New Mexico	346	461	562	707	4.9	2.0	2.9
Arizona	715	980	1,455	1,977	5.4	4.0	3.9
Utah	415	548	691	995	4.8	2.3	4.7
Nevada	245	384	581	890	7.8	4.2	5.5
Pacific	10,028	12,863	16,224	18,005	4.2%	2.3%	1.3%
Washington	1,152	1,581	2,047	2,512	5.4	2.6	2.6
Oregon	816	1,056	1,206	1,525	4.4	1.3	3.0
California	7,622	9,665	12,239	13,167	4.0	2.4	0.9
Alaska	110	167	227	268	7.2	3.1	2.1
Hawaii	328	394	506	532	3.1	2.5	0.6
Total U.S.	76,790	89,823	107,884	122,259	2.6%	1.8%	1.6%

Note: Regional sums do not add to U.S. totals due to: (1) separate estimation techniques by states, and (2) different timing in benchmarking procedures between the state and national estimates.

Source: Authors' analysis of BLS data.

Average wage growth (as opposed to median) is usually expected to be fairly brisk over a recovery, generally rising with the growth of productivity. But in the 1990s recovery, national average weekly earnings grew at 0.2% annually, and, while only a few states experienced negative growth, average wage growth was tepid given the purported strength of the recovery. The strong growth rates in the Northeast and California decelerated; by 1996, the California weekly earnings level was only $5.00 (less than 1%) above its 1989 value. Many Midwestern and most Southern states experienced flat or low (less than 0.5%) earnings growth. In the Pacific region, Washington and Oregon had relatively high growth rates, but both states failed to make up the ground they lost over the 1980s.

TABLE 7.6 Unemployment rates by state and division, 1979-97

	1979	1989	1993	1994*	1997*	Percentage-point change		
						1979-89	1989-93	1994-97
NORTHEAST	6.6%	4.5%	7.3%	6.5%	5.4%	-2.1	2.8	-1.1
New England	5.5	3.8	6.8	5.9	4.4	-1.7	3.0	-1.5
Maine	7.2	4.1	7.9	7.4	5.4	-3.1	3.8	-2.0
New Hampshire	3.1	3.5	6.6	4.6	3.1	0.4	3.1	-1.5
Vermont	5.3	3.7	5.4	4.7	4.0	-1.6	1.7	-0.7
Massachusetts	5.5	4.0	6.9	6.0	4.0	-1.5	2.9	-2.0
Rhode Island	6.7	4.1	7.7	7.1	5.3	-2.6	3.6	-1.8
Connecticut	5.1	3.7	6.2	5.6	5.1	-1.4	2.5	-0.5
Middle Atlantic	7.0%	4.7%	7.5%	6.7%	5.7%	-2.3	2.8	-1.0
New York	7.1	5.1	7.7	6.9	6.4	-2.0	2.6	-0.5
New Jersey	6.9	4.1	7.4	6.8	5.1	-2.8	3.3	-1.7
Pennsylvania	6.9	4.5	7.0	6.2	5.2	-2.4	2.5	-1.0
MIDWEST	5.5%	5.4%	6.1%	5.1%	4.0%	-0.1	0.7	-1.1
East North Central	6.1	5.7	6.5	5.5	4.3	-0.4	0.8	-1.2
Ohio	5.9	5.5	6.5	5.5	4.6	-0.4	1.0	-0.9
Indiana	6.4	4.7	5.3	4.9	3.5	-1.7	0.6	-1.4
Illinois	5.5	6.0	7.4	5.7	4.7	0.5	1.4	-1.0
Michigan	7.8	7.1	7.0	5.9	4.2	-0.7	-0.1	-1.7
Wisconsin	4.5	4.4	4.7	4.7	3.7	-0.1	0.3	-1.0
West North Central	4.0%	4.5%	5.0%	4.2%	3.5%	0.5	0.5	-0.7
Minnesota	4.2	4.3	5.1	4.0	3.3	0.1	0.8	-0.7
Iowa	4.1	4.3	4.0	3.7	3.3	0.2	-0.3	-0.4
Missouri	4.5	5.5	6.4	4.9	4.2	1.0	0.9	-0.7
North Dakota	3.7	4.3	4.3	3.9	2.5	0.6	0.0	-1.4
South Dakota	3.6	4.2	3.5	3.3	3.1	0.6	-0.7	-0.2
Nebraska	3.1	3.1	2.6	2.9	2.6	0.0	-0.5	-0.3
Kansas	3.3	4.0	5.0	5.3	3.8	0.7	1.0	-1.5
SOUTH	5.4%	5.7%	6.6%	5.9%	4.9%	0.3	0.9	-1.0
South Atlantic	5.5	4.8	6.3	5.7	4.6	-0.7	1.5	-1.1
Delaware	8.2	3.5	5.3	4.9	4.0	-4.7	1.8	-0.9
Maryland	5.9	3.7	6.2	5.1	5.1	-2.2	2.5	0.0
DC	7.3	5.0	8.5	8.2	7.9	-2.3	3.5	-0.3
Virginia	4.7	3.9	5.0	4.9	4.0	-0.8	1.1	-0.9
West Virginia	6.7	8.6	10.8	8.9	6.9	1.9	2.2	-2.0
North Carolina	4.8	3.5	4.9	4.4	3.6	-1.3	1.4	-0.8
South Carolina	5.1	4.7	7.5	6.3	4.5	-0.4	2.8	-1.8
Georgia	5.1	5.5	5.8	5.2	4.5	0.4	0.3	-0.7
Florida	6.0	5.6	7.0	6.6	4.8	-0.4	1.4	-1.8
East South Central	6.1%	6.3%	6.5%	5.5%	5.4%	0.2	0.2	-0.1
Kentucky	5.6	6.2	6.2	5.4	5.4	0.6	0.0	0.0
Tennessee	5.8	5.1	5.7	4.8	5.4	-0.7	0.6	0.6
Alabama	7.1	7.0	7.5	6.0	5.1	-0.1	0.5	-0.9
Mississippi	5.8	7.8	6.3	6.6	5.7	2.0	-1.5	-0.9

(cont.)

TABLE 7.6 *(cont.)* Unemployment rates by state and division, 1979-97

| | 1979 | 1989 | 1993 | 1994* | 1997* | Percentage-point change | | |
						1979-89	1989-93	1994-97
SOUTH *(cont.)*								
West South Central	4.7%	6.8%	7.0%	6.5%	5.3%	2.1	0.2	-1.2
Arkansas	6.2	7.2	6.2	5.3	5.3	1.0	-1.0	0.0
Louisiana	6.7	7.9	7.4	8.0	6.1	1.2	-0.5	-1.9
Oklahoma	3.4	5.6	6.0	5.8	4.1	2.2	0.4	-1.7
Texas	4.2	6.7	7.0	6.4	5.4	2.5	0.3	-1.0
WEST	6.0%	5.3%	8.1%	7.2%	5.6%	-0.7	2.8	-1.6
Mountain	5.0	5.5	5.9	5.3	4.3	0.5	0.4	-1.0
Montana	5.1	5.9	6.0	5.1	5.4	0.8	0.1	0.3
Idaho	5.6	5.1	6.1	5.6	5.3	-0.5	1.0	-0.3
Wyoming	3.1	6.3	5.4	5.3	5.1	3.2	-0.9	-0.2
Colorado	4.8	5.8	5.2	4.2	3.3	1.0	-0.6	-0.9
New Mexico	6.6	6.7	7.5	6.3	6.2	0.1	0.8	-0.1
Arizona	5.0	5.2	6.2	6.4	4.6	0.2	1.0	-1.8
Utah	4.3	4.6	3.9	3.7	3.1	0.3	-0.7	-0.6
Nevada	5.0	5.0	7.2	6.2	4.1	0.0	2.2	-2.1
Pacific	6.4%	5.2%	8.8%	8.0%	6.1%	-1.2	3.6	-1.9
Washington	6.8	6.2	7.5	6.4	4.8	-0.6	1.3	-1.6
Oregon	6.8	5.7	7.2	5.4	5.8	-1.1	1.5	0.4
California	6.2	5.1	9.2	8.6	6.3	-1.1	4.1	-2.3
Alaska	9.3	6.7	7.6	7.8	7.9	-2.6	0.9	0.1
Hawaii	6.4	2.6	4.2	6.1	6.4	-3.8	1.6	0.3
TOTAL U.S.	5.8%	5.3%	6.8%	6.1%	4.9%	-0.5	1.5	-1.2

* Unemployment rates for 1994 and beyond are not directly comparable to those from earlier years because of changes in BLS survey methodology.

Source: Authors' analysis of BLS data from Labstat Website.

Looking at levels and growth rates of median hourly wages by state (**Table 7.8**) allows us to track the wage trends of middle-wage workers. Similarly, we can track the wages of low-wage workers (**Table 7.9**) by looking at wage levels at the 20th percentile (80% of the workforce earns a higher wage than these workers). Note that, while the wage percentile tables in Chapter 3 separated males and females, here they are combined. This practice generates larger sample sizes to allow for state-level analysis while still capturing the broad trends.

Comparing the 1980s trends in Table 7.8 with the weekly averages in Table 7.7 reveals that median hourly wages, for the most part, grew more slowly than average weekly wages. In other words, when the average weekly earnings were falling in a state, the median tended to fall even faster; when the average grew in

TABLE 7.7 Average weekly wages, 1979-96 (1996 dollars)

	1979	1989	1996	Annual growth rates 1979-89	1989-96
NORTHEAST					
New England					
Maine	$428	$467	$459	0.9%	-0.3%
New Hampshire	462	524	533	1.3	0.2
Vermont	445	474	471	0.6	-0.1
Massachusetts	515·	614	653	1.8	0.9
Rhode Island	466	514	523	1.0	0.2
Connecticut	553	669	704	1.9	0.7
Middle Atlantic					
New York	$585	$664	$708	1.3%	0.9%
New Jersey	568	652	691	1.4	0.8
Pennsylvania	539	543	557	0.1	0.4
MIDWEST					
East North Central					
Ohio	$570	$535	$534	-0.6%	0.0%
Indiana	547	509	509	-0.7	0.0
Illinois	592	589	602	0.0	0.3
Michigan	642	603	606	-0.6	0.1
Wisconsin	517	492	500	-0.5	0.3
West North Central					
Minnesota	$519	$539	$555	0.4%	0.4%
Iowa	492	448	455	-0.9	0.2
Missouri	513	509	512	-0.1	0.1
North Dakota	456	412	408	-1.0	-0.1
South Dakota	416	385	399	-0.8	0.5
Nebraska	456	430	448	-0.6	0.6
Kansas	486	474	473	-0.2	0.0
SOUTH					
South Atlantic					
Delaware	$560	$566	$591	0.1$	0.6%
Maryland	517	571	583	1.0	0.3
DC	698	781	855	1.1	1.3
Virginia	494	532	539	0.8	0.2
West Virginia	541	481	463	-1.2	-0.6
North Carolina	447	470	489	0.5	0.6
South Carolina	445	457	462	0.3	0.2
Georgia	481	513	529	0.6	0.4
Florida	469	488	493	0.4	0.1

(cont.)

TABLE 7.7 *(cont.)* Average weekly wages, 1979-96 (1996 dollars)

	1979	1989	1996	Annual growth rates	
				1979-89	1989-96
SOUTH *(cont.)*					
East South Central					
Kentucky	$500	$ 462	$470	-0.8%	0.2%
Tennessee	473	480	499	0.1	0.6
Alabama	483	477	484	-0.1	0.2
Mississippi	424	415	420	-0.2	0.2
West South Central					
Arkansas	$435	$424	$429	-0.3%	0.2%
Louisiana	524	481	472	-0.9	-0.3
Oklahoma	503	475	449	-0.6	-0.8
Texas	534	529	541	-0.1	0.3
WEST					
Mountain					
Montana	$475	$419	$407	-1.2%	-0.4%
Idaho	475	442	449	-0.7	0.2
Wyoming	566	468	440	-1.9	-0.9
Colorado	526	534	548	0.2	0.4
New Mexico	483	454	456	-0.6	0.1
Arizona	509	506	507	0.0	0.0
Utah	498	471	473	-0.6	0.0
Nevada	526	519	534	-0.1	0.4
Pacific					
Washington	$585	$526	$555	-1.1%	0.8%
Oregon	536	494	520	-0.8	0.7
California	570	606	611	0.6	0.1
Alaska	854	723	624	-1.7	-2.1
Hawaii	503	526	526	0.5	0.0
Total U.S.	$534	$549	$557	0.3%	0.2%

Source: Authors' analysis of BLS data.

a state, the median generally grew less. For example, while the average weekly earnings grew 0.6% annually in California from 1979 to 1989, the median hourly wage was flat. Over the 1990s recovery, California's weekly wage was stagnant (1989-96), and the median dropped 1.4% per year (1989-97). This is the characteristic pattern of wage growth in a period of increasing inequality.

Table 7.8 reveals that, while the national median hourly wage declined 0.2%

TABLE 7.8 State hourly median wages (50th percentile), all workers, 1979-97 (1997 dollars)

	1979	1989	1992	1997	Annual growth rates		
					1979-89	1989-97	1992-97
NORTHEAST							
New England	$11.11	$12.81	$12.38	$12.07	1.4%	-0.7%	-0.5%
Maine	9.35	10.37	10.15	10.04	1.0	-0.4	-0.2
New Hampshire	10.63	12.36	11.56	11.57	1.5	-0.8	0.0
Vermont	9.97	10.80	10.78	10.23	0.8	-0.7	-1.0
Massachusetts	11.20	13.12	12.82	12.64	1.6	-0.5	-0.3
Rhode Island	10.74	11.46	11.34	11.08	0.6	-0.4	-0.5
Connecticut	11.91	13.68	13.60	13.07	1.4	-0.6	-0.8
Middle Atlantic	$12.00	$12.63	$12.26	$11.91	0.5%	-0.7%	-0.6%
New York	11.96	12.85	12.63	11.88	0.7	-1.0	-1.2
New Jersey	12.27	13.64	13.64	12.89	1.1	-0.7	-1.1
Pennsylvania	11.91	11.16	11.28	11.19	-0.6	0.0	-0.2
MIDWEST							
East North Central	$12.58	$11.35	$11.25	$11.14	-1.0%	-0.2%	-0.2%
Ohio	12.45	11.24	11.15	10.94	-1.0	-0.3	-0.4
Indiana	11.35	10.27	10.08	10.30	-1.0	0.0	0.4
Illinois	12.84	11.94	11.66	11.77	-0.7	-0.2	0.2
Michigan	13.36	11.87	11.53	11.58	-1.2	-0.3	0.1
Wisconsin	11.98	10.67	10.58	11.14	-1.2	0.5	1.0
West North Central	$11.12	$10.36	$9.93	$10.49	-0.7%	0.2%	1.1%
Minnesota	11.93	11.49	11.20	11.75	-0.4	0.3	1.0
Iowa	11.17	9.97	9.61	10.05	-1.1	0.1	0.9
Missouri	11.11	10.34	9.56	10.73	-0.7	0.5	2.3
North Dakota	10.42	9.22	8.65	8.94	-1.2	-0.4	0.7
South Dakota	9.19	8.59	8.70	8.96	-0.7	0.5	0.6
Nebraska	10.49	9.42	9.47	9.53	-1.1	0.1	0.1
Kansas	10.93	10.50	10.03	10.20	-0.4	-0.4	0.3
SOUTH							
South Atlantic	$10.44	$10.52	$10.34	$10.46	0.1%	-0.1%	0.2%
Delaware	11.69	11.82	12.04	11.29	0.1	-0.6	-1.3
Maryland	12.60	12.75	12.31	12.75	0.1	0.0	0.7
DC	13.04	12.91	12.66	12.63	-0.1	-0.3	-0.1
Virginia	11.08	11.75	11.36	11.23	0.6	-0.6	-0.2
West Virginia	12.26	9.48	9.01	9.81	-2.5	0.4	1.7
North Carolina	9.53	9.76	9.63	10.09	0.2	0.4	0.9
South Carolina	9.23	9.72	9.66	9.98	0.5	0.3	0.6
Georgia	10.27	10.50	10.27	10.90	0.2	0.5	1.2
Florida	9.73	10.08	9.68	9.87	0.4	-0.3	0.4

(cont.)

TABLE 7.8 *(cont.)* State hourly median wages (50th percentile), all workers, 1979-97 (1997 dollars)

	1979	1989	1992	1997	Annual growth rates 1979-89	1989-97	1992-97
SOUTH *(cont.)*							
East South Central	$10.30	$9.38	$9.19	$9.60	-0.9%	0.3%	0.9%
Kentucky	11.08	10.04	9.85	9.95	-1.0	-0.1	0.2
Tennessee	10.00	9.31	9.14	9.82	-0.7	0.7	1.4
Alabama	10.49	9.63	9.22	9.41	-0.8	-0.3	0.4
Mississippi	8.87	8.35	8.50	8.86	-0.6	0.7	0.8
West South Central	$10.71	$9.85	$9.77	$9.63	-0.8%	-0.3%	-0.3%
Arkansas	8.97	8.56	8.65	8.59	-0.5	0.0	-0.2
Louisiana	10.80	9.35	9.56	9.34	-1.4	0.0	-0.5
Oklahoma	11.17	10.00	9.69	9.16	-1.1	-1.1	-1.1
Texas	10.86	10.13	10.04	9.89	-0.7	-0.3	-0.3
WEST							
Mountain	$11.55	$10.56	$10.39	$10.16	-0.9%	-0.5%	-0.4%
Montana	11.41	9.67	9.45	9.11	-1.6	-0.7	-0.7
Idaho	10.94	9.48	9.59	9.76	-1.4	0.4	0.4
Wyoming	12.89	10.63	9.74	9.87	-1.9	-0.9	0.3
Colorado	12.29	11.18	11.16	11.45	-0.9	0.3	0.5
New Mexico	10.99	9.33	9.81	9.76	-1.6	0.6	-0.1
Arizona	11.16	10.81	10.64	9.82	-0.3	-1.2	-1.6
Utah	11.65	10.56	9.79	10.15	-1.0	-0.5	0.7
Nevada	11.49	11.38	11.11	10.42	-0.1	-1.1	-1.3
Pacific	$12.87	$12.71	$12.33	$11.52	-0.1%	-1.2%	-1.4%
Washington	13.39	12.35	12.43	12.23	-0.8	-0.1	-0.3
Oregon	12.72	11.82	11.34	10.81	-0.7	-1.1	-1.0
California	12.78	12.80	12.41	11.43	0.0	-1.4	-1.6
Alaska	18.16	15.31	14.83	13.95	-1.7	-1.2	-1.2
Hawaii	11.51	12.17	12.35	10.94	0.6	-1.3	-2.4
TOTAL U.S.	$11.46	$11.18	$11.16	$10.82	-0.2%	-0.4%	-0.6%

Source: Authors' analysis of CPS ORG data.

annually during the 1980s, there was a great deal of variation among the states. Median wages fell in every Midwestern and Western state (except Hawaii) over the 1980s, with particularly sharp declines in the Mountain states. In Utah, for example, the median wage was 19 cents higher than the national level in 1979, but by 1989, after falling 1.0% per year, it was 62 cents below. Keeping with the general regional trend over the 1980s, Northeastern states enjoyed relatively

TABLE 7.9 State hourly wage rates for low-wage (20th percentile) workers, 1979-97 (1997 dollars)

	1979	1989	1992	1997	Annual growth rates 1979-89	1989-97	1992-97
NORTHEAST							
New England	$7.44	$8.34	$7.97	$7.63	1.2%	-1.1%	-0.9%
Maine	6.80	7.29	6.79	6.75	0.7	-0.9	-0.1
New Hampshire	7.33	8.17	7.59	7.60	1.1	-0.9	0.0
Vermont	6.75	7.49	7.04	6.76	1.0	-1.3	-0.8
Massachusetts	7.53	8.74	8.26	7.95	1.5	-1.2	-0.8
Rhode Island	7.33	7.63	7.52	6.89	0.4	-1.3	-1.7
Connecticut	7.87	9.06	8.61	7.98	1.4	-1.6	-1.5
Middle Atlantic	$7.64	$7.54	$7.35	$7.06	-0.1%	-0.8%	-0.8%
New York	7.63	7.59	7.56	6.95	0.0	-1.1	-1.7
New Jersey	7.67	8.37	8.15	7.70	0.9	-1.0	-1.1
Pennsylvania	7.65	6.93	6.84	6.93	-1.0	0.0	0.3
MIDWEST							
East North Central	$7.80	$6.68	$6.75	$6.96	-1.5%	0.5%	0.6%
Ohio	7.61	6.71	6.61	6.61	-1.2	-0.2	0.0
Indiana	7.33	6.36	6.54	7.01	-1.4	1.2	1.4
Illinois	8.13	7.02	6.95	7.03	-1.5	0.0	0.2
Michigan	8.14	6.75	6.72	7.03	-1.9	0.5	0.9
Wisconsin	7.56	6.49	6.90	7.33	-1.5	1.5	1.2
West North Central	$7.18	$6.41	$6.32	$6.77	-1.1%	0.7%	1.4%
Minnesota	7.56	7.16	6.90	7.20	-0.5	0.1	0.8
Iowa	7.18	6.17	6.16	6.74	-1.5	1.1	1.8
Missouri	7.10	6.30	6.00	6.76	-1.2	0.9	2.4
North Dakota	6.79	5.95	5.68	6.01	-1.3	0.1	1.1
South Dakota	6.58	5.61	5.97	6.22	-1.6	1.3	0.8
Nebraska	6.98	6.10	6.30	6.38	-1.3	0.6	0.3
Kansas	7.31	6.39	6.40	6.53	-1.3	0.3	0.4
SOUTH							
South Atlantic	$6.92	$6.64	$6.57	$6.75	-0.4%	0.2%	0.6%
Delaware	7.74	7.42	7.90	7.11	-0.4	-0.5	-2.1
Maryland	7.83	7.86	7.68	7.51	0.0	-0.6	-0.5
DC	8.56	7.90	8.16	7.24	-0.8	-1.1	-2.4
Virginia	7.03	7.09	6.75	7.04	0.1	-0.1	0.9
West Virginia	7.20	5.40	5.61	5.85	-2.8	1.0	0.8
North Carolina	6.79	6.48	6.46	6.74	-0.5	0.5	0.8
South Carolina	6.66	6.23	6.01	6.61	-0.7	0.8	1.9
Georgia	6.89	6.57	6.54	6.90	-0.5	0.6	1.1
Florida	6.74	6.54	6.27	6.27	-0.3	-0.5	0.0

(cont.)

TABLE 7.9 *(cont.)* State hourly wage rates for low-wage (20th percentile) workers, 1979-97 (1997 dollars)

	1979	1989	1992	1997	Annual growth rates 1979-89	1989-97	1992-97
SOUTH *(cont.)*							
East South Central	$6.75	$5.82	$5.77	$6.23	-1.5%	0.9%	1.6%
Kentucky	7.02	5.81	5.87	6.45	-1.9	1.3	1.9
Tennessee	6.80	6.07	5.86	6.54	-1.1	0.9	2.2
Alabama	6.72	5.99	5.79	6.06	-1.1	0.1	0.9
Mississippi	6.47	5.20	5.41	5.86	-2.2	1.5	1.6
West South Central	$6.90	$5.95	$5.85	$6.05	-1.5%	0.2%	0.7%
Arkansas	6.64	5.61	5.75	5.91	-1.7	0.7	0.5
Louisiana	6.86	5.62	5.62	5.89	-2.0	0.6	0.9
Oklahoma	7.14	6.20	5.93	5.99	-1.4	-0.4	0.2
Texas	6.92	6.04	5.91	6.12	-1.4	0.2	0.7
WEST							
Mountain	$7.30	$6.45	$6.47	$6.62	-1.2%	0.3%	0.5%
Montana	6.99	5.97	5.91	6.00	-1.6	0.1	0.3
Idaho	7.01	5.88	5.96	6.40	-1.7	1.1	1.4
Wyoming	7.79	6.17	5.91	6.00	-2.3	-0.3	0.3
Colorado	7.54	6.58	6.88	7.24	-1.4	1.2	1.0
New Mexico	6.88	5.72	5.78	6.05	-1.8	0.7	0.9
Arizona	7.27	6.61	6.60	6.18	-0.9	-0.8	-1.3
Utah	7.35	6.61	6.27	6.85	-1.1	0.4	1.8
Nevada	7.62	7.22	6.97	7.16	-0.5	-0.1	0.5
Pacific	$8.06	$7.35	$7.12	$6.61	-0.9%	-1.3%	-1.5%
Washington	8.44	7.29	7.77	7.18	-1.4	-0.2	-1.6
Oregon	8.14	7.11	6.94	6.90	-1.3	-0.4	-0.1
California	8.01	7.34	7.03	6.41	-0.9	-1.7	-1.8
Alaska	11.40	9.49	9.24	8.42	-1.8	-1.5	-1.8
Hawaii	7.01	7.54	8.15	6.94	0.7	-1.0	-3.2
TOTAL U.S.	$7.33	$6.71	$6.68	$6.74	-0.9%	0.1%	0.2%

Source: Authors' analysis of CPS ORG data.

large real wage gains over the period, particularly in New England, where the median grew 1.4% annually.

Despite the recovery over the 1990s, only 17 states — mostly concentrated in the West North Central division of the Midwest — experienced median hourly wage increases between 1989 and 1997. The geographical pattern of these gains shifted notably relative to the 1980s: median wages fell in the Northeast and increased slightly in the Midwest. Western states, however, continued to lose ground, and wage losses even accelerated for most states in the Pacific region.

As noted throughout the book, labor market tightening, low rates of inflation, and the increase in the minimum wage have led to gains in national wage levels over the last few years for which we have data. To examine this phenomenon at the state level, we break from our usual peak-to-peak analyses and look at real wage trends (roughly) from trough to peak, 1992-97 (while the official trough occurred in early 1991, the unemployment trough occurred in 1992). For the median worker in the Midwest and much of the South, wages grew as the economy expanded. But for workers in the Pacific region, median wages did not respond at all to economic growth. In fact, median wages fell more quickly in the Pacific division (including California) as the expansion proceeded. By 1997, the median worker in California earned $1.37 less per hour than in 1989.

The pattern of wage growth for low-wage workers (i.e., workers at the 20th percentile of the wage scale; Table 7.9) was similar to that of the median. Here too, the 1980s were characterized by gains in the Northeast and losses elsewhere, and in the 1990s gains went mostly to low-wage workers in the Midwest and parts of the South. There are, however, some indications that the earnings of low-wage workers grew more than those of higher-paid workers in some areas, particularly over the 1990s expansion. For example, in the South Central divisions of the country, low-wage workers experienced much faster wage growth than the rest of the country, due in part to the fact that the minimum wage increases of the 1990s affected a larger share of the workforce in these low-wage states.

This last point — the differences in the shares of low-wage workers by state — is examined in **Table 7.10**, which shows the percent of workers in different wage ranges in 1997. The wage categories are chosen both to represent the share of workers covered by the minimum wage (which was $4.75 for the first two-thirds of the year, and $5.15 for the last third), as well as the share earning poverty-level wages. (As explained in Chapter 3, this is wage level needed to lift a family of four above the poverty line with full-time, full-year work.)

The table shows that 7.7% of the national workforce earned the minimum wage or less in 1997, with shares above the national average in the deep South and below-average shares in New England. The relatively large share of minimum wage workers in Mississippi, for example, means that the minimum wage increases in the 1990s had a greater impact there than in higher-wage states. Moving up the wage scale allows us to examine which states have high concentrations of low-wage workers (column 3, "Low-Wage Share"). As expected, the majority of Southern states have higher-than-average shares, but states in the West North Central division of the Midwest also have a larger share of low-wage workers than the national average. In the West, Montana has the largest share of low-wage workers, with close to two-fifths of the workforce there in poverty-level wage category.

Figures 7B through **7E** summarize much of the above information on state-level labor market trends. These figures show the relationship between changes in unemployment and changes in the wages of low-wage (Figures 7B and 7C) and median-wage (Figures 7D and 7E) workers for the periods 1979-89 and 1989-97. (The changes in unemployment are in percentage points; changes in wages are the percent changes over the period.) One would expect the relationship between these two variables to be an inverse one, with falling unemployment leading to wage growth. This relationship will be diminished, however, if other factors, such as the decline in the real value of the minimum, the fall in union bargaining power, or the shift to poorer-quality jobs dominates the increase in labor demand. Note that each state is weighted equally in the graphs, so the line through the graph reflects the experience of the average state, not the average worker.

The two figures for low-wage workers (those at the 20th percentile) show the expected pattern but with a much more favorable outlook in the 1990s relative to the 1980s. Each dot represents the intersection for each state of the change in unemployment and the change in low-wage levels over the period. Therefore, the upper-left quadrant of each graph shows states where unemployment fell and real wages grew; the lower-right quadrant shows the opposite. In the 1980s, most states fell into the bottom two quadrants, where falling wages were associated with both declining and growing unemployment. Only a few states were in the upper left portion of the graph.

But in the 1990s, the most populated quadrant was the upper left, where states experienced labor market tightening accompanied by wage growth. As pointed out in the discussion of the previous table, the increases in the minimum wage in the 1990s played a role here as well. Of the 24 states in the upper left corner, nine are in the Southern region, where the increases were most strongly felt. Even so, there were numerous states (including New York and California) in the bottom right quadrant, and a few in the lower left (falling unemployment *and* wage decline).

The beneficial effects of falling unemployment and the minimum wage increases are not so evident with regard to state median wages (Figures 7D and 7E). Here the scatter plots for the two time periods appear fairly similar, with most states in the bottom half of the graph, meaning median wages fell in states where unemployment was rising as well as states where unemployment declined. Taken together, the figures suggest that falling unemployment and the minimum wage increases helped to raise low wages but not median wages. Thus, by lift-

TABLE 7.10 Wage distribution by state and division, 1997

	$5.15 or less	$5.16-7.79	Low-wage share*	$7.80-9.99	$10.00+	Total
NORTHEAST						
New England	4.6%	16.5%	21.1%	13.4%	65.5%	100.0%
Maine	6.5	23.2	29.7	18.1	52.2	100.0
New Hampshire	4.6	16.8	21.3	16.6	62.0	100.0
Vermont	6.5	23.6	30.1	15.1	54.8	100.0
Massachusetts	4.0	14.9	18.9	12.5	68.6	100.0
Rhode Island	5.9	21.7	27.6	12.1	60.3	100.0
Connecticut	4.3	14.2	18.4	12.5	69.1	100.0
Middle Atlantic	7.2%	17.7%	24.9%	12.4%	62.6%	100.0%
New York	8.1	17.6	25.7	12.1	62.2	100.0
New Jersey	5.2	15.3	20.5	11.6	67.9	100.0
Pennsylvania	7.4	19.6	27.0	13.5	59.5	100.0
MIDWEST						
East North Central	6.7%	19.8%	26.5%	14.6%	58.9%	100.0%
Ohio	8.3	20.7	29.0	13.6	57.4	100.0
Indiana	6.0	21.0	27.0	17.3	55.7	100.0
Illinois	6.6	19.2	25.8	13.6	60.6	100.0
Michigan	6.6	18.8	25.5	13.8	60.7	100.0
Wisconsin	4.3	19.8	24.1	17.1	58.9	100.0
West North Central	6.4%	22.9%	29.3%	15.6%	55.2%	100.0%
Minnesota	4.8	19.0	23.8	14.9	61.3	100.0
Iowa	6.4	24.2	30.6	18.0	51.4	100.0
Missouri	6.5	21.6	28.1	14.1	57.7	100.0
North Dakota	9.7	31.2	40.9	15.2	43.9	100.0
South Dakota	8.2	29.9	38.0	19.0	42.9	100.0
Nebraska	7.7	27.1	34.8	17.8	47.4	100.0
Kansas	6.9	25.1	32.0	15.0	53.0	100.0
SOUTH						
South Atlantic	7.8%	21.2%	29.0%	15.4%	55.6%	100.0%
Delaware	6.0	17.9	23.8	15.4	60.8	100.0
Maryland	5.5	16.5	22.0	12.2	65.8	100.0
DC	6.8	15.6	22.4	12.0	65.6	100.0
Virginia	6.4	18.9	25.3	14.9	59.9	100.0
West Virginia	11.9	25.4	37.3	12.9	49.8	100.0
North Carolina	7.1	23.1	30.2	16.6	53.2	100.0
South Carolina	8.5	22.1	30.6	17.6	51.8	100.0
Georgia	7.9	19.2	27.1	15.5	57.5	100.0
Florida	9.2	24.0	33.2	16.0	50.8	100.0

(cont.)

TABLE 7.10 *(cont.)* Wage distribution by state and division, 1997

	$5.15 or less	$5.16-7.79	Low-wage share*	$7.80-9.99	$10.00+	Total
SOUTH *(cont.)*						
East South Central	9.4%	25.2%	34.6%	17.0%	48.5%	100.0%
Kentucky	7.3	24.2	31.5	17.6	50.9	100.0
Tennessee	7.7	25.0	32.7	17.6	49.8	100.0
Alabama	10.7	25.3	36.1	16.5	47.4	100.0
Mississippi	13.8	26.6	40.4	15.6	43.9	100.0
West South Central	10.9%	24.7%	35.6%	15.6%	48.8%	100.0%
Arkansas	12.4	29.0	41.4	18.8	39.8	100.0
Louisiana	12.7	25.1	37.9	15.0	47.1	100.0
Oklahoma	10.5	27.5	38.0	16.4	45.5	100.0
Texas	10.4	23.7	34.1	15.3	50.7	100.0
WEST						
Mountain	7.3%	23.5%	30.7%	15.6%	53.6%	100.0%
Montana	9.9	29.8	39.7	14.9	45.4	100.0
Idaho	8.0	25.4	33.4	17.2	49.4	100.0
Wyoming	10.1	26.0	36.1	13.5	50.4	100.0
Colorado	5.0	19.0	24.0	14.8	61.2	100.0
New Mexico	11.0	24.7	35.6	14.9	49.5	100.0
Arizona	8.4	26.4	34.8	15.3	49.9	100.0
Utah	6.2	23.9	30.1	16.4	53.5	100.0
Nevada	5.6	20.5	26.1	18.2	55.7	100.0
Pacific	8.0%	20.2%	28.2%	12.0%	59.8%	100.0%
Washington	5.8	17.1	22.9	13.4	63.8	100.0
Oregon	4.4	23.2	27.6	15.0	57.4	100.0
California	9.0	20.6	29.6	11.3	59.1	100.0
Alaska	2.6	13.0	15.5	11.8	72.7	100.0
Hawaii	3.7	22.8	26.5	14.9	58.6	100.0
TOTAL U.S.	7.7%	21.0%	28.6%	14.4%	57.0%	100.0%

* The low-wage share is the percent of workers earning less than $7.79 an hour. This is the wage required to lift a family of four above the poverty line with full-time, full-year employment.

Source: Authors' analysis of CPS ORG data.

FIGURE 7B Changes in low wages and unemployment, 1979-89

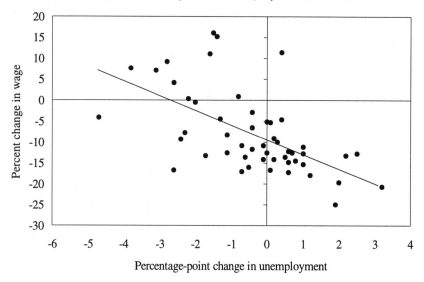

Source: See Table 7.6 and 7.9.

FIGURE 7C Changes in low wages and unemployment, 1989-97

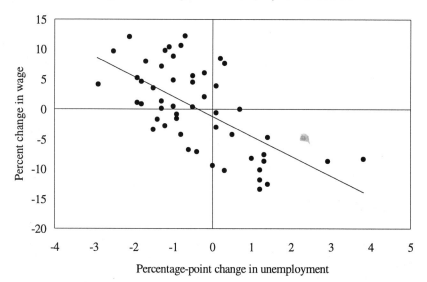

Source: See Table 7.6 and 7.9.

FIGURE 7D Changes in median wages and unemployment, 1979-89

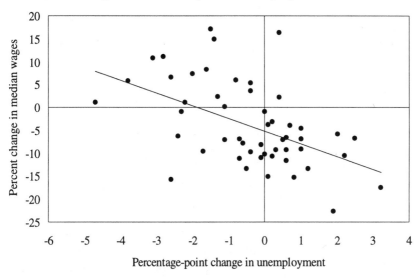

Source: See Table 7.6 and 7.8.

FIGURE 7E Changes in median wages and unemployment, 1989-97

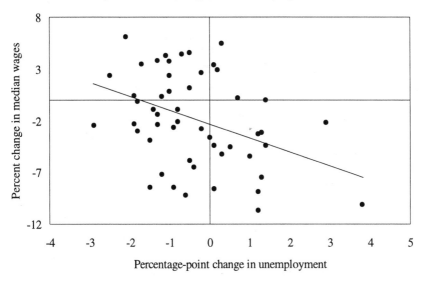

Source: See Table 7.6 and 7.8.

ing those at the bottom of the wage scale relative to those in the middle, this pattern of wage growth helped to lower wage inequality in the bottom half of the wage distribution.

Despite falling overall unemployment rates, some groups of persons are always at a disadvantage in the labor market. Young, minority workers with no more than high school degrees often have high rates of joblessness, even when the overall economy is growing. As stressed in Chapter 6, this reality poses a stiff challenge to the welfare-to-work component of welfare reform, since many women leaving the welfare rolls for the workforce fit this low-wage labor market profile.

Table 7.11 examines the rates of unemployment and underemployment (this latter concept adds discouraged job seekers and marginally employed persons to the unemployed; see table note) among young persons (18-35-year old), with at most a high school degree. The top panel is for all persons, with black and Hispanic workers in the bottom two panels. Here again we pool data across three years in order to generate large enough samples; nevertheless, only a subset of states had large enough minority samples to allow for reliable estimates.

The table shows that, while the national unemployment rate for all females age 18-35 over this time period was 7.0% (see addendum, Table 7.11), those with less than high school degrees had rates ranging from 12.1% in Utah to 29.2% in Louisiana. For black females with less than a high school degree, rates of unemployment were as high as 51.1% in California, while underemployment rates ranged from 40% to 70%.

For young Hispanic females, these indicators were less negative; in California their unemployment rate was 18.8% for those with less than a high school education and 11.8% for high school graduates; both of these rates were close to the levels for all young women in the state (this is partly due to the fact that these young Hispanic women constitute a large share of the overall group in California).

Even so, these rates, especially those for African American women, suggest that, despite recent labor market tightening, the low-wage labor market in these states may be hard pressed to handily absorb those leaving welfare for work. In a very meaningful sense, workers with such low-wage profiles face a permanent recession.

For male workers age 18-35, the national unemployment rate was 6.8% in 1995-97. As with females, the unemployment rate for young, non-college-educated males was two to three times this overall rate. Here again, large differences are evident between black and Hispanic young male job seekers. In New York, for example, among high school dropouts, unemployment rates for young

Hispanic males were one-third the rate of young African American males (10.6% as opposed to 34.1%). The gap was smaller among blacks and Hispanics with high school degrees, due to the large difference in unemployment rates by education in New York.

Poverty rates vary greatly by region and area

Figure 7F shows the trend in the percent of people who are poor — the poverty rate — by region for the period 1971-96; **Table 7.12** presents the regional rates at various economic peaks.

While the trend in regional rates follows the familiar cyclical pattern — rising over economic downturns and falling over recoveries — some interesting differences are displayed in the figure, particularly toward the end of the period. Following the deep recession of the early 1980s, poverty rates in the Northeast fell steeply; by the 1989 peak, this was the only region where the poverty rate — 10.0% — was below its 1979 level of 10.4% (Table 7.12). Over the much milder (from a national perspective) recession of the early 1990s, however, poverty rates increased most steeply in the Northeast and West, and they have fallen little since. By 1996, for the first time since these regional data have been collected, Western poverty rates — 15.4% — were above those in the South (15.1%). At the same time, above-average wage, income, and employment gains in the Midwest led to a relatively large 1.2 percentage-point decline in poverty in that region.

Table 7.13 examines these recent developments in state-level poverty rates. Here again, we combine two years of data for each state to generate more reliable rates. Poverty rates grew in each part of the country over the 1990-91 recession, and, in most states, they either grew further or failed to decline over the early years of the recovery (1992-93). For example, in New York, poverty increased from 13.0% in 1988/89 to 14.8% in 1990/91 and to 16.1% in 1992/93. Only in 1995/96 did New York poverty finally respond to the recovery.

Other states followed a similar pattern. Connecticut, one of the richest states in terms of per capita income, had steadily increasing poverty rates over the 1990s recovery, and by the end of the period was the state with the single largest increase in poverty rates (7.3 percentage points). California poverty also grew over the period, with the largest jump coming in 1992/93.

Turning to the level of poverty rates at the end of the period, Table 7.13 shows that states in the deep South, such as Louisiana (20.1% in 1995/96) and Mississippi (22.1%), had relatively large shares of state residents with incomes below the poverty level. Conversely, many Northeastern states had poverty rates that were half of this magnitude — even Connecticut, despite the large increase

TABLE 7.11 Unemployment and underemployment, 18-35-year-olds, by sex, education, and race 1995-97 (pooled)

	Female				Male	
	Unemployment		Underemployment*		Unemployment	
State	Less than high school	High school	Less than high school	High school	Less than high school	High school
NORTHEAST						
New England						
Maine	n.a.	7.1%	32.8%	19.3%	19.3%	7.0%
New Hampshire	n.a.	7.0	21.8	12.8	12.0	4.7
Vermont	n.a.	6.3	31.3	14.4	16.5	6.8
Massachusetts	13.1%	6.7	22.5	12.9	14.1	7.1
Rhode Island	15.4	9.3	30.2	19.3	13.2	8.1
Connecticut	17.2	8.1	28.4	16.0	26.1	8.7
Middle Atlantic						
New York	21.8%	9.6%	36.6%	18.6%	17.5%	9.8%
New Jersey	18.0	8.7	28.5	15.5	17.7	9.4
Pennsylvania	18.0	8.3	30.8	16.7	22.0	8.3
MIDWEST						
East North Central						
Ohio	21.1%	7.9%	33.7%	14.6%	20.2%	7.4%
Indiana	18.5	6.5	32.0	12.4	11.8	4.9
Illinois	19.9	7.9	31.5	15.0	15.5	7.7
Michigan	19.2	8.0	32.5	16.2	16.4	7.7
Wisconsin	15.2	5.3	27.6	11.7	12.6	6.1
West North Central						
Minnesota	n.a.	4.0%	22.9%	10.6%	12.9%	6.8%
Iowa	14.7%	6.2	25.8	14.5	13.1	6.5
Missouri	12.6	7.9	22.1	14.8	17.2	5.6
North Dakota	n.a.	5.2	14.4	12.4	10.5	4.5
South Dakota	11.3	5.9	21.4	11.9	9.8	5.2
Nebraska	12.2	4.6	22.1	12.0	n.a.	3.4
Kansas	15.0	6.7	31.4	14.3	13.3	5.8
SOUTH						
South Atlantic						
Delaware	n.a.	6.4%	26.0%	14.2%	12.8%	6.3%
Maryland	21.1%	9.5	33.5	16.2	15.8	8.4
DC	34.3	21.9	54.3	35.6	26.3	18.5
Virginia	20.6	6.9	33.0	14.3	8.9	5.0
West Virginia	26.6	12.2	46.2	25.3	26.1	11.4
North Carolina	14.9	8.8	26.6	15.7	9.5	5.8
South Carolina	21.0	11.0	33.6	18.4	10.6	7.2

(cont.)

344

TABLE 7.11 *(cont.)* Unemployment and underemployment, 18-35-year-olds, by sex, education, and race 1995-97 (pooled)

| | Female | | | | Male | |
| | Unemployment | | Underemployment* | | Unemployment | |
State	Less than high school	High school	Less than high school	High school	Less than high school	High school
SOUTH						
South Atlantic (cont.)						
Georgia	21.2%	7.7%	33.0%	14.0%	10.3%	6.8%
Florida	17.7	7.7	31.2	14.6	12.2	6.3
East South Central						
Kentucky	17.6%	8.8%	32.5%	17.7%	18.6%	6.4%
Tennessee	19.4	7.3	33.6	14.9	12.9	6.8
Alabama	16.0	11.2	27.5	21.2	22.4	13.1
Mississippi	22.4	11.2	33.8	21.3	15.6	9.4
West South Central						
Arkansas	20.6%	10.4%	36.2%	18.9%	14.1%	7.3%
Louisiana	29.2	11.1	46.0	19.7	17.5	6.0
Oklahoma	17.2	7.1	26.7	15.1	12.1	6.3
Texas	18.1	8.7	31.0	16.9	11.8	8.4
WEST						
Mountain						
Montana	17.2%	8.7%	34.9%	20.1%	17.2%	10.0%
Idaho	20.6	5.8	34.5	14.0	12.8	7.1
Wyoming	15.5	8.1	29.0	19.9	12.9	6.8
Colorado	14.6	5.7	26.2	13.1	12.9	5.4
New Mexico	22.9	10.0	38.1	19.9	16.2	9.8
Arizona	14.7	7.0	27.1	14.6	10.9	5.2
Utah	12.1	4.1	24.2	9.4	7.7	4.1
Nevada	13.0	8.5	27.1	15.5	10.9	7.4
Pacific						
Washington	18.0%	10.1%	32.0%	20.4%	15.7%	8.9%
Oregon	14.9	7.6	28.4	16.1	13.4	9.1
California	19.6	10.8	35.2	20.3	12.4	9.7
Alaska	17.8	10.2	34.1	20.1	15.1	8.1
Hawaii	n.a.	10.7	29.1	19.8	17.4	12.7

(cont.)

TABLE 7.11 *(cont.)* Unemployment and underemployment, 18-35-year-olds, by sex, education, and race 1995-97 (pooled)

	Female				Male	
	Unemployment		Underemployment*		Unemployment	
State	Less than high school	High school	Less than high school	High school	Less than high school	High school
BLACK						
New York	38.4%	16.2%	60.2%	26.5%	34.1%	17.1%
New Jersey	33.1	13.9	50.0	21.4	35.5	18.0
Pennsylvania	n.a.	19.7	40.9	30.5	44.9	21.7
Ohio	33.7	15.2	44.0	26.6	39.5	13.7
Illinois	41.7	17.4	59.4	29.0	37.1	22.3
Michigan	36.4	17.4	52.5	28.2	28.3	17.7
Maryland	n.a.	12.8	49.5	21.5	n.a.	13.8
DC	41.3	23.8	59.5	37.7	34.8	20.2
Virginia	35.1	15.4	45.9	25.8	n.a.	9.4
North Carolina	28.8	15.7	41.5	24.7	22.0	11.6
South Carolina	28.5	16.7	39.6	27.3	n.a.	10.4
Georgia	33.7	11.4	47.9	20.5	19.2	11.7
Florida	24.3	13.0	39.9	22.2	16.9	11.7
Alabama	24.4	19.1	43.1	32.8	34.6	15.1
Mississippi	28.4	18.6	42.3	31.4	29.9	15.6
Arkansas	47.0	20.5	65.2	33.9	n.a.	18.6
Louisiana	37.2	18.7	56.1	32.2	37.2	10.0
Texas	26.4	13.9	44.3	25.4	28.2	14.6
California	51.1	25.0	70.3	38.0	38.0	21.2
HISPANIC						
New York	18.8%	13.6%	31.8%	22.0%	10.6%	10.8%
New Jersey	16.0	11.3	23.1	20.7	16.3	10.8
Illinois	12.6	n.a.	21.2	14.5	8.5	6.3
Florida	19.4	8.3	33.8	13.5	11.6	6.0
Texas	18.8	11.0	32.0	20.6	10.3	8.3
New Mexico	25.3	7.1	42.1	17.2	12.3	10.4
Arizona	13.4	n.a.	25.7	20.6	10.8	n.a.
California	18.8	11.8	34.6	22.2	10.2	9.2

Addendum: Un- and underemployment rates for all persons (all education levels), 18-35, 1995-97

	Unemployment			Underemployment		
U.S.	All	Black	Hispanic	All	Black	Hispanic
Females	7.0%	14.0%	11.0%	13.5%	23.3%	20.2%
Males	6.8%	13.9%	8.5%	12.0%	21.9%	15.5%

* Underemployment refers to persons who are either unsuccessfully seeking work (i.e., unemployed), are not seeking work due to discouragment about their job prospects, are working part time involuntarily, or have sought work in the past year but are not currently looking for other reasons, such as lack of child care.

Source: Authors' analysis of monthly CPS data.

FIGURE 7F Poverty rates by region, 1971-96

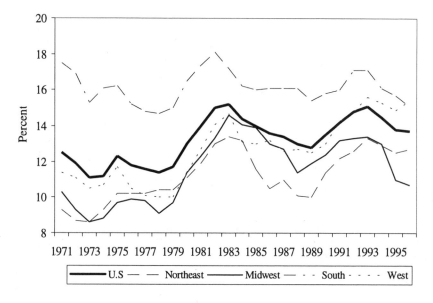

Source: See Table 7.12.

TABLE 7.12 Poverty rates for persons by region

Year	U.S.	Northeast	Midwest	South	West
1973	11.1%	8.6%	8.6%	15.3%	10.5%
1979	11.7	10.4	9.7	15.0	10.0
1989	12.8	10.0	11.9	15.4	12.5
1996	13.7	12.7	10.7	15.1	15.4
Percentage-point changes					
1973-79	0.6	1.8	1.1	-0.3	-0.5
1979-89	1.1	-0.4	2.2	0.4	2.5
1989-96	0.9	2.7	-1.2	-0.3	2.9

Source: U.S. Bureau of the Census, Poverty Website.

347

TABLE 7.13 Poverty by state, 1989-96, two-year averages

	1988-89	1990-91	1992-93	1994-95	1995-96*	Percentage-point change 1988/89 to 1995/96
NORTHEAST						
New England						
Maine	11.8%	13.6%	14.5%	10.3%	11.2%	-0.6
New Hampshire	7.2	6.8	9.3	6.5	5.9	-1.4
Vermont	8.1	11.8	10.3	9.0	11.5	3.4
Massachusetts	8.7	10.9	10.5	10.4	10.6	1.9
Rhode Island	8.3	9.0	11.8	10.5	10.8	2.6
Connecticut	3.5	7.3	9.2	10.3	10.7	7.3
Middle Atlantic						
New York	13.0%	14.8%	16.1%	16.8%	16.6%	3.6
New Jersey	7.2	9.5	10.6	8.5	8.5	1.3
Pennsylvania	10.4	11.0	12.6	12.4	11.9	1.6
MIDWEST						
East North Central						
Ohio	11.5%	12.5%	12.8%	12.8%	12.1%	0.6
Indiana	11.9	14.4	12.0	11.7	8.6	-3.4
Illinois	12.7	13.6	14.6	12.4	12.3	-0.4
Michigan	12.7	14.2	14.5	13.2	11.7	-0.9
Wisconsin	8.1	9.6	11.8	8.8	8.7	0.6
West North Central						
Minnesota	11.4%	12.5%	12.3%	10.5%	9.5%	-1.9
Iowa	9.9	10.0	10.9	11.5	10.9	1.1
Missouri	12.7	14.1	15.9	12.5	9.5	-3.2
North Dakota	11.9	14.1	11.7	11.2	11.5	-0.4
South Dakota	13.7	13.7	14.7	14.5	13.2	-0.5
Nebraska	11.6	9.9	10.5	9.2	9.9	-1.7
Kansas	9.5	11.3	12.1	12.9	11.0	1.6
SOUTH						
South Atlantic						
Delaware	9.3%	7.2%	9.0%	9.3%	9.5%	0.1
Maryland	9.4	9.5	10.8	10.4	10.2	0.8
DC	16.6	19.9	23.4	21.7	23.2	6.6
Virginia	10.9	10.5	9.6	10.5	11.3	0.4
West Virginia	16.8	18.0	22.3	17.7	17.6	0.8
North Carolina	12.4	13.8	15.1	13.4	12.4	0.0
South Carolina	16.3	16.3	18.9	16.9	16.5	0.2
Georgia	14.5	16.5	15.6	13.1	13.5	-1.1
Florida	13.1	14.9	16.7	15.6	15.2	2.2

(cont.)

TABLE 7.13 *(cont.)* Poverty by state, 1989-96, two-year averages

	1988-89	1990-91	1992-93	1994-95	1995-96*	Percentage-point change 1988/89 to 1995/96
SOUTH *(cont.)*						
East South Central						
Kentucky	16.9%	18.1%	20.1%	16.6%	15.9%	-1.0
Tennessee	18.2	16.2	18.3	15.1	15.7	-2.5
Alabama	19.1	19.0	17.4	18.3	17.1	-2.1
Mississippi	24.6	24.7	24.7	21.7	22.1	-2.6
West South Central						
Arkansas	20.0%	18.5%	18.8%	15.1%	16.1%	-3.9
Louisiana	23.1	21.3	25.5	22.7	20.1	-3.0
Oklahoma	16.0	16.3	19.3	16.9	16.9	0.9
Texas	17.6	16.7	17.9	18.3	17.0	-0.6
WEST						
Mountain						
Montana	15.1%	15.9%	14.4%	13.4%	16.2%	1.1
Idaho	12.5	14.4	14.2	13.3	13.2	0.8
Wyoming	10.3	10.5	11.8	10.8	12.1	1.8
Colorado	12.3	12.1	10.4	8.9	9.7	-2.6
New Mexico	21.3	21.7	19.5	23.2	25.4	4.2
Arizona	14.1	14.3	15.6	16.0	18.3	4.2
Utah	9.0	10.6	10.1	8.2	8.1	-0.9
Nevada	9.7	10.6	12.3	11.1	9.6	-0.1
Pacific						
Washington	9.2%	9.2%	11.7%	12.1%	12.2%	3.1
Oregon	10.8	11.4	11.6	11.5	11.5	0.7
California	13.1	14.8	17.3	17.3	16.8	3.8
Alaska	10.8	11.6	9.7	8.7	7.7	-3.1
Hawaii	11.2	9.4	9.6	9.5	11.2	0.0
TOTAL U.S.	12.9%	13.9%	15.0%	14.2%	13.8%	0.9

* A moving average was taken for the last two-years due to lack of 1997 data.

Source: U.S. Bureau of the Census, Poverty Website.

noted above, ended the period with a poverty rate of 10.7%, less than half that of Mississippi. (However, since the price of living is presumably lower in Mississippi than Connecticut, this gap is somewhat smaller than these rates suggest.) New Mexico, in part due to its large population of Native Americans (who are overrepresented among the poor), had the highest poverty rate in the nation in 1995/96 — more than one-quarter of its residents were poor.

Figure 7G and **Table 7.14** shift the geographical focus on poverty from regions and states to residence. Census data allow for the comparison of poverty rates in metropolitan and nonmetropolitan (or rural) areas. Within metropolitan areas, poverty rates in central cities can be compared with those in surrounding areas. The last column in the table compares city and rural poverty rates.

In 1959, national poverty rates were dominated by very high levels of rural poverty. As shown in the figure, rural poverty rates fell by more than half over the 1960s and 1970s. Poverty in urban areas, after falling in the 1960s, began to increase at rates well above the national average. As the last column of Table 7.14 shows, the urban poverty rate was about half that of rural areas in 1959, but by the end of the period urban poverty rates were 3.7 points above rural rates. Nevertheless, it would be a mistake to envision poverty as an "inner-city" problem; rural poverty rates remain well above the national average.

The suburbs have consistently been the area with the lowest rates of poverty, although in the most recent period suburban poverty grew by 1.4 points. Urban poverty increased by about the same magnitude: 1.5 points. As the figure shows, urban poverty has drifted up consistently since the late 1960s and, by the end of the period, was 1.3 percentage points higher than its 1959 level.

The regressivity of state tax liabilities

As pointed out in Chapter 2, state and local taxes are significantly more regressive than federal taxes, meaning that tax liability as a share of income falls as income increases. Most of state tax revenue is derived from sales taxes — a highly regressive revenue source — and property taxes, which, though less so than sales taxes, are also regressive. Evidence of state-tax regressivity is shown in **Table 7.15**, which presents state-level effective tax rates (liability as a share of income) by income quintile in 1995.

Note that in each state effective tax rates decline as income grows. For example, in the state of Washington, one of the most regressive, families in the bottom fifth paid 17% of their income in 1995 in state and local taxes, while the wealthiest families — those in the top 1% — paid 3.6%. In Nevada, families in the top 1% paid less than 2% of their income in state and local taxes, while

FIGURE 7G Poverty rates by metro/nonmetro area, 1959-96

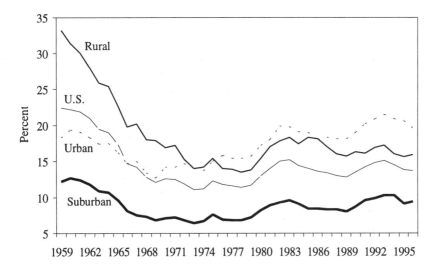

Source: Authors' analysis of U.S. Bureau of the Census (1998) data.

TABLE 7.14 Poverty rates by metro/nonmetro areas

Year	City	Suburbs	Rural	U.S.	City/rural difference
1959	18.3%	12.2%	33.2%	22.4%	-14.9%
1973	14.0	6.4	14.0	11.1	0.0
1979	15.7	7.2	13.8	11.7	1.9
1989	18.1	8.0	15.7	12.8	2.4
1996	19.6	9.4	15.9	13.7	3.7
Percentage-point changes					
1959-73	-4.3	-5.8	-19.2	-11.3	-14.9
1973-79	1.7	0.8	-0.2	0.6	1.9
1979-89	2.4	0.8	1.9	1.1	0.5
1989-96	1.5	1.4	0.2	0.9	1.3

Source: U.S. Bureau of the Census, Poverty Website.

TABLE 7.15 State and local taxes in 1995 (effective rates)*

	Lowest 20%	Second 20%	Middle 20%	Fourth 20%	Top 20% Next 15%	Top 20% Next 4%	Top 20% Top 1%
NORTHEAST							
New England							
Maine	11.6%	9.7%	9.9%	10.1%	9.4%	8.2%	7.2%
New Hampshire	9.0	6.7	5.7	5.6	4.7	3.8	3.2
Vermont	9.4	8.5	9.6	8.4	8.0	7.0	6.9
Massachussetts	11.4	10.2	9.6	8.7	8.0	7.0	6.0
Rhode Island	12.8	10.9	9.9	9.4	8.7	7.6	7.5
Connecticut	11.3	9.5	9.5	8.8	7.8	6.1	4.9
Middle Atlantic							
New York	16.1%	13.9%	13.5%	12.6%	11.4%	9.8%	8.9%
New Jersey	15.6	10.0	9.1	8.4	8.0	7.0	6.2
Pennsylvania	13.2	10.7	9.8	8.9	7.7	6.2	4.5
MIDWEST							
East North Central							
Ohio	11.6%	10.0%	9.6%	9.1%	8.1%	7.2%	6.3%
Indiana	12.6	10.3	9.4	8.3	7.3	6.0	4.9
Illinois	13.5	10.3	9.4	8.3	7.3	5.7	4.9
Michigan	13.2	11.4	10.2	9.1	7.8	6.5	5.0
Wisconsin	13.6	12.1	12.0	11.1	9.8	8.1	6.4
West North Central							
Minnesota	10.9%	10.9%	10.4%	9.7%	8.7%	8.0%	7.8%
Iowa	12.3	11.0	10.2	9.7	8.7	7.5	6.1
Missouri	11.5	10.2	9.6	8.8	7.7	6.5	5.5
North Dakota	10.6	8.7	7.8	7.3	6.5	5.7	5.2
South Dakota	11.7	8.9	7.8	6.6	5.7	4.0	2.6
Nebraska	10.8	10.1	9.7	9.1	8.3	7.2	6.4
Kansas	10.9	9.7	9.3	8.8	7.8	6.6	5.9
SOUTH							
South Atlantic							
Delaware	6.3%	6.5%	6.2%	6.0%	5.8%	5.2%	4.9%
Maryland	10.8	10.7	9.8	9.0	8.2	6.7	5.6
DC	10.5	10.0	9.5	9.1	8.0	6.4	6.4
Virginia	9.6	8.8	8.3	7.6	6.8	5.9	5.0
West Virginia	10.6	9.4	8.6	8.2	7.8	6.9	5.7
North Carolina	9.6	9.7	9.1	8.7	7.7	6.7	6.0
South Carolina	8.0	7.0	7.8	7.8	7.0	6.3	5.6
Georgia	11.1	9.9	9.3	8.4	7.4	6.3	5.7
Florida	14.0	9.8	7.6	6.4	5.3	4.1	3.2

(cont.)

TABLE 7.15 *(cont.)* State and local taxes in 1995 (effective rates)*

	Lowest 20%	Second 20%	Middle 20%	Fourth 20%	Top 20% Next 15%	Next 4%	Top 1%
SOUTH *(cont.)*							
East South Central							
Kentucky	10.4%	10.5%	10.2%	9.9%	8.7%	7.4%	5.7%
Tennessee	12.3	9.3	7.6	6.4	5.3	3.9	3.2
Alabama	11.5	10.3	9.0	7.8	6.5	5.2	3.6
Mississippi	12.1	9.7	9.6	9.1	7.7	6.4	5.4
West South Central							
Arkansas	12.0%	10.5%	9.6%	9.0%	8.1%	6.8%	5.7%
Louisiana	13.4	11.2	10.4	8.8	7.4	5.6	4.8
Oklahoma	9.9	10.0	9.4	8.9	7.6	6.1	5.0
Texas	13.8	10.4	8.5	7.3	6.1	4.9	4.0
WEST							
Mountain							
Montana	7.6%	6.5%	6.6%	6.9%	6.6%	5.9%	5.5%
Idaho	9.2	9.2	9.0	8.8	8.2	7.1	6.8
Wyoming	8.2	6.5	5.7	4.7	3.8	3.0	2.7
Colorado	9.9	9.0	8.4	7.7	6.6	5.6	5.1
New Mexico	15.0	12.6	11.0	10.0	8.9	7.5	6.7
Arizona	11.3	9.5	8.5	7.7	6.5	5.7	5.3
Utah	12.0	11.2	10.6	9.8	8.4	7.0	5.7
Nevada	8.9	5.6	4.7	4.1	3.4	2.5	1.6
Pacific							
Washington	17.0%	12.2%	10.4%	8.9%	7.2%	5.4%	3.6%
Oregon	10.8	9.1	9.2	9.2	8.5	7.6	7.0
California	12.0	9.0	8.5	8.1	7.8	7.4	8.1
Alaska	6.9	3.7	2.7	2.4	2.0	2.0	2.1
Hawaii	11.0	10.1	9.7	8.6	7.9	6.9	6.2
U.S. AVERAGE	12.4%	10.3%	9.4%	8.6%	7.7%	6.5%	5.8%

* The rates are the ratio of average tax liability to pre-tax family income by income class, after deducting the federal offset from state tax liability (since taxpayers can deduct state and local income and property taxes from their federal liability).

Source: Citizens for Tax Justice and Institute on Taxation and Economic Policy.

families in the bottom fifth paid 8.9%. Delaware has a relative flat tax structure; low-income families pay only a slightly larger share of their income in taxes than families in the top fifth. But, as shown in the final row ("U.S. Average"), most states and localities have a more regressive tax structure, as the average effective rate falls from 12.4% for the bottom fifth to 5.8% for the top 1%.

Conclusion

The data from individual regions and states show a high degree of variation, but these general points emerge: (1) most workers in regions and states with strong employment growth and low unemployment did not escape wage stagnation and decline; (2) while the states of the Northeast and California did relatively well during the expansion of the 1980s, they suffered relatively more in terms of income, wages, employment, and poverty in the 1990s; and (3) in the 1990s, low-wage workers in numerous states, particularly those in the South and Midwest, benefited from a tightening labor market and the increases in the minimum wage.

CHAPTER 8

International comparisons:

less-than-model behavior

IN THIS CHAPTER, WE COMPARE THE ECONOMIC PERFORMANCE OF THE UNITED STATES to that of 19 other rich, industrialized countries belonging to the Paris-based Organization for Economic Cooperation and Development (OECD). The comparison has two purposes. First, it provides an independent yardstick for gauging the strengths and weaknesses of the U.S. economy. In the preceding chapters, we have judged current economic outcomes using historical data for the United States as a benchmark. In this chapter, for a more limited number of economic indicators, we can compare the U.S. economy with other, similar economies that are facing the same global conditions with respect to trade, investment, technology, the environment, and other factors that shape economic opportunities. Second, the international comparisons shed light on an important debate about the advisability of exporting the "U.S. model" to other economies. In particular, with unemployment rates in the late 1990s low in the United States and generally high in Europe, many have argued that Europe should emulate key features of the U.S. economy, including weaker unions, lower minimum wages, less-generous social benefit systems, and lower taxes.

The international comparisons underline several features of postwar economic development in the United States and the rest of the OECD. First, the 1990s have been a period of slow growth in national income and productivity in all of the OECD economies, including the United States. Income and productivity growth over the last decade have generally trailed the rates obtained in the 1970s and 1980s and are far below those of the "Golden Age" from the end of World War II through the first oil shock in 1973. Second, the United States has consistently ranked in the middle or near the bottom of the OECD countries with respect to income and productivity growth. Third, the U.S. economy has consistently produced the highest levels of economic inequality, including the highest poverty rate, among the rich, industrialized economies. Moreover, inequality in the United States (along with the United Kingdom) has shown a strong tendency to rise, even as inequality was relatively stable or declining in most of the rest of the OECD. Fourth, economic mobility for those at the bottom, a factor that in principle could counteract the effects of inequality, is actually *lower* in the United States than in other OECD economies.

Incomes and productivity: United States loses the edge

For the entire postwar period, the United States has provided an average standard of living that is among the highest in the world. **Tables 8.1** and **8.2** summarize data from 1960 through 1996 on the most common measure of average living standards, per capita income, or the total value of goods and services produced in the domestic economy per member of the population. Table 8.1 converts the value of foreign goods and services, measured in foreign currency, to U.S. dollars using the market-determined exchange rate in each year. By this measure, in 1960, the United States had the second-highest standard of living (after Switzerland) among the 20 countries in the table. The United States was well ahead of most of the European economies that were still rebuilding themselves after World War II. Per capita income grew rapidly in the United States in the 1960s and 1970s, but rose even more rapidly in almost all the other economies. As a result, all of the OECD economies narrowed the income gap with United States. In the 1980s and again in the 1990s, growth in per capita income decelerated sharply throughout the OECD, including the United States. In these last two sluggish decades, growth in U.S. per capita income was close to the bottom of the rates for the rich countries. By 1996, the slower relative U.S. growth had left per capita income in the United States ($28,553) below that of Norway ($39,806), Switzerland ($38,425), Denmark ($33,367), Sweden ($32,125), Finland ($31,737), and Japan ($31,624).

Admittedly, there are problems with using market exchange rates to convert the cost of goods and services in other countries to a U.S. value. If the citizens of every country faced the same prices for the goods and services that they purchased with their incomes, then a simple conversion using market exchange rates would be sufficient for making comparisons. In reality, however, prices vary considerably across countries. For example, land and housing prices are generally much lower in the wide-open United States, Canada, and Australia than they are in more crowded European countries. Market exchange rates can also fluctuate widely in response to short-term international capital flows and other macroeconomic fac-

TABLE 8.1 Per capita income, using market exchange rates,*
1960-96 (1996 dollars)

Country	Per capita income				Annual growth rates (%)		
	1960	1979	1989	1996	1960-79	1979-89	1989-96
United States	**$14,836**	**$23,040**	**$26,641**	**$28,553**	**2.3%**	**1.5%**	**1.0%**
Japan	6,178	20,222	27,559	31,624	6.4	3.1	2.0
Germany**	10,814	20,108	24,241	26,464	3.3	1.9	1.3
France	10,743	21,279	24,840	26,243	3.7	1.6	0.8
Italy	8,460	18,062	22,668	24,327	4.1	2.3	1.0
United Kingdom	10,718	16,320	20,337	21,740	2.2	2.2	1.0
Canada	11,097	20,822	24,980	24,886	3.4	1.8	-0.1
Australia	$10,619	$17,450	$20,778	$23,028	2.6%	1.8%	1.5%
Austria	9,565	19,736	23,911	26,623	3.9	1.9	1.5
Belgium	9,610	19,044	22,992	24,956	3.7	1.9	1.2
Denmark	14,325	24,894	29,780	33,367	3.0	1.8	1.6
Finland	11,987	23,727	32,596	31,737	3.7	3.2	-0.4
Ireland	5,641	11,030	14,355	21,799	3.6	2.7	6.1
Netherlands	10,936	19,320	22,032	25,140	3.0	1.3	1.9
New Zealand	10,510	13,786	15,618	16,823	1.4	1.3	1.1
Norway	12,739	25,584	32,154	39,806	3.7	2.3	3.1
Portugal	2,391	6,013	7,795	9,007	5.0	2.6	2.1
Spain	4,971	11,688	14,772	16,536	4.6	2.4	1.6
Sweden	15,822	26,809	32,039	32,125	2.8	1.8	0.0
Switzerland	23,250	33,691	39,313	38,425	2.0	1.6	-0.3
Average excluding U.S.	$9,128	$18,967	$23,717	$25,969	3.9%	2.3%	1.3%

* At 1990 price levels and exchange rates.
** Eastern and western Germany.

Source: Authors' analysis of OECD (1998) data.

tors, and thus they may not accurately reflect long-term differences in national prices. To correct for this shortcoming, Table 8.2 uses an alternative set of criteria for converting the value of each country's goods and services into U.S. dollars. These alternative exchange rates, known as purchasing-power parities (PPPs), are not based on international currency market exchange rates but, rather, on the price of buying the same "basket" of goods and services in all countries. PPPs are, therefore, an indicator of the relative price of consumption and arguably a better measure of relative living standards than market exchange rates.

When per capita income is measured on a PPP basis, the United States appears to provide an average standard of living that is well above that of most

TABLE 8.2 Per capita income, using purchasing-power-parity exchange rates,* 1960-96 (1996 dollars)

Country	Per capita income				Annual growth rates (%)		
	1960	1979	1989	1996	1960-79	1979-89	1989-96
United States	**$13,797**	**$22,672**	**$27,007**	**$28,752**	**2.6%**	**1.8%**	**0.9%**
Japan	4,508	14,959	20,386	23,289	6.5	3.1	1.9
Germany**	9,928	17,925	21,144	23,059	3.2	1.7	1.2
France	8,380	16,720	19,880	20,583	3.7	1.7	0.5
Italy	7,128	15,037	18,590	20,227	4.0	2.1	1.2
United Kingdom	9,791	14,922	18,556	18,715	2.2	2.2	0.1
Canada	9,738	18,310	21,986	21,905	3.4	1.8	-0.1
Australia	—	—	—	—	—	—	—
Austria	$7,890	$16,214	$19,514	$21,375	3.9%	1.9%	1.3%
Belgium	8,568	17,006	20,512	21,829	3.7	1.9	0.9
Denmark	9,690	16,631	19,892	22,401	2.9	1.8	1.7
Finland	—	—	—	—	—	—	—
Ireland	—	—	—	—	—	—	—
Netherlands	8,839	15,818	18,039	20,881	3.1	1.3	2.1
New Zealand	—	—	—	—	—	—	—
Norway	8,356	16,715	21,006	24,364	3.7	2.3	2.1
Portugal	—	—	—	—	—	—	—
Spain	—	—	—	—	—	—	—
Sweden	9,508	16,111	19,254	19,293	2.8	1.8	0.0
Switzerland	—	—	—	—	—	—	—
Average excluding U.S.	$7,743	$16,060	$19,982	$21,637	3.9%	2.2%	1.1%

* 1993 benchmark EKS.
** Western Germany only.

Source: Authors' analysis of BLS (1998) data.

of the rest of the OECD economies. This suggests that consumption goods (housing, food, transportation, clothing, and others) are generally cheaper in the United States than the other economies, helping to raise the national standard of living relative to other "more expensive" economies. The pattern of growth in per capita income, however, differs little when PPPs are used instead of market exchange rates. Across almost all of the economies in Table 8.2, including the United States, growth in per capita income decelerated sharply in the 1980s and again in the 1990s. Throughout the period 1960-96, the U.S. growth rate was consistently in the middle or the bottom of the pack.

The main determinant of an economy's current and future standard of living is the level and rate of growth of productivity — the value of goods and services

TABLE 8.3 Relative productivity levels, 1960-95 (U.S.=100)

Country	1960	1973	1987	1995
United States	**100**	**100**	**100**	**100**
Japan	21	45	58	68
Germany*	52	69	84	101
France	54	73	96	102
Italy	40	64	78	90
United Kingdom	58	66	79	84
Canada	79	79	86	85
Australia	73	70	77	76
Austria	44	64	79	83
Belgium	49	68	89	97
Denmark	48	63	68	74
Finland	37	55	64	74
Ireland	31	42	59	84
Netherlands	58	77	95	98
New Zealand	—	—	—	—
Norway	48	56	76	88
Portugal	22	37	40	38
Spain	23	44	57	70
Sweden	58	73	78	79
Switzerland	71	76	76	86
Average excluding U.S.	47	61	73	80

* Western Germany.

Source: Conference Board (1997).

that the economy can produce on average in an hour of work. Productivity is, therefore, the starting point in any explanation of differences in the level and growth of income across countries. **Table 8.3** presents data on the productivity level of the same economies examined in Tables 8.1 and 8.2. In each of the four years covered, each country's productivity level is expressed as a percentage of the corresponding productivity level in the United States. In 1960, the U.S. economy was far more productive than the others, producing almost five times more goods and services in an hour than Japan and almost twice as much in an hour as Germany, France, or the United Kingdom. The nearest competitors were other economies that had escaped massive dislocation during World War II: Canada (79% of the U.S. level), Australia (73%), and Switzerland (71%). Between 1960 and 1995, all of the economies narrowed the productivity gap with the United States. By 1995, four of the economies — France (102%), Germany

TABLE 8.4 Labor productivity growth per year,* 1960-96

Country	1960**-73	1973-79	1979-96**
United States	**2.6%**	**0.3%**	**0.8%**
Japan	8.4	2.8	2.2
Germany***	4.5	3.1	1.1
France	5.3	2.9	2.2
Italy	6.4	2.8	2.1
United Kingdom	4.1	1.6	1.8
Canada	2.9	1.5	1.0
Australia	3.2%	2.4%	1.3%
Austria	5.7	3.1	2.3
Belgium	5.2	2.7	2.0
Denmark	3.9	2.3	2.1
Finland	5.0	3.2	3.6
Ireland	4.8	4.3	3.9
Netherlands	4.9	2.6	1.6
New Zealand	2.1	-1.1	1.3
Norway	3.8	2.7	1.8
Portugal	7.5	0.5	2.4
Spain	6.0	2.8	2.8
Sweden	3.7	1.4	2.0
Switzerland	3.3	0.8	0.4
Average excluding U.S.	5.7%	2.5%	1.9%

*   Business sector.
** Or closest available year.
*** First two columns refer to western Germany; third column is calculated
     as the weighted average of western German productivity growth between
     1979 and 1991 and combined eastern and western German productivity
     growth between 1991 and 1994.

Source: OECD (1997).

(101%), the Netherlands (98%), and Belgium (97%) — had essentially attained
U.S. productivity levels.

Table 8.4 and **Figure 8A** summarize the international trends in productivity growth rates. The pattern of productivity growth closely resembles that of
per capita income, which is not surprising given the close connection between
the two concepts. The first key feature of productivity growth is the dramatic
slowdown after the mid-1970s. Productivity across the OECD economies was
much more rapid in the 1960s than it has been in the 1980s and 1990s. A second
feature of international productivity growth is that the United States has been

FIGURE 8A Productivity growth rates, 1960-96

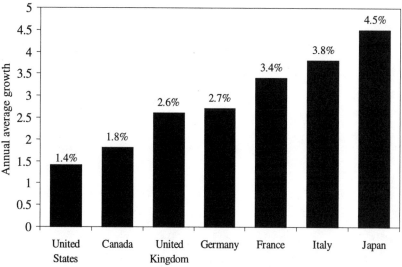

Source: Authors' analysis of OECD (1997).

among the poorest performers over the whole period. Traditionally, economists have excused the poor U.S. performance by arguing that it is much harder to lead than to follow, to innovate than to imitate. In this view, productivity growth is faster outside the United States because other economies are engaged in a constant game of catchup that involves the rapid assimilation of technological improvements pioneered in the United States. While this view may have made sense as late as the 1960s or 1970s, the data on productivity levels in Table 8.3 suggest that, by the mid-1990s, several European economies had matched or exceeded U.S. productivity levels, and many others had narrowed the gap considerably. If U.S. productivity growth rates continue to lag behind those in other OECD economies, economists may have to allow that features intrinsic to European economies provide them with an important edge over the United States when it comes to productivity growth. Certainly, the ability of France, Germany, the Netherlands, and Belgium to match U.S. productivity levels in the 1990s suggests that these countries' comprehensive welfare and collective-bargaining systems have not stymied income growth or improvements in economic efficiency relative to the more free-market United States.

TABLE 8.5 Real compensation growth per year,* 1979-96

Country	1979-89	1989-96
United States	**-0.3%**	**0.1%**
Japan	1.4	0.7
Germany**	1.2	-0.1
France	1.1	1.1
Italy	1.4	0.7
United Kingdom	2.1	0.5
Canada	0.5	0.5
Australia	0.3%	0.6%
Austria	1.9	1.3
Belgium	0.9	1.7
Denmark	0.3	1.6
Finland	3.0	2.3
Ireland	1.6	1.4
Netherlands	0.0	0.4
New Zealand	0.1	-0.8
Norway	0.4	1.4
Portugal	0.1	3.5
Spain	0.1	1.8
Sweden	1.3	0.8
Switzerland	1.7	0.7
Average excluding U.S.	1.2%	0.7%

* Compensation per employee in business sector.
** Growth rate for western Germany, 1979-91; eastern and western Germany, 1992-96.

Source: Authors' analysis of OECD data.

Workers' wages and compensation: slow, unequal growth

Wages and other work-related benefits are by far the most important source of income for the vast majority of people in the United States and the other comparison countries. The level, growth, and distribution of wages and benefits are therefore important starting points for international economic comparisons.

Table 8.5 shows the annual growth rate of total compensation (wages plus fringe benefits) in the private sector for 20 countries in the 1980s and 1990s. In both decades, growth rates have varied considerably across countries. In the 1980s, the United States put in the worst performance, with average wages falling about 0.3% per year; while wages grew most in Finland (3.0% per year) and

TABLE 8.6 Relative hourly compensation of manufacturing production workers, 1979-96 (using market exchange rates, U.S.=100)

Country	1979	1989	1996
United States	**100**	**100**	**100**
Japan	60	88	118
Germany*	125	124	180
France	85	90	120
Italy	78	101	99
United Kingdom	63	74	80
Canada	87	103	94
Australia	83	87	94
Austria	88	99	141
Belgium	131	108	146
Denmark	116	102	137
Finland	77	118	133
Ireland	54	67	78
Netherlands	126	105	131
New Zealand	52	55	62
Norway	114	128	142
Portugal	19	21	32
Spain	59	63	76
Sweden	125	123	139
Switzerland	117	117	160
Average excluding U.S.	83	96	122

* Western Germany.

Source: Authors' analysis of BLS and OECD data.

the United Kingdom (2.1% per year). In the 1990s, average compensation in the United States was almost stagnant, with an annual growth rate of just 0.1%. Over the same period, compensation growth was worse in New Zealand (-0.8% per year) and unified Germany (-0.1% per year). Nevertheless, in most economies in the 1990s, wages grew much more rapidly than in the United States.

The most extensive international data on compensation covers the narrower group of workers in manufacturing. **Tables 8.6** and **8.7** compare hourly compensation in manufacturing in 19 OECD countries to the corresponding levels in the United States in 1979, 1989, and 1996. In Table 8.6, we have converted the national compensation rates into U.S. dollars using market exchange rates. Since market exchange rates reflect the relative value of American goods, services

TABLE 8.7 Relative hourly compensation of manufacturing production workers, 1979-96 (using purchasing-power parities, U.S.=100)

Country	1979	1989	1996
United States	**100**	**100**	**100**
Japan	49	61	75
Germany*	86	111	133
France	66	86	93
Italy	87	100	93
United Kingdom	62	76	76
Canada	81	92	105
Australia	71	79	90
Austria	72	92	107
Belgium	91	107	121
Denmark	71	78	92
Finland	59	80	103
Ireland	50	65	76
Netherlands	87	101	107
New Zealand	55	56	60
Norway	70	90	96
Portugal	31	34	40
Spain	58	70	76
Sweden	78	88	94
Switzerland	75	87	98
Average excluding U.S.	68	84	94

* Western Germany.

Source: Authors' analysis of BLS and OECD data.

(including labor), and assets in international markets, the compensation figures here capture the relative costs to an employer of hiring U.S. labor. In 1996, 11 of the 19 countries had total compensation levels in manufacturing that were higher than those in the United States. The differences in compensation costs were substantial, ranging from 18% greater in Japan (118) to 80% higher in Germany (180%), with most European manufacturing competitors paying 30% to 40% more than their competitors in the United States. At least among the rich, industrialized countries, the United States has become a low-wage country.

In Table 8.7, we have converted the national compensation rates into U.S. dollars using purchasing power parities. As with the per capita income figures calculated using PPPs in Table 8.2, these compensation figures probably better reflect the ability of the compensation levels in each country to guarantee a specific standard of living. When PPPs are used to adjust national compensation, U.S. workers fare better in the international comparison. In 1979, manufacturing compensation on a PPP basis was higher in the United States than in every other country examined here. Only one country, Belgium (91), was within 10% of the U.S. level. All of the economies, however, closed the compensation gap between 1979 and 1996. By 1996, manufacturing compensation in the United States (100) had fallen behind that of Germany (133), Belgium (121), Austria (107), the Netherlands (107), Canada (105), and Finland (103).

Table 8.8 looks more carefully at growth in manufacturing compensation, on a PPP basis, over the periods 1979-89 and 1989-96. The table examines growth in compensation over the two periods separately for all employees and for production workers only. During the 1980s, the United States had one of the lowest rates of growth in hourly compensation in manufacturing, just 0.4% per year. Only Canada (0.2% per year) and Denmark (0.1% per year) did worse. Over the same period, hourly compensation for production workers in the United States actually fell 0.6% per year, compared to an average growth in the other advanced economies of 1.5% per year. Production worker compensation also fell in New Zealand (-0.6% per year) and Denmark (-0.1% per year), but rose in every other country examined here. In the 1990s, the United States turned in the worst performance in compensation rates for all employees, with a 0.3% per year growth rate. At the same time, compensation for production workers in the United States fell 0.3% per year. Hourly compensation for production workers grew in every other country except Italy, where it fell 0.4% per year. The positive growth rates in hourly compensation for all employees (which include both production, or nonsupervisory, workers and nonproduction, or supervisory, workers) and the negative growth rates for production workers in the United States are another manifestation of growing inequality in the United States over the 1980s. In short, the hourly compensation data suggest that manufacturing compensation is growing more slowly and more unequally in the United States than it is in other OECD countries.

Table 8.9 takes a broader look at international earnings inequality, using data on full-time employees in all sectors of the economy. The table measures inequality as the ratio of earnings of high-wage workers (those making more than 90% of the total workforce) to the earnings of low-wage workers (those making more than only 10% of the workforce). By this measure, in the early 1980s, Canada and the United States were the most unequal of the OECD countries. The ratio of earnings of the 90th-percentile worker to those of the 10th-percentile worker (the "90-10 ratio") was 4.01 in Canada and 3.65 in the United States, well above most of the rest of the economies in the table. As the last two

TABLE 8.8 Real hourly compensation growth in manufacturing, 1979-96

Country	1979-89		1989-96	
	All employees	Production workers	All employees	Production workers
United States	**0.4**	**-0.6**	**0.3**	**-0.3**
Japan	1.8	1.4	2.6	2.5
Germany*	2.4	2.0	2.6	2.1
France	1.9	2.2	0.9	1.7
Italy	1.0	1.6	1.4	-0.4
United Kingdom	2.8	1.7	1.5	0.8
Canada	0.2	0.1	0.8	1.3
Australia	—	0.5	—	1.3
Austria	—	1.9	—	1.9
Belgium	1.1	0.9	1.7	1.4
Denmark**	0.1	-0.1	2.0	1.9
Finland	—	2.8	—	3.2
Ireland	—	1.8	—	1.0
Netherlands	0.9	0.5	1.1	0.3
New Zealand	—	-0.6	—	0.2
Norway	0.9	0.9	1.4	1.1
Portugal	—	1.3	—	1.5
Spain	—	1.2	—	1.7
Sweden	1.0	0.8	0.5	0.8
Switzerland	—	1.2	—	0.4
Average excluding U.S.	1.8	1.5	2.0	1.6

* Western Germany.
** Figure for all workers in second period is 1989-93.

Source: Authors' analysis of BLS and OECD data.

columns of the table indicate, inequality grew steadily in the United States throughout the 1980s and 1990s. As a result, by the mid-1990s, the United States had surpassed Canada as the OECD country with the greatest degree of earnings inequality among full-time workers.

The pattern of changes in inequality in the rest of the OECD economies was complex. In the 1980s, inequality grew in the United Kingdom (4.9 points per year), Canada (4.4), Japan (1.5), Australia (1.3), and Finland (1.2); it was relatively flat in Sweden (0.9), Austria (0.6), France (0.4), Denmark (0.4), and Norway (-0.7); and inequality fell sharply in Italy (-7.8) and Germany (-3.8). In the

TABLE 8.9 Earnings inequality growth, 1979-97

Country	Earnings inequality*			Annual point change x 100	
	Early-1980s	Late-1980s	Mid-1990s	Early 1980s to late-1980s	Late 1980s to mid-1990s
United States	**3.65**	**4.14**	**4.43**	**5.0**	**3.6**
Japan	3.01	3.16	3.02	1.5	-2.4
Germany**	2.69	2.46	2.32	-3.8	-3.5
France	3.24	3.28	3.06	0.4	-3.2
Italy	2.94	2.16	2.80	-7.8	16.0
United Kingdom	2.79	3.28	3.37	4.9	1.1
Canada	4.01	4.40	4.20	4.4	-5.2
Australia	2.74	2.87	2.92	1.3	0.8
Austria	3.45	3.51	3.66	0.6	2.9
Belgium***	—	1.99	2.07	—	1.4
Denmark	2.14	2.18	—	0.4	—
Finland	2.46	2.57	2.34	1.2	-3.7
Ireland	—	—	—	—	—
Netherlands	—	2.61	2.59	—	-0.3
New Zealand	—	2.92	3.40	—	5.3
Norway	2.06	1.98	—	-0.7	—
Portugal	—	3.49	4.05	—	13.9
Spain	—	—	—	—	—
Sweden	2.04	2.12	2.21	0.9	1.5
Switzerland	—	2.70	2.75	—	0.9

*   Measured as the ratio of the earnings of the 90th-percentile worker to the 10th-percentile worker, i.e., the 90-10 ratio.
**   Western Germany.
*** Data are for the 80-10 ratio.

Source: Authors' analysis of OECD data.

1990s, inequality grew sharply in Italy (16.0) and Portugal (13.9) and less in New Zealand (5.3), Austria (2.9), Sweden (1.5), Belgium (1.4), and the United Kingdom (1.1, a significant deceleration from the 4.9 points of the 1980s). Over the same period, inequality changed relatively little in Switzerland (0.9), Australia (0.8), and the Netherlands (-0.3), and actually declined in Canada (-5.2), Finland (-3.7), Germany (-3.5), France (-3.2), and Japan (-2.4). In short, since the end of the 1970s, earnings inequality has grown substantially in the United States, the United Kingdom, and New Zealand, but has fluctuated within a much narrower band in most of the rest of the more regulated OECD economies.

One of the most troubling aspects of U.S. inequality is that it can imply a low standard of living for those at the bottom, despite the generally high average

FIGURE 8B Hourly wages at 10th percentile, indexed to U.S., 1991

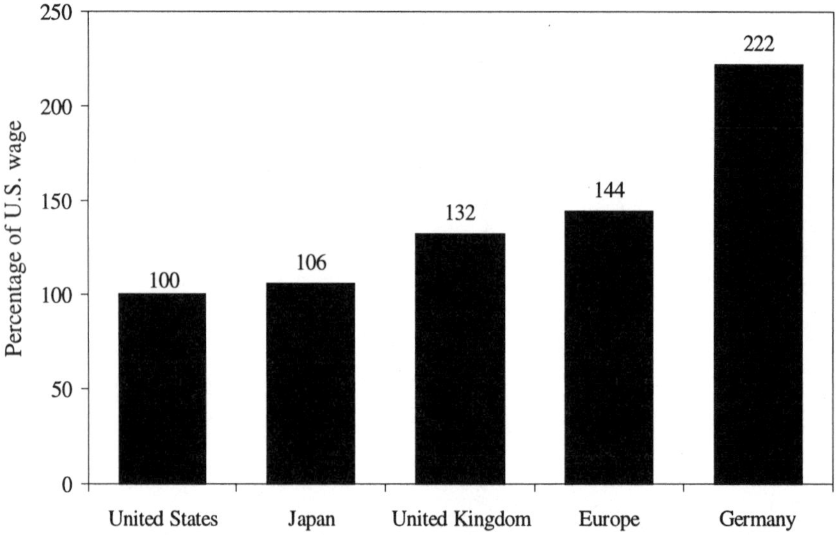

Source: Freeman (1995).

living standards for the U.S. economy as a whole. **Figure 8B** shows that, despite relatively high levels of average productivity in the U.S. economy, workers at the 10th percentile of the earnings distribution make considerably less in absolute terms than workers at a similar position in the earnings distribution of other rich, industrialized countries. On a purchasing-power basis (which, compared to market exchange rates, tends to raise the earnings of U.S. workers relative to workers in other countries), a low-wage worker in Germany, for example, makes more than twice as much as a low-wage worker in the United States. The typical low-wage worker in an advanced European economy earns 44% more than in the United States. The large dispersion of earnings in the United States relative to other countries leaves U.S. low-wage workers with very low earnings, despite living in the country with one of the world's highest income levels.

Boosters of the U.S. labor market model often argue that greater economic mobility in the United States counteracts any negative effects of higher U.S. inequality in any given year. **Table 8.10** reproduces results from an OECD analysis that bears on this claim. For each of seven countries, including the United States, the OECD identified workers from national surveys whose earnings placed them among the poorest 20% of full-time workers in 1986. The OECD used the same surveys to examine how these same workers were faring five years later, in

TABLE 8.10 Earnings mobility of low-paid workers

| Country | 1991 earnings status of 1986 low-paid* workers | | | |
	No longer employed full time	Still low paid*	Moved to second fifth	Moved to upper 60%
United States	**41.4%**	**30.6 %**	**16.7%**	**11.3%**
Germany**	39.3	27.4	16.8	16.6
France	22.5	35.7	23.8	18.0
Italy	8.3	43.8	25.1	22.8
United Kingdom	12.9	35.8	27.8	23.6
Denmark	26.7%	32.1%	20.5%	20.7%
Finland	26.3	28.8	20.1	24.8
Sweden	27.6	35.5	18.4	18.4

* The bottom 20% of workers.
** Western Germany.

Source: Authors' analysis of OECD (1996).

1991. In the United States, 41.4% were no longer employed full time, 30.6% still had earnings in the bottom 20% of all full-time workers, 16.7% had moved up to the second fifth of the earnings distribution, and 11.3% had joined the top 60% of earners. This U.S. record for mobility compares poorly to that of the other seven economies. The United States had the lowest share of workers moving to the second fifth of earners and the lowest share moving into the top 60%; it also had the highest share of workers no longer employed full time. By these figures, the United States economy appears to offer *less mobility* than that of Germany, France, Italy, the United Kingdom, Denmark, Finland, and Sweden, all economies known for a much greater degree of government intervention in the labor market than experienced in the United States.

Household income: slow, unequal growth

The per capita income figures in Tables 8.1 and 8.2 were economy-wide, annual averages. Since individuals make many important decisions about consumption as part of a family or broader household, and since, as we have seen, averages can be deceiving, we now turn to international comparisons of the distribution of household income. Since labor compensation accounts for the largest share

TABLE 8.11 Household income inequality, relative to national median income

Country	Year	Percent of national median		Ratio of 90th to 10th percentile	Gini coefficient**
		10th percentile*	90th percentile*		
United States	**1991**	**36%**	**208%**	**5.78**	**0.343**
Japan	1992	46	192	4.17	0.315
Germany***	1989	54	172	3.21	0.261
France	1984	55	193	3.48	0.294
Italy	1991	56	176	3.14	0.255
United Kingdom	1991	44	206	4.67	0.335
Canada	1991	47	183	3.90	0.285
Australia	1989	45%	193%	4.30	0.308
Austria	1987	56	187	3.34	—
Belgium	1992	58	163	2.79	0.230
Denmark	1992	54	155	2.86	0.239
Finland	1991	57	158	2.75	0.223
Ireland	1987	50	209	4.18	0.328
Netherlands	1991	57	173	3.05	0.249
New Zealand	1987-88	54	187	3.46	—
Norway	1991	56	158	2.80	0.233
Portugal	—	—	—	—	—
Spain	1990	49	198	4.04	0.306
Sweden	1992	57	159	2.78	0.229
Switzerland	1982	54	185	3.43	0.311
Average excluding U.S.	—	51%	186%	3.73	0.290

* The 10th percentile household receives a higher income than 10% of the population, but less than 90% of the population; the 90th percentile household receives a higher income than 90% of the population, but less than 10% of the population.
** The Gini coefficient equals 0 when income is perfectly equally distributed; it equals 1 when all income is concentrated at the top of the income distribution.
*** Western Germany.

Source: Gottschalk and Smeeding (1997).

of household income, the basic pattern of inequality that we observed with earnings repeats itself here: income inequality is high (and rising) in the United States compared to the rest of the OECD. U.S. inequality yields poverty rates that are higher, and living standards that are lower at the bottom, than those in comparable economies. As we saw with earnings, income mobility appears to be *lower* in the United States than in other OECD countries.

Table 8.11 uses two measures of household income inequality for 19 OECD

FIGURE 8C Household income inequality, national median income = 100

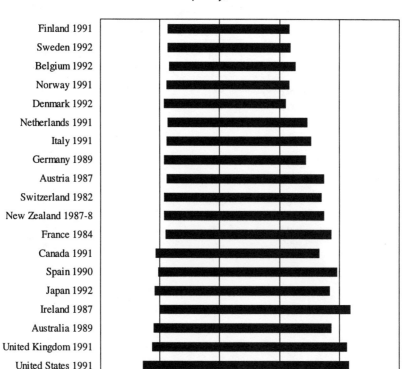

Source: Gottschalk and Smeeding (1997).

countries. The first measure is the "90-10 ratio" for household income, which is calculated exactly as for workers' earnings in Table 8.9. The 90-10 ratio gives the ratio of income received by the 90th-percentile household (receiving income greater than 90% of all households) to the income received by the 10th-percentile household (receiving more than 10%, but less than 90%, of all households). The second inequality measure is the Gini coefficient, a special inequality scale ranging from zero (perfect equality of income across households) to one (all income is concentrated at the very top of the income distribution). The United States has the most unequal household income by both measures (see also **Figure 8C**). In the United States, a household in the 10th percentile of the income distribution receives just 36% of the income of the median household (the household exactly in the middle of the income distribution). In the other 18 econo-

371

TABLE 8.12 Household income inequality, relative to U.S. median income

Country	Year	Percent of U.S. median		Ratio of real national median to real U.S. median
		10th percentile*	90th percentile*	
United States	**1991**	**36%**	**208%**	**1.00**
Japan	1991	43	176	0.92
Germany**	1989	41	133	0.77
France	1984	39	137	0.71
Italy	—	—	—	—
United Kingdom	1991	33	156	0.76
Canada	1991	52	201	1.10
Australia	1989	38%	165%	0.86
Austria	1987	—	—	—
Belgium	1992	43	120	0.74
Denmark	1992	46	131	0.85
Finland	1991	50	138	0.88
Ireland	—	—	—	—
Netherlands	1991	44	133	0.77
New Zealand	—	—	—	—
Norway	1991	51	143	0.91
Portugal	—	—	—	—
Spain	—	—	—	—
Sweden	1992	47	132	0.83
Switzerland	—	—	—	—
Average excluding U.S.	—	41%	155%	0.84

*   The 10th percentile household receives a higher income than 10% of the population, but less than 90% of the population; the 90th percentile household receives a higher income than 90% of the population, but less than 10% of the population.
** Western Germany.

Source: Gottschalk and Smeeding (1997).

mies, the 10th percentile household receives between 44% (United Kingdom) and 58% (Belgium) of the median national income. At the other extreme, the 90th percentile household in the United States makes 208% of the median national income, a level matched only by Ireland (209%) and the United Kingdom (206%), with most other countries finding themselves somewhere between 155% (Denmark) and 185% (Switzerland).

The income inequality in Table 8.11 compares the position of low- and high-income households relative to the median income in each country. We can

FIGURE 8D Household income inequality, U.S. median income = 100

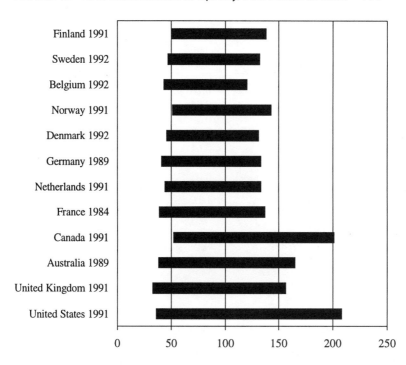

Source: Gottschalk and Smeeding (1997).

also compare the incomes of low- and high-income households to the median in the United States. This allows us to compare the absolute standard of living of low- and high-income households across countries. **Table 8.12** and **Figure 8D** present the results of this exercise. Despite the high median income in the United States, inequality in the United States is so severe that low-income households in the United States are actually worse off than in every other country in the table except the United Kingdom (which has a lower median household income and a relatively high level of income inequality). Not surprisingly, high-income households are much better off in the United States (208% of the median income) than in the rest of the countries (except Canada, which trails only slightly behind the United States at 201% of the U.S. median).

Table 8.13 shows that, since the end of the 1970s, income inequality has been growing in most rich, industrialized countries. In absolute terms (see the last column of Table 8.13), the annual increase in income inequality has been strongest in Sweden, the United States, Australia, Japan, the Netherlands, and

TABLE 8.13 Change in income inequality after 1979

		Annual change in Gini coefficient*	
Country	Period	Relative (percent)	Absolute (point change)
United States	**1979-95**	**0.79**	**0.35**
Japan	1979-93	0.84	0.25
Germany**	1979-95	0.50	0.13
France	1979-89	0.40	0.12
Italy	1980-91	-0.64	-0.58
United Kingdom	1979-95	1.80	0.22
Canada	1979-95	-0.02	0.00
Australia	1981-89	1.16	0.34
Austria	—	—	—
Belgium	—	—	—
Denmark	1981-90	1.20	—
Finland	1979-94	-0.10	-0.02
Ireland	—	—	—
Netherlands	1979-94	1.07	0.25
New Zealand	—	—	—
Norway	1979-92	0.22	0.05
Portugal	—	—	—
Spain	—	—	—
Sweden	1979-94	1.68	0.38
Switzerland	—	—	—

* Measured as the relative change in the Gini coefficient, where growth reflects more inequality.
** Western Germany.

Source: Authors' analysis based on Gottschalk and Smeeding (1997).

the United Kingdom. Income inequality has grown more slowly in Germany, France, and Norway and has been basically unchanged in Canada and Finland. Income inequality has fallen over the same period in Italy (though the more recent earnings data in Table 8.9 suggest that subsequent income data may show a large jump in inequality by the mid-1990s). Given the lower initial levels of inequality in most countries other than the United States, the absolute increases in other economies represent much larger relative increases in inequality than they would in the United States.

Since most studies of international poverty use relative income inequality to measure national poverty rates, higher inequality translates almost directly

TABLE 8.14 Poverty rates*

Country	Year	Percentage in poverty			Rank		
		Total	Elderly	Children	Total	Elderly	Children
United States	**1994**	**19.1%**	**19.6%**	**24.9%**	**1**	**3**	**1**
Japan	1992	11.8	18.4	12.2	4	4	7
Germany**	1989	7.6	7.5	8.6	8	10	9
France	1984	7.5	4.8	7.4	9	15	11
Italy	1991	6.5	4.4	10.5	14	16	8
United Kingdom	1991	14.6	23.9	18.5	2	1	2
Canada	1991	11.7	5.7	15.3	5	14	4
Australia	1989	12.9%	21.6%	15.4%	3	2	3
Austria	—	—	—	—	—	—	—
Belgium	1992	5.5	11.9	4.4	16	8	15
Denmark	1992	7.5	11.3	5.1	9	10	13
Finland	1991	6.2	14.4	2.7	15	5	17
Ireland	1987	11.1	7.6	13.8	6	11	5
Netherlands	1991	6.7	4.1	8.3	11	17	10
New Zealand	—	—	—	—	—	—	—
Norway	1991	6.6	13.5	4.9	13	6	14
Portugal	—	—	—	—	—	—	—
Spain	1990	10.4	11.4	12.8	7	9	6
Sweden	1992	6.7	6.4	3.0	11	13	16
Switzerland	—	—	—	—	—	—	—
Average excluding U.S.	—	9.8%	12.2%	11.3%	—	—	—

* Measured as share below 50% of the median adjusted disposable personal income for individuals. Elderly are 65 and older; children are 17 and under.
** Western Germany.

Source: Smeeding (1997).

into higher levels of poverty in these international studies. **Table 8.14** summarizes international data from the 1990s on poverty rates for the population as a whole, for the elderly (65 and older), and for children (17 and under). Following the standard methodology, the table defines the poverty rate as the share of households receiving 50% or less of the median household income in each country. In the United States, this threshold amounts to an income that is close to the official U.S. poverty line. (The data in Table 8.12, which compare the income of the 10th-percentile household in each country to the U.S. median income, provide an indication of the absolute standard of living of low-income families across the OECD countries.) Like the official U.S. definition, the poverty rates in Table 8.14 take into account cash transfers and are adjusted for family size, but, unlike the U.S. definition, they also account for taxes and the value of food stamps.

The United States, with 19.1% of its total population living in poverty, has the highest level of overall poverty among the 16 countries examined here. The next closest is the United Kingdom, with a 14.6% poverty rate. Nine of the 16 countries have poverty rates below 8% — less than half the U.S. rate. The United States does a little better with respect to poverty among the elderly. About 19.6% of Americans age 65 and older live in poverty by this international definition, a smaller share than in the United Kingdom (23.9%) and Australia (21.6%), but the U.S. rate is still above those in the remaining 13 economies. The United States also suffers from the highest rate of child poverty, with almost one in four children (24.9%) under the age of 18 living in poverty by the international definition. Rates in the rest of the countries range from 2.7% (Finland) to 18.5% (United Kingdom).

International differences in labor market institutions such as minimum wages and unions explain a large part of the differences in international poverty rates, but variations across countries in tax and transfer programs for low-income households are also important. **Table 8.15** illustrates the net effect of national tax and transfer programs on poverty rates for the population as a whole, the elderly, and children in 15 countries. For the population as a whole, the "pre" column gives the poverty rate determined by the workings of the labor market, that is, before taxes on gross incomes and before income received from government assistance programs. The United States, which has the highest overall poverty level in Table 8.14, has, at 26.7%, a lower "market-determined" poverty level than do Sweden (34.1%), Ireland (30.3%), the United Kingdom (29.2%), Belgium (28.4%), Spain (28.2%), and Denmark (26.9%). The U.S. tax and transfer system, however, reduces this market-determined poverty rate only to 19.1% (a 28.5% reduction in the number of persons in poverty). The tax and transfer systems in all the other countries in the table reduce poverty by substantially higher margins, from 44.4% in Australia to 80.6% in Belgium. The U.S. tax and transfer system works best at reducing poverty among the elderly, due primarily to the workings of the Social Security program, which along with these other programs reduces poverty among the elderly by 66.6%. This sizable reduction, however, is the second smallest in the table, just better than the United Kingdom, which achieved only a 65.1% reduction in poverty among the elderly.

The U.S. tax and transfer system does far worse in reducing poverty among children, only managing to lower the market-determined poverty rate from 28.7% to 24.9%, a mere 13.2% reduction in child poverty rates. Only Italy, with a final child poverty rate of 10.5%, produced a smaller reduction (4.5%) in child pov-

TABLE 8.15 The impact of taxes and transfers on poverty rates*

	Year	All persons			Elderly			Children		
		Pre**	Post**	Change (%)	Pre**	Post**	Change (%)	Pre**	Post**	Change (%)
United States	1994	**26.7%**	**19.1%**	**-28.5%**	**58.7%**	**19.6%**	**-66.6%**	**28.7%**	**24.9%**	**-13.2%**
Japan	—	—	—	—	—	—	—	—	—	—
Germany***	1989	22.0	7.6	-65.5	65.8	7.5	-88.6	11.7	8.6	-26.5
France	1984	21.6	7.5	-65.3	79.9	4.8	-94.0	27.4	7.4	-73.0
Italy	1991	18.4	6.5	-64.7	55.7	4.4	-92.1	11.0	10.5	-4.5
United Kingdom	1991	29.2	14.6	-50.0	68.5	23.9	-65.1	28.7	18.5	-35.5
Canada	1991	23.4	11.7	-50.0	58.2	5.7	-90.2	22.7	15.3	-32.6
Australia	1989	23.2%	12.9%	-44.4%	70.2%	21.6%	-69.2%	20.5%	15.4%	-24.9%
Austria	—	—	—	—	—	—	—	—	—	—
Belgium	1992	28.4	5.5	-80.6	88.9	11.9	-86.6	17.2	4.4	-74.4
Denmark	1992	26.9	7.5	-72.1	69.9	11.3	-83.8	17.1	5.1	-70.2
Finland	1991	15.6	6.2	-60.3	43.8	14.4	-67.1	11.6	2.7	-76.7
Ireland	1987	30.3	11.1	-63.4	54.9	7.6	-86.2	30.3	13.8	-54.5
Netherlands	1991	22.8	6.7	-70.6	65.5	4.1	-93.7	15.2	8.3	-45.4
New Zealand	—	—	—	—	—	—	—	—	—	—
Norway	1991	21.8	6.6	-69.7	68.0	13.5	-80.1	12.7	4.9	-61.4
Portugal	—	—	—	—	—	—	—	—	—	—
Spain	1990	28.2	10.4	-63.1	68.2	11.4	-83.3	20.7	12.8	-38.2
Sweden	1992	34.1	6.7	-80.4	91.6	6.4	-93.0	18.4	3.0	-83.7
Switzerland	—	—	—	—	—	—	—	—	—	—
Average excluding U.S.	—	23.8%	9.2%	-61.7%	67.5%	10.1%	-84.9%	19.2%	11.0%	-38.1%

*   Measured as share below 50% of the median adjusted disposable personal income for individuals. Elderly are 65 and older; children are 17 and under.
** "Pre" refers to pre-tax, pre-transfer income; "post" refers to post-tax, post-transfer income.
*** Western Germany.

Source: Smeeding (1997).

erty. The tax and transfer systems in the rest of the OECD countries reduced child poverty between 24.9% (Australia) and 83.7% (Sweden).

As with earnings, some have argued that, while inequality in the United States may be higher than in other economies, the U.S. economy also offers greater opportunities for low-income households to improve their economic circumstances. **Table 8.16** and **Figure 8E** present the results of an international study of the economic mobility of poor families with children in the mid-1980s that assesses the validity of this claim.

The first column of Table 8.16 gives the poverty rates for families with children in each of the countries in the study. As in Table 8.14, poverty rates in

TABLE 8.16 Poverty rates and transitions out
of poverty for families with children, mid-1980s

Country	Poverty rate*	Transition rate**	Percent of families poor in all 3 years of a 3-year period
United States	**20.3%**	**13.8%**	**14.4%**
White	15.3	17.0	9.5
Black	49.3	7.7	41.5
Germany***	7.8	25.6	1.5
Ethnic German	6.7	26.9	1.4
Immigrants	18.0	20.0	4.0
France (Lorraine)	4.0	27.5	1.6
Canada	17.0	12.0	11.9
Ireland	11.0%	25.2%	n.a.
Netherlands	2.7	44.4	0.4
Sweden	2.7	36.8	n.a.

* Measured as percent of families with income below 50% of that country's median income in year 1.
** Measured as percent of families who were poor in year 1 who had more than 60% of median income in year 2.
*** Western Germany.

Source: Duncan et al. (1991).

the United States are higher than in the other countries examined here. This is particularly true for black families in the United States, whose poverty rate was 49.3%. The second column ("transition rate") shows the percent of poor families in the first year of the study who escaped poverty by the second year. The third column reports the share of families that were poor in all three years of the three-year period examined.

Figure 8E displays some of the same data. The horizontal axis of Figure 8E is the percent of families who were poor in the first year of the study (column 1, Table 8.16). The vertical axis is the percentage of poor families who escaped poverty by the second year (column 2, Table 8.16).

Most of the countries in Figure 8E show relatively low poverty rates and relatively high "escape" rates. France (Lorraine region), for example, has a family poverty rate of 4% in the first year, with 27.5% of the poor in that year escaping poverty by the next year. However, the U.S. position in the figure reveals both high poverty and *low mobility*. The U.S. overall poverty rate (20.3%) is the highest in the table, and the escape rate of 13.8% is the second lowest. The situation for U.S. blacks is particularly severe. As noted above, the poverty rate

FIGURE 8E Poverty rates and transitions out of poverty, families with children, mid-1980s

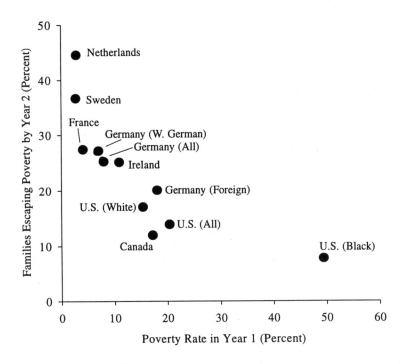

Source: Duncan et al. (1991).

for black families is 49.3%, the highest in the table. Blacks in the United States also have the lowest probability of escaping poverty; only 7.7% of the poor in the first year had left poverty by the second year. Only the Canadian poor are less likely than the U.S. poor (overall) to leave poverty. In fact, even foreigners within Germany, who have higher poverty rates than U.S. whites, have higher escape rates than the U.S. poor.

The third column of Table 8.16 provides further evidence of low economic mobility in the United States compared to the other countries in the table. The probability of a poor family with children remaining poor for the full length of the three-year period of the study was highest in the United States, at 14.4% (41.5% for black families in the United States). The rate for Canada (11.9%) was slightly lower than the U.S. average; the rate for other countries in the study was much lower — below 5.0% in every case where data were available.

Employment and hours worked: strength of the U.S. model?

The per capita income figures in Tables 8.1 and 8.2 appear, at face value, to be at odds with the international estimates of productivity levels in Table 8.3. Per capita income in the United States — the value of goods and services produced in one year per person — is generally much higher relative to the other OECD economies than is the U.S. productivity level —the value of goods and services produced in an one hour of work in the United States. These differences between per capita income and productivity levels (gross national product per hour worked) stem from two important differences across countries: the share of the total population in employment, and the average number of hours worked each year by those with jobs.

The U.S. economy employs a greater share of its working-age population, and its workers work, on average, more hours per year, than is the case in any other rich, industrialized economy. This raises per capita income in the United States relative to other economies with roughly similar productivity levels but lower levels of employment and lower average annual hours worked. Supporters of the U.S. model have long argued that the U.S. ability to generate a greater volume of work, whether measured in terms of number of jobs or hours of work, is a major feature of the U.S. model. In this section, we take a closer look at international employment rates, average hours worked, and unemployment rates. The United States does indeed employ a greater share of its working-age population than any of the 10 economies in **Table 8.17** for which comparable data are available. In 1996, the United States employed 70.9% of its male working-age population (second only to Japan with 74.9%) and ranked first with respect to female employment, with 56.0% of women employed. Employment rates can vary because of differences across economies in school enrollment rates for adults, early retirement rates, and women's nonmarket responsibilities, especially child care. As we shall see below, however, one of the most important determinants of the differences in employment rates across the 10 economies in Table 8.17 is the unemployment rate.

Table 8.17 shows a different pattern over time for employment rates of men and women. Among working-age men, employment rates fell in every country during the 1980s and in every country except the Netherlands in the 1990s. The decline in male employment between 1979 and 1996 was smallest in the United States (1.3 percentage points in the 1980s and 1.6 percentage points in the 1990s). Declines in employment over the entire period were much higher in several European economies, most notably France (-12.0 percentage points), Sweden (-11.9 percentage points), Italy (-9.8 percentage points), Germany (-9.7 percentage points), and the United Kingdom (-8.8 percentage points). Among work-

TABLE 8.17 Employment rates

	Employment rate*			Change	
	1979	1989	1996	1979-89	1989-96
Men					
United States	**73.8%**	**72.5%**	**70.9%**	**-1.3**	**-1.6**
Japan	78.2	75.1	74.9	-3.1	-0.2
Germany**	69.8	65.9	60.1	-3.9	-5.8
France***	69.6	61.2	57.6	-8.4	-3.6
Italy****	66.3	59.9	56.5	-6.4	-3.4
United Kingdom***	74.5	70.4	65.7	-4.1	-4.7
Canada	73.4	71.4	65.2	-2.0	-6.2
Australia	75.3%	71.9%	67.9%	-3.4	-4.0
Netherlands***	74.3	65.0	66.9	-9.3	1.9
Sweden***	73.7	70.9	61.8	-2.8	-9.1
Women					
United States	**47.5%**	**54.3%**	**56.0%**	**6.8**	**1.7**
Japan	45.7	47.4	47.7	1.7	0.3
Germany**	38.4	39.7	41.2	1.3	1.5
France***	40.5	41.2	40.3	0.7	-0.9
Italy****	27.3	28.6	28.4	1.3	-0.2
United Kingdom***	45.3	49.1	50.1	3.8	1.0
Canada	45.3	53.7	52.1	8.4	-1.6
Australia	40.7%	48.6%	50.4%	7.9	1.8
Netherlands***	29.2	37.4	44.9	8.2	7.5
Sweden***	57.2	61.7	54.2	4.5	-7.5

*   Total employment as a percentage of working-age population.
**   Data for western Germany; 1996 column is preliminary figure for 1994.
***   Data for 1996 are preliminary.
**** Data in 1996 column are preliminary data for 1995.

Source: Authors' analysis of BLS (1997).

ing-age women, employment rates rose between 1979 and 1996 in every country but Sweden (-3.0 percentage points from a high base in 1979) and France (-0.2 percentage points). The largest increases occurred in the Netherlands (15.7 percentage points from a very low base in 1979), Australia (9.7 percentage points), the United States (8.5 percentage points), Canada (6.8 percentage points), and the United Kingdom (4.8 percentage points).

Table 8.18 reports the average number of hours worked per year by employees in 15 OECD countries. Workers in the United States worked, on aver-

TABLE 8.18 Average annual hours worked, 1979-95

	1979	1990	1995	Change 1979-95
United States	**1905**	**1943**	**1952**	**47**
Japan*	2126	2031	1898	-228
Germany**	1764	1616	1559	-205
France	1813	1668	1631	-182
Italy	1788	—	—	—
United Kingdom	1821	1773	1735	-86
Canada	1802	1738	1737	-65
Australia	1904	1869	1876	-28
Austria	—	—	—	—
Belgium	—	—	—	—
Denmark	—	—	—	—
Finland	1868	1764	1775	-93
Ireland	—	—	—	—
Netherlands	—	—	—	—
New Zealand	—	1820	1843	—
Norway	1516	1432	1424	-92
Portugal*	—	—	2009	—
Spain	1988	1829	1807	-181
Sweden	1451	1480	1544	93
Switzerland*	—	—	1639	—
Average excluding U.S.	1900	1812	1752	-166

* Figure in 1995 column refers to 1994 data.
** Western Germany.

Source: OECD (1996).

age, more hours per year (1,952) than workers in any of the other countries, even more than the historic leader in hours worked, Japan (1,898). Between 1979 and 1995, as nearly every other country reduced its average hours worked per year, the United States increased its average by 47 hours. (Sweden also increased its average hours worked (93), but only to a level that kept it next to the bottom in average hours worked per year – 1,544 hours, or less than 80% of the U.S. level.) **Figure 8F** reveals one important reason for international difference in hours worked: statutory annual vacation policies in European countries that exceed the average days provided by U.S. employers. The U.S. average, about 16 days per year, is below the statutory minimum in all but two of the countries in the figure.

FIGURE 8F Legally mandated paid vacation in European countries

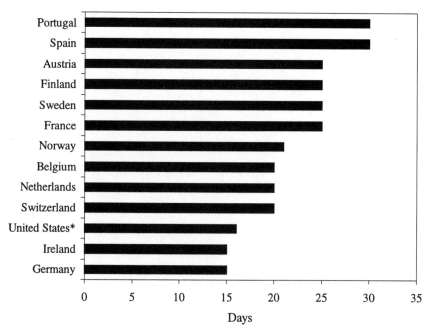

* Average, not legally mandated.
Source: Authors' analysis of Leete-Guy and Schor (1992).

The data on employment rates and average hours worked suggest that more U.S. workers (as a share of the U.S. working population) contribute more hours on average to GDP than is the case in most other OECD countries. The calculations in **Table 8.19** summarize data similar to that presented in Tables 8.17 and 8.18 and help to reconcile the differences between the U.S. and the other economies' productivity levels, on the one hand, and their per capita income, on the other. German productivity rates, for example, are 101% of those in the United States (see column 1), but fewer Germans work, which reduces per capita income 13% in Germany relative to the United States. Those Germans who do work on average work fewer hours than in the United States, which further reduces per capita income in Germany 6% relative to the United States. The basic lesson of the employment and hours data, and the exercise in Table 8.19, is that an important portion of the apparently higher standard of living in the United States comes not from working harder or smarter than other comparable economies, but simply from working more and longer.

The capacity of the U.S. economy to sustain higher employment rates and

TABLE 8.19 Impact of productivity, employment,* and hours differences

	Output per hour worked as % of U.S.	Effect of		Per capita income as % of U.S.
		Employment* (%)	Hours (%)	
United States	**100%**	**0%**	**0%**	**100%**
Japan	68	5	9	82
Germany**	101	-13	-6	82
France	102	-19	-5	78
Italy	90	-11	-7	72
United Kingdom	84	-8	-5	71
Canada	85	-10	4	79
Australia	76%	-4%	3%	75%
Austria	83	-6	-1	76
Belgium	97	-21	-1	75
Denmark	74	5	2	80
Finland	74	-11	2	66
Ireland	84	-29	5	60
Netherlands	98	-7	-17	73
New Zealand	70	-2	-4	64
Norway	88	-1	-8	79
Portugal	43	-3	3	43
Spain	70	-29	13	54
Sweden	79	-6	-1	72
Switzerland	86	2	3	91

* Combined effects of differences in unemployment rate, labor force participation rate, and age composition of total population.
** Western Germany only.

Note: The data in Table 8.19 differ from those in Tables 8.17 and 8.18 and are therefore not directly comparable. In Table 8.19, for example, Japanese employment rates and hours worked appear to be higher than in the United States. We place more weight on the data from the OECD in Tables 8.17 and 8.18 than on the data from the Conference Board in Table 8.19, but nevertheless believe that the exercise in Table 8.19 provides a helpful illustration of the impact of international differences in employment rates and hours worked.

Source: Conference Board (1997).

higher volumes of work (measured in the total hours of annual employment) is an important accomplishment of the U.S. economy. **Table 8.20**, nevertheless, attempts to put U.S. job creation into historical and international context. The table shows the annual employment growth rate in 20 OECD economies over two periods, 1979-89 and 1989-96. Two features stand out. First, the U.S. employment growth rate during the incomplete 1990s business cycle (1.0% per

TABLE 8.20 Employment, 1979-96

	Employment (thousands)			Employment change (thousands)		Annual growth rate (%)	
	1979	1989	1996	1979-89	1989-96	1979-89	1989-96
United States	**98,859**	**117,265**	**125,467**	**18,405**	**8,203**	**1.7%**	**1.0%**
Japan	55,640	62,250	65,465	6,610	3,215	1.1	0.7
Germany*	—	—	—	0	0	0.4	-0.0
France	21,796	22,275	22,233	479	(42)	0.2	-0.0
Italy	20,217	20,560	19,947	343	(614)	0.2	-0.4
United Kingdom	24,601	26,160	25,731	1,559	(429)	0.6	-0.2
Canada	10,624	12,928	13,439	2,304	510	2.0	0.6
Australia	6,006	7,587	8,096	1,580	509	2.4%	0.9%
Austria	3,350	3,366	3,487	16	121	0.0	0.5
Belgium	3,675	3,683	3,673	9	(10)	0.0	-0.0
Denmark	2,377	2,507	2,471	129	(36)	0.5	-0.2
Finland	2,046	2,242	1,943	195	(299)	0.9	-2.0
Ireland	1,150	1,092	1,277	(58)	185	-0.5	2.3
Netherlands	5,142	5,490	6,101	349	611	0.7	1.5
New Zealand	1,413	1,429	1,614	16	185	0.1	1.8
Norway	1,841	1,985	2,054	144	69	0.8	0.5
Portugal	3,780	4,318	4,180	538	(138)	1.3	-0.5
Spain	11,997	12,103	11,979	106	(124)	0.1	-0.1
Sweden	3,964	4,225	3,817	260	(408)	0.6	-1.4
Switzerland	3,112	3,725	3,808	613	83	1.8	0.3
Average excluding U.S.	—	—	—	—	—	0.8%	0.2%

* Growth rate for western Germany, 1979-91; eastern and western Germany, 1992-96.

Source: Authors' analysis of OECD (1997).

year) has been slower than over the 1979-89 business cycle (1.7% per year). Second, the U.S. "jobs machine" is less effective at creating jobs in the 1990s than Ireland (2.3%, after net job losses in the 1980s), New Zealand (1.8%, after stagnant job creation in the 1980s), and the Netherlands (1.5%). The U.S. performance is also not substantially better over the 1980s and 1990s than that of Australia, Japan, or Canada.

The employment growth data, therefore, suggest that the current U.S. job creation rate is not particularly high either by its own historical terms or when compared with several other economies with very different labor market institutions. These job creation data are consistent with the earlier data on employment rates, which showed that the U.S. was not able to prevent the male employment rate from falling in the 1980s and 1990s (though it did a better job than other

TABLE 8.21 Unemployment rates, 1979-96 (percent of civilian labor force)

	Standardized unemployment*		
	1979	1989	1996
United States	**5.8%**	**5.3%**	**5.4%**
Japan	2.1	2.3	3.4
Germany	—	—	8.9
Western Germany	2.7	5.6	7.2
France	5.3	9.3	12.4
Italy	5.8	10.0	12.0
United Kingdom	4.7	7.3	8.2
Canada	7.5	7.5	9.7
Australia	6.1%	6.2%	8.6%
Austria	—	—	4.4
Belgium	9.1	7.5	9.8
Denmark	—	7.4	6.9
Finland	6.5	3.3	15.3
Ireland	—	14.7	11.6
Netherlands	5.8	6.9	6.3
New Zealand	—	7.1	6.1
Norway	2.0	5.0	4.9
Portugal	—	4.9	7.3
Spain	7.7	17.2	22.1
Sweden	2.1	1.6	10.0
Switzerland	—	—	—
Average excluding U.S.	4.4%	6.9%	9.1%

* Unemployment based on comparable definitions.

Source: OECD (1997).

economies) and that several economies raised their female employment rates by larger margins than did the United States over the same period.

Table 8.21 reports the unemployment rate in 20 OECD countries for 1979, 1989, and 1996. A few countries have relatively low unemployment rates in 1996, with the lowest rates in Japan (3.4%), Austria (4.4%), Norway (4.9%), the United States (5.4%), New Zealand (6.1%), the Netherlands (6.3%), Denmark (6.9%), and western Germany (7.2%). Most, however, have unemployment rates above 8.0%. Moreover, in every country for which data are available, except the United States, the unemployment rate was higher in 1996 than it was in 1979.

Table 8.22 assesses an important claim about the causes of higher Euro-

TABLE 8.22 Unemployment rates by education level, 1994

| Country | Unemployment rate* | | | Ratio of | |
	Less than high school	High school	College	Less than high school/ college	High school/ college
United States	**12.6%**	**6.2%**	**3.2%**	**3.9**	**1.9**
Japan	—	—	—	—	—
Germany**	13.9	8.8	5.4	2.6	1.6
France	14.7	10.5	6.8	2.2	1.5
Italy	8.4	7.5	6.4	1.3	1.2
United Kingdom	13.0	8.3	3.9	3.3	2.1
Canada	14.3	9.0	7.3	2.0	1.2
Australia	10.2%	6.9%	4.5%	2.3	1.5
Austria	4.9	2.8	1.7	2.9	1.6
Belgium	12.5	7.1	3.7	3.4	1.9
Denmark	17.3	10.0	5.3	3.3	1.9
Finland	22.7	16.4	8.5	2.7	1.9
Ireland	18.9	9.7	4.9	3.9	2.0
Netherlands	8.2	4.8	4.3	1.9	1.1
New Zealand	9.3	5.3	2.9	3.2	1.8
Norway	6.5	4.7	2.3	2.8	2.0
Portugal	6.0	6.2	2.5	2.4	2.5
Spain	21.3	19.4	15.0	1.4	1.3
Sweden	8.8	7.6	3.6	2.4	2.1
Switzerland	5.1	3.4	3.0	1.7	1.1
Average excluding U.S.	12.9%	9.3%	6.2%	2.3	1.6

* Standardized rate.
** Eastern and western Germany.

Source: Authors's analysis of OECD (1997).

pean unemployment — that Europe's labor market institutions, such as strong unions, high minimum wages, and generous benefits have priced less-skilled workers out of jobs. If this were the case, we would expect the unemployment rates of less-educated workers and better-educated workers to be relatively close to one another in the United States, where relatively weak unions, low minimum wages, and stingy benefits would have less of an effect on the employment prospects of less-educated workers (that is, wages can fall so as to promote more jobs for the less skilled). Conversely, we would expect the unemployment rates of less-educated and better-educated workers to be relatively farther apart in Europe, where labor market institutions would, by conventional thinking, disproportionately hurt job creation for less-educated workers. The data in Table 8.22 run completely counter to the conventional expectation. The unemployment rate for less-than-high-school-educated workers in the United States in 1994 was 3.9 times higher than for college-educated workers. The ratio of less-educated to better-educated unemployment rates was *lower* in 17 of the remaining 18 countries in the table (Ireland had the same ratio as the United States). Thus, it appears that Europe's strong labor market institutions have not contributed to relatively higher unemployment rates among less-educated workers compared to the United States; if anything, the European institutions appear to be associated with substantially *lower* relative unemployment rates for less-educated workers.

Evaluating the U.S. model

This chapter places the performance of the U.S. economy in an international context. The data suggest that the United States suffers from greater earnings and income inequality and higher pre- and post-tax-and-transfer poverty rates than almost every other OECD economy. Low-wage workers and low-income households in the United States are almost universally worse off in absolute terms than their low-wage, low-income counterparts in other, less-affluent OECD countries. Moreover, most of these economic indicators have deteriorated in the United States in the 1980s and 1990s relative to the rest of the OECD.

Supporters of the U.S. model generally acknowledge the relative inequality of the United States, but argue that the model provides greater mobility, greater employment opportunities, and greater dynamism than do more interventionist economies. The evidence, however, provides little support for this view. First, economic mobility, at least for low-wage workers and poor families, appears to be *lower* in the United States than in most European economies.

Second, U.S. success in employment creation is often exaggerated. U.S. job growth rates in the 1990s are lackluster by its own historical standards and no better than several other OECD countries with very different kinds of labor market institutions. While the U.S. is the only economy to escape rising unemployment over the last two decades, several OECD countries still have unemployment rates near or below that of the United States. Perhaps most importantly, the pattern of unemployment rates in OECD countries is completely inconsistent with the idea that labor market institutions have priced less-educated workers out of jobs: the "flexible" U.S. labor market has the highest relative unemployment rate for less-educated workers among all the OECD countries.

Third, the data on growth rates in per capita income and productivity suggest that the U.S. economy is among the *least* dynamic of the OECD economies. In the 1980s and 1990s, nearly all the OECD economies — including the United States — appear to have suffered a dramatic deceleration in both the growth rates of per capita income and productivity. The especially slow growth rates in the United States, however, have allowed all the OECD countries to narrow the U.S. lead; several have eliminated the productivity gap altogether.

The best interpretation of the available international evidence is that all of the OECD economies are experiencing substantial difficulties in the late 1990s. Economic growth and productivity growth rates have fallen across the entire OECD in the last two decades. Inequality has risen sharply, especially in the United States, the United Kingdom, and a few other countries. Simultaneously, unemployment has increased to alarming levels in the majority of OECD economies, especially in Europe. This chapter and the rest of this book illustrate the many shortfalls of the "U.S. model" as a potential solution to the broad range of problems facing the OECD economies. The evidence in this chapter, which underscores the diversity of international experience with providing wage, income, and employment security, suggests that those who look exclusively to the United States for solutions will miss a great deal.

Family income and poverty data

by Jared Bernstein

———————————————————————————————

This appendix explains the various adjustments made to the March Current Population Survey data along with the methodology used to prepare the data in the tables discussed below.

Table 1.8: The data used for this table come from special versions of the March 1990 and 1997 CPS files.

Beginning in 1996 (with retrospective income data for 1995), the Census Bureau introduced a new method for top coded cases for four key earnings variables, the most important of which is "earnings from longest job" (others are self-employment income, farm self-employment income, and income from other wage and salary employment). Individuals who reported values above the top code on these variables were previously assigned the top code value on the public use files; from 1996 forward, they are assigned a value equal to a group-specific mean above the top code (groups are based on sex, race/origin, and worker status). This procedure creates an inconsistency when comparing these files with earlier years.

In order to generate comparable measures of income for an earlier year, the Census Bureau performed the following data reconstruction. Using their internal file for 1989 (which has higher top codes than the public use files), Census programmers determined the percent of cases that fell above their internal top code. Using the same groupings noted above, they calculated mean values on the earnings variables of cases between the external and internal top codes. They then found these same percentiles in the 1997 file and followed the same procedure, calculating the mean values between the external top code and these "ceiling" values determined from the 1989 file.

For example, for earnings from longest job in 1989, 0.1% of the weighted cases were above the internal top code. Therefore, the Census Bureau identified the 99.9th percentile on the 1997 file and calculated the means for the various groups between the external (i.e., public use) top code and this value.

We made one further adjustment to these data. The procedure as described assumes that the income of the top 0.1% did not grow even in nominal terms between 1989 and 1996. Since this is very unlikely, we assigned the real growth of that portion of the top 1% that was not top coded in either year to those in the top 0.1% in 1996.

Quintiles in the table comprise 20% of persons, not families, in each fifth.

Table 1.10: The methodology for this table is presented in Ryscavage et al. (1992). Following these authors, we capture the impact of demographic changes on household incomes by adjusting the weights of household heads to reflect demographic changes over the time periods shown in the table.

We use the following categories: *education:* high school or less, some college, and college or more; *age:* less than 25, 25-44, 45-64, and 65 and older; *family type:* married-couple households, single-headed households, individuals living alone; *race:* white, nonwhite.

In order to simulate the income effects of changing shares of the population with these characteristics between t_0 and t_1, we multiplied each head-of-household's weight by the ratio of the standardized number of households with a particular characteristic in t_0 to that in t_1. For example, to estimate the effect of the change in the age of household heads over the period 1969-79, we divided the 1979 sample into the age groups noted above, and multiplied the weight of each 1979 householder by the ratio of the weighted number of householders in that cell in 1969 to that in 1979. Both numerator and denominator are standardized by dividing each by the total number of households in their respective years. Finally, to measure the impact of all of the demographic factors taken together, we performed the same exercise but with each representing the intersection of all the variables noted above (e.g., one cell would be nonwhite, married-couple householders, age 25-34, with four or more years of college).

Two caveats should be noted with this type of analysis. First, due to correlation between some of these characteristics and income levels, there are various interactions between these demographic categories that are not reflected in the table. For example, whites tend to have higher incomes than nonwhites, and are also more likely than nonwhites to be college educated. Thus, the sum of these two effects — race and education — taken separately are likely to be larger than their combined effect, because the summative approach fails to partial out the correlation.

Second, demographic decompositions such as this one tend to suffer from an endogeneity problem. That is, the exercise assigns causation to the demographic changes under analysis, implying, for example, that the increase in single-parent families led to lower average income levels. It is possible, however, that the causality runs the other way. Say, for example, that income declines stemming from male wage declines have led to an increase in female-headed families. To the extent that this is the case, the contribution of demographic factors will be overstated.

Tables 1.16–1.20: Here again, we were confronted with the inconsistency in the data introduced by the changes made in the above discussion of Table 1.8. Since our analysis goes back to 1979, we could not use the specially constructed data files, which cover only 1989 and 1996. Therefore, we implemented the following adjustments to the March data for 1979, 1989, and 1996.

In order to create a comparable set of files, we use the assumption that the upper tail of the distribution of key variables follows the Pareto distribution. Thus, using the definition of the Pareto along with the observed distribution below the top codes, we calculated estimates of the mean values above the top code and assigned these values to the top-coded cases (see Bernstein and Gao 1998 for a further description of this approach). We implemented this procedure for the variables total earnings, interest income, and income from dividends.

Note that, in 1996, we applied these Pareto-imputed means to any person with values above the top code, despite that fact that the public use file, as described in the discussion of Table 1.8, has actual means values, at least for the earnings variables, for persons with similar characteristics above the top code.

We then constructed datasets for the three years of married couples, spouse present, where the family head was between 25 and 54 years of age. The distributional analysis places 20% of families, not persons, in each fifth. The methodology closely follows that described in Joint Economic Committee (JEC) 1992.

Husbands and wives' wages in this analysis (Table 1.18) are constructed differently than in most of the analysis in this book, i.e., they are "hour-weighted" in this section and "person-weighted" elsewhere (this follows the JEC methodology). Whereas we usually calculate averages by summing the wages and dividing by the weighted number of earners, in this case we calculate annual hours by dividing annual earnings by annual hours. Since there is a positive correlation between earnings levels and number of hours worked, hour-weighted wage levels tend to be slightly higher than person-weighted wages.

Finally, note that in the calculation of income shares in the absence of wives' earnings (Table 1.20), we determine a separate set of quintile cutoffs (based on family income minus wives' earnings) than those for actual shares. This approach simulates one choice of a counterfactual distribution.

Table 6.16: The methodology for this decomposition is taken from Danziger and Gottschalk (1995), Chapter 5. The change to be explained is the difference in poverty rates between t_0 and t_1. We first isolate the effect of average income growth by assigning the average growth between the two time periods to all families in t_0 and recalculate the poverty rate (we adjust each family's poverty line for the increase in the CPI over this period). This procedure holds the demographic composition and the shape of the income distribution constant in t_0 while allowing incomes to grow equally for all families. Thus, the difference between this simulated poverty rate and the actual t_0 poverty rate is attributable to the growth in average income.

We repeat this exercise for each demographic group in t_0 (we use the three family types in Table 6.13, two races — white and nonwhite — and three education categories of the family head — less than high school, high school and some college, and college or more). By weighting each of these simulated t_0 rates by their t_1 population shares, we can simulate a t_0 poverty rate that reflects the average income growth and demographic composition of t_1. The difference between this simulated rate and the one discussed in the above paragraph gives the contribution of demographic change over the time period. Finally, since this second simulated rate incorporates the mean growth and demographic change between the two periods, but not the change in the shape of the distribution, the difference between this second simulated rate and the actual rate for t_1 equals the change in poverty rates attributable to changes in inequality over the two periods.

Tables 7.3–7.4: In order to have enough cases to generate reliable estimates of state income levels, we pooled three years of March CPS files, with income data for the years 1978-80, 1988-90, and 1994-96. Given the inconsistency in the treatment of top codes noted above, we implemented the same Pareto procedures, on the same variables, described in the discussion of Table 1.16–1.20. The Pareto-imputed means were calculated for the national data, based on the pool distribution over the three years. These quintiles consist of 20% of persons, not families, in each fifth.

Wage analysis computations

by David E. Webster

This appendix provides background information on our analysis of wage data from the Current Population Survey (CPS), which is prepared by the Bureau of the Census for the Bureau of Labor Statistics (BLS). Specifically, for 1979 and beyond, we analyze micro data files provided by BLS that contain a full year's data on the outgoing rotation groups (ORG) in the CPS. (For years prior to 1979, we use the CPS May files; our use of these files is discussed below.) We believe that the CPS ORG files allow for a timely, up-to-date, and accurate analysis of wage trends keeping within the familiar labor force definitions and concepts employed by the BLS.

The sampling framework of the monthly CPS is a "rolling panel," in which households are in the survey for four consecutive months, out for eight, and then back in for four months. The ORG files provide data on those CPS respondents in either the fourth or eighth month of the CPS (i.e., in groups four or eight, out of a total of eight groups). Therefore, in any given month the ORG file represents a quarter of the CPS sample. For a given year, the ORG file is equivalent to three months of CPSs (1/4th of 12). For our analysis, we use a sample drawn from the full-year ORG sample, the size of which ranges from 160,000 to 180,000 observations during the 1979 to 1994 period. Due to a decrease in the overall sample size of the CPS, the ORG has been shrinking since 1994, and our current sample comes in at about 145,000 cases.

Changes in annual or weekly earnings can result from changes in hourly earnings or from more working time (either more hours per week or weeks per year). Our analysis is centered around the hourly wage, which represents the pure price of labor (exclusive of benefits), because we are interested in changing pay levels for the workforce and its subgroups. We do this to be able to clearly distinguish changes in earnings resulting from more (or less) work rather than more (or less) pay. Most of our wage analysis, therefore, does not take into account that weekly or annual earnings may have changed because of longer or shorter working hours or lesser or greater opportunities for employment. An exception to this is Table 3.1, where we present annual hours, earnings, and hourly weighted wages from the March CPS.

In our view, the ORG files provide a better source of data for wage analysis than the traditionally used March CPS files. In order to calculate hourly wages from the March CPS, analysts must make calculations using three retrospective variables: the annual earnings, weeks worked, and usual weekly hours worked in the year prior to the survey. In contrast, respondents in the ORG are asked a set of questions about hours worked, weekly wages, and (for workers paid by the hour) hourly wages in the week prior to the survey. In this regard, the data from the ORG are likely to be more reliable than data from the March CPS. See Bernstein and Mishel 1997 for a detailed discussion of these differences.

Our subsample includes all wage and salary workers with valid wage and hour data, whether paid weekly or by the hour. Specifically, in order to be included in our subsample, respondents had to meet the following criteria:

- age 18-64;

- employed in the public or private sector (self-employed were excluded);

- hours worked within the valid range in the survey (1-99 per week, or hours vary – see discussion below); and,

- either hourly or weekly wages within the valid survey range (top coding discussed below).

For those who met these criteria, an hourly wage was calculated in the following manner. If a valid hourly wage was reported, that wage was used throughout our analysis. For salaried workers (those who report only a weekly wage), the hourly wage was their weekly wage divided by their hours worked. Outliers, i.e., persons with hourly wages below 50 cents or above $100 in 1989 CPI-U-X1-adjusted dollars, were removed from the analysis. These yearly upper and lower bounds are presented in **Table B-1**. CPS demographic weights were applied to make the sample nationally representative.

The hourly wage reported by hourly workers in the CPS is net of any overtime, tips, or commissions (OTTC), thus introducing a potential undercount in the hourly wage for workers who regularly receive tips or premium pay. OTTC is included in the usual weekly earnings of hourly workers, which raises the

TABLE B-1 Wage earner sample, hourly wage upper and lower limits, 1973-97

Year	Lower	Upper
1973	$ 0.19	$ 38.06
1974	0.21	41.85
1975	0.23	45.32
1976	0.24	47.90
1977	0.25	50.97
1978	0.27	54.44
1979	0.30	59.68
1980	0.33	66.37
1981	0.36	72.66
1982	0.39	77.10
1983	0.40	80.32
1984	0.42	83.79
1985	0.43	86.77
1986	0.44	88.39
1987	0.46	91.61
1988	0.48	95.40
1989	0.50	100.00
1990	0.53	105.40
1991	0.55	109.84
1992	0.57	113.15
1993	0.58	116.53
1994	0.60	119.52
1995	0.61	122.90
1996	0.63	126.53
1997	0.65	129.45

Source: Author's analysis.

possibility of assigning an imputed hourly wage to hourly workers based on the reported weekly wage and hours worked per week. Conceptually, using this imputed wage is preferable to using the reported hourly wage because it is more inclusive. We have chosen, however, not to use this broader wage measure, because the extra information on OTTC seems unreliable. We compared the imputed hourly wage (reported weekly earnings divided by weekly hours) to the reported hourly wage; the difference presumably reflects OTTC. This comparison showed that significant percentages of the hourly workforce appeared to receive negative OTTC. These error rates range from a low of 0% of the hourly workforce in the period 1989-93 to a high of 16-17% in 1973 to 1988, and persist across the survey change from 1993 to 1994. Since negative OTTC is clearly implausible, we rejected this imputed hourly wage series and rely strictly on the hourly rate of pay as reported directly by hourly workers, subject to the sample criteria discussed above.

For tables that show wage percentiles, we "smooth" hourly wages to compensate for "wage clumps" in the wage distributions. The technique involves creating a categorical hourly wage distribution, where the categories are 50-cent intervals, starting at 25 cents. We then find the categories on either side of each decile and perform a weighted, linear interpolation to locate the wage precisely on the particular decile. The weights for the interpolation are derived from differences in the cumulative percentages on either side of the decile. For example, suppose that 48% of the wage distribution of workers by wage level are in the $9.26-9.75 wage "bin," and 51% are in the next higher bin $9.76-10.25. The weight for the interpolation (in this case the median or 50th percentile) is: $\dfrac{(50\text{-}48)}{(51\text{-}48)}$ or 2/3. The interpolated median equals this weight, times the width of the bin ($.50), plus the upper bound of the previous bin ($9.75), or $10.08 in this example.

For the survey years 1973-88, the weekly wage is top coded at $999.00 (an extended top code value of $1,923 is available in 1986-88). Particularly for the later years, this truncation of the wage distribution creates a downward bias in the mean wage. We dealt with the top-coding issue by imputing a new weekly wage for top-coded individuals. The imputed value is the Pareto-imputed mean for the upper tail of the weekly earnings distribution, based on the distribution of weekly earnings up to the 80th percentile. This procedure was done for men and women separately. The imputed values for men and women appear in **Table B-2**. A new hourly wage, equal to the new estimated value for weekly earnings, divided by that person's usual hours per week, was calculated.

As noted above, we extend our analysis back to 1973 by using the May CPS files, which typically have sample sizes of about 35,000 meeting our criteria. Given these relatively small samples, we pool the 1973 and 1974 May CPS for our wage analysis of education and experience by race.

In January 1994, a new survey instrument was introduced into the CPS; many labor force items were added and improved. This presents a significant challenge to the researcher who wishes to make comparisons over time. The most careful research on the impact of the survey change has been done by BLS researcher Anne Polivka (1996, 1997). Interestingly, Polivka does not find that the survey changes had a major impact on broad measures of unemployment or wage levels, though significant differences did surface for some subgroups (e.g., weekly earnings for those with less than a high school diploma and advanced

TABLE B-2 Pareto-imputed mean values for top-coded weekly earnings, and share top coded, 1973-97

	Share			Value	
Year	All	Men	Women	Men	Women
1973	0.11%	0.17%	0.02%	$1,370	$1,342
1974	0.16	0.26	0.01	1,390	1,302
1975	0.21	0.35	0.02	1,413	1,323
1976	0.30	0.51	0.01	1,392	1,316
1977	0.36	0.59	0.04	1,388	1,313
1978	0.38	0.65	0.02	1,380	1,297
1979	0.57	0.98	0.05	1,389	1,301
1980	0.72	1.23	0.07	1,382	1,287
1981	1.05	1.82	0.10	1,410	1,281
1982	1.45	2.50	0.18	1,431	1,306
1983	1.89	3.27	0.25	1,458	1,307
1984	2.32	3.92	0.42	1,472	1,336
1985	2.78	4.63	0.60	1,491	1,344
1986	0.02	0.03	0.00	2,437	2,466
1987	0.02	0.03	0.00	2,413	2,472
1988	0.02	0.04	0.01	2,410	2,461
1989	0.45	0.78	0.07	2,769	2,557
1990	0.55	0.94	0.10	2,805	2,579
1991	0.65	1.10	0.15	2,824	2,616
1992	0.71	1.17	0.20	2,802	2,629
1993	0.79	1.31	0.22	2,833	2,648
1994	1.20	1.90	0.42	2,922	2,721
1995	1.27	2.05	0.41	2,903	2,693
1996	1.34	2.16	0.45	2,932	2,714
1997	1.64	2.56	0.63	2,951	2,777

Source: Author's analysis.

degrees, the unemployment rate of older workers). However, a change in the reporting of weekly hours did call for the alteration of our methodology. In 1994 the CPS began allowing people to report that their usual hours worked per week vary. In order to include nonhourly workers who report varying hours in our wage analysis, we estimated their usual hours using a regression-based imputation procedure, where we predicted the usual hours of work for "hours vary" cases based on the usual hours worked of persons with similar characteristics. An hourly wage was calculated by dividing weekly earnings by the estimate of hours for these workers. The share of our sample that received such a wage is presented in **Table**

TABLE B-3 Share of wage earners
assigned an hourly wage from
imputed weekly hours, 1994-97

Year	Percent hours vary
1994	2.1%
1995	2.1
1996	2.5
1997	2.5

Source: Author's analysis.

B-3. The reported hourly wage of hourly workers was preserved.

Demographic variables are also used in the analysis. Education up to 1992 refers to years of school completed. Our race variable comprises four mutually exclusive categories:

- white, non-Hispanic;
- black, non-Hispanic;
- Hispanic, any race;
- all others.

Beginning in 1992, the CPS employed a new coding scheme for education, which is essentially the respondent's highest degree achieved. In order to create a consistent time series on wages, we developed a methodology to impute years of education completed given the categories on the 1992-97 files. Our imputation was facilitated by the 1990 February CPS, which contains both the old and new education coding. In order to impute years of education completed for 1992 through 1997, we regressed years of education on education categories (the new coding) plus a set of controls including age (and age-education interactions), region, urban status, and five occupations. Beginning with this edition of *State of Working America,* we ran separate models for the four racial groups described above, by gender. This improved method has a minor effect on the education distribution of minorities near the bottom of the labor market.

We employ these imputations in various tables in Chapter 3, where we present wage trends by education over time. While we are confident that our imputations do a good job of representing the trend in wages by education level, we are less confident regarding predictions of educational attainment. Therefore, we do not use imputed years of education to estimate the shares of workers in different education categories to bridge the coding change.

The measurement of inflation

by Dean Baker

Throughout this book, the CPI-UX1, the Bureau of Labor Statistics' standard measure of consumer inflation, has been used to deflate nominal dollar amounts. In recent years many economists have been critical of this measure, arguing that it overstates the true rate of increase in the cost of living by 0.8-1.6% annually. While there is some validity to the criticism, many of the claims are grossly exaggerated, and little effort has been devoted to examining the ways in which the CPI-U might understate inflation. Furthermore, the implications of a significant CPI overstatement of inflation for past living standards are highly implausible.

Critics generally contend that the following four factors contribute to an overstatement of inflation in the CPI:

1. the CPI does not measure the impact of consumers switching to goods that rise less rapidly in price;

2. the CPI does not pick up the effect of consumers switching to discount stores;

3. the quality adjustments in the CPI are inadequate;

4. the CPI does not pick up new goods when they first appear on the market.

The first bias is real, but most research on the topic estimates its size at only about 0.2% annually.

The second source of bias is almost certainly much smaller, as can be illustrated with some crude numbers. At most, only about 20% of the index consists of goods that can be sold at discount stores (food, appliances, apparel, etc.), and the bias can apply only to the portion of these sales that *switches* in a given year to a discount store. The amount that switches in a year can probably not exceed 2% of the total sales in this category. This means that 0.4% of the entire index (2% of 20%) might switch in a given year. Quality-adjusted savings (i.e., adjusting for any quality differences between service and convenience at the different types of stores) on these sales of 10% would imply an upward bias of 0.04%. By contrast, many of the CPI's critics have counted this bias as 0.2-0.4% annually, as much as 10 times higher than the true measure.

The same sort of exaggerations characterize claims about the other biases in the CPI. The CPI already includes extensive adjustments for quality change. It is indeed possible that it does not fully pick up improvements in quality, but some research has indicated that it overstates improvement in quality in certain cases (Gordon 1990.) It also does a far better job in recent years of picking up price declines in new products. Since 1980, new products have been rotated into the index over a five-year period. Prior to that year, new products could be introduced only as the entire survey was revised, or about every 15 years.

There are also reasons for believing the CPI understates the true increase in the cost of living. Higher legal expenses incurred because people are more worried about being sued would not enter the CPI unless hourly fees actually increase. Similarly, if health insurance premiums rise across the board because a small portion of the population is getting sicker, the CPI would not pick up the increase. There are enough of these heretofore unexamined factors that make it far too early to conclude that the CPI overstates the true increase in the cost of living.

It is also important to note the implication of a significant upward adjustment in the CPI. By all measures, the CPI would have overstated inflation more in the past than it does at present, implying that the decline in income growth over the last 15 years has been even more dramatic than previously thought. For example, if the CPI currently overstates inflation by 1.0% annually, then the 1.0% annual decline in the median male wage over the last 15 years would be adjusted to instead show a constant real wage over this period. However, since this degree of bias would imply a CPI overstatement of around 2% in the 1960s, the 2% annual real wage growth of that era would be revised up to over 4.0%. Another inescapable implication of this new perspective on income growth is that the levels from which income has grown must have been far lower than is generally believed. Reasonable extrapolations based on a CPI bias of 1.0% imply that most Americans must have been living below the current poverty level as recently as 1960, and had a living standard that was only about 80% of the current poverty level in 1953 (Baker 1996). This account of the recent past does not seem plausible, and it provides further grounds for believing that the standard CPI remains the best measure of consumer inflation.

Table notes

FREQUENTLY CITED SOURCES

The following abbreviations are used throughout the table notes.

ERP—President of the United States. Economic Report of the President.

P-60 Series—U.S. Department of Commerce, Bureau of the Census, Series P-60, various dates.

SCB—U.S. Department of Commerce, Survey of Current Business, monthly.

Employment and Earnings—U.S. Department of Labor, Employment and Earnings, monthly and historical supplements.

NIPA—U.S. Department of Commerce, National Income and Product Accounts, revisions as of spring 1998.

INTRODUCTION

A   *Wage Growth in the 1990s.* The wage data underlying the annualized changes in the top panel of the table are from the CPS ORG; see Appendix B. Wage data for the first six months of 1998 are seasonally adjusted using the ARIMA-X-11 procedure as described in BLS publication *Employment and Earnings*. However, female wages at the 20th and 90th percentile had no identifiable seasonal component and are thus not seasonally adjusted.

Unemployment rate data (panel two) for All, Black, and Hispanic are from the BLS Labstat web site (the BLS allows Hispanics to be in any racial group); data for the first half of 1998 are seasonally adjusted. Unemployment data for 18-35-year-old blacks or Hispanics with high school degrees are derived by the authors from the CPS monthly microdata. In this table, we match the BLS definition of Hispanics, noted above. Elsewhere in the book, Hispanics are an exclusive category unless otherwise noted. These values are seasonally adjusted using a multiplicative ratio to moving average procedure, since we did not have enough years of data to apply X-11 methods.

The real minimum wage (panel 3) deflates the nominal minimum in each time period by the CPI-U. Since the nominal minimum wage was $4.25 for three-quarters of 1996 and $4.75 for the last quarter, we used a weighted average — $4.38 — as the value of the minimum for that year.

The CPI-U is also from the BLS Labstat, and data for the first half of 1998 are seasonally adjusted.

B   *Family Income and Hours Worked in the 1990s, Middle-Income, Married-Couple Families.* See notes for Tables 1.16, 1.17 (in Appendix A), and for Figure 1I.

C   *Wealth, Profitability, and CEO Pay Trends.* Wealth data from Tables 5.3 and 5.6. Return on capital and capital share of income based on data described in note to Table 1.15. CEO pay based on data presented in Figure 3P and Table 3.51. Growth in NYSE stock prices from *ERP* (1997), Table B-95, p. 390, deflated by the CPI-UX1.

CHAPTER 1

1.1   *Median Family Income.* Census homepage, Historical Income Tables, Families, Table F7 (http://www.census.gov/hhes/income/histinc/f07.html).

1.2   *Annual Growth of Median Family Income.* Yearly dollar change is annual average of total dollar change in period from sources listed in Table 1.1. Family-size-adjusted income is average family income of the middle fifth adjusted for family size using the official poverty equivalence scale. Census homepage, Historical Income Tables, Families, Table F-14.

1.3   *Median Family Income by Age of Householder.* Census homepage, Historical Income Tables, Families, Table F11 (http://www.census.gov/hhes/income/histinc/f11.html).

1.4   *Median Family Income by Race/Ethnic Group.* Census homepage, Historical Income Tables, Families, Table F5 (http://www.census.gov/hhes/income/histinc/f05.html).

1.5   *Median Family Income by Family Type.* Census homepage, Historical Income Tables, Families, Table F7 (http://www.census.gov/hhes/income/histinc/f07.html).

1.6   *Shares of Family Income Going to Various Income Groups and to Top 5%.* Census homepage, Historical Income Tables, Families, Table F2 (http://www.census.gov/hhes/income/histinc/f02.html).

1.7   *Real Family Income Growth by Income Group.* Census homepage, Historical Income Tables, Families, Table F1 (http://www.census.gov/hhes/income/histinc/f01.html).

1.8   *The Growth of Income Inequality, 1989-96, Using Comparable Data.* See Appendix A.

1.9   *Distribution of Real Consumption Expenditure.* U.S. Department of Labor (1995e), Tables 2-16 and 2-19. The equivalence scale used is derived from the official poverty scales.

1.10   *The Impact of Demographic Change on Household Income.* See Appendix A.

1.11   *Distribution of Persons, Households, and Families by Income Level.* P-60, No. 197, pp. B-2, B-4, U.S. Bureau of the Census (1991), and, for 1996, unpublished data provided by Jack McNeil of the Census Bureau. For relative incomes, family incomes for different size families are made comparable using equivalence scales as in Ruggles (1990), and single individuals are treated as one-person families.

1.12 *Sources of Income Growth of Top Fifth.* Authors' analysis of specially constructed March CPS dataset to account for omissions and undercounts of various income components (e.g., capital gains; see Appendix A, Mishel et al. 1996). Families with negative incomes are excluded. Each fifth has 20% of persons, not 20% of families.

1.13 *Shares of Market-Based Personal Income by Type.* From NIPA Table 2.1. The earliest data available are for 1959.

1.14 *Shares of Income by Type and Sector.* Based on NIPA Table 1.15. The "Corporate and Business" sector includes "corporate," "other private business," and "rest of world." The "government/nonprofit" sector includes the household, government enterprise, and government sectors, all of which generate no capital income.

1.15 *Profit Rates at Business Cycle Peaks.* Methodology is presented in Baker (1996); actual values are from unpublished tabulations.

1.16-
1.20 See Appendix A.

1.21 *Changes in Family Hours Worked by Family Type.* Authors' analysis of March Demographic Files. Income fifths use Census income and are defined separately for each family type. Related subfamilies are included with the primary family in the household, both for income and hours calculations.

1.22 *Median Income by Male 10-Year Birth Cohorts.* Census homepage, Historical Income Tables, Persons, Table P7 (http://www.census.gov/hhes/income/histinc/p07.html).

1.23 *Income Mobility.* Unpublished tabulations of the Panel Study of Income Dynamics by Peter Gottschalk. Family heads are less than 62 years of age over the full period. Quintiles are constructed such that 20% of persons, not 20% of families, are in each group. Quintile cutoffs are income-to-needs ratio, using the official poverty lines, so these rates are adjusted for family-size differences. Family income in 1994 is from the 1995 early release of the PSID, which does not include Social Security income. However, since the sample selection excludes families where the household head is 63 or over, this omission is unlikely to affect the results.

1.24 *Income Mobility Over the 1970s and 1980s.* See note to Table 1.23.

CHAPTER 2

2.1 *Federal vs. State and Local Tax Burdens.* NIPA Tables 1.1, 3.2, and 3.3.

2.2 *Tax Revenue in OECD Countries.* OECD (1997c), Table 3, p. 75. Includes Social Security.

2.3 *Average After-Tax Family Income Growth.* Authors' calculations based on pre-tax adjusted family income and effective tax rates from Congressional Budget Office (1998), Table A-1, p. 36 and earlier unpublished CBO data.

2.4 *Shares of After-Tax Income for All Families.* Authors' calculations based on pre-tax adjusted family income and effective tax rates from CBO (1998) and earlier unpublished data. The sum of the shares is forced to sum to 100%, which is not the case in the original data due to the exclusion of families and persons with zero or negative income from the lowest quintile and the inclusion of these same families and individuals in the "all" category.

2.5 *The Effects of Tax and Income Changes on After-Tax Income Shares.* See notes to Table 2.4.

2.6 *Effect of 1993 Tax Law on 1999 Tax Liabilities and Rates.* Authors' analysis using unpublished CBO estimates of tax liability under pre- and post-OBRA changes and CBO projections for pre-tax income for 1999.

2.7 *Effective Federal Tax Rates.* Data for 1977-92 from U.S. House of Representatives (1991, 73) and unpublished data supplied by Frank Sammartino of CBO. Data for 1999 from CBO (1998), Table A-3, pp. 40-41.

2.8 *Estimated Effective Federal Tax Rates on 1998 Income Under Prevailing Tax Law.* From unpublished tables by Citizens for Tax Justice (1997), based on CBO data; CTJ has adjusted 1998 corporate income tax data to be consistent with earlier years. Figures here use income from 1998 and tax code from each year. These figures, therefore, differ from Table 2.7, which uses income from each year together with the tax code applicable in that year.

2.9 *Effective Federal Tax Rate for a Family of Four With One Earner.* Department of Treasury (1995), Table 4.

2.10 *Effect of Federal Tax Changes on Family Tax Payments.* Unpublished data from Citizens for Tax Justice, October 1997.

2.11 *Effective Tax Rates for Selected Federal Taxes.* Unpublished CBO tables, June 26, 1995 and CBO (1998), Table A-3, pp. 40-41.

2.12 *Changes in Effective Federal Taxes.* See notes to Table 2.11.

2.13 *Taxed and Untaxed Corporate Profits.* NIPA Tables 1.1 and 1.16. Taxes include federal, state, and local combined. Actual profits are taxed profits plus net interest (interest paid minus interest received) and the difference between the allowance for inventory investment and capital depreciation allowed in the tax code, on the one hand, and actual inventory investment and capital depreciation, on the other. The idea for this analysis is based on an unpublished paper by Thomas Karier. Only nonfinancial corporations are included because banks do not pay net interest — they *receive* net interest.

2.14 *Corporate Profits Tax Rates.* NIPA Tables 1.1 and 1.16.

2.15 *Effective State and Local Tax Rates in 1995 as Percentage Shares of Income for Nonelderly Married Couples.* Citizens for Tax Justice and Institute on Taxation & Economic Policy (1996), Appendix I, p. 52.

2.16 *Types of Federal vs. State and Local Taxes as a Percent of Revenue at Each Level.* NIPA Tables 3.2 and 3.3.

2.17 *Types of Taxes as a Percent of GDP.* NIPA Tables 1.1, 3.2, and 3.3.

CHAPTER 3

3.1 *Trends in Average Wages and Average Hours.* The 1967-73 and 1973-79 trends are from unpublished tabulations provided by Kevin Murphy from an update of Murphy and Welch (1989). These data are based on the March CPS files. Hours of work were derived from differences between annual, weekly, and hourly wage trends. The Murphy and Welch data include self-employment as well as wage and salary workers. The trends from 1979 on are based on the authors' tabulations of March CPS files using a series on annual, weekly, and hourly wages for wage and salary workers using the same sample definition as used in the CPS ORG wage analysis (see Appendix B). The weekly and hourly wage data are "hour weighted," obtained by dividing annual wages by weeks worked and annual hours worked (weeks worked times hours per week). The Murphy and Welch data were bridged to the 1979 levels. Productivity data are from *ERP* (1998), Table B-49, p. 338, for the nonfarm business sector.

3.2 *Growth of Average Hourly Wages, Benefits, and Compensation.* These data are computed from NIPA data on hours worked and compensation, wages, other labor income, group health insurance, and social insurance for the public and private sectors. These data were inflation-adjusted by the NIPA Personal Consumption Expenditure (PCE, chain-weighted) index, with health insurance adjusted by the PCE medical care (chained) index.

3.3 *Growth in Private-Sector Average Hourly Wages, Benefits, and Compensation.* Based on employment cost levels from the BLS Employment Cost Index series for March 1987 to March 1997 for private industry workers (see 1997 data in U.S. Department of Labor 1997). We categorize pay differently than BLS, putting all wage-related items (including paid leave and supplemental pay) into the hourly wage. Benefits, in our definition, include only payroll taxes, pensions, insurance, and "other" benefits. It is important to use the current-weighted series rather than the fixed-weighted series because composition shifts (in the distribution of employment across occupations and industries) have a large effect. Employer costs for insurance are deflated by the medical care component of the CPI. All other pay is deflated by the CPI-UX1 for "all items." Inflation is measured for the first quarter of each year.

3.4 *Production and Nonsupervisory Workers.* Data from 1959 to 1997 from ERP (1997), Table B-47, p. 336. Data for 1947, Supplement to *Employment and Earnings* (March 1985, 5).

3.5 *Changes in Hourly Wages by Occupation.* Based on analysis of CPS wage data described in Appendix B.

3.6 *Wages for All Workers by Wage Percentile.* Based on analysis of CPS wage data described in Appendix B.

3.7 *Wages for Male Workers by Wage Percentile.* Based on analysis of CPS wage data described in Appendix B.

3.8 *Wages for Female Workers by Wage Percentile.* Based on analysis of CPS wage data described in Appendix B.

3.9 *Changes in the Gender Wage Differential.* Based on data from Tables 3.7 and 3.8. Women's employment share derived from data in *ERP* (1997), Table B-36, p. 324.

3.10 *Share of All Workers Earning Poverty-Level Hourly Wages and Multiples.* Based on analysis of CPS wage data described in Appendix B. The poverty-level wage was defined as the four-person poverty threshold in 1996 ($16,036) divided by 2,080 hours and deflated by CPI-UX1 to obtain levels for other years. We calculated more intervals than we show but aggregated for simplicity of presentation (no trends were lost).

3.11 *Share of White Workers Earning Poverty-Level Hourly Wages and Multiples.* See note to Table 3.10. These are non-Hispanic whites.

3.12 *Share of Black Workers Earning Poverty-Level Hourly Wages and Multiples.* See note to Table 3.10. These are non-Hispanic blacks.

3.13 *Share of Hispanic Workers Earning Poverty-Level Hourly Wages and Multiples.* See note to Table 3.10. Hispanics may be of any race.

3.14 *Growth of Specific Fringe Benefits.* Based on NIPA data described in note to Table 3.2 and ECI levels data described in note.

3.15 *Change in Private Sector Employer-Provided Health Insurance Coverage.* Based on tabulations of March CPS data samples of private wage and salary earners ages 18-64 who worked at least 20 hours per week and 26 weeks per year. Coverage is defined as being included in an employer-provided plan where the employer paid for at least some of the coverage.

3.16 *Change in Private Sector Employer-Provided Pension Coverage.* See note to Table 3.15.

3.17 *Dimensions of Wage Inequality.* All of the data are based on analyses of the ORG CPS data described in Appendix B. The measures of total wage inequality are natural logs of wage ratios (multiplied by 100) computed from Tables 3.6 and 3.7. The education and experience differentials are computed from regressions of the log of hourly wages on education categorical variables (high school omitted), experience as a quartic, marital status, race and region (4). The college–high school premium is simply the coefficient on "college," a category representing 16 years of schooling. The experience differentials are the differences in the value of experience (calculated from the coefficients of the quartic specification) evaluated at 5, 15, and 30 years.

The changes in within-group wage inequality reflect the growth of the "residual wage" for wage earners at the 90th, 50th, and 10th percentiles. The "residual wage" was computed as the difference between the actual and predicted wage, with the predicted wage based on the model described above. The 90th, 50th, and 10th percentile worker was approximated by workers in the following percentile wage ranges: 85-94, 45-54, 5-14. The procedure forces the growth of within-group wage inequality to reflect the experiences of high-, middle-, and low-wage workers. Procedures used by other analysts measure the growth of within-group wage inequality in a manner (by focusing on the distribution of the "residual" wage) that allows a high "residual" wage earner to be a low-, middle-, or high-wage earner.

3.18 *Change in Real Hourly Wage for All by Education.* Based on tabulations of CPS wage data described in Appendix B. The group with 17 years of schooling (college plus one) is omitted for simplicity of presentation. Since the CPS questions on educational attainment shifted in 1992, it was necessary to impute years of schooling in the data for 1992 and more recent years (see Appendix B for details). The procedure for estimating the college–high school wage premium is described in the note to Table 3.17. The shares of the workforce by education category are tabulated from the same data. We do not present 1997 data because we believe our imputations of years of schooling are not reliable for "quantity" trends.

3.19   *Change in Real Hourly Wage for Men by Education.* See note to Table 3.18.

3.20   *Change in Real Hourly Wage for Women by Education.* See note to Table 3.18.

3.21   *Educational Attainment of Workforce.* Based on analysis of CPS wage earners. The data are described in Appendix B. The categories are as follows: "Less than high school" is grade 1-12 or no diploma; "high school/GED" is high school graduate diploma or equivalent; "some college" is some college but no degree; "associate college" is occupational or academic associate's degree; "college B.A." is a bachelor's degree; and "advanced degree" is a master's, professional, or doctorate degree.

3.22   *Hourly Wages of Entry-Level and Experienced Workers by Education.* Based on analysis of CPS wage data described in Appendix B.

3.23   *Hourly Wages by Decile Within Education Groups.* Based on analysis of CPS wage data described in Appendix B.

3.24   *Decomposing the Change in Overall Wage Inequality Among Men.* All of the data are from the ORG CPS data sample described in Appendix B. The "overall" distribution in the first row of each panel is the log of the relevant hourly wage percentiles (multiplied by 100) from Table 3.7. The distribution for the "returns to skill" row in each panel is constructed in two stages. First, we fit a standard, human-capital regression equation (described in the note to Table 3.17) to the data for each year, saving the estimated coefficients from the regression and each individual's residual. Second, we compute a counterfactual wage distribution for the end-year for each period we analyze. For those years, we compute what each individual's wage would have been if he or she had the same characteristics (including residual wage) but the coefficients from the earlier year. We then compute the wage differentials from this counterfactual distribution, which represents what the wage distribution would be if only the returns to skill changed. The change in wage differentials between a beginning year's actual distribution and an end year's counterfactual distribution is the effect of changes in "returns to skill." The figures in the "other" row of each panel are simply the difference between the changes in the overall and the changes in the wage distribution due to changes in the returns to skill.

3.25   *Decomposing the Change in Overall Wage Inequality Among Women.* Based on the same procedure as described in the note to Table 3.24, using a sample of women.

3.26   *Hourly Wage Growth Among Men by Race/Ethnicity.* Based on analysis of CPS wage data described in Appendix B.

3.27   *Hourly Wage Growth Among Women by Race/Ethnicity.* Based on analysis of CPS wage data described in Appendix B.

3.28   *Employment Growth by Sector.* Employment data from *Employment and Earnings* (March 1996), Table B-1, p. 51, and Table B-12, p. 72, and *Employment and Earnings* (April 1998), Table B-1, p. 44. Hourly compensation data from BLS Employment Cost Levels data for 1997. See note to Table 3.3.

3.29   *Changes in Employment Share by Sector.* Based on data in Table 3.28.

3.30   *The Effect of Industry Shifts on the Growth of the College/High School Differential.* The industry shift effect is calculated from estimated college–high school wage differentials using the model described in the note to Table 3.17 ("industry composition actual") and a model that adds a set of industry controls (12), which gives "industry composition constant." The difference in the growth of these estimates is the industry shift effect.

3.31   *Net Trade in U.S. Manufactures by Skill Intensity and Trading Partner.* Cline (1997), Table 4.3, p. 188.

3.32   *Trade-Deficit-Induced Job Loss by Wage and Education Level.* Scott et al. (1997), Tables 1 and 2.

3.33   *Effect of Changes in Prices of Internationally Traded Manufactured Goods on Wage Inequality.* Schmitt and Mishel (1996), Table 9.

3.34   *Legal Immigrant Flow to the United States.* Borjas (1994), Table 1, p. 1668, updated for the 1990s by Steven A. Camarota of the Center for Immigration Studies based on Immigration and Naturalization Service (1997) and Hansen and Faber (1997).

3.35   *Educational Attainment of Immigrant and Native Men.* Borjas (1994), Table 4, p. 1676, updated for 1996 by Steven A. Camarota of the Center for Immigration Studies based on tabulations (following Borjas) of the March 1996 CPS for men, age 25 to 64, in the civilian sector, not self-employed and not living in group quarters.

3.36   *Union Wage and Benefit Premium.* Employment Cost Index pay level data in U.S. Department of Labor (1997), Table 13. Regression-adjusted union effect from Pierce (1998), Tables 3, 4, and 5. Wages are defined differently in the top and bottom panels, as Pierce follows the BLS definitions while the upper panel defines wages to include paid leave and supplemental pay (as described in note to Table 3.3). Pierce's estimates are based on regressions on ECI microdata for 1994.

3.37   *Union Wage Premium by Demographic Group.* Regression estimates of union wage differentials using CPS ORG data for 1997. See Appendix B for description of the data. The data in the table are the coefficients on union membership (union member or covered by a collective bargaining agreement) in a model of log hourly wages with controls for education, experience as a quartic, marital status, region, industry (12) and occupation (9), and race/ethnicity and gender where appropriate. Percent union is percent of group that are members or covered by a collective bargaining agreement tabulated from the same CPS ORG sample.

3.38   *Effect of Deunionization on Male Wage Differentials.* This analysis replicates, updates, and expands on Freeman (1991), Table 2. The analysis uses the CPS ORG sample used in other analyses (see Appendix B). The year 1978, rather than 1979, is the earliest year analyzed because we have no union membership data in our 1979 sample. The union wage premium for a group is based on the coefficient on collective bargaining coverage in a regression of hourly wages on a simple human capital model (the same one used for estimating education differentials, as described in note to Table 3.17) with major industry (12) and occupation (9) controls in a sample for that group. The change in union premium across years, therefore, holds industry and occupation composition constant. "Percent union" is the share covered by collective bargaining. Freeman's analysis assumed the union premium was unchanged over time. We allow the union premium to differ across years so changes in the union effect are driven by changes in the unionization rate and the union wage premium. The analysis compares the change in the union effect on relative wages to the actual change in relative wages (regression-adjusted with simple human capital controls plus controls for other education or occupation groups).

3.39   *Effect of Unions on Wages, by Wage Fifth.* From Card (1991), Table 8. The effect of deunionization is the change in union coverage times the union wage premium.

3.40   *Effect of Deunionization on Male Wage Inequality.* From Card (1991), Table 9; Freeman (1991), Table 6; and DiNardo, Fortin, and Lemieux (1994), Table 4.

3.41   *Value of the Minimum Wage.* Historical values of minimum wage from Shapiro (1987), p. 19.

3.42   *Characteristics of Minimum Wage and Other Workers.* Bernstein and Schmitt (1998), Table 1.

3.43   *Impact of Lower Minimum Wage on Key Wage Differentials Among Women.* The impact of the change in the minimum wage since 1979 is based on comparing the actual changes with changes from 1979 to simulated wage distributions in 1989 and 1997 where the real value of the minimum wage in 1979 is imposed on the data. This analysis is based on the CPS ORG data described in Appendix B. The simulated microdata are obtained by setting the hourly wages of those in the "sweep" (earning between the current minimum wage and the 1979 value) at the 1979 value (inflation-adjusted by CPI-UX) of the minimum wage. Those earning less than the legislated minimum wage were assigned a wage at the same proportionate distance to the 1979 level as they were to the existing minimum. In 1997, the existing minimum was based on a weighted average by month of the prevailing minimum of $4.75 for nine months and $5.15 for three months. The counterfactual returns to education were estimated on the simulated microdata with a simple human capital model and compared to the actual change (based on the same model) presented in Table 3.17. The other wage differentials are based on logged differentials computed from the actual and simulated microdata. The shares earning less than the 1979 minimum are computed directly from the data.

3.44   *Distribution of Minimum Wage Gains and Income Shares by Fifth for Various Household Types.* Bernstein and Schmitt (1998), Table 2.

3.45   *The Impact of Labor Market Institutions on Wage Differentials.* Fortin and Lemieux (1996), Table 1.

3.46   *Decomposition of Growth of Male College–Noncollege Wage Premium by Occupation.* This decomposition starts from the fact that the college–noncollege wage differential in any year is a weighted average of the college wage premium specific to each occupation (e.g., college-educated scientists relative to all non-college workers) and the weight of the occupation (its college employment) in total college employment. Changes in the college–noncollege wage differential can therefore be decomposed into changes in occupational weights (e.g., the expansion of an occupation with a higher-than-average premium expands the differential) and changes in occupation premiums. This analysis is based on a regression of log hourly wages on a simple human capital model (see note to Table 3.17) with one education categorical variable—college graduate—interacted with a dummy variable for each occupation group. The sample is described in Appendix B, except, for this analysis, those with more than a college degree are excluded. Estimates for 1979, 1989, and 1997 were used for the decomposition.

3.47   *Decomposition of Growth of Female College–Noncollege Wage Premium by Occupation.* See methodology described in note to Table 3.46.

3.48   *Utilization of Workers by Technology's Impact on Wage and Education Level.* Mishel, Bernstein, and Schmitt (1997).

3.49   *Changes in Employment Shares by Occupation for All Workers and Young College Graduates.* Based on tabulations of CPS ORG data described in Appendix B. Young college graduates defined as those with 1 to 10 years experience in order to have a sufficient sample size for each occupation group.

3.50   *Hourly Wages by Occupation for All Workers and Young College Graduates.* See note to Table 3.49.

3.51   *Executive Pay Growth.* The 1992-97 trends are based on a series of *Wall Street Journal*/William M. Mercer surveys (of 350 large companies) of CEO compensation. "Realized direct compensation" includes salary, bonus, gains from options exercised, value of restricted stock at grant and other long-term incentive award payments. The "average" is computed as the average of each quartile cutoff (25, 50, and 75), which would understate the growth relative to a true average. Cash compensation data, also from Mercer, goes back to 1989. The average compensation for 1989 is backed out of the 1992 data by extrapolating the 1989-92 trend in the Pearl Meyer/*Wall Street Journal* data.

3.52   *CEO Pay in Advanced Countries.* Total CEO compensation in dollars and the ratio of CEO to production-worker pay are from Towers Perrin (1988 and 1997). The production worker ranking is based on data from Department of Labor (1995a) for 1994.

3.53   *Demand Shifts: Changes in Pay and Education Requirements.* Update of an analysis presented in Mishel and Teixeira (1991), Tables 2 and 7. It is based on a shift-share analysis of the employment distribution of 13 major occupations and the pay and education characteristics of these occupations. The education levels are from tabulations of the CPS ORG data (as described in Appendix B) for 1995 by occupation. Wage levels are those prevailing over the 1979-93 period (from the CPS ORG data), and compensation is based on computing an occupation-specific compensation/wage ratio from ECI levels data and applying it to the wages data. The historical occupation data are from series available from *Employment and Earnings*. Future trends are based on the occupation shifts from 1996 to 2006 in Silvestri (1997), Tables 1 and 2.

3.54 *Future Labor Supply Trends.* Immigration was projected by extrapolating the 1980-88 trends in immigrant employment share of Borjas et al. (1991) to 1992. Data from Census P-25 Series, No 1104, Table 1 were used to project the net immigrant (ages 16-64) increase to 2005 (13 times annual growth). The BLS projections of labor force participation in 1998 were used to translate population growth into labor force growth. This estimate was reduced to account for the aging of the immigrant population beyond age 64, using Tables C-3 and C-4. The Census and BLS projections data for medium and high were matched.

Labor-force median age from Fullerton (1997), Table 9. Historical data on college degrees awarded are from Table 28, p. 61, of U.S. Department of Education (1997a). The projected college degrees awarded are the middle projections from Table 28, p. 61, of Department of Education (1997). Past employment is civilian employment (20 years or more) from Table B-35, p. 322, of *ERP* (1998). Future employment is estimated based on the growth in the labor force (age 20 or more) from Fullerton (1997), Table 7, and assuming the growth rate from 1996-2006 continues to 2008. The college enrollment rate is the average of those ages 18-24 using the middle alternative projection for 2008 from Table A 1.3 of Department of Education (1997a). The college-age population projection is the number of 18- to 24-year-olds from Table B4 of Department of Education (1997a).

CHAPTER 4

4.1 *Unemployment Rates.* Data for years before 1997 are from U.S. Department of Labor (1988), Table A-24, pp. 404-61, and BLS website, May 8, 1996. Data for 1997 are from Employment and Earnings, January 1998, Table 5, p. 168.

4.2 *Underemployment.* Civilian labor force and unemployed from BLS, Employment and Earnings (January 1998), Table 1, p. 162. Discouraged workers are individuals not in the labor force who wanted a job, had searched for work in the previous year, were available to work, but were not actively searching for work because of "discouragement over job prospects." "Other marginally attached" individuals are in identical circumstances, but are not actively searching for work for reasons other than discouragement, including family responsibilities, school or training commitments, or ill health or disabilities. The source for discouraged and marginal workers is BLS, Employment and Earnings (January 1998), Table 35, p. 206. "Involuntary part-time" workers cite "economic reasons for working fewer than 35 hours per week (from BLS, Employment and Earnings, January 1998, Table 20, p. 192).

4.3 *Effect of 1% Higher Unemployment Rate on Weeks Unemployed and Employed and on Annual Earnings.* Analysis of Tables 5 and 7 in Blank and Card (1993). These tables are slightly mismatched because the coefficients in their Table 7 are for the 1973-91 period, while the means in their Table 5 are for the 1967-91 period.

4.4   *Employment Growth.* Total employees on nonfarm payrolls taken from the BLS establishment survey as reported in BLS, Employment and Earnings (January 1998), Table B-1, p. 45. Total civilian employment, civilian noninstitutional population, and civilian labor force participation rate from the Current Population Survey of households as reported in BLS, Employment and Earnings (January 1998), Table 1, p. 162. Hours worked by full-time and part-time employees from NIPA Table 6.9C and full-time equivalent employees from NIPA Table 6.5C; both from Survey of Current Business, August 1997 and earlier, unpublished electronic versions of tables.

4.5   *Employment Stability for Men, 1970s versus 1980s.* Rose (1995), Table 2, p. 10.

4.6   *Employment Stability and Earnings for Men, 1970s versus 1980s.* Rose (1995), Table 8, p. 11.

4.7   *Median Job Tenure by Age.* Aaronson and Sullivan (1998), Figure 2, p. 21. Numbers corresponding to figure provided by Daniel Aaronson and Ann Ferris.

4.8   *Share of Employed Workers in Long-Term Jobs.* Farber (1997b), Table 1, p. 29.

4.9   *Four-Year Job Retention Rates.* Neumark, Polsky, and Hansen (1997), Table 5.

4.10   *Rate of Job Loss by Reason.* Farber (1998), Appendix Table 3, p. 12.

4.11   *Rate of Job Loss by Occupation and Reason.* Farber (1997a), Appendix Table 5, p. 69. Table excludes other category because workers in the 1994 and 1996 Displaced Workers Survey, which provides the underlying data for the 1991-93 and 1993-95 periods respectively, do not ask workers who cite "other" reason for displacement about their occupation on the lost job.

4.12   *The Costs of Job Loss, Averages for 1980s and 1990s.* Percent out of work from Farber (1997a), Table 6, p. 49, last row; post-displacement change in earnings from Farber (1997a), Table 10, p. 55; post-displacement change in earnings compared to continuously employed from Farber (1997a), Table 14, p. 62; health insurance coverage from Gardner (1996), Table 6, p. 53.

4.13   *Perceptions of Job Security.* Aaronson and Sullivan (1998) analysis of 1997 General Social Survey data, Figure 6, p. 30. Numbers corresponding to figure provided by Daniel Aaronson and Ann Ferris.

4.14   *Workers by Work Arrangement.* EPI analysis of CPS Contingent Worker Survey data, 1995 and 1997.

4.15   *Wages of Nonstandard Workers Compared to Regular Full-Time Workers, by Sex and Work Arrangement.* Kalleberg et al. (1997) analysis of 1995 Contingent Work Survey, Table 12, p. 23.

4.16   *Percentage Share of Workers With Employer-Provided Health and Pension Benefits by Work Arrangement.* EPI analysis of 1997 Contingent Worker Survey data.

4.17   *Nonagricultural Employment by Full-Time and Part-Time Status.* Employment and Earnings (January 1998), Table 21, p. 193, and earlier issues.

4.18   *Employment in Personnel Services Industry.* Data on personnel services industry employment (SIC code 736) and total employment from the BLS web site, June 24, 1998.

4.19   *Employment in Temporary Help Industry.* Data on temporary help industry employment (SIC code 7363) and total employment from the BLS web site, June 24, 1998.

4.20   *Self-Employment.* Prior to 1989, data taken from U.S. Department of Labor (1989), Table 21, pp. 112-113; for 1989, Employment and Earnings (January 1990), Table 23, p. 189; for 1997, Employment and Earnings (January 1998), Table 15, p. 183.

4.21   *Multiple Job Holding.* All figures are for May of the given year. Data for 1973 and 1989 are from the U.S. Department of Labor (1989); 1979 are from Sekscenski (1980); 1985 from Stinson (1986); and 1997 from Employment and Earnings (June 1997), Table A-35, p. 63.

4.22   *Hours Worked by Multiple Job Holders, by Sex.* Unpublished data from BLS provided by John Stinson.

CHAPTER 5

5.1   *Growth of Household Wealth.* Net worth and asset data are from the Federal Reserve Bank, Flow of Funds Accounts, Table B.100 Balance Sheet of Households and Nonprofit Organizations, <http://www.bog.frb.fed.us/releases/z1/data.htm>, accessed May 13, 1998. Nonprofit organizations, a small component judging from the breakout on tangible assets, were included because the Federal Reserve does not give breakouts for financial assets. Data were converted to real dollars using the CPI-UX1, chained backward to the CPI-U prior to 1967. The number of households is based on Bureau of the Census (1996), Supplement, Table 1, and Bureau of the Census (1997), Table B-2, p. B-3. We use growth in families from 1949 to 1967 to proxy growth in households over this period. We estimate the number of households in 1997 by increasing the 1996 figure using the growth rate for 1989-96.

5.2   *Distribution of Income and Wealth.* Wolff (1997), Table 1, p. 27.

5.3   *Households With Low Net Wealth.* Unpublished analysis of Survey of Consumer Finance (SCF) data by Edward Wolff, May 1998.

5.4   *Percent of Total Assets Held by Wealth Class.* Wolff (1997), Table 5, p. 31.

5.5   *Changes in the Distribution of Wealth.* Unpublished analysis of SCF data by Edward Wolff, May 1998.

5.6   *Change in Wealth by Wealth Class.* Unpublished analysis of SCF data by Edward Wolff, May 1998.

5.7   *Change in Wealth by Income Class.* Wolff (1997), Table 8, p. 34.

5.8   *Wealth by Race.* Wolff (1997), Table 6, p. 32.

5.9   *Share of Households Owning Stock.* Unpublished analysis of SCF data by Edward Wolff, May 1998.

5.10   *Household Assets and Liabilities by Wealth Class.* Unpublished analysis of SCF data by Edward Wolff, May 1998.

5.11   *Concentration of Stock Ownership by Income Level.* From an unpublished analysis of SCF data by Wolff. Modeled on table presented in Poterba and Samwick (1996).

5.12   *Household Debt Burden.* Debt and asset information from the Federal Reserve Board, Flow of Funds Accounts of the United States. Total debt service payments and consumer debt service payments as percent of disposable personal income from St Louis Federal Reserve web site. Source for both: <http://www.bog.frb.fed.us/releases/z1/data.htm>, accessed May 13, 1998. Personal income for 1967-97 from *ERP* (1998), Table B-30, p. 316; for 1949, from ERP (1985), Table B-22, p. 258.

CHAPTER 6

6.1   *Percent and Number of Persons in Poverty.* U.S. Bureau of the Census, P60-198, C1.

6.2   *Persons in Poverty, by Race/Ethnicity.* U.S. Bureau of the Census, P60-198, C1.

6.3   *Percent of Children in Poverty, by Race.* U.S. Bureau of the Census, P60-198, C2.

6.4   *Family Poverty, by Race/Ethnicity of Family Head and for Different Family Types.* U.S. Bureau of the Census, P60-198, C3.

6.5   *High-Risk Factors for Poverty, Females 25 and Over.* Unpublished tabulations provided by the Census Bureau, poverty division.

6.6   *1992 Poverty Rates Under Official and Alternative Measures.* Table 5-8, National Research Council (1995). Proposed measure "alternative 1" is used, which employs a scale economy factor of 0.75. This factor is used to construct equivalence scales for families of different sizes. The "alternative 2" scale factor, 0.65, leads to a higher overall poverty rate (19.0%) than alternative 1.

6.7   *Demographic Characteristics of Poor Persons Under Alternative Definitions.* Tables 5-6 and 5-8, National Research Council (1995). See note to Table 6.6.

6.8   *Poverty Rates When (Nonmedical) Noncash Benefits Are Included.* U.S. P60-182RD (Table 1) and P60-198 (Table 5).

6.9   *Percent of Persons with Low Relative Income, by Race, Adjusted for Family Size.* U.S. Bureau of the Census (1991) and unpublished data provided by Jack McNeil. Family incomes for different size families are made comparable using equivalence scales as in Ruggles (1990). Single individuals are treated as one-person families.

6.10   *Poverty Gap: Aggregates and Means.* Unpublished data provided by the Center on Budget and Policy Priorities.

6.11   *Poor Persons Below 50% of Poverty Level.* Census homepage, Historical Poverty Tables, Persons, Table 22 (http://www.census.gov/hhes/poverty/histpov/hstpov22.html).

6.12   *Changes in Poverty Rates and Growth Indicators.* Poverty rates: see note to Table 6.1; productivity: *ERP* (1998), Table B-49; per capita income, *ERP* (1998), Table B-31; unemployment, *ERP* (1998), Table B-42; Gini coefficient, see note to Table 1.6.

6.13   *Changing Family Structure and Poverty.* U.S. Bureau of the Census, P60-198, C1.

6.14   *Changes in Family Structure and Poverty.* See note to Table 6.13. This conventional shift-share analysis assigns the increase in poverty rates to "between" and "within" factors. To the extent that either of these factors is endogenous to poverty changes, e.g., if increasing poverty rates *led* to family structure changes, this simple decomposition will fail to account for such behavioral changes.

6.15   *Educational Level of Family Heads and Poverty, Families With Children.* Authors' analysis of March CPS data. Education coding changes for 1996 column from highest grade completed to highest level of attainment.

6.16   *Decomposing Changes in Poverty Rates Into Demographic and Economic Factors.* See Appendix A.

6.17   *Poverty-Reducing Effects of Taxes and Transfers.* P-60, No. 182-RD and No. 198, Table 5 (definitions 2, 8, 10, and 14).

6.18   *Family Income Components of Prime-age Families.* Authors' analysis of March CPS data. Prime-age families are those headed by a person age 25-54, and exclude single person units and families with negative incomes. Since the analysis focuses on the bottom 20%, we did not adjust income components for changes in top codes.

6.19   *Work Experience of the Poor.* 1979: P-60, No. 130, p. 58; 1989: P-60, No. 168, p. 65; 1989: P-60, No. 185, p. 89; 1996: unpublished tabulation provided by Census Bureau, poverty division.

6.20   *Annual Average Hours Worked, Low-Income Families, by Family Type and Income Quintile.* See note to Table 1.21.

6.21   *Characteristics of Low-Wage Workers.* Authors' analysis of CPS ORG data; see Appendix B.

6.22   *Unemployment and Underemployment Rates, 1997, by Sex and Race.* Authors analysis of CPS monthly data.

6.23   *Annualized Changes in Hourly Wages of Low-Wage Workers.* See Appendix B.

CHAPTER 7

7.1   *Median Family Income by Region.* Census homepage, Historical Income Tables, Families, Table F6 (http://www.census.gov/hhes/income/histinc/f06.html).

7.2   *Median Income for Four-Person Families, by State.* Census homepage, Historical Income Table (http://www.census.gov/hhes/income/4person.html).

7.3   *Income Inequality by State, Late 1970s to Mid-1990s.* See Appendix A.

7.4   *Income Inequality by Selected States, Top 5% to Bottom 20%.* See Appendix A.

7.5   *Nonfarm Payroll Employment, by State.* U.S. Bureau of Labor Statistics homepage, Nonfarm Payroll Statistics from the Current Employment Statistics (State and Area), generated by Yonatan Alemu, using Selective Access, http://stats.bls.gov/sahome.html.

7.6   *Unemployment Rates by State and Division.* BLS Homepage, Local Area Unemployment Statistics (ftp://ftp.bls.gov/pub/time.series/la/).

7.7   *Average Weekly Wages, by State.* Data from the BLS ES-202 Survey, Census of Establishments Covered by Unemployment Insurance, provided by BLS.

7.8   *State Hourly Median Wages (50th Percentile), All Workers.* See Appendix B.

7.9   *State Hourly Wage Rates for Low-Wage (20th Percentile) Workers.* See Appendix B.

7.10   *Wage Distribution by State and Division.* See Appendix B.

7.11   *Unemployment and Underemployment, 18-35-Year-Olds, by Sex, Education, and Race.* Authors' analysis of CPS monthly data; three years of data are combined to generate samples large enough for reliable estimation.

7.12   *Poverty Rates for Persons by Region.* Census Poverty homepage, Historical Poverty Tables, Persons, Table 9 (http://www.census.gov/hhes/poverty/histpov/hstpov9.html).

7.13   *Poverty by State, Two-Year Averages.* Census Poverty homepage, Historical Poverty Tables, Persons, Table 19 (http://www.census.gov/hhes/poverty/histpov/hstpov19.html).

7.14   *Poverty Rates by Metro/Nonmetro Areas.* Census Poverty homepage, Historical Poverty Tables, Persons, Table 8 (http://www.census.gov/hhes/poverty/histpov/hstpov8.html).

7.15   *State and Local Taxes in 1995 (Effective Rates).* Citizens for Tax Justice and Institute on Taxation and Economic Policy (1996).

CHAPTER 8

8.1   *Per Capita Income, Using Market Exchange Rates.* OECD (1998), Table 20, p. 146. Converted to 1996 dollars, from 1990 dollars in original, using the CPI-UX1 from the *Economic Report of the President* (1998), Table B-62, p. 352. Population (1989) weighted average.

8.2   *Per Capita Income, Using Purchasing-Power-Parity Exchange Rates.* BLS (1998a), Table 1. Population (1989) weighted average.

8.3   *Relative Productivity Levels.* Conference Board (1997), Table 1, p. 6.

8.4   *Labor Productivity Growth per Year.* Data in first column begin in 1960 or earliest available year: 1961 for Australia and Ireland; 1962 for Japan and the UK; 1964 for Spain; 1965 for France and Sweden; 1966 for Canada and Norway; 1967 for New Zealand; 1969 for the Netherlands; and 1970 for Belgium. Data in last column end in

1996 or latest available year: 1993 for Portugal; 1994 for Germany, Austria, and Norway; 1995 for Japan, Italy, the United Kingdom, Australia, Finland, Ireland, New Zealand, Spain, Sweden, and Switzerland. First two columns refer to western Germany. The third column is calculated as the weighted average of west German productivity growth between 1979 and 1991 and total German productivity growth between 1991 and 1994. OECD (1997a), Annex Table 58, p. A66. Employment (1989) weighted average.

8.5   *Real Compensation Growth per Year.* Nominal compensation per employee in the business sector from OECD (1995), Annex Table 12, p. A15 and OECD (1997a), Annex Table 12, p. A15 deflated by changes in consumer prices from OECD (1997a), Annex Table 16, p. A19. Employment (1989) weighted average.

8.6   *Relative Hourly Compensation of Manufacturing Production Workers (Using Market Exchange Rates).* Hourly compensation costs in national currency for production workers in manufacturing from BLS (1998b), Table3, converted to U.S. dollars using market exchange rates from OECD (1998), Table 2, p. 174-5. Manufacturing employment (1990) weighted average.

8.7   *Relative Hourly Compensation of Manufacturing Production Workers (Using Purchasing Power Parities).* Hourly compensation costs in national currency for production workers in manufacturing from BLS (1998b), Table3, converted to U.S. dollars using purchasing power parities for GDP from OECD (1998), Table 3, p. 174-5. Manufacturing employment (1990) weighted average.

8.8   *Real Hourly Compensation Growth in Manufacturing.* Compensation for all workers in manufacturing is hourly compensation in manufacturing, on a national currency basis, from BLS (1998c), Table 7, p. 22; compensation for production workers is hourly compensation costs in national currency for production workers in manufacturing from BLS (1998b), Table 3. Both are deflated using consumer price indexes derived from OECD (1997a), Table 16, p. A19, except for the United States, which uses the CPI-UX1 from *ERP* (1998), Table B-62, p. 352. Manufacturing employment (1990) weighted average.

8.9   *Earnings Inequality Growth.* Unpublished OECD data, updating OECD (1996), Table 3.1, pp. 61-62. The first column refers to 1979, the second to 1989, and the last to 1997, except: Japan, 1995; Germany, 1983, 1993; France, 1996; Italy, 1993; Canada, 1981, 1990, 1994; Australia, 1995; Austria, 1980, 1994; Belgium, 1995; Denmark, 1980; Finland, 1980, 1995; Netherlands, 1994; New Zealand, 1988; Norway, 1980, 1991; Portugal, 1993; Sweden, 1980, 1995; and Switzerland, 1991, 1996.

8.10   *Earnings Mobility of Low-Paid Workers.* OECD (1996), Table 3.10, pp. 95-6.

8.11   *Household Income Inequality, Relative to National Median Income.* Gottschalk and Smeeding (1997), Figure 2. Population (1989) weighted average.

8.12   *Household Income Inequality, Relative to U.S. Median Income.* From Gottschalk and Smeeding (1997), Figure 4. Population (1989) weighted average.

8.13   *Change in Income Inequality After 1979.* Relative changes in the Gini coefficient taken from Gottschalk and Smeeding (1997), Appendix Table A-1. Absolute changes calculated from relative changes in Gottschalk and Smeeding (1997), Appendix Table A-1 and Gini coefficients in Gottschalk and Smeeding (1997), Figure 2; for Japan, 1992 Gini coefficient estimated using average of 1990 and 1993; for Germany, 1990 coefficient estimated using 1989; for Norway, 1992 coefficient used for 1991.

8.14   *Poverty Rates.* Smeeding (1997), Table 1. Population (1989) weighted average.

8.15   *The Impact of Taxes and Transfers on Poverty Rates.* Smeeding (1997), Table 7. Population (1989) weighted average.

8.16   *Poverty Rates and Transitions Out of Poverty for Families With Children, Mid-1980s.* Duncan et al. (1991), Table 1.

8.17   *Employment Rates.* BLS (1997), Tables 4 and 5.

8.18   *Average Annual Hours Worked per Person in Employment.* OECD (1996), Table G, p. 179. Employment (1989) weighted average.

8.19   *Impact of Productivity, Employment, and Hours Differences.* Conference Board (1997), Table 3, p. 9. The data in Table 8.19 differ from those in Tables 8.17 and 8.18 and are therefore not directly comparable. In Table 8.19, for example, Japanese employment rates and hours worked appear to be higher than in the United States. We place more weight on the data from the OECD in Tables 8.17 and 8.18 than on the data from the Conference Board in Table 8.19, but nevertheless believe that the exercise in Table 8.19 provides a helpful illustration of the impact of international differences in employment rates and hours worked.

8.20   *Employment.* Calculated from employment indexes in OECD (1997a), Annex Table 20, p. A23. Employment (1989) weighted average.

8.21   *Standardized Unemployment Rates.* OECD (1997a), Annex Table 22, p. A25. Population (1989) weighted average.

8.22   *Unemployment Rates by Education Level.* OECD describes educational categories as: "Less than upper secondary," "Upper secondary," and "Tertiary." OECD (1997b), Table D, pp. 175-6. Population (1989) weighted average.

Figure notes

INTRODUCTION

A   See note for Figure 3I.

CHAPTER 1

1A   *Median Family Income.* See note to Table 1.1.

1B   *Annual Growth of Median Family Income.* See note to Table 1.1.

1C   *Average Number of Persons per Family.* Census homepage, Historical Time Series, Households, Table 6 (http://www.census.gov/population/socdemo/hh-fam/htabHH-6.txt).

1D   *Ratio of Family Income of Top 5% to Lowest 20%.* Census homepage, Historical Income Tables, Families, Table 3 (http://www.census.gov/hhes/income/histinc/f03.html).

1E   *Family Income, Average Annual Change.* Census homepage, Historical Income Tables, Families, Table 3 (http://www.census.gov/hhes/income/histinc/f03.html).

1F   *Income Shares in the Corporate Sector.* See note to Table 1.14.

1G   *Corporate Sector Profit Rates.* See note to Table 1.15.

1H   *Working Wives' Contribution to Family Income.* Hayge (1993) and unpublished updates.

1I   *The Effect of Wives' Earnings on Family Income, Prime-Age Families.* See Appendix A.

1J   *Median Family Income by Age of Householder.* See note to Table 1.3.

1K   *Percent Staying in Same Fifth in Each Pair of Years, 1968-69–1990-91.* Gottschalk and Danziger (1998).

CHAPTER 2

2A   *Federal Tax Burden.* See note to Table 2.7.

2B   *Effective Federal Tax Rate for Family of Four.* See note to Table 2.9.

2C   *Personal Income Tax Burden.* See note to Table 2.11.

2D   *Payroll Tax Burden.* See note to Table 2.11.

2E   *Corporate Tax Burden.* See note to Table 2.11.

2F   *Excise Income Tax Burden.* See note to Table 2.11.

2G   *Taxed and Untaxed Corporate Profits as a Percent of GDP.* See note to Table 2.13.

2H   *Corporate Profits Taxes.* See note to Table 2.14.

2I   *Total Tax Receipts as a Percent of GDP.* Update by original authors of Bajika and Steuerle (1991).

2J   *Federal Revenue Sources.* See note to Table 2.16.

2K   *State and Local Revenue Sources.* See note to Table 2.16.

CHAPTER 3

3A   *Hourly Wage and Compensation Growth of Production/Nonsupervisory Workers.* See note to Table 3.4. Hourly compensation was estimated based on multiplying hourly wages by the ratio of compensation to wages for all workers in each year. The compensation/wage ratio is drawn from the NIPA data used in Table 3.2.

3B   *Hourly Wages for Men by Wage Percentile.* See note to Table 3.7.

3C   *Hourly Wages for Women by Wage Percentile.* See note to Table 3.8.

3D   *Share of Workers Earning Poverty-Level Wages.* See note to Table 3.10.

3E   *Share of Workers Earning Poverty-Level Wages, by Race/Ethnicity.* See note to Tables 3.11, 3.12, and 3.13.

3F   *Share of Pension Participants Primarily in Defined-Contribution Plans.* From Employment Benefit Research Institute (1998), Table 4.

3G   *Men's Wage Inequality.* Based on ratios of wages by decile in annual data presented in Table 3.7.

3H   *Women's Wage Inequality.* Based on ratios of wages by decile in annual data presented in Table 3.8.

3I   *Productivity and Average and Median Compensation.* Average hourly productivity and compensation are for the nonfarm business sector from *ERP* (1998), Table B-49, p. 338. The median compensation of men and all workers is derived by multiplying the compensation/wage ratio (based on the NIPA data discussed in the note to Table 3.2) and the median wage series for "all" and for "men" in Tables 3.6 and 3.7. All compensation series are deflated by the CPI-UX1. The real average hourly compensation series will, therefore, differ (grow faster) from that published by BLS (which is deflated by the CPI).

3J   *College–High School Wage Premium.* Differentials estimated with controls for experience (as a quartic), region (4), marital status, and race/ethnicity, and education is specified as dummy variables for less than high school, some college, college, and advanced degree. Estimates were made on the CPS ORG data as described in Appendix B. Originally presented in Mishel and Bernstein (1996).

3K   *Entry-Level Wages of Male and Female High School Graduates.* See note to Table 3.22.

3L   *Entry-Level Wages of Male and Female College Graduates.* See note to Table 3.22.

3M   *Reading and Mathematics Proficiency by Race.* From Department of Education (1997b), pp. 80, 86.

3N   *Union Coverage in the United States.* Hirsch and Macpherson (1998), Table 1a.

3O   *Real Value of the Minimum Wage.* See note to Table 3.41.

3P   *Ratio of CEO to Average Worker Pay.* The ratio of CEO to average worker pay is based on the CEO pay data presented in Table 3.51 and the production worker wage series (converted to compensation and annualized by multiplying by 2,080 hours) presented in Table 3.4. To obtain the historical data on CEO compensation, the Pearl Meyers/*Wall Street Journal* series was used to extend the William M. Mercer/*Wall Street Journal* series backwards.

3Q   *College Degrees as Share of Employment.* See note to Table 3.54.

CHAPTER 4

4A   *Underemployment.* See note to Table 4.2.

4B   *Median Job Tenure by Age.* See note to Table 4.7.

4C   *Job Leavers.* Data on job leavers and the total unemployed from BLS web site, July 6, 1998.

4D   *Workers by Work Arrangement.* See note to Table 4.14.

4E   *Employment in Temporary Help Industry.* See note to Table 4.19.

CHAPTER 5

5A   *Growth of Household Wealth Per Household.* See note to Table 5.1.

5B   *Share of Total Household Wealth Held by Richest 1% of Individuals.* Wolff (1992), Table 1.

5C   *Distribution of Wealth.* See note to Table 5.5.

5D   *Growth of U.S. Stock Market.* Standard & Poor's Composite Index from *ERP* (1998), Table B-95, p. 390, deflated by the CPI-UX1.

5E   *Share of Total Stock Market Gains, by Wealth Class.* Authors' calculations using data in Table 5.10.

5F   *Concentration of Stock Ownership.* See note to Table 5.11.

CHAPTER 6

6A   *Poverty Rate.* See note to Table 6.1.

6B   *Poverty Rates by Price Index.* Census Poverty Homepage, Historical Poverty Tables, Experimental Measures, Table 3 (http://www.census.gov/hhes/poverty/histpov/ rdp03.html).

6C   *Relative Poverty Rates for Children, Mid-1980s to Mid-1990s.* Smeeding (1997).

6D   *Percent of Poor Persons Below 50% of Poverty Level.* See note to Table 6.11.

6E   *Predicted vs. Actual Poverty Rates.* Author's update of Blank (1991). Independent variables in the model include male unemployment, growth in the CPI, the ratio of the poverty line to mean household income, the ratio of transfers to GNP, and the poverty rate, lagged one year. Fitted values are used through 1983; forecasted values are used from 1984 forward.

6F   *Family Poverty and Income Changes Among the Lowest 20% of Families.* Family poverty rates are from P60-198, Table C3; average income for the bottom 20% of families is from Census homepage, Historical Income Tables, Families, Table 3 (http://www.census.gov/hhes/income/histinc/f03.html).

6G   *Prime-Age Workers With Low Earnings and Full-Time/Year-Round Attachment.* Data for 1974-89 from P60-178, Table 3; data for 1996 provided by Jack McNeil of the Census Bureau.

6H   *Workers in Families With Children, With Low Earnings and Full-Time/Year-Round Attachment.* See note to Figure 6G.

6I   *Real Hourly Wages of Low-Wage Workers.* Authors' analysis of CPS ORG data; see Appendix B.

CHAPTER 7

7A   *Median Family Income by Region.* See note to Table 7.1.

7B   *Changes in Low Wages and Unemployment.* See notes to Table 7.6 and 7.9.

7C   *Changes in Low Wages and Unemployment.* See notes to Table 7.6 and 7.9.

7D   *Changes in Median Wages and Unemployment.* See notes to Table 7.6 and 7.8.

7E   *Changes in Median Wages and Unemployment.* See notes to Table 7.6 and 7.8.

7F   *Poverty Rates by Region.* See note to Table 7.12.

7G   *Poverty Rates by Metro/Nonmetro Area.* See Table 7.14; Missing values for the years 1960-66 were interpolated by regressing annual data for 1967 forward on the national poverty rate, a trend, and an AR(1) term.

CHAPTER 8

8A *Productivity Growth Rates.* Annual averages calculated from OECD (1997a), Annex Table 58, p. A66.

8B *Hourly Wages at Tenth Percentile, Indexed to United States.* Data for the United States, Germany, Advanced Europe, and the United Kingdom taken from Freeman (1998), p. 29; data for Japan from Freeman (1995), p. 66.

8C *Household Income Inequality, Relative to National Median Income.* See note to Table 8.11.

8D *Household Income Inequality, Relative to U.S. Median Income.* See note to Table 8.12.

8E *Poverty Rates and Transitions Out of Poverty, Families With Children.* See note to Table 8.16.

8F *Legally Mandated Paid Vacation in European Countries.* Leete-Guy and Schor (1992), p. 19.

Bibliography

Aaronson, Daniel, and Daniel G. Sullivan. 1998. "The Decline of Job Security in the 1990s: Displacement, Anxiety, and Their Effect on Wage Growth." *Economic Perspectives*, First Quarter, pp. 17-43.

Bajika, Jon, and C. Eugene Steuerle. 1991. "Individual Income Taxation Since 1948." *National Tax Journal*, vol. 44, no. 4, pp. 451-75.

Baker, Dean. 1996. "Trends in Corporate Profitability: Getting More for Less?" Technical Paper. Washington, D.C.: Economic Policy Institute.

Bernstein, Jared, and Danielle Gao. 1998. *Pareto Imputations of Capped Values in the March CPS*. Technical Paper. Washington, D.C.: Economic Policy Institute. Forthcoming.

Bernstein, Jared, and John Schmitt. 1998. *Making Work Pay: The Impact of the 1996-97 Minimum Wage Increase*. Washington, D.C.: Economic Policy Institute.

Blank, Rebecca M. 1991. "Why Were Poverty Rates So High in the 1980s?" National Bureau of Economic Research, Working Paper No. 3878. Cambridge, Mass.: NBER.

Blank, Rebecca M., and David Card. 1993. "Poverty, Income Distribution, and Growth: Are They Still Connected?" *Brookings Papers on Economic Activity*, No. 2. Washington, D.C.: Brookings Institution.

Bluestone, Barry M., Edith Rasell, and Lawrence Mishel. 1996. *Living Standards Chartbook*. Washington, D.C.: Economic Policy Institute, forthcoming.

Borjas, George J. 1994. "The Economics of Immigration." *Journal of Economic Literature*, Vol. 32, No. 4, pp. 1667-1717.

Camarota, Steven A. 1998. Unpublished tabulations.

Card, David. 1991. "The Effect of Unions on the Distribution of Wages: Redistribution or Relabelling?" Working Paper No. 287. Princeton, N.J.: Department of Economics, Princeton University.

Center on Budget and Policy Priorities. 1998. *Poverty Tables*. Washington, D.C.: CBPP.

Citizens for Tax Justice and Institute on Taxation & Economic Policy. 1996. *Who Pays? A Distributional Analysis of the Tax Systems in All 50 States*. Washington, D.C.: Citizens for Tax Justice and Institute on Taxation & Economic Policy.

Cline, William R. 1997. *Trade and Income Distribution*. Washington, D.C.: Institute for International Economics.

Conference Board. 1997. "Perspectives on a Global Economy, Understanding Differences in Economic Performance." Report Number 1187-97-RR. New York: Conference Board.

Congressional Budget Office. 1998. *Estimates of Federal Tax Liabilities for Individuals and Families by Income Category and Family Type for 1995 and 1999*. Washington, D.C.: Congressional Budget Office.

Danziger, Sheldon, and Peter Gottschalk. 1995. *America Unequal*. New York, N.Y.: Harvard/ Russell Sage Foundation.

DiNardo, John, Nicole M. Fortin, and Thomas Lemieux. 1994. "Labor Market Institutions and the Distribution of Wages, 1973-1992: A Semiparametric Approach." Unpublished.

DiNardo, John, Nicole M. Fortin, and Thomas Lemieux. 1996. "Labor Market Institutions and Gender Differences in Wage Inequality." Paper presented at the Industrial Relations Research Association Meetings, San Francisco, January.

Duncan, Greg, et al. 1991. "Poverty and Social Assistance Dynamics in the United States, Canada and Europe." Paper presented at the Joint Center for Political and Economic Studies Conference on Poverty and Public Policy, Washington, D.C.

Economic Report of the President. Annual. Washington, D.C.: U.S. Government Printing Office.

Employment Benefit Research Institute. 1998. Agenda background material for "The National Summit on Retirement Savings," Washington, D.C., June 4-5.

Farber, Henry S. 1997a. *The Changing Face of Job Loss in the United States, 1981-95*. Princeton, N.J.: Princeton University.

Farber, Henry S. 1997b. *Trends in Long Term Employment in the United States, 1979-96*. Industrial Relations Section Working Paper No. 384. Princeton, N.J.: Princeton University.

Faber, Henry S. 1998. *Has the Rate of Job Loss Increased in the Nineties?* Industrial Relations Section Working Paper No. 394. Princeton, N.J.: Princeton University.

Fortin, Nicole M., and Thomas Lemieux. 1996. "Labor Market Institutions and Gender Differences in Wage Inequality." Presented at the Industrial Relations Research Association Annual Meeting, San Francisco, Calif., January.

Freeman, Richard. 1991. "How Much Has De-unionization Contributed to the Rise in Male Earnings Inequality?" National Bureau of Economic Research, Working Paper No. 3826. Cambridge, Mass.: NBER.

Freeman, Richard. 1995. "The Limits of Wage Flexibility to Curing Unemployment. *Oxford Review of Economic Policy*, vol. 11, no. 1, pp. 63-72.

Freeman, Richard. 1997. "Low Wage Employment: Is More or Less Better?" Harvard University, unpublished paper.

Freeman, Richard. 1998. "The Facts About Rising Economic Disparity." In James A. Auerbach and Richard S. Belous, eds., *The Inequality Paradox: Growth and Income Disparity.* Washington, D.C.: National Policy Association.

Fullerton, Howard N., Jr. 1997. Labor Force 2006: Slowing Down and Changing Composition. *Monthly Labor Review.* Vol. 120, No. 11, pp. 23-38

Gardner, Jennifer M. 1995. "Worker Displacement: A Decade of Change." *Monthly Labor Review*, Vol. 118, No. 4, pp. 45-57.

Gottschalk, Peter, and Sheldon Danziger. 1998. "Family Income Mobility—How Much Is There and Has It Changed?" In James A. Auerbach and Richard S. Belous, eds., *The Inequality Paradox: Growth of Income Disparity.* Washington, D.C.: National Policy Association.

Gottschalk, Peter, and Timothy M. Smeeding. 1997. "Empirical Evidence on Income Inequality in Industrialized Countries," Luxembourg Income Study Working Paper No. 154.

Hansen, Kristin A., and Carol Faber. 1997. *Current Population Reports.* Report No. P20-494.

Hayghe, Howard V. 1993. "Working Wives' Contributions to Family Incomes." *Monthly Labor Review*, Vol. 116, No. 8, pp. 39-43.

Hirsch, Barry T., and David A. Macpherson. 1998. *Union Membership and Earnings Data Book: Compilations from the Current Population Survey (1998 Edition).* Washington, D.C.: Bureau of National Affairs.

Immigration and Naturalization Service. 1997. *Statistical Yearbook of the Immigration and Naturalization Service 1996.* Washington, D.C.: U.S. Government Printing Office.

Joint Economic Committee. 1992. *Families on a Treadmill: Work and Income in the 1980s.* Washington, D.C.: JEC.

Leete-Guy, Laura, and Juliet B. Schor. 1992. *The Great American Time Squeeze: Trends in Work and Leisure, 1969-89.* Washington, D.C.: Economic Policy Institute.

Mishel, Lawrence, and Jared Bernstein. 1994. "Is the Technology Black Box Empty? An Empirical Examination of the Impact of Technology on Wage Inequality and the Employment Structure." Presented to the Labor Economics Workshop, Harvard University. Unpublished.

Mishel, Lawrence, and Jared Bernstein. 1996a. "Did Technology's Impact Accelerate in the 1980s?" Paper presented at the Industrial and Relations Research Association meetings, San Francisco, Calif., January.

Mishel, Lawrence, and Jared Bernstein. 1996b. "Technology and the Wage Structure: Has Technology's Impact Accelerated Since the 1920s?" Paper presented at the National Bureau of Economic Research Labor Studies Workshop, Cambridge, Mass., July.

Mishel, Lawrence, and Ruy Teixeira. 1991. *The Myth of the Coming Labor Shortage: Jobs, Skills, and Incomes of America's Workforce 2000.* Washington, D.C.: Economic Policy Institute.

Murphy, Kevin, and Finis Welch. 1989. "Recent Trends in Real Wages: Evidence from Household Data." Paper prepared for the Health Care Financing Administration of the U.S. Department of Health and Human Services. Chicago, Ill.: University of Chicago.

National Research Council. 1995. *Measuring Poverty: A New Approach.* Washington, D.C.: National Research Council.

Neumark, David, Daniel Polsky, and Daniel Hansen. 1997. *Has Job Stability Declined Yet? New Evidence for the 1990s.* Working Paper No. 6330. Cambridge, Mass.: National Bureau of Economic Research.

Organization for Economic Cooperation and Development. 1995.*Economic Outlook.* Paris: OECD.

Organization for Economic Cooperation and Development. 1996. *Employment Outlook.* Paris: OECD.

Organization for Economic Cooperation and Development. 1997a. *Economic Outlook.* Paris: OECD.

Organization for Economic Cooperation and Development. 1997b. *Employment Outlook.* Paris: OECD.

Organization for Economic Cooperation and Development. 1997c. *Revenue Statistics 1965-1996.* Paris: OECD.

Organization for Economic Cooperation and Development, Statistics Directorate. 1998. *National Accounts, Main Aggregates, Volume 1, 1960-96.* Paris: OECD.

Pierce, Brooks. 1998. "Compensation Inequality." U.S. Department of Labor, Bureau of Labor Statistics, Washington, D.C. Manuscript.

Rose, Stephen J. 1995. *Declining Job Security and the Professionalization of Opportunity.* Research Report No. 95-04. Washington, D.C.: National Commission for Employment Policy.

Ruggles, Patricia. 1990. *Drawing the Line: Alternative Poverty Measures and Their Implications for Public Policy.* Washington, D.C.: Urban Institute.

Ryscavage, Paul, Gordon Green, Edward Welniak, and John Coder. 1992. *Studies in the Distribution of Income.* U.S. Department of Commerce, Bureau of the Census, Series P-60, No. 183. Washington, D.C.: U.S. Government Printing Office.

Schmitt, John, and Lawrence Mishel. 1996. "Did International Trade Lower Less-Skilled Wages During the 1980s? Standard Trade Theory and Evidence." Technical Paper. Washington, D.C.: Economic Policy Institute.

Scott, Robert E., Thea Lee, and John Schmitt. 1997. *Trading Away Good Jobs: An Examination of Employment and Wages in the U.S., 1979-94.* Briefing Paper. Washington, D.C.: Economic Policy Institute.

Sekscenski, Edward S. 1980. "Women's Share of Moonlighting Nearly Doubles During 1969-79." *Monthly Labor Review,* Vol. 103, No. 5.

Shapiro, Isaac. 1987. *No Escape: The Minimum Wage and Poverty*. Washington, D.C.: Center on Budget and Policy Priorities.

Silvestri, George T. 1997. "Occupational Employment Projections to 2006." *Monthly Labor Review*. Vol. 120, No. 11, pp. 58-83.

Smeeding, Timothy M. 1997. "Financial Poverty in Developed Countries: The Evidence from LIS," Luxembourg Income Study Working Paper No. 155.

Stinson, John F., Jr. 1986. "Moonlighting by Women Jumped to Record Highs." *Monthly Labor Review*, Vol. 109, No. 11.

Towers, Perrin and Company. Various years. Worldwide Total Remuneration.

U.S. Department of Commerce, Bureau of the Census. Current Population Reports. Various dates. *Marital Status and Living Arrangements*. P-20 Series. Washington D.C.: U.S. Government Printing Office.

U.S. Department of Commerce, Bureau of the Census. Current Population Reports. Various dates. P-60 Series. Washington, D.C.: U.S. Government Printing Office.

U.S. Department of Commerce, Bureau of the Census. Current Population Reports. 1990. *Trends in Income, by Selected Characteristics: 1947 to 1988*. P60 Series, No. 167. Washington, D.C.: U.S. Government Printing Office.

U.S. Department of Commerce, Bureau of the Census. Current Population Reports. 1991. *Trends in Relative Income: 1964 to 1989*. P60 Series, No. 177. Washington, D.C.: U.S. Government Printing Office.

U.S. Department of Commerce, Bureau of the Census. Current Population Reports. 1995. *Household and Family Characteristics*. P20 Series. Washington, D.C.: U.S. Government Printing Office.

U.S. Department of Commerce, Bureau of the Census. Current Population Reports. 1996. *A Brief Look at Postwar U.S. Income Inequality*. P60 Series, No.191. Washington, D.C.: U.S. Government Printing Office.

U.S. Department of Commerce, Bureau of the Census. Current Population Reports. 1997. *Money Income in the United States: 1996*. P60 Series, No.197. Washington, D.C.: U.S. Government Printing Office.

U.S. Department of Education, National Center for Education Statistics. 1997a. *Projections of Education Statistics to 2008*. NCES 98-016. Washington, D.C.: U.S. Government Printing Office.

U.S. Department of Education, National Center for Education Statistics. 1997b. *The Condition of Education 1997*. NCES 97-388. Washington, D.C.: U.S. Government Printing Office.

U.S. Department of Labor. 1995e. *Report on the American Workforce*. Washington, D.C.: U.S. Government Printing Office.

U.S. Department of Labor. Bureau of Labor Statistics (BLS). 1988. *Labor Force Statistics Derived from the Current Population Survey, 1948-87*. Washington, D.C.: U.S. Government Printing Office.

U.S. Department of Labor, BLS. 1989. *Handbook of Labor Statistics.* Bulletin No. 2340. Washington, D.C.: U.S. Government Printing Office.

U.S. Department of Labor, BLS. 1995a. *International Comparisons of Hourly Compensation Costs for Production Workers in Manufacturing 1975-94, Supplementary Tables for BLS Report 893 June 1995.* Washington, D.C.: U.S. Government Printing Office.

U.S. Department of Labor, BLS. 1995b. *Monthly Labor Review.* Washington, D.C.: Bureau of Labor Statistics.

U.S. Department of Labor, BLS. 1997. *Employer Costs for Employee Compensation-March 1997.* No. 97-371. Washington, D.C.: U.S. Government Printing Office.

U.S. Department of Labor, BLS. Various years. *Productivity and Costs.* Washington, D.C.: U.S. Government Printing Office.

U.S. Department of Labor, BLS, Office of Productivity and Technology. 1997. *Comparative Civilian Labor Force Statistics, Ten Countries, 1959-96.* Washington, D.C.: Bureau of Labor Statistics.

U.S. Department of Labor, BLS, Office of Productivity and Technology. 1998a. *Comparative Real Gross Domestic Product Per Capita and Per Employed Person, Fourteen Countries, 1960-1996.* Washington, D.C.: Bureau of Labor Statistics.

U.S. Department of Labor, BLS, Office of Productivity and Technology. 1998b. *International Comparisons of Hourly Compensation Costs for Production Workers in Manufacturing, 1975-1996, Supplementary Tables.* Washington, D.C.: Bureau of Labor Statistics.

U.S. Department of Labor, BLS. 1998c. *International Comparisons of Manufacturing Productivity and Unit Labor Cost Trends, 1996.* Washington, D.C.: Bureau of Labor Statistics.

U.S. Department of the Treasury, Internal Revenue Service. 1998. *Publication 15, Circular E, Employer's Tax Guide.* Washington, D.C.: Internal Revenue Service.

U.S. Department of the Treasury, Office of Tax Analysis. 1995. *Average and Marginal Federal Income, Social Security, and Medicare Tax Rates for Four-Person Families at the Same Relative Positions in the Income Distribution, 1955-95.* Washington, D.C.: U.S. Government Printing Office.

Wolff, Edward N. 1992. "Changing Inequality of Wealth." Paper presented at the American Economic Association Meetings, Boston, Mass., January.

Wolff, Edward N. 1993. *The Rich Get Increasingly Richer: Latest Data on Household Wealth During the 1980s.* Briefing Paper. Washington, D.C.: Economic Policy Institute.

Wolff, Edward N. 1994. "Trends in Household Wealth in the United States, 1962-1983 and 1983-1989." *Review of Income and Wealth,* Series 40, No. 2.

Wolff, Edward N. 1996. "Trends in Household Wealth During 1989-1992." Paper submitted to the Department of Labor. New York, N.Y.: New York University.

Wolff, Edward N. 1997. "Recent Trends in the Size Distribution of Household Wealth." New York University, manuscript.

Index

EPI Publications

GETTING PRICES RIGHT
The Debate Over the Consumer Price Index
edited by Dean Baker
0-7656-0222-9 (paper) $19.95
0-7656-0221-0 (cloth) $50.95

RECLAIMING PROSPERITY: A Blueprint for
Progressive Economic Reform
edited by Todd Schafer & Jeff Faux
Preface by Lester Thurow
1-56324-769-0 (paper) $19.95
1-56324-768-2 (cloth) $62.50

THE NEW AMERICAN WORKPLACE: Transforming Work Systems in the United States
by Eileen Appelbaum & Rosemary Batt
0-87332-828-0 (paper) $18.95
0-87332-827-2 (cloth) $45.00

U.S. TRADE POLICY AND GLOBAL GROWTH
New Directions in the
International Economy
edited by Robert A. Blecker
1-56324-531-1 (paper) $22.95
1-56324-530-2 (cloth) $52.50

THE MACROECONOMICS OF SAVING,
FINANCE, AND INVESTMENT
edited by Robert Pollin
0-472-10787-9 (cloth) $52.00

RISKY BUSINESS
Private Management of Public Schools
by Craig E. Richards, Rima Shore,
& Max B. Sawicky
0-944826-68-7 (paper) $19.95

BEWARE THE U.S. MODEL
Jobs & Wages in a Deregulated Economy
edited by Lawrence Mishel & John Schmitt
0-944826-58-X (paper) $24.95

SCHOOL CHOICE
Examining the Evidence
edited by Edith Rasell & Richard Rothstein
0-944826-57-1 (paper) $17.95

UNIONS AND ECONOMIC COMPETITIVENESS
edited by Lawrence Mishel & Paula B. Voos
0-87332-828-0 (paper) $20.95
0-87332-827-2 (cloth) $46.95

HOW TO ORDER

All orders for EPI books, studies, working papers,
and briefing papers should be addressed to:

EPI Publications
1660 L Street NW, Suite 1200, Washington, D.C. 20036

or call: **800-EPI-4844** (202-331-5510 in Washington area)

Orders can be faxed to: (202) 775-0819.

EPI will send a complete catalog of all publications. Discounts are available to
libraries and bookstores and for quantity sales.
EPI's website contains executive summaries and introductions to recent EPI books and
studies. Publications can be ordered from the website as well. The address is:

http://www.epinet.org

RECENT EPI STUDIES

LIVING STANDARDS & LABOR MARKETS

MAKING WORK PAY
The Impact of the 1996-97
Minimum Wage Increase
by Jared Bernstein & John Schmitt
60 pages, $12, 1998

DEFUSING THE BABY BOOMER TIME BOMB
Projections on Income in the 21st Century
by Dean Baker
44 pages, $12, 1998

NONSTANDARD WORK, SUBSTANDARD JOBS
Flexible Work Arrangements in the U.S.
by Arne L. Kalleberg et al.
94 pages, $12, 1997

MANAGING WORK AND FAMILY
Nonstandard Work Arrangements Among
Managers and Professionals
by Roberta M. Spalter-Roth et al.
70 pages, $12, 1997

THE PROSPERITY GAP
A Chartbook of American
Living Standards
by Edith Rasell, Barry Bluestone, &
Lawrence Mishel
110 pages, $15, 1997

WHERE'S THE PAYOFF?
The Gap Between Black
Academic Progress and Economic Gains
by Jared Bernstein
55 pages, $12, 1995

COST AND QUALITY MATTERS: Workplace
Innovations in the Health Care Industry
by Ann Greiner
86 pages, $12, 1995

RAISING THE FLOOR:
The Effects of the Minimum Wage
on Low-Wage Workers
by William E. Spriggs & Bruce W. Klien
92 pages, $12, 1994

THE SKY HASN'T FALLEN
An Evaluation of the Minimum
Wage Increase
by Jared Bernstein & John Schmitt
16 pages, $5, 1997

LOW-WAGE LABOR MARKET INDICATORS BY CITY AND STATE
The Constraints Facing Welfare Reform
by Jared Bernstein
100 pages, $10, 1997

FAMILY FRIEND OR FOE?
Working Time, Flexibility,
and the Fair Labor Standards Act
by Lonnie Golden
24 pages, $5, 1997

GOVERNMENT & THE ECONOMY

MONOPOLY.COM
Will the WorldCom-MCI Merger
Tangle the Web?
by Jeff Keefe
36 pages, $12, 1998

BAD DEAL OF THE CENTURY
The Worrisome Implications of
the WorldCom-MCI Merger
by Dan Schiller
28 pages, $12, 1998

WHERE'S THE MONEY GONE?
Changes in the Level and Composition
of Education Spending, 1967-91
by Richard Rothstein with
Karen Hawley Miles
98 pages, $12, 1995

WHERE'S THE MONEY GOING?
Changes in the Level and Composition
of Education Spending, 1991-96
by Richard Rothstein
28 pages, $12, 1997

GROWING STATE ECONOMIES
How Taxes and Public Services Affect
Private-Sector Performance
by Timothy J. Bartik
70 pages, $12, 1996

THE PUBLIC INVESTMENT DEFICIT:
Two Decades of Neglect
Threaten 21st Century Economy
by Dean Baker
22 pages, $5, 1998

THE PRIVATIZATION OF PUBLIC SERVICE
Lessons From Case Studies
by Elliott Sclar
28 pages, $12, 1997

DO STATE & LOCAL TAX INCENTIVES WORK?
by Robert G. Lynch
34 pages, $12, 1996

ROBBING THE CRADLE? A Critical
Assessment of Generational Accounting
by Dean Baker
51 pages, $12, 1995

SUSTAINABLE ECONOMICS

CLEARING THE AIR
The Impact of Air Quality
Regulations on Jobs
by Eli Berman & Linda T.M. Bui
36 pages, $12, 1997

FALLING PRICES: Cost of Complying With
Environmental Regulations Almost Always
Less Than Advertised
by Hart Hodges
15 pages, $5, 1997

**A NEW LOOK AT ENVIRONMENTAL
REGULATION AND COMPETITIVENESS**
by Eban Goodstein
21 pages, $5, 1997

JOBS AND THE ENVIRONMENT
The Myth of a National Trade-Off
by Eban Goodstein
44 pages, $12, 1995

TRADE & COMPETITIVENESS

TRADING AWAY GOOD JOBS
An Examination of Employment and
Wages in the U.S., 1979-94
*by Robert E. Scott, Thea Lee, & John
Schmitt*
13 pages, $5, 1997

AMERICAN JOBS AND THE ASIAN CRISIS
The Employment Impact of the Coming
Rise in the U.S. Trade Deficit
by Robert E. Scott & Jesse Rothstein
13 pages, $5, 1998

JOBS ON THE WING:
Trading Away the Future
of the U.S. Aerospace Industry
by Randy Barber & Robert E. Scott
96 pages, $12, 1995

**JAPANESE AUTO TRANSPLANTS AND THE
U.S. AUTOMOBILE INDUSTRY**
by Candace Howes
102 pages, $12, 1993

**NEW PRIORITIES IN FINANCING
LATIN AMERICAN DEVELOPMENT:**
Balancing Worker Rights, Democracy,
and Financial Reform
by Jerome Levinson
64 pages, $12, 1994

POLITICS & PUBLIC OPINION

VOLATILE VOTERS:
Declining Living Standards and
Non-College-Educated Whites
by Ruy A. Teixeira & Joel Rogers
46 pages, $10, 1996

WHO JOINED THE DEMOCRATS?
Understanding the 1996 Election Results
by Ruy A. Teixeira
7 pages, $5, 1996

ABOUT EPI

The Economic Policy Institute was founded in 1986 to widen the debate about policies to achieve healthy economic growth, prosperity, and opportunity in the difficult new era America has entered.

Today, America's economy is threatened by slow growth and increasing inequality. Expanding global competition, changes in the nature of work, and rapid technological advances are altering economic reality. Yet many of our policies, attitudes, and institutions are based on assumptions that no longer reflect real world conditions.

Central to the Economic Policy Institute's search for solutions is the exploration of policies that encourage every segment of the American economy (business, labor, government, universities, voluntary organizations, etc.) to work cooperatively to raise productivity and living standards for all Americans. Such an undertaking involves a challenge to conventional views of market behavior and a revival of a cooperative relationship between the public and private sectors.

With the support of leaders from labor, business, and the foundation world, the Institute has sponsored research and public discussion of a wide variety of topics: trade and fiscal policies; trends in wages, incomes, and prices; the causes of the productivity slowdown; labor-market problems; rural and urban policies; inflation; state-level economic development strategies; comparative international economic performance; and studies of the overall health of the U.S. manufacturing sector and of specific key industries.

The Institute works with a growing network of innovative economists and other social science researchers in universities and research centers all over the country who are willing to go beyond the conventional wisdom in considering strategies for public policy.

Founding scholars of the Institute include Jeff Faux, EPI president; Lester Thurow, Sloan School of Management, MIT; Ray Marshall, former U.S. secretary of labor, professor at the LBJ School of Public Affairs, University of Texas; Barry Bluestone, University of Massachusetts-Boston; Robert Reich, former U.S. secretary of labor; and Robert Kuttner, author, editor of *The American Prospect,* and columnist for *Business Week* and the Washington Post Writers Group.

For additional information about the Institute, contact EPI at 1660 L Street, NW, Suite 1200, Washington, DC 20036, (202) 775-8810.

ABOUT THE AUTHORS

LAWRENCE MISHEL is the research director of the Economic Policy Institute. He is the co-author of the previous versions of *The State of Working America*, as well as *The Myth of the Coming Labor Shortage* (with Ruy Teixeira) and *Manufacturing Numbers*, and the editor (with Paula Voos) of *Unions and Economic Competitiveness*. He holds a Ph.D. in economics from the University of Wisconsin, and his articles have appeared in a variety of academic and nonacademic journals. His areas of research are labor economics, wage and income distribution, industrial relations, productivity growth, and the economics of education. In some circles he is known as the coach of the red team in the Takoma Park Babe Ruth Baseball League.

JARED BERNSTEIN is a labor economist with the Economic Policy Institute. He is the co-author of three previous editions of *The State of Working America*. He specializes in the analysis of wage and income inequality, with an emphasis on low-wage labor markets and poverty, and his articles have appeared in popular and academic journals. Between 1995 and 1996, he held the post of deputy chief economist at the U.S. Department of Labor, where, among other topics, he worked on the initiative to raise the minimum wage. Mr. Bernstein holds a Ph.D. in social welfare from Columbia University.

JOHN SCHMITT is a labor economist with the Economic Policy Institute. He has written for general and academic publications on wage inequality, the minimum wage, unemployment, and economic development. He is a co-author of *The State of Working America 1996-97*. Mr. Schmitt has an A.B. from the Woodrow Wilson School of Public and International Affairs at Princeton University and an M.Sc. and Ph.D. in economics from the London School of Economics. He has traveled, studied, and worked extensively in Latin America, most recently in El Salvador, where he conducted economic research with a Fulbright grant and later worked for the United Nations Peace-Keeping Mission (ONUSAL).